A FURTHER RANGE

*Studies in Modern Spanish Literature
from Galdós to Unamuno*

In Memoriam Maurice Hemingway

edited by
Anthony H. Clarke

UNIVERSITY
of
EXETER
PRESS

First published in 1999 by
University of Exeter Press
Reed Hall, Streatham Drive
Exeter, Devon EX4 4QR
www.ex.ac.uk/uep/

© The individual contributors 1999

British Library Cataloguing in Publication Data
A catalogue record of this data is available from the British Library

ISBN 0 85989 575 0

Typeset in Caslon in Great Britain by Exe Valley Dataset Ltd, Exeter

Printed and bound in Great Britain by
Short Run Press Ltd, Exeter

Contents

Foreword

Not long after Maurice Hemingway's death it became apparent to those of us working in the same field, or one very adjacent to Maurice's, that there would be strong support for the idea of a scholarly publication in honour and memory of the man and his work. In July 1995 there took place in Santiago de Compostela, at the invitation of that most 'acogedora' of universities, a symposium or small-scale conference on and around the figure of Emilia Pardo Bazán, as a spontaneous gesture to mark Maurice's stature as a scholar and his personal link with Santiago and Galicia. Two years later the fruits of this symposium, plus at least as many articles again—contributed by colleagues who could not attend the original conference—were published as *Estudios sobre Emilia Pardo Bazán. In Memoriam*, edited by Professor J.M. González Herrán, who had been the guiding force behind these two projects.

While the above conference and publication were in preparation, plans were going ahead in the UK for a similar 'In Memoriam' volume, without the relevant conference. At the reception after the memorial service for Maurice at the University of Exeter there was some initial talk of a possible scholarly publication to pay tribute to Maurice's special place and contribution in the world of Hispanic Studies. In subsequent discussions with Prof. Herrán and with Maurice's colleagues in the Exeter Department it was decided that there would be a volume on Pardo Bazán—the one described above—and another volume, not only including Pardo Bazán but also reflecting the wider range of Maurice's involvement with peninsular Spanish literature. The rationale is obvious: there were many of Maurice's colleagues who were not *Pardobazanistas* but who were academics working on late nineteenth- and/or early twentieth-century Spanish literature. It would have been a great pity had these colleagues been debarred from collaborating in an appropriate 'In Memoriam' volume simply because of the nature of their own specializations or because the decision had been taken to confine the homage to one volume on Pardo Bazán. Thus, for the best of reasons, there came about two book-length publications in honour and memory of Maurice Hemingway; it is the second of these which you now peruse.

In no sense do the two publications attempt to compete with each other, since each one fulfils a different function and need. Some of you may not know the Santiago volume, in which case I commend it to you as a much-needed showcase for current work on Pardo Bazán, but more especially as an emotional yet scholarly response to a special set of circumstances. The additional material, over and above the nineteen articles on Pardo Bazán and her work, gives a personal touch and a sense of Maurice's humane approach to teaching and to scholarship. The presentation by Darío Villanueva, the Editor's note, the Bibliography and the brief account of his academic career and leisure interests by Richard Hitchcock, all work together to evoke something of Maurice's special place in our minds, meriting simultaneously our respect and affection. However, nowhere does the remembered image of Maurice come across more strongly than in the hitherto unpublished piece by him which fittingly rounds off the volume: 'Emilia Pardo Bazán, *Los Pazos de Ulloa*: punto de vista y psicología'. As J.M. González Herrán explains, this essay was recreated and translated from a taped lecture by Maurice, possibly given to his undergraduate students at Exeter, and dating from 1977. There is an uncanny sense of Maurice talking to you, even though the Spanish words are not his own. In this short piece is to be found part of the explanation of what Maurice stood for as a scholar.

And so to the present volume. The first part of the title deserves a word or two of clarification. Robert Frost's sixth book of poems was entitled *A Further Range* (1937), expressing thus not merely the idea of another series of poems, but also, and more importantly, of poetry moving and being within other dimensions or horizons. In appropriating Frost's title, I have simply sought to suggest a further offering of articles in honour and memory of Maurice Hemingway, wishing to follow the fine example of the Santiago volume, and, at the same time, to express something of what Maurice himself achieved through his teaching, his scholarship and his publications; something which undoubtedly reached out towards and frequently attained 'a further range'.

It is not part of my brief—nor indeed do I see it as appropriate—for me to describe all the articles contained in this volume, and to single out individual articles for comment and attention would be invidious. What must be said, however, is that scholars working in the fields touched on by these articles will recognize quickly the nature and relevance of the contribution. The fourteen articles here published cover between them the scholarly range for which Maurice himself was principally known. Pardo Bazán and Galdós comprise the majority of the studies (including one article on both Galdós and Pardo Bazán), with coverage being appropriately extended to take in Padre Coloma's *Pequeñeces*—Maurice was invariably drawn to the religious dimension of Spanish nineteenth-century literature—and an introduction to Insúa's prose fiction, especially relevant because of Maurice's own championship of the cause of Insúa through the publication of his pioneering bibliography. The remaining two articles—on the crucial transitional phase of the novel in Spain in the early years of this century and Unamuno's representation of personality as viewed through the language and theories of modern physics—are germane to Maurice's literary and psychological interests not only in their own right, but also to the extent to which they reflect the new directions of Spanish prose fiction and drama during the period which was Maurice's own main area of scholarly involve-ment. Without Galdós it is difficult to envisage Unamuno; without Galdós, Clarín and Pardo Bazán it is difficult to envisage the 'turn of the novel' in the first few years of this century in Spain.

No contributor here represented was asked to ensure that his/her article conformed to a specific scholarly range. All, as I subsequently came to believe, wrote <u>for</u> Maurice, in the sense that they instinctively chose a subject which they saw as potentially a <u>Maurice</u> topic: one which would have interested him personally as a scholar and, indeed, in some cases, one which he would have been pleased to take on himself. In closing, I remember keenly the words with which José Manuel González Herrán ended his note on Maurice in the *Bulletin of Hispanic Studies*. He evoked the moment when Maurice boarded the plane to leave Santiago and Galicia for what was to be the last time; the farewell was 'Hasta siempre, Maurice'. Academics can salute their peers in various ways, but there is truly no better way than using the familiar tools of one's trade—and of <u>his</u> trade—to say 'Hasta siempre, Maurice'.

Anthony H. Clarke

Addendum

In the Introduction to Maurice Hemingway's edition of the *Poesías inéditas u olvidadas de Emilia Pardo Bazán* (Exeter Hispanic Texts, LI, University of Exeter Press, 1996) mention is made of an autograph item in Maurice's private collection which, after his death, was passed on to the Casa-Museo Emilia Pardo Bazán, La Coruña. In recognition of a uniquely handsome gesture I should set the record straight by saying that the item—a postcard with a short autograph poem by Doña Emilia—was given to me by an assiduous collector of original autograph material when I informed him that I was acquainted with a scholar who would prize the item perhaps more than anyone else. The collector neither knew of Maurice nor recognized the name of Pardo Bazán, until I put him in the picture. The fact that the autograph postcard might be worth several hundred pounds was not sufficient to outweigh the pleasure of passing it on to the most appropriate person. His own fascination with autograph material would be echoed by that of Maurice when it joined <u>his</u> collection in Exeter. Little did we know then that Maurice was to enjoy it for so short a time.

Editorial Note

The Editor and Publisher wish to record their gratitude for the help and advice given by Dr Richard Hitchcock and Professor Alex Longhurst in the later stages of the production of this book. Although they expressly wished not to figure on the title page, their involvement and commitment were such that, in all fairness, this should have been the case.

Introduction

My pleasant duty is to write an introduction to this collection of essays, brought together to commemorate the scholastic life and achievement of a friend and colleague of over twenty-five years' standing. Maurice Hemingway has deserved the attention that he has received since that sad day in July 1994, when death intervened to cut short an academic career of extraordinary quality. His impact on the Department of Spanish in the University of Exeter had been substantial and was increasing as each year passed. His burgeoning reputation as an international scholar brought renown to Exeter, and his diplomatic and linguistic skills were used with greater frequency by his adopted alma mater in later years, when, for example, he formed part of goodwill missions to the University of Rennes. His dedication to his University and to his Department were typical of the unstinting commitment of his generation of scholars. He may have been critical of particulars, but he was loyal, because he had an underlying faith in the efficacy of his discipline, and of the system within which, under certain constraints, he was able to pursue his chosen career.

Maurice Hemingway commenced his employment in the days when subject specialisms were sacrosanct. One was hired on the basis of a literary or linguistic specialism, and this was usually identified as a circumscribed area within which most, if not all, of one's teaching commitments were expected to fall. It was made quite clear to Maurice that his position in the Department of Spanish at Exeter was that of a nineteenth-century literary expert. He was still labouring, when he arrived, to finish his DPhil in Oxford, which was duly awarded in 1977. He was not prepared, however, to sacrifice thoroughness for the gratification of an immediate qualification, and he set about broadening his knowledge of late nineteenth-century literature. A fluent French speaker and Francophile, he devoured French literature as he sought to place the work of his own chosen Spanish author, the

Condesa Emilia Pardo Bazán, within a European literary context. His visit to her Library in the Pazo de Meirás whilst still a research student led to an early bibliographical publication in the *Bulletin of Hispanic Studies*, and to the solid realization that her own literary formation was by no means insular. When the book of the thesis was published with the title *Emilia Pardo Bazán: The Making of a Novelist* in 1983, its favourable reception indicated that other specialists acknowledged the European dimension whose presence Maurice had striven to demonstrate in Emilia Pardo Bazán's *oeuvre*. Evidence of the abiding critical esteem in which this work is held is its planned translation into Spanish through the auspices of his friends and colleagues in the University of Santiago de Compostela. The publication of his book began a fruitful period in which he produced further closely argued studies of her work and may be said to have contributed, in large measure, to the high regard in which Emilia Pardo Bazán is nowadays held. Although by inclination a literary critic, Maurice never relinquished his bibliographical pursuits, and his purchase of eight letters and two cards to Luis Vidart led to their exemplary publication in the *Anales Galdosianos* in 1986. He bequeathed these letters to the Casa-Museo Emilia Pardo Bazán in La Coruña, and they were ceremoniously handed over in July 1995.

Maurice, however, had no one-track mind. A narrow specialism did not suffice to meet his teaching commitments in the days of expansion in the 1980s, and so he methodically amplified his own knowledge of Spanish literature in the period approximately spanning the years 1860–1920. A course on the Regionalist novel, for example, took him from Fernán Caballero via Valera, Alarcón, and Pereda, to Alas, Palacio Valdés, Pérez Galdós, Narcís Oller, and perhaps most surprisingly of all Blasco Ibáñez. He would start with Fernán Caballero's dictum: 'España comienza a dejar de ser', would pause to consider the impact of the flood of translations of French, English and German novels, including those of Scott, Goethe, Dumas, and Eugène Sue, and would then revert to a detailed analysis of *La Gaviota* as the first important 'novela de costumbres'. Gradually, 'home-grown' products usurped foreign imports, as the Spanish reading public developed a taste for Pereda, whom he characterized as first and foremost a *costumbrista*. A theme that Maurice would then go on to develop was the considerable dependence of the revival of the novel in the nineteenth century on the growth of *costumbrismo*. In his discussion of Pereda's works, for example, he paid due attention to his defence of regionalism, while linking it to a political current. He characterized Valera differently: in *Juanita la larga*, Valera delighted in creating a subjective, idealized vision of his childhood home—no kind of faithful mirror of Andalucían life here, but a form of paradise regained through the imagination.

Exhaustive reading informed his teaching which was distinguished in his later years, both by the time-honoured pedagogic practice of circulating amongst his audience extracts of the works being discussed, and by the imaginative use of visual aids, including original manuscript material, slides and photographs (of the Albufera for the novels of Blasco Ibáñez), and *gaucho* artefacts, when he later ventured into Latin American literature.

Maurice was scrupulous in scene-setting, and he took particular care over this when, for example, breaking what for him was new ground, the Valencian novels of Blasco Ibañez. He examined the ways in which the regional theme, encapsulating a specifically Valencian way of life, blended into the universal one of man's condition in general. As he composed his lectures on nineteenth-century writers, and on later Latin American novelists such as García Márquez and Cortázar, he became absorbed by them, drawn into their ethos. He gave them every chance to speak to him, but his critical acumen never deserted him. After going down countless literary channels over a period spanning a dozen to fifteen years, he returned to Emilia Pardo Bazán with a more profound admiration, and to *Los pazos de Ulloa* in particular. Dona Emilia, he would conclude in terms of warm approval, created a novel of astonishing pathos and humour, wherein Galician life is filtered through the consciousness of Julián, such that Julián himself, the medium, became more important than Galicia, the message.

He never forewent his rigorous scholarly procedures. In the last few years of his life, he assembled a collection of the novels of Alberto Insúa, publishing a detailed bibliography of the latter's works, posthumously, in *Revista de Literatura*. After his death, it was learnt that a publishing house in the United Kingdom had agreed to publish a book of his entitled *The Fiction of Alberto Insúa*, a project which Maurice was never able to undertake.

The other activity which was not sacrificed even after Maurice took sickness retirement from active university teaching, was his supervision of research students. He liked to keep abreast of his students' works; for one he read the novels of Bryce Echenique; for another he scoured the voluminous short writings of Emilia Pardo Bazán; he received work and discussed it with his postgraduate students until he was just too infirm to continue to do so. This devotion to the cause of the encouragement and enlightenment of the next generation of scholars was for him the other side of the same intellectual coin. Literature needed first to be read, and then expounded. The stimulus was communicated to others who would then continue to carry the same torch.

In Exeter, his dedication to teaching and research bore fruit; and this volume reflects the vitality of that heritage.

Richard Hitchcock
Exeter, September 1998

Contributors

Julia Biggane (Department of Hispanic Studies, University of Aberdeen)

Peter Bly (Department of Spanish and Italian, Queen's University, Kingston, Canada)

Jean-François Botrel (Université de Haute Bretagne, Rennes)

Rodolfo Cardona (Department of Spanish, Boston University)

Anthony H. Clarke (Department of Hispanic Studies, University of Birmingham)

Nelly Clémessy (Université de Nice)

David Henn (Department of Spanish and Latin-American Studies, University College, London)

José Manuel González Herrán (Departamento de literatura española, Universidad de Santiago de Compostela)

Richard Hitchcock (Department of Spanish, University of Exeter)

Alex Longhurst (Department of Spanish, University of Exeter)

Frank McQuade (formerly Department of Spanish, University of Leeds)

Eamonn J. Rodgers (Department of Modern Languages, Spanish and Latin-American Studies, University of Strathclyde)

Alison Sinclair (Clare College, University of Cambridge)

Eric Southworth (St Peter's College, University of Oxford)

1

The Turn of the Novel in Spain
From Realism to Modernism in Spanish Fiction

Alex Longhurst

The year 1902 is generally reckoned to be the point at which Spanish fictional narrative breaks new ground. That the appearance of radically new kinds of novels by Unamuno, Baroja, Valle and Azorín, all in that *annus mirabilis,* marks the beginning of a new age for the Spanish novel has by now been repeated *ad nauseam.*[1] Yet in a sense this is an oversimplification: not only because, other than furnishing a convenient *terminus a quo,* it fails to explain anything, but also because it ignores the wider context of a developing genre with its community of writers, publishers and readers. In retrospect, 1902 may be seen as a special year in terms of publications; but it may be a mistake to treat it as unheralded apocalypse. That the wind was blowing from a different direction few today would want to question; but who pulled on the tiller for the vessel to begin its wondrous turn is not an easy matter upon which to decide.

The modern Spanish novel (Realist, post-Romantic, that is) is an especially interesting case, since it develops late and in the virtual absence of an autochthonous tradition, something which is not true of the English or the French novel. Within Spanish literature itself— ignoring, that is, the highly influential translations of Scott, Dickens, Balzac and other foreign writers—the *costumbristas* are the only close forerunners of the Realist fiction-writers of the second half of the nineteenth century, and a novelist like Galdós appears to create a new genre almost in a void, with only the distant Cervantes, in his own national culture and language, to inspire him. And even Baroja, who starts his career a quarter of a century later, seems to belong more in the English nineteenth-century narrative tradition than in the Spanish. What I am saying in effect is that the historical process that took the novel from Realism to Modernism was rather more condensed in Spain than it was in England or France. When the novel takes a Modernist turn in these countries, it does so after the best part of a century since its beginnings with Stendhal, Balzac, Austen and Thackeray (not to mention such sturdy eighteenth-century predecessors as Diderot, Defoe, Fielding). In Spain we have but three decades of continuous Realist fiction before the turn comes, yet come it does at about the same time as in other European countries. The critical decade, as I shall argue, is that of the 1890s, which means that, in Spain at any rate, the first Modernist manifestations come hard on the heels of the great Realist novels of the 1880s.

European Modernism has tended to be associated above all with the literary production of the period from World War I to the Great Depression, and it is true that many of the great experimental novels that have since become part of the Modernist canon were published during that period (*Les Caves du Vatican* [1914], *Portrait of the Artist as a Young Man* [1916], *Demian* [1919], *Ulysses* [1922], *Confessions of Zeno* [1923], *The Magic Mountain* [1924], *The Trial* [1925], *Les Faux-monnayeurs* [1925], *A la Recherche du temps perdu* [1913–1927], *To the Lighthouse* [1927], *Point Counter Point* [1928], *The Man without Qualities* [1930], to name but a handful). What we can immediately say about these and many other works of the period (one could add Unamuno's *Niebla* and Pérez de Ayala's later novels) is that they are incontrovertibly and self-consciously different— explorations rather than reactions. For that reason they are un-mistakably non-realist. Yet many other works of fiction written well before the First World War may share the same kinds of assumptions about art without showing the same manifestly differentiating features. Kafka, Proust and Joyce are in far less danger of being misunderstood than earlier novelists who may well have made similar aesthetic assumptions but whose work appears on the surface to be applying the old formula, with no visible signs of aesthetic rebellious-ness. Some thirty years ago Frank Kermode divided Modernism into two phases, Paleo-Modernism and Neo-Modernism, the former being associated with the production of the period 1907–1925 and the latter with a much later, post-World War II phenomenon (which has subsequently been loosely termed post-Modernism). Kermode saw the 1890s as a precursor of Modernism, but Malcolm Bradbury had no problem in pushing back the early manifestations of Modernism to the 1890s, if we judge according to certain essential features which emphasize 'the perceptual resources of the artist himself as a high subjective consciousness; [...] the heightened resonance that might be attached to certain observed objects; [...] presentation through the consciousness of characters rather than through an objective presentation of material; [...] the direction of art as the writer's essential subject matter'.[2] If we look for these kinds of underlying assumptions as the indicators of a fundamental change of direction in literary production, it is not difficult to identify works that signal an aesthetic shift long before the First World War. David Daiches, for example, convincingly placed Joseph Conrad, whose most significant work was published between 1900 and 1911, alongside Joyce, Lawrence and Virginia Woolf as part of the great modern quartet that transformed the English novel.[3] And if we look beyond creative literature, the Modernist milestones of the late nineteenth century are many and incontestable: Nietzsche published his most influential works in the 1870s and 1880s; Bergson began his campaign against Determinism in 1889 with his *Essai sur les données immédiates de la conscience* which was to culminate in his famous *L'Évolution créatrice* (1907); Dilthey effectively demolished Hippolyte Taine's brand of Positivism in 1900 with his essay *The Origin of Hermeneutics*; and in that same year Freud published *The Interpretation of Dreams*. In 1902 the brilliant French mathematician Henri Poincaré published a widely-read book, *La Science et l'Hypothèse*, in which he defended the role of intuition and creative thought in science and argued that scientific explanations of phenomena were not truths but conventions, hypothetical metaphors. All this signals the end of standard nineteenth-century ways of thinking across a range of disciplines.

If we accept Paul Valéry's idea that a literary mode or age (*époque*) is first and foremost a reaction, then we must presumably infer that Modernism was a reaction against Realism and Naturalism and their philosophical fellow-travellers Positivism and Determinism. But there is, in any case, plenty of evidence that this is how the early Modernists themselves perceived the situation. Those who decried such nineteenth-century doctrines and practices are legion. Shortly before his death, Flaubert—hardly a Modernist but so often now-adays quoted as a precursor—denounced Zola's brand of Naturalism because it neglected 'poetry and style' in favour of materialism. Thomas Hardy said much the same thing in his pointedly titled essay 'The Science of Fiction' (1891):

> The fallacy [of scientific realism] appears to owe its origins to the just perception that with our widened knowledge of the universe and its forces, and man's position therein, narrative, to be artistically convincing, must adjust itself to the new alignment, as would also artistic works in form and colour, if further spectacles in their sphere could be presented. Nothing but the old illusion of truth can permanently please, and when the old illusions begin to be penetrated, a more natural magic has to be supplied.[4]

What Hardy is saying, then, is that the old Realist illusion of historicity is crumbling, and that Naturalism, the 'more natural magic', is but an attempt to bolster it. Joseph Conrad, too, a major figure caught between two styles who could never bring himself to abandon the history-likeness of the novel, an idea which he persistently defended, insisted nevertheless that the novel 'puts to shame the pride of documentary history' because as 'a form of imagined life' it transcended the uncertainty of document and factual reconstruction. While accepting Henry James's contention that the novelist acted as a historian, he added that fiction, by going beyond the reading of documents, was nearer the truth:

> Henry James claims for the novelists the standing of the historian as the only adequate one, as for himself and before his audience. I think that the claim cannot be contested, and that the position is unassailable. Fiction is history, human history, or it is nothing. But it is also more than that; it starts on firmer ground, being based on the reality of forms.[5]

What we have here, in a nutshell, is the parting of the ways between an art that aspired to measure itself against reality (Realism) and an art that stated its own separateness. With Conrad we are at the very beginning of this process: fiction is a form, not just a record; that is why his narrator, Marlow, is both eye-witness and creator, interpreting, manipulating, distorting the narration of events. The events are treated as if they were history; but their form of presentation precludes certainty and objectivity. Gide, who in 1891 had defended Symbolism as closer to the real than Realism because the symbol, unconstrained by historical time, was closer to the underlying truth of phenomena, had changed his mind by 1895 and was arguing (in *Paludes*) that, far from being a transmitter of a truth, a literary text is semantically open-ended, dependent on the particularities of a given reader. This relativism is of course one of the basic characteristics of Modernism. Just a few years later Gide turned his attention to Realism and Naturalism, denouncing the art of the Goncourt brothers as 'a diminution of life'. This rejection of both Realism and Symbolism was to reappear in *Les Faux-monnayeurs* (1925), but it is clear that it was already laid down in Gide's artistic canon by 1900. Later writers were to insist that reality — whatever it may be — can be experienced but not described, and that to expect a novel to represent it is fundamentally to misjudge the possibilities of the genre. Virginia Woolf wrote about this at some length, regretting the misapplied skills of novelists such as Wells, Bennett and Galsworthy:

> If we fasten, then, one label on all these books, on which is one word, materialists, we mean by it that they write of unimportant things; that they spend immense skill and immense industry making the trivial and the transitory appear the true and the enduring.[6]

Novelists, argued Virginia Woolf, are trapped by convention into believing that their plots have a 'likeness to life'. But the more they try to make them like life the less they are like life, because life is very far from being 'like this'. What we have is realities rather than reality, worlds refracted by our consciousness on the basis of innumerable and unco-ordinated sense impressions. Realism falsified life because, in the words of Virginia Woolf,

> Life is not a series of gig lamps symmetrically arranged; life is a luminous halo, a semi-transparent envelope surrounding us from the beginning of consciousness to the end. Is it not the task of the novelist to convey this varying, this unknown and uncircumscribed spirit, whatever aberration or complexity it may display, with as little mixture of the alien and external as possible? We are not pleading merely for courage and sincerity; we are suggesting that the proper stuff of fiction is a little other than custom would have us believe it.[7]

This is much the same argument that Unamuno used in his repeated denunciations of the Realist aesthetic: that by concentrating on the external realities that we *appear* to have in common we are in fact eschewing the reality of our existence. We have to move from the inner to the outer world and not vice versa. Unamuno's best known formulation of his ideas on the novel was made in *Tres novelas ejemplares y un prólogo* (1920) where he speaks of the 'hombre numénico' who is obliged to live in a 'mundo fenoménico'. What the true novelist should aspire to is to create inner worlds and not seek inspiration in the street, the public square, and the café.

Unamuno realized full well that Realism ('realismo' with a small r for him) was a catch-all,[8] but it did not stop him from constantly contraposing the 'cosa puramente externa, aparencial, cortical y anecdótica' of 'el llamado realismo' and his own brand of 'realidad real' which he equated with the creative impulse which comes not from observation of external detail but from the imagination of the artist who transforms his dreams into art: '¿o es que la *Odisea*, esa epopeya que es una novela, y una novela real, muy real, es menos real cuando nos cuenta prodigios de ensueño que un realista excluiría de su arte?'[9] In effect, Unamuno is judging the authenticity of art by an appeal to 'internalism', and as an explanation of his own work it is not unconvincing. But the trouble with this kind of argument is that it can be made to apply to almost any writer whom we decide to rescue from an apparently discredited literary mode, which is precisely what Unamuno does with Balzac: 'Balzac no era un hombre que hacía vida de mundo ni se pasaba el tiempo tomando notas de lo que veía en los demás o de lo que les oía. Llevaba el mundo dentro de sí' (OC, II, 976). By 1920, of course, the Modernist approach to fiction was in full spate; indeed, we are by then at the threshold of the avant-garde movement which can be regarded as the terminal form of early twentieth-century Modernism and was to provoke a return to documentary Realism in the 1930s. The essence of Unamuno's ideas on the novel as found in *Tres novelas ejemplares y un prólogo* is not at all exceptional, even if his expression of those ideas remains as always highly idiosyncratic. Yet there is other evidence to suggest that we do not have to wait until 1920 or even until 1910 (Virginia Woolf's famous choice of date when 'human character changed') to observe a new aesthetic of fictional narrative at work. What had happened, rather, is that there had been no sudden discontinuity, that Realism had evolved into 'realisms' with a diversity of qualifying adjectives, multiple approaches each claiming to be more real, or more faithful to the human situation, or more aware of the possibilities of art and the role of the artist.[10]

In Spain, as in England, the Modernist turn is perhaps less immediately perceptible than in France. Coming under the spell of German idealism, Spain produced neither a stout defender of philosophical Positivism nor a first-rank practitioner of full-blown Naturalism. Despite the shocked reaction of the Conservative Catholic intelligentsia, Pardo Bazán's *La cuestión palpitante* was every bit as much a mis-representation of Zola's ideas as a defence of Realism seen from a Liberal-Catholic point of view. The materialist Determinism of Zola (irrespective of whether he himself believed in it) did not take root in Spain, and even depictions of low life, poverty or sexual impropriety—plenty of the latter—were offered without any theoretical underpinning. Ángel Ganivet's very early (virtually contemporaneous) analysis of Naturalist inroads into Spanish fiction is both interesting and largely convincing. In his youthful treatise *España filosófica contemporánea* (presented unsuccessfully for a doctorate) he wrote:

Después de algunas escasas muestras de la novela histórica, de la sentimental y de la de costumbres, se ha impuesto la psicológica o analítica tan defendida por Zola. En este punto, como en tantos otros, vivimos bajo influencias extrañas a nuestra historia y a nuestro carácter; pero la influencia hasta la hora presente no ha sido tan decisiva que se extienda en toda su amplitud. La doctrina del fundador de la novísima escuela literaria se condensa en tres afirmaciones: el organismo humano, como todos los demás, se rige por leyes fatales, siendo una especie de máquina cuyo motor es el temperamento, el cual explica la gran variedad de las funciones individuales; para estudiar la vida del hombre, hemos de valernos del método mismo de la ciencia positiva, de la observación y del análisis, ya que el experimento no sea posible; para exponer el resultado de nuestro estudio, nos serviremos del lenguaje más acomodado a la realidad y más apto para expresarla fielmente, desechando el auxilio de la imaginación, que es un colaborador pernicioso. Fácilmente se nota que la novela española contemporánea coincide en sus tendencias con estas dos últimas conclusiones, aunque moderándolas prudentemente, pero difiere de la primera por completo. El fondo filosófico de la novela naturalista es un positivismo radical que no acepta ningún novelista español digno de esta consideración. Alarcón, Pereda, Trueba, Pardo Bazán y la mayor parte de ellos son espiritualistas. Valera, Galdós y otros lo son también, aunque también propenden al escepticismo.[11]

I have quoted at length because this seems to me the most revealing analytical synopsis by a contemporary observer. Ganivet not only gives us a penetrating definition of Naturalism, but he also tells us that in its purest form it does not exist in Spain. The closest we get to a Spanish version of authentic Naturalism, I suggest, are the Valencian novels of Blasco Ibáñez and the novels of Zamacois, but in the case of Blasco, despite some semblance of Determinism, his best work still sits comfortably within the robust Spanish tradition of the regionalist novel, and in the case of Zamacois, for whom admittedly a stronger case has been made, his Naturalism is too limited, too synonymous with eroticism, to be wholly convincing.[12] Even after 1900 and the appearance of the *noventaiochistas*, Spanish narrative continued to be dominated by novelists whom we may, *grosso modo*, term Realist, Galdós, Pardo Bazán, Palacio Valdés, Blasco Ibañez and many other minor figures who have been largely forgotten since. Among the younger writers Baroja is often referred to as a continuator of Realism, but this is wholly misleading and comes about as a result of comparing his work with the much more visibly experimental novels of the later Unamuno, Azorín, or Pérez de Ayala. If instead of looking at the peaks of experimentalism we search instead for more subtle changes in approaches to novel-writing, and perhaps, too, in the apparently unconnected but often revealing comments of writers, a different picture begins to emerge, one in which Modernism appears as a reaction, certainly, but more through a process of incubation than through revolutionary upheaval. It is like a child who rebels against the father because of his upbringing, not in spite of it. Modernism, at any rate in fiction (and it is in fiction that European Modernism had its clearest and widest manifestations), would then appear, not as a reminiscence of Romanticism or a sequel to Symbolism, but rather as the offspring of Realism itself, wayward and rebellious, but an issue nonetheless.

Manuel Fernández Cifuentes has shown how the concept of the novel underwent such changes in critical reviews and theoretical writings during the period 1900–1914 that one can justifiably speak of a breakdown of the concept. The appeal to 'realism' was frequent, but the word had become polysemic, being used for very different kinds of novels and often being qualified by epithets such as 'nuevo', or 'viril', or 'español', or by phrases such as 'todo vida' (of a novel by Baroja) and 'sin un átomo de vida verdadera' (of a novel by the more traditional Ricardo León).[13] Ortega realized that the word had been emptied of meaning, 'una de tantas vagas palabras con que hemos ido tapando en nuestras cabezas los huecos de ideas exactas'.[14] Gómez de la Serna (of all people) argued that the literature of the bourgeoisie had turned its back on reality and become too literary, and that a new less 'literary' literature had come to take its place: 'la nueva literatura tiende a ser lo menos literaria posible'.[15] Since the literature of the bourgeoisie had been the Realist novel *par excellence*, we can see that the traditional correspondence between Realism and reality, according to which the novel, though not a copy of an external reality, was in some way informed by it, clearly no longer applied. All these comments come from the period 1909–1912, and while they offer no consensus as to what had replaced, or should replace, previous practice, they do afford a clear indication that a change had already taken place. Since Valle-Inclán, Azorín, Baroja and Pérez de Ayala had been publishing novels that did not fit the Realist paradigm, one could reasonably infer that their work, even if commercially far less successful than that of the Realists and their epigones, had not gone unnoticed (something we know in any case from press reviews of the time) and had sparked off a debate, indeed a polemic, about the aesthetics of the genre that was well and truly raging in the years before the First World War.[16]

This, however, would only be half the story, for the fact is that we can find comments on the perceived inadequacies of traditional Realism and of a new aesthetic orientation to replace it rather earlier than those just referred to, suggesting that it was not simply a case of the novels published from 1902 onwards being solely responsible for bringing about the critical perception of a changing aesthetic. In 1894, for example, Emilia Pardo Bazán referred to Naturalism as already belonging to literary history and having been replaced by new tendencies.[17] Largely for quasi-religious reasons, Naturalism (as advocated by Zola and the Goncourt brothers) had always been a polemical issue in Spain, but no one could seriously doubt the impact which the doctrine had, not as doctrine, but as an approach to narrative. As Jean-François Botrel puts it, after examining 13,000 titles of the 1880–1890 decade, 'De lo observado a través de la producción bibliográfica sacamos [...] la impresión que existió en España un movimiento isócrono con la fase del "naturalismo triunfante" señalada para Europa [..], pero de forma dispersa, sin verdadera coherencia doctrinal ni fuerzas, no tanto para defenderlo como para realizarlo'.[18] Given that the doctrine of Naturalism had few adherents in Spain, and that it is in the praxis that we have to seek out its influence, it is interesting to see Unamuno in 1898 approaching the question from the other end, that is, explaining why Naturalism has failed.

In an article entitled 'Notas sobre el determinismo en la novela' (1898), Unamuno offers an interesting critique of Zola's approach to the novel. Although his lack of sympathy towards Determinism is not hard to detect, he does not in point of fact reject Zola for being a Determinist. On the contrary, he is prepared to accept Determinism as a working hypothesis: 'Admitamos provisoriamente lo que se llama solución determinista y veamos si cabe encarnarla en el arte' (OC, IX, 770). Determinism, according to Unamuno, is no more than a statistical science that deals in averages (e.g. the occurrence of crime in a given social milieu) and tells us nothing about a particular individual. To apply the concepts of Determinism to the novel is misguided because 'el arte es un saber intuitivo' (OC, IX, 771). Zola's personages are constructed according to pre-set rules, and although they might at first sight offer a greater impression of reality, 'nunca tendrán la vida que el artista presta a lo intuido en la realidad' (OC, IX, 771). While stating that 'el naturalismo novelesco [...] ha fracasado' (OC, IX, 773), Unamuno believes that it has done the genre a service because the reading public, accustomed to a type of fiction carefully constructed on the basis of documents taken from reality, is unlikely to accept a 'ficción desenfrenada' (OC, IX, 772). Indeed, he welcomes the careful documentation of the Naturalist novel as a 'gran progreso' and compares it with his own attempt at 'anovelar la historia' in his *Paz en la guerra*. It is clear, therefore, that Unamuno does not reject Naturalism because it falsified reality; he criticized it, rather, because it failed to communicate a 'sensación de vida' (OC, IX, 770). What Naturalism did was *to falsify art* by trying to turn itself into something that it could not be: a science based on logical abstraction. Art cannot fail to neglect the individual precisely because life is not a scientific abstraction but the reflection of our own individual consciousness: 'El arte debe proceder como la naturaleza, en el orden del ser intuitivamente reflejado en nosotros, no en el orden del conocer discursivamente expuesto' (OC, IX, 771–2). Here we have, in a nutshell, what was soon to become one of the central tenets of Modernism: the primacy of the individual consciousness as a source of all interpretations of the world, a principle that was at work long before Joyce comically enunciated it in the opening lines of *A Portrait of the Artist as a Young Man*.[19]

At about this same time Pío Baroja was writing of the importance of the unconscious in modern art. His theme was that art and science were going their separate ways, in itself a manifest indication of the perceived decline, or rejection, of Naturalism. Influenced perhaps by Claude Bernard's *Introduction á la médecine expérimentale*, Baroja always retained a respect for experimental science, but never made Zola's 'mistake' (warned against by Bernard himself) of applying its methods to a non-science. Writing in 1899, Baroja's thesis is that science has come to so dominate the life of humanity that art has nowhere left to hide. The result has been that modern artists, especially writers, have turned their attention to areas where science finds it difficult to operate, namely the world of the unconscious, of sensations, of hidden impulses. Art—and Baroja seems almost to regret this—has become irrational, or, as he says, 'inconsciente'. Whereas in past ages 'el genio era casi siempre consciente', now 'el arte actual nace de lo subconsciente'.[20] We can see just how close Baroja's analysis of the modern world is to Unamuno's. In the 1898 article referred to above, Unamuno had written:

Querer racionalizarlo todo en el arte es excluir de él lo *irracional*, factor importantísimo de la vida real. Empleo aquí *irracional* en el sentido que esta voz recibe en matemáticas. Sucede como con lo imaginario. La raíz cuadrada de dos es en matemáticas una cantidad imaginaria, un número indeterminable, inconmensurable con la unidad, y, sin embargo, no hay nada que pueda determinarse gráficamente con mayor sencillez, puesto que se reduce a la diagonal del cuadrado de la unidad. No por cálculo, por intuición se logra fijarlo, y fijarlo si no científica, artísticamente por lo menos.

El arte es un saber intuitivo, gráfico podría decir, que nos presenta realidades que la ciencia, que sólo opera con cantidades abstractas [...], no consigue determinar. (OC, IX, 771)

Six months later Baroja wrote:

> El arte moderno busca el producir impresiones, sencillas y vagas, y huyendo de los grandes ideales de la ciencia, perfecciona la técnica del arte, que es precisamente la parte científica de éste.
>
> El arte ha ganado en sinceridad, pero ha perdido en inteligencia. El arte antiguo hablaba al entendimiento; el moderno, más carnal, habla sólo a la sensualidad y a la subconsciencia.
>
> A las regiones superiores del espíritu sedujo la Ciencia; al arte le han quedado las regiones inferiores del alma, una segunda personalidad inferior, llamada subconsciencia; ese reflejo oscuro de la vida es quien goza de la obra de arte moderna. (OC, VIII, 851)

Where Unamuno writes 'irracional', Baroja writes 'subconsciente', that which cannot be logically proven but our experience tells us exists; where Unamuno uses 'racionalizar', Baroja uses 'hablar al entendimiento'; where Unamuno writes 'cantidades abstractas', Baroja prefers 'grandes ideales de la ciencia'; and where Unamuno speaks of 'saber intuitivo', Baroja, the enthusiast of Dostoyevski, speaks of 'ese reflejo oscuro de la vida'; almost a case, a Spaniard might say, of 'los mismos perros con distintos collares'. Furthermore, in a declaration about the aims of art that almost exactly parallels the definition (quoted above) of Unamuno's, to the effect that art should aspire to be like nature in the sense that it is an intuitive reflection on, not an explanation of, our being, Baroja wrote: 'El artista moderno no es, respecto a la Naturaleza, un espejo que trate de reflejarla: es más bien un instrumento delicado que vibra con sus latidos y amplifica sus vibraciones' (OC, VIII, 851). Virginia Woolf would doubtless have approved.

Writing in that same year (1899) for a French publication about the Spanish literary scene, Baroja refers to the instability and rapid turnover of ideas of an artistic culture that does not seem to know where it is going. Of the generation of Realists, enthusiasts of Zola, 'ya casi no queda nada', he writes. 'La señora Pardo Bazán, Picón, Narciso Oller, son los únicos escritores de los primeros días del naturalismo que todavía trabajan con éxito.' But these writers belong to a generation that now appears old-fashioned: '[...] aunque muestran alguna benevolencia hacia las ideas liberales, son, en el fondo, reaccionarios; pertenecen a la vieja España, sombría y religiosa'. One writer, however, escapes from this general put-down, but what is interesting is why Baroja finds in him an exception:

Pérez Galdós, el único de nuestros escritores verdaderamente grande y abierto, ha logrado dar un impulso a la literatura española dirigiéndola a nuevos principios, como lo prueban las obras de evolución reciente hacia un misticismo realista.[21]

Whatever it is that Baroja means by 'misticismo realista', what is important for him is that Galdós is not simply applying the old formula but has evolved a new approach in recent years. Galdós is therefore no longer classed as a 'Naturalist' alongside various others of his generation; he is the exception. Clearly for Baroja, as for Unamuno, the ideas and the modes of writing that had dominated the later decades of the century had, by the late 1890s, run their course.[22]

In this same article of 1899 Baroja uses the term *modernista*, although in a very loose way, including in it a variety of writers of all genres and styles. Of these writers only Benavente stands out, he says, although he does also single out Valle-Inclán and Rueda as promising writers of great style. And in another article, also of 1899, he wrote:

Hay un sinfín de tendencias y de corrientes artísticas. El arte y la literatura varían como la moda. Seguir la moda en el traje es ser elegante; seguirla en literatura es ser modernista.

El modernista, el adorador de lo nuevo, no encuentra, como el elegante, una sola moda que adoptar, sino muchas en el mismo momento.[23]

Four years later, Baroja returned to the subject of *modernismo* in a much more positive and revealing, though perhaps no more precise, treatment of the subject. The article is in effect a stout defence of a kind of *modernismo* that is not quite the same as that which he had mentioned, unenthusiastically, in his 1899 articles. Now, in 1903, he launches uncompromisingly into a denunciation of those who think 'modernistas' are sexual deviants with long hair and flamboyant dress habits. Those who hold such opinions are branded as imbeciles who fail to realize that the inspiration of the 'modernista' movement is to be found in the strong men of art and letters: Dickens, Ibsen, Dostoyevski, Nietzsche, Rodin. This may seem somewhat like a list of Baroja's favourites, and no one to my knowledge has claimed Dickens for Modernism, but the inclusion of Dostoyevski and Nietzsche is enormously significant, since these two are of course widely regarded among scholars as the progenitors, or at the very least the clearest precursors, of Modernism. That a young, obscure writer in a backward, peripheral country should have realized the enormous impact that these two writers were having and were to continue to have on an emerging generation of writers says something about the Spanish intellectuals' extraordinary openness to foreign influences at the turn of the century.[24] What characterizes the 'estilo modernista', which for Baroja, quite clearly, is not simply a style of writing but an approach to writing, is rebellion, that is to say, disconformity from established norms. What is new is the freedom to create, freedom from doctrinal encumbrances or even conventional expectations that dictated what art should be: 'Antes, una época tenía su estilo; [...] Hoy cada individuo es una época' (OC, VIII, 845). Baroja rejects the criticisms of those who, using traditional criteria of style, find fault with the younger writers; his riposte to them is simple: 'se debe escribir como se siente'. In one important respect Baroja's article reads like a Modernist manifesto, namely, in its insistence on the primacy of the artistic self: 'el escritor debe presentarse tal como es' (OC, VIII, 846). Which is not to say that the artistic revelation of the self comes easily to the writer; on the contrary, that inner I that lies deep within our consciousness or even subconsciousness is difficult to locate:

> Lo difícil es esto, llegar a descubrir el Yo, parir la personalidad, grande o pequeña, de ruiseñor o de buho, de águila o de insecto, cuando se tiene. El estilo debe ser expresión, espontánea o rebuscada, eso es lo de menos, pero expresión fiel de la forma individual de sentir y pensar. (OC, VIII, 846)

Baroja's conviction that literature was undergoing a profound change is also evidenced by his opinion that two virtually unknown writers of outstanding talent will in the end gain the recognition they deserve. These two writers, who according to Baroja were 'en discordancia completa con el momento histórico en que nacen y con la sociedad

14

que los rodea' (OC, V, 54–5), were indeed ahead of their time. Silverio Lanza and Ángel Ganivet, wrote Baroja, 'no han conocido aún los favores de la crítica ni del público, pero una reacción va iniciándose en la juventud presente, que hará que estos grandes desconocidos sean, al fin, los triunfadores', (OC, V, 55). Baroja had in fact written, at the astonishingly early age of seventeen, a laudatory and perceptive piece on Silverio Lanza in 1890 (mischievous, too, since he calls upon the 'editor', J.B. Amorós, to publish more of the 'deceased' writer's works).[25] In that piece he had said:

> Creo yo que Silverio Lanza no pertenece a ninguna escuela literaria. Su talento imaginativo, su poder cerebral, no sé explicarme, vamos, le impide ser naturalista (Perdón). Su pesimismo filosófico unido a su escepticismo, le prohíbe el ser idealista. (HS, I, 92)

In other words, he belonged to neither of the two major fictional currents prevalent in 1890. Nor of course would the Modernists shortly to come on the scene.

Other writers and commentators were making similar or even identical points to those made by Unamuno and Baroja. As early as 1897, Azorín, who was the literary critic *par excellence* among the younger writers, had singled out Benavente as bringing a new approach to the theatre that contrasted sharply with that of Echegaray. Menéndez y Pelayo, on the other hand, remained Azorín's *bête noire* for his positivistic approach to history and literature based on the accumulation of external data. But, above all, Azorín singled out Baroja, from the very beginning of the latter's novelistic career, as representing the new art whose essence lay in capturing the sensation of reality, not in its description.[26] In an article interestingly entitled 'Orgías del yo', written as early as 1900 when all the fiction Baroja had published amounted to *Vidas sombrías, La casa de Aizgorri,* some other short stories and parts of *Silvestre Paradox* in serial form, Azorín wrote of him that what he could not experience with his excessively cerebral personality he could nevertheless capture in his vibrant prose: '¿No es esto una compensación extraña? Ser incapaz para la vida y ofrecer la más aguda sensación de vida; encontrarse embargado para vivir tal estado psicológico, y pintarlo con la más abrumadora limpieza'.[27] The poetic qualities that Azorín finds in Baroja ('poesía hondamente trágica') may perhaps call to mind the aspirations of Symbolism rather than the innovations of

Modernism, but what is clear at any rate is that, in Azorín's view, Baroja's attempt to 'experimentar todas las sensaciones', to look for 'los matices de las cosas', represented a radically new approach to fictional prose. Blasco Ibañez, by contrast, was said to represent 'la modalidad antigua' (OC, VIII, 133). Three years later Azorín insisted on the novelty of Baroja:

> Nuestra tradición no es la sencillez y la transparencia. Propendemos a lo inextricable y a lo difuso [...] Pues Baroja ha traído a la novela esta simplicidad que es preciso traer a todos los géneros. *Camino de perfección* es su obra maestra. Todo el ambiente de la España contemporánea está encerrado en pocas páginas: las llanuras inacabables, rojizas; las ciudades vetustas, ruinosas; los caminos viejos de herradura; los mesones y ventas; las callejuelas sombrías; los casinos de los pueblos; las procesiones de penitentes; las melopeas subyugadoras de la música religiosa... Y esta visión del novelista produce un efecto penetrante, doloroso; porque Baroja logra en sus descripciones, no trasladar un aspecto cualquiera de las cosas o del paisaje, sino aquel matiz que marca precisamente su cualidad dominante. (OC, VIII, 127–8)[28]

Pérez de Ayala, another perceptive observer of the cultural scene, was too young to be writing before 1900, but by 1903 he was already pointing, like Baroja before him, to the diversity of approaches and the fragmentation of novelistic styles following the demise of what he called the 'escuela naturalista':

> Ya sé yo que es fácil y acomodaticio aferrarse a una idea y juzgar por modo escolástico; pero lo considero absurdo, sobre todo en una época como la nuestra, de tan grande diferenciación de tendencias, en todas las cuales late un espíritu interior de anarquismo estético. En la novela, sobre todo, se ha llegado al triunfo completo del individualismo *atómico* a partir de la bancarrota de la escuela naturalista. Hoy cada autor escribe sus novelas sin prejuicios de técnica ya definida ni preocupaciones de bando, y el público los alienta a todos. No hay una novela concebida *específicamente* y que predomine como escuela de *moda* sobre todas las demás; hay la novela *in genere,* que cada cual entiende a su modo.[29]

Once again, the views expressed by Pérez de Ayala coincide to a degree with those of other commentators, especially in noting, firstly, the collapse of the old aesthetic, and secondly, that the new aesthetic, if there is one, is inherent in the individual writer or the individual work. A year later he insists on this: 'No es atrevimiento asegurar que la novela está en decadencia. [...] cada autor la entiende a su modo y existe tal variedad de tendencias y de procedimientos, tal disparidad y falta de cohesión, que el esfuerzo del revistero literario se pierde en complejidades y complicaciones'(OC, I, 1203–4). What is just as interesting as the fact that there is a multiplicity of approaches is Pérez de Ayala's explicitly stated belief that the novel must evolve or die, and that this evolution must perforce be a movement 'del objetivismo impersonal de los naturalistas al egoísmo psicológico e incoherente de la vida, ampliamente y humanamente considerados' (OC, I, 1203). Pérez de Ayala does not go so far as to say that the evolution has already happened (though there were certainly by now clear examples of 'egoísmo psicológico'), but that the rupture has occurred he appears not to doubt, and it has occurred in the recent past ('no hace muchos años').[30]

The preceding comments of fiction writers and critics (most were both) writing around the turn of the century strongly suggest that during the 1890s there had been a noticeable change in aesthetic climate which, among other things, brought about a reorientation in the art of fictional narrative. What examples of the fiction of the period can be offered as an illustration of this change of direction? Given the robustness and success of the realist novel one would not expect a sudden decline in this mode of literature. We could reasonably begin to look for signs of restlessness or heterodoxy within the Realist tradition itself. The case of Galdós is as important as any and more than most, given both his position and his sensitivity to the literary scene. It seems clear that something significant does indeed happen to Galdós's novelistic production in the 1890s, as Baroja said. The novel I should like to look at briefly is a well-known one that has received much comment, *Misericordia*. I choose this because it is a work whose theme or content could easily have qualified it for a Naturalist label, but whose treatment of such a theme simply precludes such a denomination.

Misericordia still evinces many characteristics typical of both nineteenth-century fiction and of Galdós's earlier manner. The opening of the novel, with its careful scene-setting which serves to establish a precise environment—in a novel where the external environment does figure prominently—is almost a model of nineteenth-century practice, in which it is entirely normal to home in on the characters from a distance via the description of the landscape or other physical environment. We have, too, the use of an inorganic I-narrator, with his occasional first-person interventions, old-fashioned pretence at non-omniscience in what is fully omniscient narration, and quaint apostrophes to the reader of the 'pues, señor' type.[31] We also have, as in so much of Galdós's work, the depiction of the economic decline of the middle classses and their desperate attempts to maintain appearances, though here in extreme form. Finally, we have in this novel probably the best descriptions of urban low life—vagrants, paupers, panhandlers, ragamuffins, cripples genuine and simulated, and their haunts—in the whole of nineteenth-century Spanish fiction, descriptions which, despite the undoubted element of implied protest at social injustice, are carried out with a complete lack of sentimentality and idealization. Galdós's picture of the indigent and the wretched is not a pretty one, socially or morally; what we are shown is human degradation. It is this aspect of the novel that brings it close to the Naturalist ambition to study society the better to understand it and thereby improve it. Yet, paradoxically, Galdós's novel of 1897 is far removed from the scientific aspirations of the authentic Naturalist novel. And the reason for this is that *Misericordia* is as much, if not more, a study in fabulation as a depiction of mendicity in late nineteenth-century Madrid.

It would appear that in this novel Galdós is giving his characters greater autonomy, that is, greater freedom to use their inventive capacity, than in many previous ones. This is indirectly reflected in a hitherto untypical use of *style indirect libre*, albeit a tentative one.[32] Rather more obviously and importantly this new approach is enshrined in the imaginative behaviour of the characters, primarily, but not exclusively, in that of the protagonist herself. There is in Spanish literature an obvious precedent to what Benina does. Faced with a problem not of his making, Sancho Panza created a fictitious version of Dulcinea on the basis of what he had heard Don Quixote say and later had to confront a 'real life' princess. Galdós's novel requires that Benina create Don Romualdo out of thin air, but since the real Don Romualdo who will eventually turn up has strong connections with the Casa de la Misericordia, the logically-minded reader will reasonably infer that the choice of name was a subconscious memory on the part of Benina. But that inference, logical though it is, would miss the point of Benina's inventiveness, or rather of the author's use of the characters in this novel.

Finding herself in a quandary, like Sancho before her, Benina invents a benefactor, and having invented him gets into ever deeper water by having to maintain the fiction. Benina's invention, with all its attendant detail which she provides with relish, is described by the narrator as a 'simulacro perfecto de la verdad', words with which Galdós inaugurates a gently ironic game with his characters and novelesque material. The phrase, after all, is the ultimate description of a Realist novel, a perfect simulacrum, one that stands in for the real thing, reminding us of Thackeray's dictum 'the Art of Novels is to represent Nature'. Benina does what a storyteller does: embroider the fiction with the trappings of reality, in her case a whole household composed of individuals with their own peculiar characteristics; in other words, she is inventing her own novel. Galdós has, of course, allowed the character to go far beyond the necessary white lie to explain the provenance of the money; Benina is in effect using poetic licence through a feat of imagination. As the narration progresses, the narrator increasingly emphasizes the imaginative capacity of the characters. Almudena's conjurings enthral Benina, not because they are true but because they deserve to be: '[...] Benina se embelesaba oyéndole, y si a pie juntillas no le creía, se dejaba ganar y seducir de la ingenua poesía del relato, pensando que si aquello no era verdad, debía serlo. [...] lo que contaba Almudena era de lo que *no se sabe*. ¿Y no puede suceder que alguno sepa lo que no sabemos los demás?'(OC, V, 1910). Furthermore, the characters imagine another world, a parallel world of which they have but a dim awareness, as we have of dreams. These are worlds that, like dreams, intrude but are not understood, 'cosas verdaderas de otro mundo que se vienen a éste', in Benina's words. The 'otro mundo' is marvellously ambiguous and hints at a playful author, for he, too, has two worlds to contend with and imports truths from one to the other, except that 'éste', the world that Benina knows, is for the real author the world of his fictions, that is, of his imagination, but composed in part of 'cosas verdaderas'. If the *Reyes Magos* existed in the real world, why should there not be other 'Reyes *de ilusión*' to succour the needy, asks Benina. Galdós writes the phrase in italics, that is to say it is given the appearance of a written, authorial statement. It is almost as if Galdós were by implication claiming an author's right to fabulate. Fabulation, not just representation, is what he is paradoxically defending in this most naturalistic of his novels. And he does so ingeniously by proxy, that is to say through the medium of his characters, who engage in make-believe.

Several times throughout the novel Galdós refers to the powerful imagination of his characters. Obdulia and Frasquito, like the two central characters Benina and Almudena, are great inventors of stories. Obdulia refers to her 'facultad de figurarme las cosas que no he visto nunca' (OC, V, 1922). She does not need to visit Paris, she explains, because she has already imagined herself there, so she would prefer Germany or Switzerland. Her 'delirio imaginativo' (OC, V, 1923) is so contagious (the word is the narrator's) that it affects her admirer too. Not that Frasquito de Ponte needs any encouragement to give free rein to his imagination; for if Obdulia lives in a dreamworld, her admirer 'casi le superaba en poder imaginativo' (OC, V, 1917). And, as if to remind us of the characterizing trait of the personage, the phrase 'poder imaginativo' is repeated but a few pages later (OC, V, 1920). Doña Paca, too, allows her imagination to run away with her and invents escapades and misdemeanours for her maidservant that have no basis in the latter's life. But the two women share a strange ability to intuit the future. For just as Benina expects a miracle (and unwittingly invents the miracle-worker), so Doña Paca accurately sees in a dream the source of her future economic salvation. Indeed, Doña Paca has great difficulty in distinguishing fact from fiction. She cannot accept what Don Romualdo and even Frasquito say of Benina: 'El aturdimiento, el vértigo mental de Doña Paca fueron tan grandes, que su alegría se trocó súbitamente en tristeza, y dio en creer que cuanto decían allí era ilusión de sus oídos; ficticios los seres con quienes hablaba, y mentira todo[...]' (OC, V, 1968).

At this juncture, Doña Paca completely and amusingly rejects the 'truth' in favour of the 'fiction', that is to say she opts to accept the ideal version created by Benina's fertile imagination rather than the mundane version created by a non-too-spiritual man of the cloth who brings economic salvation but no spiritual enrichment:

> Yo le suplico a usted, mi Sr. D. Romualdo —dijo Doña Francisca
> enteramente trastornada ya—, que no crea nada de eso; que no haga
> ningún caso de las Beninas figuradas que puedan salir por ahí, y se
> atenga a la propia y legítima Nina; a la que va de asistenta a su casa
> de usted todas las mañanas, recibiendo allí tantos beneficios, como
> los he recibido yo por conducto de ella. Ésta es la verdadera; ésta la
> que hemos de buscar y encontraremos con la ayuda del Sr. de Cedrón
> y de su digna hermana Doña Josefa, y de su sobrina Doña Patros...
> Usted me negará que la conoce, por hacer un misterio de su virtud y
> santidad; pero esto no le vale, no señor. (OC, V, 1968)

There is of course no Doña Josefa or Doña Patros; but Benina's
invention is so ingrained in Doña Paca's imagination that it cannot
be displaced by the new Don Romualdo. Rather than accept Don
Romualdo's own account she prefers to reassert Benina's, as she does
at the end to the very progenitor of the tale herself:

> Pues el milagro es una verdad, hija, y ya puedes comprender que nos
> lo ha hecho tu D. Romualdo, ese bendito, ese arcángel, que en su
> modestia no quiere confesar los beneficios que tú y yo le debemos... y
> niega sus méritos y virtudes... y dice que no tiene por sobrina a Doña
> Patros... y que no le han propuesto para Obispo... Pero es él, es él,
> porque no puede haber otro, no, no puede haberlo, que realice estas
> maravillas. (OC, V, 1982)

In the end Doña Paca will deny her loyal servant, but what Galdós
makes very clear is that she denies her because of the direct
intervention of her daughter-in-law, Juliana, who is the one character
in the novel who is guided solely by practical, down-to-earth,
materialistic considerations:

> Sentíase [Doña Paca] oprimida bajo la autoridad que las ideas de
> Juliana revelaban con sólo expresarse, y ni la ribeteadora se daba
> cuenta de su influjo gobernante, ni la suegra de la pasividad con que
> se sometía. Era el eterno predominio de la voluntad sobre el capricho,
> y de la razón sobre la insensatez'. (OC, V, 1977)

Thus, Benina's banishment from the Juárez household is not just a
monument to ingratitude but is also presented as the triumph of
reason over imagination.

It is, of course, Benina who has been given the major responsibility
for fabulation, but she is aided, significantly, by a companion who

cannot observe the external world. In his Moorish/Jewish persona of Mordejai, Almudena becomes another fabulator. In the world of material objects Almudena can only distinguish dark masses against the light, 'pero en lo de los mundos misteriosos que se extienden encima y debajo, fuera y dentro del nuestro, sus ojos veían claro' (OC, V, 1912). Thus, for the purposes of telling his tales, Mordejai can see perfectly clearly, whether it is a matter of angels, or Moorish horseriders with their white cloaks fluttering in the wind, or indeed the regal *Samdai* and his dazzling entourage. Mordejai's tales are so entrancing that his audience of deprived women is captivated: 'Oían esto las tres mujeres embobadas, mudas, fijos los ojos en la cara del ciego, entreabiertas las bocas. [...] no se hallaban dispuestas a creer y acabaron creyendo' (OC, V, 1913). The point about the fables invented by Benina and Almudena is not so much that they are plausible (Almudena's are scarcely so), but that they are appealing. Galdós does not make Benina say that she believes Almudena's fabulous conjurations and magic formulae, but rather that she is sufficiently fascinated by the Moor's account to believe in *the possibility of their effects*. Here Galdós seems to be hinting at what is after all an ancient quality of a good storyteller, namely that the impact of the tale depends less on a close relationship to reality and more on the teller's persuasive imagination.

Paradoxically, yet in another sense logically, the biggest fabulator of all can bring about change in other people's lives but not in her own. Although we are, of course, dealing here with a saintly and Christ-like figure, as the constant biblical echoes make perfectly clear, she is a heterodox one from a narrowly religious point of view. The saviour that Benina so convincingly invents leaves her as baffled and confused as the princess Dulcinea left Sancho bewildered and frustrated at the prospect of three thousand three hundred lashes to disenchant someone he had wilfully fabricated in the first place. Benina could more easily believe in the Don Romualdo of her imagination than in the Don Romualdo of flesh and blood: '[...] encaminóse a San Sebastián, pensando por el camino en D. Romualdo y su familia, pues de tanto hablar de aquellos señores, y de tanto comentarlos y describirlos, había llegado a creer en su existencia' (OC, V, 1929). It is the appearance of the real priest that creates the problem for Benina, not because she is afraid of being found out, but rather because she finds it difficult to reconcile those two worlds mentioned earlier. Time and again the narrator emphasizes the confusion in her mind. The first time the appearance of the priest is reported to her this confusion lasts a mere instant ('confusa un instante por la rareza del caso, lo dio pronto al olvido'), but when more and more outsiders appear to appropriate her invention her perplexity grows. She is described as experiencing 'una gran confusión o vértigo en su cabeza', and '[...] confusa, sintiendo que lo real y lo imaginario se entrelazaban en su cerebro' (OC, V, 1951); and again, '[...] sintió [...] que se renovaba en su mente la extraña confusión y mezcolanza de lo real y lo imaginado' (OC, V, 1958); and yet again, 'tenía [...] un espantoso lío en la cabeza con aquel dichoso clérigo, tan semejante [...] al suyo, al de su invención' (OC, V, 1959). The repeated references to the difficulty of distinguishing between invention and reality are not, of course, casual and add up to a very clear pointer to what is in the novelist's mind.

Seeing Don Romualdo in the flesh brings with it astonishment ('llegó al mayor grado de confusión y vértigo de su mente') but also the final realization on the part of Benina that her invention has its own autonomy, is no longer, that is, dependent on her. For a moment she feels compelled to run after the disappearing priest to claim him back as hers: 'Dígame si es usted el mío, mi D. Romualdo, u otro' (OC, V, 1961).[33] But she desists, as if realizing the futility of this and recognizing that she has lost her patent: 'Volvióse a casa muy triste, y ya no se apartó de su mente la idea de que el benéfico sacerdote alcarreño no era invención suya, de que todo lo que soñamos tiene su existencia propia, y de que las mentiras entrañan verdades' (OC, V, 1961). In the end she is left to ponder which is the real version and which is the fake, but she cannot tell. This is where *Misericordia* so accurately foreshadows the Modernist preoccupation with the nature of the relationship between art and reality, between the world and the book. What Galdós seems to imply through his characters is that what ultimately matters in art is the creative force of the imagination. In *Misericordia*, reality is shaped by the imagination as much as imagination by reality. Obliquely, but inescapably, the novelist is claiming the right to indulge his inventive capacity free from the shackles of any doctrine that proposed turning the genre into a quasi-scientific endeavour. What is remarkable is that in a novel so rooted in the miseries and sufferings taken from the real world, Galdós managed to stake a powerful claim for the liberating role of the imagination in our lives. And in so doing he proves that art does not have to be escapist to be imaginative.

If Galdós's *Misericordia* shows an older writer who is adapting and evolving the Realist formula to break new ground, there is an almost exactly contemporaneous case of a younger writer who, not having formed part of the Realist tradition, nevertheless does much the same thing as Galdós, although rather more brashly. If there is a clear case of hybridization in fin de siècle Spanish literature between nineteenth-century (Realist) storytelling and twentieth-century (Modernist) fictionalizing, I suggest it is to be found in Ángel Ganivet's *Los trabajos del infatigable creador Pío Cid*. Ganivet's philosophical forays, *España filosófica contemporánea* and *Idearium español*, reveal an eclectic and often uneasy mixture of Positivist, Idealist and even at times traditional Catholic thought. The same, in literary rather than philosophical terms, applies to his two Pío Cid novels, *La conquista del reino de Maya* and *Los trabajos del infatigable creador Pío Cid*. *Los trabajos* is at times, and for pages at a time, a perfectly typical Realist account of changing human relationships in a situation governed by economic, political and emotional circumstances, and also evinces some recourse to chance to spur on the storyline. Much of the narrative has a this-happened-then-that linear structure and is in standard omniscient form despite a first-person narrator who comes and goes. Some of the pages that deal with the to-ings and fro-ings of the characters in Madrid and the domestic tensions of the Pío Cid household could have come straight out of the Galdós of the middle period. And yet, of course, no one could possibly mistake Ganivet's novel for a well-wrought Realist product. It is not merely that plot has been wholly replaced by incident, which it has, but that the manner of presentation of these incidents often intrudes into the narrative, drawing attention to the mechanics of fiction rather than contributing to the credibility of the account. The personalized narrator (called Ángel, as we later learn) who introduces the story goes to great lengths to authenticate the account he is about to relate by explaining his sources and his own knowledge of the hero. But the fact is that for virtually every assertion of historicity there is an ironic comment or giveaway remark that completely sabotages the stated aim. Verisimilitude is not an authorial objective; rather is there a deliberate attempt to create a constant tension between truth and invention, between the narrator's role as witness and *histor*, on the one hand, and his role as progenitor of verbal inventions, on the other. The procedure recalls Conrad's use of Marlow as a kind of artificial reconstructor, except that Ganivet's procedure altogether lacks Conrad's subtlety. Ganivet does not merely question the objectivity of the narrator but the whole status of the tale. Having been at some pains to explain the origins of the biography of Pío Cid, Ganivet's narrator continues:

> Comprenderá el amable lector lo difícil que ha de ser a un historiador o novelista habérselas con un héroe de tan repelosa catadura. Un hombre que no suelta prenda jamás, un arca cerrada como el protagonista de esta historia, es un tipo que parece inventado para poner a prueba a algún consumado maestro en el arte de evocar en letras de molde a los seres humanos. Mi obra no es una evocación, sino una modesta relación de un testigo de presencia; pero un hombre que, si no ocultó su vida, no dio a nadie noticias de ella, dejando a los curiosos el cuidado de escudriñarla, no es posible que sea enteramente conocido y justificado. Mucho me temo que, a pesar de mi buena voluntad, el malaventurado Pío Cid tenga que sufrir la pena póstuma de no ser comprendido o de que le tomen por engendro fantástico y absurdo, fundándose en lo incongruente de mi relato, que no abraza toda su vida, sino varios retazos de ella, zurcidos por mí con honradez y sinceridad, pero sin arte. (OC, II, 12–13)

As if this playing with the historicity of the account were not enough, we are shortly afterwards regaled with a chapter entitled 'El protoplasma' from a novel written by the narrator's informant, the disillusioned newspaperman Cándido Vargas, and found among the latter's documents. Despite obvious departures from historical reality identified by Ángel, the chapter is intercalated in the account because it presents Pío Cid centre-stage, but not before we learn from the putative author himself that '[...] yo estaba entonces sugestionado por la novedad naturalista; para mí una novela debía tener fisiología, mucha fisiología y muchos detalles descriptivos, y de los héroes huir como el diablo de la luz' (OC, II, 57). Cándido Vargas's own admission, added to the narrator's comment of an 'epígrafe apestosamente fisiológico', has the inevitable consequence of forcing us to see the intercalated tale as a skit on Naturalism, which indeed it is, something which becomes obvious when we read the descriptions of the characters' appearance as well as their conversation and actions, all a *reductio ad absurdum* of the Naturalists' technique of meticulous description of physiology, temperament and environment. Yet even before we reach this point, Ganivet, through his narrator Ángel, has made it clear in the opening pages of the book that his approach to the biographical reconstruction of the personage is going to be wholly different from those currently in vogue. Although initially tempted to 'satisfacer mi curiosidad de novelista incipiente y utilizarle en una obra de psicología novelesca al uso', he later changed his mind and instead of employing 'los procedimientos literarios que las escuelas en boga preconizan', in which the subject is dissected as if he were a guinea-pig, he decided to write 'una biografía escrita con amor' (OC, II, 9–10).

From the very beginning, then, Ganivet insists in a lighthearted but pointed way that his novel has nothing to do with Naturalism, that it is self-consciously different from current fashion. This alleged departure from contemporary norms is to be observed in a number of features of the novel, including the extravagance and fertile imagination of the protagonist, utterly unorthodox in his actions and ideas. But beyond the sheer tongue-in-cheek extravaganza of the hero's disquisitions and behaviour, behind whom we detect an inventive but whimsical author, there is also the aspect already indirectly alluded to, namely the creation of a fiction which ironically draws attention to itself as fiction rather than as fact. There are numerous instances of this, but one in particular stands out. Some hours before his departure for Madrid after the election campaign in Granada, Pío Cid, accompanied by Ángel, attends a literary circle. Among the various readings that take place that evening there is one of a newly written tale intended by its author for a collection of *Tragedias vulgares* which he is about to publish. This is the story of Juanico el ciego and his daughter Mercedillas. There is no suggestion that the tragic tale of the blind man is anything but fiction, yet at the end of the reading Pío Cid announces that he had not only personally known the blind man and Mercedillas but that he could add certain obscure biographical details unknown to the author of the tale. These details, taken from 'life', only serve to suggest to Ángel that the tale bears a resemblance to the Oedipus myth and could be further elaborated to illustrate the principle of the Fates, while the author of the tale expresses his desire to incorporate Pío Cid's additions, something which the latter warns against on the grounds that 'cuando un escritor cambia de punto de vista, ha de cambiar también de procedimiento, no debe remendarla, sino destruirla y hacer otra nueva' (OC, II, 436). Not content with turning the episode into a life-versus-literature debate in which the reader cannot tell what is truth and what is fiction, Ganivet muddies the waters further by making a by now grown-up Mercedes and her seducer join the train in which, twenty-four hours later, Pío Cid and Ángel are travelling to Madrid. Having recognized her, Pío Cid informs his companion, whose later comment in his role as narrator is pointed enough: 'Era la primera vez en mi vida que veía enlazarse el arte con la realidad' (OC, II, 464). If we bear in mind that the private exchange which takes place between Mercedes and Pío Cid in the railway carriage while Ángel and Mercedes's companion repair to the station buffet is reported verbatim by Ángel, we may begin to see the point of the ironic game that Ganivet is playing with his characters, both hero and narrator. The character Ángel, as the name implies, represents the author in his function as storyteller: he relates, but he also knows everything there is to know about his tale. That is a 'realidad'. But in the story itself the inventiveness or creative labours ('trabajos') are ascribed to the hero. That, of course, is a fiction. Ganivet playfully intertwines the two levels of the story, that of the adventures of Pío Cid and that of the reconstruction of the bio-graphy, but in essence the biography consists of Pío Cid's own inventions, a virtual autobiography or self-creation, in turn a reflection of the ineluctable truth that a writer's autobiography is in his books. Ganivet constantly insists that what we are reading is, paradoxically, both true and contrived, as, for example, in the episode of the encounter with the daughter of Juanico el ciego:

Nuestro encuentro fue providencial, y más que suceso verídico parecerá a muchos combinación novelesca, no sólo por la perspicacia que demostró Pío Cid al reconocer a Mercedes, sino por la circunstancia singular de estar nosotros al tanto de su historia por el relato que de ella nos hizo Antón del Sauce. En este concurso de felices coincidencias no ha de verse sin embargo la mano de un novelista; ha de verse la mano oculta que gobierna las cosas humanas, la cual quiso darle a Mercedes un amigo y defensor que luchara contra la fatalidad misteriosa que llevaba dentro de su ser la hija del desgraciado Juan de la Cruz. (OC, II, 476–7)

27

The 'fatalidad misteriosa' is no longer the hereditary or environmental Determinism of the Naturalists; it is mysterious only because
a novelist does not declare his hand. As Ángel ironically implies, we
the readers (and we must not forget that the story of Mercedes starts
off as a tale that is read and discussed) look for reasons why a
character behaves in a particular way, whereas the real reason is
staring us in the face. I have no wish to claim that Ganivet's novel is
some kind of latter-day or post-Modernist fabrication in which a
novelist does little more than contemplate his fictional navel; rather
do I see it as a claim, or recognition, comically realized, that the
novel aspires to entertain by creating alternative worlds through an
effort of the imagination, not by pretending to study the real one.
Ganivet has abandoned the tenets on which the modern novel had
been built, but without having fully abandoned its modes of narration.[34]

The third novelist I should like to refer to is Pío Baroja. Despite his
unassailable position within Spain as the country's premier novelist
of the first half of the twentieth century, he does not enjoy a similar
reputation abroad, nor has scholarly criticism on the whole been as
successful in explaining his novelesque creations as in the case of
Unamuno's or Valle-Inclán's. Many still labour under the misappre-
hension that Baroja came late to the art of fiction after having tried
his hand at medicine, business and journalism. This is hugely
misleading, for, journalism apart (all major writers were forced to be
journalists of one kind or another at the turn of the century),[35]
Baroja was a writer long before he was anything else. He was barely
seventeen when he wrote a long series of articles on Russian
literature published in *La Unión Liberal* in early 1890, and although
much of his material was culled from Vicomte de Vogüé's *Le Roman
russe*, it still evinces a strong interest in literary affairs. Between the
ages of twenty and twenty-one he published some two dozen *cuentos*,
and a year later, while practising as a country doctor, he published
another two dozen or so. He continued writing short stories right
through the 1890s and even after his début as a novelist in 1900. By
the time *Camino de perfección* was published in 1902 (after
serialization in 1901 in *La Opinión*), Baroja, at the age of twenty-
nine, had been writing in public for not less than twelve years.[36]
Baroja's formation and emergence as a writer belong incontestably to
the 1890s.

If ever a major Spanish writer was schooled to take over the Naturalist mantle in Spain, then that writer, with his deep agnosticism, his early interest in physiology, and his branching out into psycho-physics, was Pío Baroja.[37] Yet, as we have seen, Baroja did not consider himself a Naturalist. Like Unamuno, he dismissed neither Naturalism nor its high priest Zola (although he later described Daudet and the Goncourt brothers as literary pygmies); he merely considered the movement *passé*. In his early stories Baroja sought other effects, and the influence of Poe is probably discernible. In 'Noche de Vela' (1893), for example, the description of the dying girl is so oblique that it makes us wonder whether we are witnessing a scene that is meant to be real or whether the delirious 'father' is imagining the whole thing. A passing reference to 'escribía [...] junto a su mesa' suggests that he is a writer, but he is not writing; he is pacing up and down in despair listening to the 'gorgoteo siniestro, semejante al que produce el agua al salir de una botella'. The reference to a bottle is suggestive enough, so is the 'insensibilidad' to which his 'exceso de dolor' drives him. And why does Baroja use the reflexive form of the verb in 'Hubo un momento en que se creyó que su hija se moría'? Or why are the sounds of the street at dawn described as 'ruidos extraños' (just as the earlier sound emanating from the alcove was a 'ruido extraño') when on the contrary they should have been entirely familiar? Or, indeed, why is there an apparent description of the moment of death ('cayó para atrás y quedó inmóvil, con los ojos abiertos'), followed *in the same sentence* by a description of recovery ('cesó el delirio, la hija abrió los ojos') which contains a patent contradiction? It would have been interesting to know the reaction of an 1893 reader to this tale, but at least we know what the editor of the newspaper *La Justicia* thought of its short-story writer: he sacked him. Baroja's manner of narrating in his earliest work is a world away from standard Realism, and it immediately raises the question of the status of the story. Nineteenth-century fiction by and large had emulated the methods of history in trying to sustain the illusion of truth. We read a Realist novel *as if* it were true. 'Noche de vela' does not appear to be at all concerned with history-likeness or external truth. On the contrary, it deliberately eschews such a truth by putting obstacles in our path, by hinting that the tale is other than it seems to be. Whether we choose to interpret it as a case of a drunken writer deliriously imagining the

29

whole thing (no dying girl because 'estaba solo'), or whether we see the account as simply being refracted through the fertile imagination of a writer struggling to give form to his nebulous, embryonic inspiration, does not substantially affect the issue. The fact remains that the reality is now in the telling, not in the tale; it is a purely 'poetic' reality.

Not all of Baroja's early stories are as ambiguous as 'Noche de vela'; but quite a number share this apparent compulsion to go beyond external appearances through the use of an array of techniques and an ever-recurring theme: death. One of these techniques is the use of a *ritornello*. In 'Melancolía' (1893) the 'Y estaba triste' refrain is used to encapsulate the painful insight of the man who has been successful at everything, including the acquisition of knowledge, yet who hankers after, in his words, 'precisamente lo que no tengo', but who does not know what it is that he is missing and suffers accordingly. We, the readers, are obliged as it were to share that same experience through our enforced frustration. In 'La muerte y la sombra' (1894) much of the story is a description of the colours, sounds and sensations of the countryside as night approaches. The refrain 'y la sombra vencía a la luz', an obvious biblical reversal, is used not only to announce the onset of dusk as father and son make their way home after working in the fields, but also the ebbing away of life from the young man dying from an unspecified disease, so that the 'agonía de la tarde' is inseparable from the dying moments of the man, who looks longingly at nature wishing to surrender his consciousness to the clouds, the wind and the sea, 'la materia eterna e infinita'. And nature in turn seems to be watching him expectantly: 'Los árboles de las cumbres alzaban al cielo sus descarnados brazos de espectro.' At the moment of death 'una estrella corrió por el cielo dejando una brillante ráfaga luminosa'. Far from a Naturalistic description of death with all the physiological paraphernalia, what we have here is an attempt to render the dying moments of a character in pantheistic, quasi-mystical terms. In *Romancero gitano* Federico García Lorca was to treat the death of a child in similar fashion, with the Moon acting as the agent of nature in claiming back a life.

The attempt to capture mental states indirectly through the phantasmagoric description of nature is a Barojan technique frequently used in the stories of the 1890s, and one which will reappear strongly in *Camino de perfección* (1902), in which the countryside is seen through the eyes of the neurotic painter Fernando Ossorio. An allied technique is that of combining unusual perceptions or sensations with memory. In 'Día de niebla' (1894), for example, the account begins as an objective, impersonal description of a seascape on a foggy evening. Gradually we move from description to sensation as sounds and smells intrude; the waves and their agitated motion are then described as the mind of a god and we sense the presence of an observer, which is immediately confirmed as, seated on a rock watching the crashing waves, this observer suddenly hears a scream 'como salido de una garganta humana; aquella nota de dolor se perdió como un átomo de tristeza en la tristeza inmensa de la noche'. But if we expect a dramatic dénouement we are mistaken, for it is only now, in the closing paragraph, that we discover that the terrifying scream heard on a foggy evening in the craggy foreshore is but a distant memory ('recuerdo de lejanas épocas') that is reactivated when the narrator sits alone in his country house and in the silence of the night hears the creaking doors and rustling leaves. The experience has been modulated both by memory and by circumstance and we simply cannot tell whether it was real or imagined. The point, both in this and other Barojan stories, would seem to be that for a writer, *qua* writer, there can be no difference between the real and the imagined.

Occasionally Baroja will use a variety of techniques simultaneously. This is the case in 'El reloj' (1899), where we find the use of a *ritornello*, the effects of alcohol, an unusual setting, and the encompassing silence to evoke a premonition of death. The narrator, 'emborrachado por [...] tristezas y por el alcohol', imagines himself in a castle, where the grandfather clock, 'alto y estrecho como un ataúd', marks the hours with its metallic ticking. The imagined experience of living in the darkened castle away from human foibles seems at first to quieten the narrator's tortured soul, to make him forget his 'locas esperanzas' and 'necias ilusiones', but the encompassing silence induces terror as he feels cut off from the living world and is compelled to implore nature to communicate to him through the sounds of the trees, the leaves and the rain, and the moon to lift the veil of mist from his eyes 'turbios por la angustia de la muerte'. But all is silence, and the *ritornello* (the ticking clock) which had earlier indicated a living time makes its final appearance in altered form: '*Y el reloj sombrío que mide indiferente las horas tristes se había parado para siempre.*'[38]

In these and other stories of the 1890s Baroja seems consciously to move away from a positivistic treatment of phenomena and from a Realist or Naturalist mode of presentation. One could, perhaps, posit a Symbolist influence, given the poem-like structure of many of these stories. Baroja's early style of writing was not appreciated at the time, except by commentators such as Azorín and Unamuno, both of whom wrote early complimentary pieces on him, but these were writers who would have been sympathetic to his breaking of old moulds. These early characteristics of Baroja's narrative prose, and especially his attempt to convey abnormal, irrational or obsessive experiences and imaginings, survived into the novel that catapulted him to fame among the literary intelligentsia of Madrid, *Camino de perfección*, but before then he published two novels that confirm the move away from dominant nineteenth-century modes. *Aventuras, inventos y mixtificaciones de Silvestre Paradox* (1900–1), the first of Baroja's novels to see the light of day, albeit in serial form, is, as well as a Pickwickian account of the life of bohemian intellectuals in fin de siècle Madrid, a skit on Positivism. Indeed, much of the story is a satire of nineteenth-century *cientifismo* and pseudo-scientific theorizing that Baroja knew at first hand but found indigestible, as we know from his autobiographical writings. Although not directly mentioned, Naturalism itself rates at least two oblique but inescapable references. The first is to the Naturalist penchant for describing crimes and criminals with meticulous attention to detail. When Silvestre is hired to provide copy for a publication pointedly entitled *Los crímenes modernos. Historia, caracteres, rasgos y genialidades de los criminales de nuestra época*, he burns the candle at both ends enthusiastically describing all the perversions of the criminal mind and the grisly details of their crimes for the benefit of the bourgeois reader, who 'repantigado en su butaca, podía refocilarse leyendo tan amenos horrores' (OC, II, 105), as the narrator comments tongue-in-cheek. The other reference is via a passing but obviously satirical remark on Émile Zola to the effect that even he cannot compete with the ghastly account of degenerate behaviour offered by Ossorio of his family (OC, II, 128).

It is not, however, Naturalism but rather Positivism and its stable-mate Determinism that are the butts of Baroja's satire. This is apparent from the very first page of the novel, in which the initial description of the person of the caretaker takes the form of a description of the clothes that appear at the window: he is a *gorrito*, a *bufanda* and a *chaleco* rather than a person. This is immediately followed by the grotesque introduction of the central character:

CARACTERES ANTROPÓLOGICOS

Pelo:	rojizo
Barba:	idem
Ojos:	castaños
Pulsaciones:	82
Respiraciones:	18 por minuto
Talla:	1,51

Braquicefalia manifiesta

Ángulo facial: Goniómetro de Broca, 80,02

Individuo esencialmente paradoxal. (OC, II, 10)[39]

For Silvestre, knowledge is collection and classification. He is a collector of odds and ends which for the caretaker represent 'el caos' but for him represent the means to an understanding of the world. His aunt, too, had a classification mania in the best nineteenth-century biological tradition: 'Tenía la chifladura clasificadora y coleccionista; para ella el mundo era una inmensa buhardilla que había que ordenar y clasificar; guardaba lo que encontraba en varios paños, hacía un envoltorio, al envoltorio le ponía una etiqueta con su letrero'(OC, II, 22). His uncle's approach to boiling an egg is un-yieldingly, but comically, scientific, as is Silvestre's similar approach to brewing coffee, described by the narrator as of 'una exactitud matemática'. From his own father, a geologist and naturalist, Paradox had learnt to collect fossils and geological specimens, that is, to observe and to gather data, and thence to build a scientific picture of the world, except that Silvestre is really a dreamer masquerading as a scientist: '[...] era interesantísimo para un espíritu observador como el de Silvestre adivinar, por la clase de papel que aún cubría la pared, dónde había estado la sala, dónde la cocina y el comedor, y reconstruir, de una manera más o menos fantástica, las escenas que allí se habrían desarrollado' (OC, II, 16). From his elders, Silvestre learns how to classify knowledge and apply science, except that his knowledge is useless and his inventions droll. He is the ultimate quack scientist who does not just produce mad inventions but whose scientific database is a mere jumble of scraps and museum pieces.

There is a good deal more to Paradox's pseudo-Positivism than an 'espíritu observador' and a habit of accumulating scientific bric-à-brac. His taxidermy, for example, exactly parallels Positivist law-making. The orthodox Positivist started from an accumulation of observed data and then proceeded through a process of induction to formulate the general laws that were supposed to explain the observed facts; that is, from the observation of the world's *external* manifestations the Positivist moved to a consideration of what the world was really like, of its *internal* mechanisms.[40] For Silvestre, taxidermy is not just a matter of observing the animal's external features and reproducing them accurately; it behoves the scientist, in this case in the guise of taxidermist, to go beyond the external, observable universe and explain its inner essence:

> Porque disecar—decía Paradox—no es rellenar la piel de un animal de paja y ponerle después ojos de cristal. Hay algo más en la disecación: la parte del espíritu; y para definir esto—añadía—hay que dar idea de la actitud, marcar la expresión propia del animal, sorprender su gusto, dar idea de su temperamento, de su idiosincrasia, de las condiciones generales de la raza y de las particulares del individuo.
>
> Y como muestra de sus teorías enseñaba su buho, un bicho huraño, grotesco y pensativo, que parecía estar recitando por lo bajo el soliloquio de Hamlet, y la obesa avutarda, toda candor, pudor y cortedad, y su caimán, que colgaba del techo por un alambre, con su sonrisa macabra, llena de doblez y de falsía, y sus ojos entornados, hipócritas y mefistofélicos. (OC, II, 51)

Baroja's satire, as he transforms positivistic science into a search for the soul of stuffing, is unmistakable, as is his mockery of *cientifismo*, apparent in many passing ironic remarks on pseudo-scientific pursuits (e.g. 'No en balde se pasa un hombre la vida estudiando la clasificación de Cuvier'). As if all this were not enough, Baroja at one point turns his mock-scientist into a mock-philosopher. Reading, or perhaps more accurately mis-reading, the German idealists, Silvestre Paradox convinces himself that Krause and other epígones had failed to do justice to the great German philosophers and that he, Paradox, would show the scientific relevance of Kant, Hegel, and Schopenhauer:

'[...] se persuadió a sí mismo de que todas las verdades enunciadas por los filósofos favoritos debían de agruparse formando un sistema o cuerpo de doctrina en armonía con los hechos y con los descubrimientos de la ciencia moderna' (OC, II, 68). The marriage of science and philosophy is to take the form not of a written commentary ('le parecía vulgar y anticuado escribir sus ideas'), but of a geometric representation. Baroja's *reductio ad absurdum* of pseudo-science reaches a peak of mockery in this section of the novel. Silvestre's mathematically conceived metaphysics is a farrago of mumbo-jumbo, non-sequiturs, diagrams, symbols and neologisms, but presented in such a deadpan way paragraph after paragraph, that it is made to sound realistic. It is, of course, nothing of the sort, for the ambitious cosmology is based on spurious links between the opening verse of St John's gospel, a sprouting potato which Silvestre finds at the bottom of his wardrobe, and a hotchpotch of evolutionary theory and Kantian- and Schopenhauerian-derived pseudo-concepts such as *Voluntad-nouménica* and *Reflejo-nouménico,* not to mention circles, polygons, dots, crosses and coloured dashes. From this extraordinary attempt to explain the self, matter, consciousness, free will, life and everything, the narrator extracts the simplest of conclusions: 'Paradox era, por tanto, determinista' (OC, II, 70). Here we have Baroja revealing the butt of his satire: deterministic systems. Despite the grotesque distortion, so close to the real object is Baroja's satire that he even makes Paradox emulate his Positivist models by doing, in a mock-serious way of course, what Positivist thinkers had been doing, namely, using their systems as predictive tools: '[...] Silvestre se creyó en el caso de señalar algunas consecuencias de su sistema y augurar para el porvenir una época de la desaparición del egoísmo agresivo, en que el hombre tendría un máximum de libertad, de alegría, de vida y de luz; un mínimum de dogma, de ley, de tristeza y de oscuridad' (OC, II, 70). Here we can see the novelist having a passing dig at the utopias predicted by evolutionary sociologists and political thinkers.

The allegedly unscientific nature of Determinist or Positivist systems of thought is cleverly mirrored in the narrative structure adopted for the novel. The narrator, or compiler of facts as he calls himself, makes much of the lengths to which he has gone to ascertain the data of his biography. Having drawn a blank in his researches, he comes across a distinguished university professor who

35

had known Paradox and who hands over his notes on the personage, 'datos seguros, irrebatibles e indiscutibles' (OC, II, 17). Such is the good professor's ability to authenticate the biography, that he is even able to expound scientifically the various etymologies of the hero's curious surname (which needless to say are given tongue-in-cheek by Baroja). Unfortunately, having provided his scientifically irrefutable information, the professor privately lets it be known to the compiler that he rather fears that

> los datos suministrados por él resulten falsos, y que toda la historia aquí contada no sea más que pura mixtificación. Ha añadido que puros indicios le hacen suponer que Silvestre Paradox no se llamaba Silvestre, ni siquiera Paradox. ¿Es verdad, es mentira todo esto? Lo ignoramos. (OC, II, 45)

The biography is thus immersed in complete uncertainty, not to say scepticism, about its origins, an epistemological doubt about the nature of art and writing that was about to become one of the characteristic qualities of Modernist endeavour. Furthermore, when the professor later reappears as a personage in Paradox's biography, he turns out to be not the dispassionate and objective man of science we had been led to believe he was, but rather a complete charlatan whose magnum opus was a treatise on the morphology of words according to their resemblance to the songs of birds and the cries of animals with the lexical complexity of a language being determined by the region's fauna. Baroja is incorrigible in his insistence on reducing scientific plausibility to farce.

In this, his only comic novel, therefore, Baroja has offered us an ingenious debunking of pseudo-scientific systems of thought that were all the rage in the latter half of the nineteenth century in the whole of Europe but more incongruously in a scientifically backward Spain, systems of thought that made false claims to science and to the advancement of knowledge and that promised to transform society. It is not science itself that Baroja is mocking; the touches of parody in which the novel abounds indicate that his ridicule is aimed at precisely those whom he denounced in his autobiographical writings for claiming to be men of science when they were simply 'mixtificadores', a particularly common breed in late nineteenth-century Spain, described aptly enough by a word which does not exist. Just a few short years after he completed his medical studies, Determinism for Baroja had become a joke.

Baroja's second novel (the first if we go by earliest appearance in book form), also reveals a stance which appears to question Determinist explanations. *La casa de Aizgorri* (1900) is an altogether different kind of work, serious, sentimental, and full of vague, atmospheric symbolism heavy with foreboding. Yet it maintains a thesis which is anti-Determinist and arrived at, moreover, within an exploration of Determinism itself. Space rules out a detailed examination, so I shall limit myself to the briefest of treatments of the theme of this frustrated play which became a novel in dialogue form.

There are a number of features in this work which appear to resist logical explanation (including at one point a 'stream of consciousness' utterance that defies decoding), but the main lines of its thesis seem reasonably clear. The central theme is that of degeneracy, real or imagined. Águeda detects signs of abnormality in her father and brother (or half-brother, for this, oddly, is left in doubt) and ascribes this to the effects of alcoholism brought about by the distillery which has been in family ownership for three generations. This idea of family degeneracy is also sustained by the father, who speaks of madness in his family and who is portrayed as an alcoholic tormented by bouts of guilt-ridden anxiety over the loss of someone whom he has mistreated (possibly his dead wife, but again this is never explained). The heroine dates her initial awareness of degeneracy to her very first meeting with her brother when she was at the impressionable age of fourteen and he was nine (another unexplained oddity) and she was able to observe his sadistic cruelty towards animals and even herself. Águeda's belief in a degeneracy handed down from generation to generation has been provoked by the family doctor's previous attempt to explain the perverse behaviour of the boy as the possible result of an inherited condition and his reference now to the damaging effects of alcohol in the community. His declaration that '[el alcohol] no mata, pero hace degenerar a la descendencia' (OC, I, 21) confirms Águeda in her suspicion that she is just such a degenerate product and that therefore she cannot marry the man who aspires to her hand and whose love she would wish to return. It is at this point in the novel that the statement on Determinism reaches its maximum expression. Águeda is convinced ('tengo la certidumbre') that she has inherited a mental affliction induced in turn by a distorted environment, the distillery. Her fears are rendered in poetic language but the thrust is clear:

> ÁGUEDA: [...] De noche me despierto con sobresalto y veo caras que me contemplan, y siento que algo me acecha y me espía... Salgo al balcón de mi cuarto y veo la fábrica con sus ventanas iluminadas, ojos inyectados de fiera, que buscan una presa en la negrura de la noche. Y luego veo el río a la luz de la luna y me turba, y contemplo el cielo estrellado, y el corazón me palpita con fuerza ante un peligro que no comprendo.
>
> DON JULIÁN: ¿No puedes dominar esas impresiones?
>
> ÁGUEDA: No. Las domino a veces por un esfuerzo de voluntad, pero vuelven a renacer. Ahora mismo, cualquier cosa se me figura que puede tener influencia en mi vida: una estrella que corre, una luz que se apaga. Lucho contra todas esas ideas; pero temo, ahora más que nunca, quedar vencida, y que, en un momento de terror, me envuelvan completamente esas alas negras. (OC, I, 25)

In fact Don Julián, the doctor, despite his unwitting contribution to Águeda's predicament, rejects his own previous theoretical suppositions about inherited mental illness and declines to be persuaded by the diagnosis of her condition. His suggestion to Mariano, Águeda's suitor, that the malady may exist only in her imagination is countered by the latter's remark that this is all that is needed to explain her terrifying ordeal. Here we have the crux of the matter: whether Águeda's condition has a physiological cause, in which case the deterministic thesis will be upheld, or whether she is suffering from a self-induced delusion.[41] It is Mariano, rather than the doctor, who, refusing to accept the inevitability of Águeda's condition, determines to remove the imagined cause of her affliction. Yet paradoxically, when Baroja makes him express his resolution, he does so in Darwin-speak:

> MARIANO: [...] Ahora empezará la lucha. Veremos quien vence. [...] Águeda lo quiere. Antes de ser mía exige que esta fábrica se cierre. Lo quiere. Eso basta. (Se detiene a contemplar el retrato que se halla sobre el sitial.) Aquí está el fundador, Machín de Aizgorri, el guerrero que sembró el espanto en toda Guipúzcoa. ¡Pobre

hombre! ¡Cómo degeneró tu casta! Al cabo de cientos de años la savia enérgica de los Aizgorri no produce más que plantas enfermas y venenosas. Pero entre su floración malsana hay un lirio blanco y puro, y ése yo lo arrancaré de la casa de Aizgorri y lo llevaré donde hay sol y alegría y amor. Sí, Machín; no me importa ese gesto adusto ni ese ademán altivo. Tu nieta, descendiente de los más nobles hidalgos, será la mujer de un fundidor, hijo de ferrones. Sí, lo será, lo será. (OC, I, 32)

The distillery is indeed destroyed, first by flooding, which ruins all the stock in the cellars, and then by fire, which destroys not just the factory but the entire village. The obvious religious symbolism of these agents of purification should nevertheless not obscure the fact that what Baroja seems to be emphasizing in Águeda's recovery is not so much the intervention and impact of external events as the process of self-healing. Terrified of being left on her own with a dying father she nevertheless brings herself to agree to her brother's departure (clearly an intended symbol, given the associations with his arrival), and hours later recovers her composure at the side of her father's corpse by an effort of the will:

Águeda se asoma a la puerta de la alcoba y mira, y al darse cuenta de que la muerte ha pasado por allí, cierra los ojos y espera algo, algo que va a caer sobre su alma, a hundirla para siempre en el abismo de la locura. Y Águeda nota que retozan en su alma las sonrisas de las fantasías enfermas, las largas y vibrantes carcajadas; pero de pronto un impulso enérgico le dice que su razón no vacila, y ante lo inexplicable y ante la muerte, su espíritu se recoge y se siente con energía, y, victoriosa de sus terrores, entra con lentitud en la alcoba de su padre, se arrodilla junto a la cama y reza largo tiempo por el alma del muerto. (OC, I, 37)

This reconciliation with the phenomenon of death, in clear contrast with her earlier experience of it when, upon her mother's death, 'veía sombras que se echaban sobre mí' (OC, I, 25), is the first step in the recovery of her sanity. Later, when a hostile crowd of striking workers invades her house, she summons up the courage to cross the dike— which she has earlier associated with her terrors—in the darkness and join Mariano in his 'legitimate' enterprise of the iron foundry.

Águeda is thus shown to have recovered her will and established control over her environment. Moreover, the doctor, who had been responsible for stating the theory of degeneracy, turns up at the foundry in a symbolic gesture of solidarity with those who assert their freedom to overcome adversity. The sentimental epilogue leaves us in no doubt: natural and supernatural terrors are left behind. Águeda no longer feels doomed to producing congenitally defective children, and in forging the remaining flywheel and fulfilling the commercial contract against all the odds, the characters prove their ability to control their destiny. Both congenital and environmental Determinism are refuted, and they are refuted, simplistically perhaps but significantly for our purposes, through man's creative endeavour as symbolized by the final scene in which the four characters who refuse to succumb tamely to the pressures of their environment forge not just a piece of machinery to serve man but a whole new future. The creative will provides the solution to the terrors of the night, man-made or not—that seems to be Baroja's thesis in a work which, though scarcely typical of his fiction, is nevertheless highly revealing of his early preoccupations.[42]

I hope that the preceding excursion through the work, both critical and creative, of Spanish writers in the 1890s and early years of the 1900s has shown some pointers to the modifications that fictional narrative was undergoing at the turn of the century. The well-known landmarks of Modernist fiction, whether in Spain or in the rest of Europe, were still to appear and tend to be associated with the period of the First World War and its aftermath—in Spain, Unamuno's *Niebla* appeared in 1914.[43] But the aesthetic assumptions had already changed and can be traced back to the decline of Realism and Naturalism in the 1890s. The comments of the observers of the time show remarkable agreement in pointing to the collapse of the literary conventions that had governed narrative art for thirty years, while the works of fiction themselves evince clear attempts at innovation. If we use Malcolm Bradbury's list of features quoted at the beginning of this essay, we will see that all of them apply to a greater or lesser degree. In the first place, the reliance on *artistic perception* rather than external description is a category sufficiently broad to cause few problems. All three of the writers we have looked at go far beyond documentary realism and offer us an approach based on transcending an encompassing material reality. Even in Galdós, the most objective writer of the three, history-likeness has become attenuated in favour of a rather more poetic and visionary presentation. The connection with the real has certainly not been lost, but the artist himself seems to see in that reality a world that is too complex to be explained away. Galdós's later novels, of which *Misericordia* is probably the best example, speak to us less of ideological confrontations and social deficiencies and more of humankind's potential to rise above material adversity through creative will power (as indeed Galdós himself was called upon to do as a result of his economic problems). In the second place, conferring a *heightened resonance* to certain observed objects is of course a technique most obvious in Baroja, who uses it constantly in his short stories, but there are examples, too, in Galdós and Ganivet. In *Misericordia*, coins, the ultimate symbol of materialist values, are made to acquire an almost mystical role in the characters' lives and search for survival, and so to a degree are other objects of food and raiment that can no longer be taken for granted. And beyond this there is the heightened consciousness of a vision of the world seen through the inner eyes of a blind man: he it is who sees the 'real' Benina even though he cannot see her physically. In an apparent reaction against the Positivist tendency to reduce all spiritual values to the material, Galdós, through his two central characters of Benina and Almudena, is raising the material to the spiritual. In Ganivet we find a similar heightened consciousness, if not of objects certainly of the people observed by Pío Cid: he has the mysterious power of sensing the quality of a person, knowing people from the inside upon acquaintance, anticipating their reactions, judging their capacities and thereby ascribing them a role.

But it is Malcolm Bradbury's third and fourth descriptors that most clearly point to the future. In *Misericordia* the consciousness of characters plays an enlarged role. Galdós, as we have seen, is by now using *style indirect libre* and allowing his characters a far greater say, for even if the novel is not in dialogue form as was *Realidad* seven years earlier, the direct interventions of the narrator are much reduced compared to earlier fiction, and the thoughts and speeches of the characters, as well as their own inventions, are greatly increased. Instead of being told what the characters think, we are more often shown them thinking. In Ganivet's novel, presentation through consciousness also takes the form of allowing his protagonist

41

to talk endlessly about his singular view of the world and to contrive situations, while in Baroja we often observe the world through the minds of characters who are in some way abnormal, drunk, anxious, fearful, suffering from a neurosis, or at the point of death. Finally, that a revaluation of narrative art is under way is incontestable. To say that art has become 'the writer's essential subject matter' (in Bradbury's phrase) would perhaps be too bold a claim to make of any of the three novelists under scrutiny here, but that the fictions in some way incorporate or reflect the creative world of the artist is both true and enormously suggestive of Modernist preoccupations with the nature and function of art. The very stuff of *Misericordia* is the characters' disposition to fabulate; without their inventiveness, their imaginative capacity, there would be no novel; and Benina's 'perfect simulacrum' is a tale within a tale. In *Los trabajos del infatigable creador Pío Cid* Ganivet virtually allows his character to invent the fictions, that is, the incidents that add up to the novel, while at the same time ironically playing with the idea of fiction-as-fact and fact-as-fiction. And in Baroja, too, we have characters who are in some way creative agents who transform reality, whether it is a writer as in 'Noche de vela', a quack inventor and philosopher as in *Silvestre Paradox*, or, as in *La casa de Aizgorri*, a family of mental degenerates who evoke a world of madness, phantoms and terrors, in turn banished by a different kind of artistic creativity. In all these works we can observe a conscious movement away from the kind of fiction that had reached its zenith as recently as the preceding decade and which lesser writers, perhaps encouraged by the huge commercial success of the translations of Zola's novels in Spain during the late 1890s, were still assiduously cultivating.

There is, of course, a great deal more to say about this decade, not least the change of orientation of another leading Realist and one-time defender of Naturalism, Emilia Pardo Bazán. Here one would necessarily have to defer to the scholar to whom this volume pays homage. For it was Maurice Hemingway who, in an important study of this novelist, showed conclusively the shift of emphasis in her middle-period work, from *Insolación* (1889) to *Memorias de un solterón* (1896).[44] From a Naturalist-inspired desire to render and explain the external world, Pardo Bazán moved to an increasingly un-Zolaesque search for interior meaning and the exploration of the human psyche. In tracing the evolution of Pardo Bazán, Hemingway showed the inadequacy of making too sharp a distinction between the fiction of the late nineteenth and that of the early twentieth centuries. In subscribing to this point of view myself, I would suggest that the samples of fiction of the period 1893–1900 that we have looked at here evince several of the features that were shortly to characterize the Modernist novel. These works were in a very real sense pioneering and help to establish the links between two distinct literary worlds that perhaps were not so antagonistic after all.

2

Looking for Scapegoats

Pardo Bazán and the War of 1898

David Henn

In April 1899, almost exactly a year after the United States Congress had declared war on Spain, Emilia Pardo Bazán published an article entitled 'Asfixia' in the weekly magazine *La Ilustración Artística*. This piece, written against the background of Spain's swift and humiliating defeat in the Spanish–American War and the consequent loss of Cuba, Puerto Rico, and the Philippines, deals with two issues. The first concerns what Pardo Bazán perceived as the asphyxiating silence with which Spain's leading writers, especially the novelists, had responded to the national catastrophe of 1898. The second part of the article involves a brief assessment of the current state of the Carlist question, a discussion prompted by the fact that the pro-Spanish community in Cuba had, according to a report received by Pardo Bazán, aligned itself with the cause of the pretender to the Spanish throne. Thus the Unionists of Cuba, in a desperate attempt to rescue themselves from the seeming horrors of the present situation (a former colony now independent, but effectively under the control of the United States), were prepared to clutch at the straw of an increasingly enfeebled dynastic movement that was commonly associated, even by most conservative Spaniards, with an ideology and a spirit that were very much part of a bygone age.

Yet while the Unionists of Cuba were looking to a past cause to rescue them from their present plight, it is interesting to note that this article of Pardo Bazán opens with the suggestion that the current predicament of the mother country is simply the product of the past, a distant past, now exacting its tribute from the present. Thus she begins her article with an anguished question which is then followed by a tantalizingly undeveloped statement: '¿Dónde hay cosa más actual que las desdichas de España? Actual, sí, y al mismo tiempo ¡tan antigua! No viene de ayer, ni de anteayer... De siempre, o por lo menos de épocas que ya no alcanza la memoria.'[1]

The Galician author then proceeds to inform her readers that such thoughts occur to her while she is in the process of consulting a dozen or more books on the subject of the situation of contemporary Spain, in preparation for a lecture that she is shortly to give in Paris. It is at this point that Pardo Bazán decries the lack of any pertinent response from those she terms 'los literatos de gran renombre en España', having noted that the Spanish books piled on her desk are largely by little-known writers (p. 61). (It transpires from the sixteen items listed in the bibliography to Pardo Bazán's Paris lecture that two of the works she presumably had on her desk were Unamuno's *En torno al casticismo*, which was serialized in *La España Moderna* in the first half of 1895, and Maeztu's *Hacia otra España*, which had just been published.)

In the remainder of the first part of her article for *La Ilustración Artística*, Pardo Bazán signals the urgent need for the publication of essays that would expose problems and inspire a dynamic response. A nation that she describes as backward, floundering, and disheartened requires 'una literatura de acción, estimulante y tónica, despertadora de energías y fuerzas, remediadora de daños' (p. 62). But, as Pardo Bazán gloomily proceeds to suggest, the Spanish people will not read such material, nor indeed any other kind of 'concerned' literature. In fact, she ventures to suggest that were it not for the Spanish-American market, the Spanish publishing industry would be at a pretty pass. The author goes on to note that the Spanish press will not concern itself with any kind of debate on the national situation, preferring instead to give the reading public the journalistic fodder that it craves: namely, lengthy reports on bullfights and accounts of political machinations in far-off provinces, of street disturbances, of marital dramas, of crimes of passion, and so on. According to Pardo Bazán, the press fails to deal with those issues that might be regarded as tedious: education; agriculture; cultural matters; economic problems, or plans for curing the ailing body politic (pp. 62–3).

There is no doubt that the Galician novelist is, in this central part of her article, indulging in a degree of exaggeration. Yet she is also undoubtedly uttering some home truths. The concern, at times verging on despair, that Pardo Bazán reveals in much of this magazine article was to re-emerge within a week or so in a much more profound, sharply focused, and systematically developed form when she became the first Spaniard to address the prestigious, Paris-based 'Société de Conférences'. Thus it was abroad that Pardo Bazán chose to proclaim her anguish at the straits of her native country, to suggest how Spain had sunk to such depths, and to propose remedial action. Here, in effect, she chose to break what she perceived as the silence of the Spanish literary establishment, particularly that of the unnamed 'prosistas famosos' (p. 61).

Yet Pardo Bazán's Paris lecture is only part of her considered response to the events of 1898 and to the process that, in her opinion, culminated in the military and political catastrophe of that year. For almost two decades she had been a social commentator, a literary critic, and a polemicist whose published output in these fields had been quite phenomenal. However, Pardo Bazán was still known principally as a writer of fiction, and as such she reacted to the trauma of 1898 with a novel that is very much a companion-piece to her Paris lecture. This work is *El Niño de Guzmán*, which was serialized in *La España Moderna* in early 1899. So, by the spring of that year the Galician author had produced two significant responses to the disasters of the previous summer, each of which contained clear and forceful indications of the process that she regarded as having led to such a calamitous turn of events.

Yet neither the Paris lecture nor the work of fiction was particularly out of character in that neither indicated the acquisition by the author of dramatically new insights nor the injection into her fiction or discursive prose of themes, issues, or concerns that had not already been touched on or even dwelt upon in her previous writing. However, the novel and the lecture of early 1899 do reveal one profoundly significant change of tack on the part of the author. In her writings of the 1880s and much of the 1890s Pardo Bazán had focused on what she saw as the inherent weaknesses of the Spanish body politic as it emerged from the Revolution of 1868 and the republican experiment of 1873–4, only to lead to the relatively stable but also, in her opinion, disastrously ineffectual period of the Restoration settlement. But by 1899 she had extended the scope of her historical and cultural deliberations by viewing the foundering state of Restoration politics in the context of the *whole* of the nineteenth century and also, even more ambitiously, in the context of the very origins of the modern Spanish state.

Pardo Bazán's lecture to the 'Société de Conférences' was delivered in French. Several months later, French and Spanish versions of the talk were published in Madrid, in the same volume. The title and subtitle of the Spanish version, *La España de ayer y la de hoy: (La muerte de una leyenda)* correspond exactly to those of the French original. The lecture is not long (about 7,000 words) and in its opening paragraphs it focuses immediately on the substance of the 'legend' mentioned in the subtitle. Indeed, Pardo Bazán starts with the statement that French travellers to Spain perceive the country through the mist of a legend, a legend which is a kind of '*romancero* rezagado y tardío' and which is the collective creation of the Spanish people.[2] This baneful legend, 'funesta leyenda' (p. 62), is presented as the direct cause of Spain's ills: 'Ha desorganizado nuestro cerebro, ha preparado nuestros desastres y nuestras humillaciones' (p. 62).

Pardo Bazán labels this legend the 'leyenda dorada', the reverse side of the 'leyenda negra' (p. 62), and then seeks to be a little more specific, suggesting that the legend is, essentially, the intoxicating power of Spain's past: 'Caracteriza a la leyenda dorada la apoteosis del pasado. El ayer se nos ha subido a la cabeza; hemos creído que bastaba evocar las blancas carabelas de los conquistadores para conservar las conquistas' (p. 63). Having touched on the period of discovery and conquest, Pardo Bazán mentions the cultural glories of Roman Spain and then, after an aside, returns to the epoch of the 'Reyes Católicos' to make some interesting assertions and surprising comparisons.

While acknowledging the attraction for modern Spaniards of the achievements of the 'Reyes Católicos' in the area of political unification, Pardo Bazán suggests that the reign of Ferdinand and Isabella undermined the 'spontaneity' of their subject peoples. After unification, the Spaniards apparently became a nation in which the vitality of the *people* was quickly sapped by the debility of the *nation*. A contrast is then made with two earlier periods that had witnessed what the author terms 'florecimientos magníficos' (p. 66), namely Roman Spain and Moslem Spain. Pardo Bazán then goes on to highlight the contrast with the condition of contemporary Spain and outlines the chronology of decline:

Eramos fuertes, temidos, estudiosos, poseíamos industria y agricultura, y son los restos de aquella vida intensa los que en parte sostiene la actual. —Dos siglos después de los Reyes Católicos, quién ignora cómo quedó España, solitaria, exhausta, famélica; cuatro siglos y medio después nada nos resta de las grandezas de antaño. (p. 66)

Yet the seeds of recovery and progress could still be found in the old traditions and values (liberty, tolerance, faith, industry, and vigour), but only if Spaniards had the energy to look for them. Instead, however, the people have enshrouded themselves in the 'leyenda dorada', which, it is suggested, was crystallized in the early nineteenth century in the War of Independence and subsequently saw its Romantic manifestation in the Carlist movement. Here Pardo Bazán proceeds to mock the dynastic cause to which she had undoubtedly been drawn, with varying degrees of enthusiasm, during the previous thirty years: a cause whose adherence to the principle of absolute monarchy she could still find attractive in times of weak government and national crisis.

Up to this point in her lecture, Pardo Bazán had largely dealt in general terms, only occasionally touching on or alluding to particular components of her 'leyenda dorada'. However, in the second half of her address the author brings her focus to bear much more sharply on the constituent parts of the legend, and also on its perceived impact on the attitudes of Spaniards. At the same time, she reiterates many of the criticisms of Spanish society and Spanish institutions that had figured, both explicitly and implicitly, in many of her works of fiction and essays of the previous twenty years.

In the first place, what constitutes the insidious legend that forms the thesis of her Paris lecture? In certain respects the answer appears to be rather humdrum, even trite:

Según la leyenda, España es, no sólo la más valerosa, sino la más religiosa, galante y caballeresca de las naciones. Según la leyenda, nos preciamos de ardientes patriotas, desdeñamos los intereses materiales y nos hincamos de rodillas ante la mujer. (p. 72)

Yet this list hardly appears to be the recipe for decline, loss of empire, national prostration, and a recent crushing defeat at the hands of a young country disdainfully referred to in Spain as a nation of pork-butchers. However, what Pardo Bazán then proceeds to do is look at the practical implications of some of these apparently entrenched beliefs.

Whilst she does not doubt that, on an individual basis, Spaniards are brave, the author notes that in modern warfare single acts of sacrifice are not enough: armies need adequate equipment, organization, and planners. Indeed, ten years earlier, in her chronicles of the Paris Universal Exposition of 1889, Pardo Bazán had observed that the Spanish Army was in such a poor state that it could not possibly win a war.[3] For this audacity she incurred the wrath of the political and military establishment. (Interestingly, Pardo Bazán had not directed her attention to the condition of the Spanish Navy; yet it was the hapless navy that suffered the most dramatic blows in the Spanish–American War. Raymond Carr observes: 'Spanish experts had argued that the Spanish fleet was superior to the U.S. fleet; its greatest weaknesses, however, were that it had never been able to afford target practice or coal good enough to keep up speed.'[4] Thus in May 1898 the Spanish Pacific squadron was destroyed in an hour, and a few weeks later the whole of the Atlantic fleet was lost, outside Santiago de Cuba, in a matter of four hours.)

In fact, Pardo Bazán informed her Paris audience that when, the previous year, the military situation had looked increasingly grave the people of Madrid had hoped for a miracle. Yet her subsequent assertion of the lack of religious faith of Spaniards suggests that such Divine intervention would hardly be merited. Contrary to the 'leyenda dorada', she affirms: 'Ya no somos un pueblo religioso, ni siquiera un pueblo que practica' (p. 73). Indeed, here Pardo Bazán specifies that while the bourgeoisie are indifferent with regard to matters of religion, the lower classes either practise in a mechanistic fashion or are uncouthly irreverent (p. 73). No mention is made of the devoutness or otherwise of the upper classes.

The myth of Spanish patriotism is dealt with in an equally brusque manner. Pardo Bazán sees her fellow Spaniards as being far more interested in bullfighting and the theatre than in national crises and disasters (pp. 74–5). However, when it comes to the supposed disdain of the Spaniard for material comforts, the author is a little more wide-ranging. What is seen to afflict the majority of her fellow countrymen (the exceptions being the Basques and Catalans) is not so much a contempt for the fruits of materialism as a revulsion at the idea of the work and application necessary for the acquisition of material benefits. Hence the preference for gambling on the lottery or the stock market. At the same time, those in power have catered for the Spaniards' apparent reluctance to engage in honest toil by creating numerous meaningless posts for friends and relatives—the so-called 'empleomanía' (p. 78).

Finally, when she turns to that part of the 'leyenda dorada' which projects the idea of the Spanish male's devotion to women, Pardo Bazán addresses a subject that had figured both explicitly and implicitly in much of her fiction of the previous two decades and which she had also discussed with some vigour in her discursive prose from the late 1880s onwards. In the Paris lecture she restates her long-held view: the Spanish female is the object of neither gallantry nor respect. Rather, she is shackled by cultural attitudes that discourage her from seeking a serious education and from becoming a productive member of society. Pardo Bazán claims that even 'progressive' Spanish males cannot permit themselves to acknowledge that a woman's place could be outside the home (p. 79).

So much for the substance and the deficiencies of the insidious legend that Pardo Bazán signals as having paved the way for the current plight of Spain. But legends are not, of course, self-propelling: to have effect they need to be transmitted and sustained. Earlier in her lecture, the author had suggested that during the course of the eighteenth century the Bourbon monarchs, as they gradually became Hispanicized, had identified themselves with the legend of a golden past and its legacy of matchless national virtues (p. 70). In the nineteenth century, according to Pardo Bazán, the legend was transmitted by the literature of the Romantic period: she specifies the work of Zorrilla and Duque de Rivas, and claims that the legend was subsequently promoted in the writing of Fernán Caballero. Moreover, Pardo Bazán suggests that the Revolution of 1868 actually led to the intensification of the 'espíritu legendista' in writers and readers alike, with even the liberal press waxing enthusiastic over those authors who supposedly captured the customs and spirit of bygone ages. She goes on to attack the parochialism of those (unnamed) writers who extolled unchanging Spanish values and at the same time scorned cultural developments taking place abroad, thus choosing the comfortable route to recognition and popularity at home (pp. 80–1).

Yet while Pardo Bazán does not claim that the promulgation in literature of 'traditional' Spanish values is responsible for the economic stagnation of the country, she does conclude her review of literature's complicity in the transmission of the 'leyenda dorada' with a condemnation of what she sees as the attack on commercial activity to be found in a large number of plays performed in the second half of the nineteenth century. In these works, which Pardo Bazán sees as 'síntomas del pacto de la literatura con el pasado' (p. 81), she asserts that business and industry are tacitly condemned by way of assaults on usury and financial dealings. Again, no authors are identified, but it is safe to assume that she has in mind the work of dramatists such as Manuel Tamayo y Baus (1829–98) and Adelardo López de Ayala (1829–79).[5]

At this stage in her deliberations, having cast her censure far and wide, Pardo Bazán confesses that she too, and especially in her youth, had been seduced by the appeal and comfort of the legend and by what she terms 'el fantasma de la tradición' (p. 82). Yet this is not, she adds, the 'genuine' tradition but rather a conventional falsehood disguised as tradition, one which creates a past that is aesthetically seductive. This appeal, furthermore, is such that it deflects the individual from an awareness of the grave practical problems afflicting contemporary Spain. Pardo Bazán had already indicated a number of these problems to her French audience and in the closing part of her lecture she identifies others. Thus she signals the high rate of illiteracy in Spain and the shambolic state of education (from the primary level to that of universities) and the resultant lack of a scientific base in the country (pp. 83–4). The author also holds forth on a topic that had already figured frequently in her fiction and other writing: the appalling state of Spanish politics, with its stifling and corrupting effect on the nation as a whole, and the manipulation and subversion of the political process by the blight of *caciquismo*. It is little wonder, she notes, that the people of Spain, unable to change a political system that so ill serves the country, should view with indifference the disasters that have beset the nation (pp. 84–86).

In her closing comments, Pardo Bazán suggests that the disaster of 1898 has also resulted in the destruction of the pernicious golden legend, but then a few sentences later, she fears that this might not be the case. And in between these two thoughts she wonders if and how an exhausted Spain will be able to recover. Ultimately, all Pardo

Bazán believes she can do is associate herself with a tiny minority of Spaniards who are prepared to reveal the extent of the damage and replace the legend with a call for renovation through practical endeavours (pp. 88–9). The extent to which she is here suggesting her common cause with some of those younger writers who would later be labelled as members of the so-called Generation of 1898 is a point to which I shall return later, albeit briefly. But for the moment I should like to pursue in a little more detail a matter that I have already touched on several times: namely, that a number of the specific problems that the Galician novelist identified in her Paris lecture as afflicting Restoration Spain were not concerns that had suddenly assailed her in the aftermath of the war with the United States. Indeed, many of the issues that Pardo Bazán had raised in Paris had, from time to time, figured in her discursive prose of the 1880s and 1890s or had surfaced in a number of her novels of that period.

At the heart of Pardo Bazán's preoccupation with the state of contemporary Spain was what she deemed to be a failed constitutional process—representative government or parliamentary democracy. However, it was not until her third novel, *La Tribuna* (1883), that she confronted the political issue. Here, against the background of the Revolution of 1868, the uncertainty that followed this, and the rise of the republican movement, the novelist exposes and satirizes the naive faith of ordinary people who believed that the republican model of government would bring about social equality and general well-being. The instability and insurrection that marked the First Republic's brief life of less than twelve months is beyond the scope of the novel, since the narrative closes on the day in February 1873 when the republic was declared. But certainly the novel's readers of ten years later would have known the broad details of events and would have been perfectly aware of the point that the author was making.

Yet the republican experiment was no more than a brief interlude in the arrangement of a monarch ruling with parliament and the army. After the restoration of the Bourbon monarchy in 1875 it was the system of constitutional monarchy and parliamentary democracy (although with a restricted franchise) that Pardo Bazán saw as being at the root of Spain's stagnation and enfeeblement in the last quarter of the nineteenth century. And whereas in the election episode of *El cisne de Vilamorta* (1885) the author suggested the frivolity of the electoral system, it was in the following novel, *Los pazos de Ulloa* (1886), that she showed with graphic detail the whole process to be a sham: with intimidation, bribery, and vote-rigging orchestrated by the local *caciques*. The issue of *caciques* manipulating and subverting the democratic process, which is dealt with at some length in *Los pazos de Ulloa*, is also touched on elsewhere in Pardo Bazán's fiction of the period. However, it is not a matter of the author suggesting that the constitutional process would work properly without their insidious interference. Rather, she uses *caciquismo* as a very handy rod with which to flay the whole system of representative government. Moreover, she makes her general position quite clear in some of her non-fictional writing of the 1880s and 1890s. Indeed, while Pardo Bazán was prepared to acknowledge that the Restoration settlement had brought political stability to Spain,[6] she believed that the price paid for this stability was the impoverishment and prostration of the country. The author labours this point in the final section of her Italian travel chronicles, *Mi romería* (1888), noting among other things that representative government has brought about 'la ruina, acabamiento y perdición de España'.[7] And a year later, in her account of her trip to the Paris Universal Exposition of 1889, the writer dismisses the parliamentary system as a defective institution and a farce.[8]

By the end of the 1880s, then, Pardo Bazán had suggested in her fiction and clearly indicated elsewhere that parliamentary democracy was principally responsible for the paralysis afflicting Restoration Spain. Indeed, the great ideological struggle that she saw taking place in 1870s and 1880s Spain was between what she termed the 'Vieja España' and the 'Nueva España', with the latter proclaiming constitutionalism as its fundamental dogma.[9] Moreover, in *La madre naturaleza* (1887) Pardo Bazán uses her protagonist and namesake (the former artillery officer, Gabriel Pardo) to symbolize the struggle between the old ways and the pressures for change. According to Gabriel, the Revolution of 1868 had unceremoniously swept away his youthful vision of 'la España histórica [...] una España épica y gloriosa'.[10] Having outgrown his subsequent emotional flirtation with Carlism and then with republicanism (two very different ideological recipes for the country), the young man soon becomes disillusioned with a third option, the Restoration version of constitutional monarchy.

However, it is not that Gabriel sees the parliamentary system as inherently flawed: he simply believes that Spain is not ready for it, and not for a very long time (I, 323).

This notion that, for whatever reasons, Spain is a special case does perhaps explain Pardo Bazán's grudging acceptance that, although France's system of representative government (a republican model, it should be noted) is a defective institution further undermined by the greed and personal ambition of politicians, this has not prevented France from recovering from the humiliation of the Franco-Prussian War and from regaining, in the closing years of the century, its erstwhile vigour and status. Indeed, during her visit to the Paris Exposition of 1889 Pardo Bazán took a keen interest in the French political scene and in one of her chronicles (dated 9 July) she described with undisguised relish the unseemly behaviour in the National Assembly. Yet this did not prevent her from proclaiming, at the end of her visit to the French capital, that France was 'una grande, poderosa, ilustrada, activa y fuerte nación' and from expressing the hope that one day Spaniards might be able to say the same of their own country.[11] But presumably the main point here is that whereas, according to Pardo Bazán, Spain has become enfeebled because of parliamentary democracy, her neighbour to the north has once again become powerful *despite* this system.

Gabriel Pardo figures prominently in *Insolación* (1889), where he is frequently scathing about the Spanish mentality and the state of contemporary Spain. Indeed, in this novel he suggests that Restoration Spain has become no more than a self-parody of its very worst, most superficial aspects (I, 418–19), and even compares it to a central African country (I, 415). This African comparison, it should be noted, is one that Pardo Bazán makes in her Paris lecture of 1899 (p. 83). Yet how, in concrete terms, was Spain to embark on the recovery that would make her a modern and respected *European* country? Gabriel Pardo has no blueprint and neither, in fact, does the author. However, in the course of her Paris lecture Pardo Bazán did identify a number of what she saw as the more obvious concrete causes of Spain's prostration. Thus, stemming from the failure of the Restoration political settlement are, according to the Galician author, the sorry state of Spanish industry and agriculture, and the total inadequacy of Spain's system of public education. Although in her novels of the 1880s and 1890s Pardo Bazán often alighted on the lack of educational opportunities for females and, by the late 1890s, translated this social and cultural issue into an economic concern (one half of the nation unable to fulfil its productive potential), she also frequently made it clear that even the level of instruction available to the more fortunate sections of the male population was far from ideal.

Yet Pardo Bazán also saw deficiencies that could not be blamed quite so readily on the failure of Restoration politics: for example, the decline in religious faith; the apparent laziness and apathy of so many Spaniards; their lack of patriotism; their parochialism and, of particular significance for the author at the close of the 1890s, the collective hankering after a glorious past, and the myth and even tyranny of that past. It was this last issue, the pernicious 'leyenda dorada', that she saw as fundamentally responsible for leading Spaniards to the calamity of 1898. And while, in her capacity as social and cultural commentator, Pardo Bazán indicated to her Paris audience of April 1899 what she saw as the constituents of this legend, it was as a novelist that she had, shortly before this date, given her Spanish readers a fictional treatment of this same theory and topic.

The first thirteen chapters of *El Niño de Guzmán* were serialized in *La España Moderna* between January and March of 1899. These chapters were published in the summer of the same year as volume eighteen of Pardo Bazán's *Obras completas*, with the title-page indicating that this was the *first part* of the novel. In a newspaper article that appeared in September, the author stated that she had the complete version of the novel in her head and planned to finish it as soon as possible.[12] However, the second part was never published, no manuscript version of it has come to light, and Pardo Bazán never again mentioned the project.

Incomplete novels are, of course, frustrating and tantalizing—especially when the first half has received the author's blessing of publication and when the whole work has not been sundered by the death, incapacity, or inactivity of the novelist. Yet an incomplete, published work such as *El Niño de Guzmán* is still, I believe, artistically valid. It is also legitimate, I am sure, to make judgements and draw conclusions on the basis of what there is of the novel: a fairly carefully developed and dramatically terminated expository half of an unfinished work of fiction.

The one hundred and fifty pages that we have of *El Niño de Guzmán* are, on the whole, the artistic expression of the principal thesis of Pardo Bazán's Paris lecture: namely, that Spaniards are intoxicated by, and culturally and psychologically dependent on, their collective vision of a glorious past; a vision that incorporates a mistaken belief in or reliance on the valour, chivalry, deep religious faith, unworldliness, and patriotism of Spaniards. Yet how can a novelist present and treat these issues? One approach might be to reveal failings in the specific areas mentioned as part of character/ narrative development. But how could the author convey the notion of a people totally obsessed with the glories and values of bygone ages? Should the characters constantly hold forth on the splendours of the past, or be seen continually immersing themselves in historical and literary accounts of momentous exploits and achievements? Such a narrative process might soon become repetitive and tedious.

Pardo Bazán resolves this problem of approach by contrasting an external perception of Spain with the internal reality of the country and its society. In fact, she uses the trusty narrative device of having an outsider bring the baggage of his preconceptions into an environment that will soon disabuse him. This outsider, the eponymous protagonist, Pedro Niño de Guzmán, has spent most of his life in northern Europe, receiving his education in Britain and Germany. But whatever the substance of his formal studies, Guzmán's cultural formation (under the guidance of a Hispanophile Irish tutor) has left him with a highly idealized view of the country of his birth. This vision of Spain is fuelled by his tutor's passion for the Romantic descriptions by foreign writers such as Washington Irving and Frédéric Ozanam, as well as by Guzmán's own immersion in the works of Fernán Caballero and his quest to understand the history of Spain and the nobility of the race through a familiarity with medieval epic poetry and Golden-Age drama. Consequently, the young man's view of Spain is gained through the lens of literature. And when, brimming with emotion, Guzmán crosses into Spain in the high summer of 1897, only to be brought down to earth as an officious customs inspector examines his trunks and suitcases and suggests that substantial duties will have to be paid, the symbolic significance of the mundane customs activity that so deflates and frustrates him soon becomes apparent.

Throughout the course of the novel the baggage of Guzmán's cultural preconceptions, enthusiastically packed by his former tutor and himself, has its contents exposed and scattered by the unpleasant reality of the Spanish homeland. Guzmán's return to Spain is, in essence, a pilgrimage: a desire for the confirmation of his faith in his national and cultural heritage. As Guzmán's aristocratic cousin, Borromeo, puts it: 'Quiere estudiar a España, recorrerla registrar [...] el solar de sus antepasados; no de los antepasados de su linaje, sino de los antepasados nacionales, nuestras glorias.'[13] Yet, in his initial contacts with this society, Guzmán swiftly experiences one disillusionment after another. Thus in the casino at San Sebastián he witnesses the frivolity and obsession with gambling of upper-class society. And although he is at first reluctant to regard San Sebastián as typical of Spain, or the patrons of the casino as representative of the higher reaches of Spanish society, Guzmán is soon persuaded by his cousin (an enlightened aristocrat) that Madrid is just as bad as the northern resort and that the aristocrats have abandoned their old values and have been corrupted by the money-loving and power-loving middle classes.

Yet in this novel Pardo Bazán does not simply rely on the limited experiences of Guzmán or the observations of Borromeo in order to indict the middle and upper reaches of Spanish society. She also reveals, through their actions, the flawed behaviour and attitudes of certain aristocrats and, in addition, uses the narratorial voice to thrust home the message. On top of this, some secondary characters appear to have as their principal purpose the role of commentators on the corruption and decline of the upper classes, and also on the ailing state of the nation.

So where is the Spain that Guzmán seeks, if indeed it exists? The answer, according to Borromeo, is that the heart of Spain is to be found in the provinces and particularly in the villages. Here, apparently, the ordinary people are the repositories of the traditional Spanish qualities that Borromeo lists as including energy, sincerity, patriotism, truth, faith, and stoicism. And here, too, the name of Unamuno comes to mind. As I mentioned earlier, Pardo Bazán does list *En torno al casticismo* in the bibliography to *La España de ayer y la de hoy*. She would undoubtedly have agreed with Unamuno's plea for the Europeanization of Spain and would certainly have concurred with his condemnation of a false tradition that seeks the past 'enterrado en libros y papeles, y monumentos, y piedras'.[14] Similarly, Pardo Bazán would have accepted Unamuno's rejection of a political system that had contaminated the national soul (p. 139). Indeed, for a moment in *El Niño de Guzmán* it seems that she is about to align herself with the Basque writer's faith in what he terms 'el pueblo desconocido' (p. 141). Yet the novel's narrator immediately makes it clear that Borromeo's belief in the copious virtues of ordinary, rural folk is simply a product of his immersion in the works of the Basque writer Antonio de Trueba (1819–89), whose short stories frequently present a mawkishly idealized view of the peasants of his native region. Thus it appears that Trueba's fiction has coloured Borromeo's perceptions just as Fernán Caballero's writing had turned the head of Guzmán.

Once again, then, a certain kind of literature is seen to bring delusion to the sentimentally susceptible reader. Indeed, in *El Niño de Guzmán* there are several pointed reminders that the two main characters, Guzmán and his cousin, had, long before they met, formed a bond through their correspondence, the letters of which revealed and reinforced their belief in the existence of a Spain that remained true to set of traditional and worthy principles. Each man was an avid reader and each had constructed this vision of Spain on the basis of literary evidence and their literary experience. Their exchange of letters had simply been an extension and reworking (and rewriting) of this experience. In effect, both Guzmán and Borromeo, cocooned in the constructs of literature, had been isolated and sheltered from the reality behind the fictitious worlds that they had so lovingly nurtured.

During the course of the narrative, Guzmán's construct is steadily undermined and then demolished, thus compelling him to subsequently and anxiously seek the true spirit of Spain in Borromeo's vision of the noble peasant class. Yet Borromeo has had no direct contact with the humble members of the section of society that he so exalts. Disfigured and misshapen from birth, he had always shunned these people, fearing that they would mock his grotesque appearance. Thus when the two men decide to venture into the countryside, to visit the sanctuary at Lezo and see its famous Christ, it comes as little real surprise to the reader when it transpires that the peasants are heavily involved in the secular pursuit of local politics and that their attitude to religion is crudely superstitious and thoroughly self-serving. Guzmán's process of disillusionment now appears to be complete.

The eponymous hero does not figure in the one remaining chapter of the narrative, and the first part of the novel is brought to a dramatic conclusion with the arrival of the news of the assassination (8 August 1897, in the Basque country) of the Prime Minister and architect of the Restoration settlement, Antonio Cánovas del Castillo. Presumably, with the disaster of 1898 still painfully fresh in her mind and, of course, with the wisdom of hindsight, Pardo Bazán is emphasizing in the final two chapters of this unfinished novel the vacuity of Guzmán's vision of the glorious, legendary Spain and the destruction of this delusion. In addition, the closing announcement of the killing of Cánovas appears to reflect the current instability in Spain—in her Paris lecture Pardo Bazán (who was a qualified admirer of the politician) stated that Cánovas 'pagó con su vida [...] el terrible momento que atravesamos' (p. 88). The Prime Minister's murder might also be intended to indicate to the characters in the novel that an era has ended or it could be perceived by them as a harbinger of disasters to come.

But in the end it is, of course, largely pointless to speculate on how this novel would have developed. In the published first part, Pardo Bazán constructed her thesis relentlessly and with unmistakable clarity and all that can be said with any certainty is that *El Niño de Guzmán* is, with some minor variations of emphasis, the artistic companion-piece to her Paris lecture of 1899. In both statements, the lecture and the novel, she condemns the sham of the so-called 'leyenda dorada' and exposes its dangers. And although in the lecture Pardo Bazán touched on some practical concerns that Spaniards needed to address, in neither work does she suggest specific approaches to these and other material problems afflicting contemporary Spain.

In 1900, in an article written at the Paris Exposition of that summer, the author asserted that in strong or even sound nations, priority was given to education, something that she describes as 'la preocupación incesante, lo sagrado'.[15] This was not, presumably, the kind of 'education' that had intoxicated and distracted so many Spaniards and brought about the delusions of Guzmán and Borromeo. But, in any case, after the publication of *El Niño de Guzmán*, Pardo Bazán did not address (or even touch on) the national issue in her full-length works of fiction. *Misterio* (1903) is an adventure story set in early nineteenth-century France, and is little more than a piece of literary escapism. However, in her last three novels: *La quimera* (1905), *La sirena negra* (1908), and *Dulce dueño* (1911) Pardo Bazán traces how the protagonist of each of these works finds redemption and personal regeneration through the discovery of Christ.[16] In fact, in the forward to the published version of her Paris lecture, Pardo Bazán did suggest that Catholicism could be a regenerating force for the Spanish race (p. 11). However, by the time she came to write her last three novels the Galician author had clearly shifted her focus from a concern with the plight of the nation to an interest in the salvation of the individual, and from wordly issues to spiritual ones.[17]

3

Ciclo Adán y Eva
La autobiografía de don Benicio Neira en versión de Emilia Pardo Bazán

Rodolfo Cardona

Las novelas de este ciclo están precedidas de un 'Prólogo en el cielo' que narra la llegada de don Benicio Neira al umbral de la gloria donde pregunta, 'Señor de cielos y tierra, ¿es verdad que voy a entrar en la mansión de los escogidos? [...] ¿Yo entre santos, mártires, confesores y vírgenes, tronos, jerarquías, potestades y dominaciones?' La voz del Espíritu de Dios le responde, 'No estarás entre los santos ni entre las vírgenes porque no lo eres. Entre los mártires y confesores bien podrías, pues algún martirio padeciste y algunas veces me confesaste.' Y añade una sorprendente declaración que sólo recientemente el Papa Juan Pablo II, en su libro *Cruzando el umbral de la esperanza*, y el nuevo catecismo llegan a aceptar: '¿Has imaginado tú que Yo crié, perfeccioné y redimí al género humano para destinarlo a condenación eterna, verle retorcerse en el fuego del Purgatorio o aullar en los braseros del Infierno?' (Hace relativamente poco tiempo que el filósofo y naturalista católico Teilhard de Chardin se encontró en apuros por declaraciones semejantes.) Pero continuemos. El Espíritu de Dios le advierte a don Benicio que 'Con todo, aún te queda una penitencia que cumplir. Antes de entrar en el goce de la beatitud, bajarás otra vez a la Tierra y escribirás tu historia para bien de algunos de tus semejantes.' De nada le sirve a don Benicio protestar que él no es escritor y menos novelista, porque la voz del Espíritu le advierte 'Obedece y calla,' dejándolo en estado de aturdimiento del que lo saca el Angelito que resulta ser Monchito, el hijo de Neira quien, muy pequeño, '[...] cayó del tercer piso de su casa por un descuido de la niñera y se hizo tortilla...' El angelito saca a su padre de este apuro conduciéndolo a Marineda e introduciéndole en casa de la escritora que ahí reside, quien se encargará de escribir por él su autobiografía en forma de novela. Y nos preguntamos ¿por qué esta estratagema? Pero la contestación tendrá que esperar.

Es posible que Unamuno obtuviera la idea para su narración 'Juan Manso' de este 'Prólogo en el cielo.' Don Benicio Neira y Juan Manso tienen mucho en común: ambos son unos 'zanguangos,' para utilizar una palabra muy usada por doña Emilia. Ninguno de los dos ha hecho nada que pueda justificar el premio de la gloria o la condenación al infierno. Por eso ambos son enviados de nuevo a la tierra para adquirir méritos. En el caso de Neira, por medio de la escritura. El escribir, o contarle a una escritora, su vida, le permitirá revivirla y analizar sus acciones y carácter para comprenderlos y ofrecerlos a sus semejantes de ejemplo; un ejemplo para evitar, naturalmente. En el caso de Manso, Dios cree necesario que reviva su vida, pero esta vez sin mansedumbre, pero con una energía y determinación tales que le permitan, al morir de nuevo, meterse en el Cielo de redón. Pero volvamos al caso de Neira que es el que nos ocupa.

¿Cómo es que no termina su cometido? ¿Por qué deja su vida inconclusa de modo que sólo llegamos al final por medio de las memorias de un amigo suyo solterón? ¿Por qué se impone doña Emilia el artificio del 'Prólogo en el cielo' que luego descarta? Aunque la escritora se impone un plan previo no lo cumple al pie de la letra, lo que demuestra, paradójicamente, la falta de un plan previo. ¿Improvisa doña Emilia sobre la marcha y cambia de narrador o de método narrativo al encontrarse en una encrucijada? Es difícil contestar estas preguntas sin antes hacer un análisis de lo que en realidad ella se propuso hacer con este ciclo novelístico bautizado 'Adán y Eva.'

Si la primera novela de este ciclo se supone que es la autobiografía de don Benicio Neira impuesta por Dios como penitencia para que pueda entrar en la gloria, ¿por qué lleva el título de *Doña Milagros?* Esta incongruencia, añadida a las apuntadas anteriormente, sólo se explica si aceptamos que esta señora constituye el eje central en la vida de don Benicio, aunque doña Milagros entra en su vida cuando éste ya ha alcanzado su madurez, y sale de ella mucho antes de su muerte. Y como ya se apuntó, el resto de su vida no está narrado por Neira sino por Mauro Pareja, alias el Abad, en una novela que lleva el título *Memorias de un solterón.* Sólo leyendo las dos novelas que comprenden el ciclo 'Adán y Eva' podemos enterarnos de la vida completa de don Benicio Neira y en este sentido, por fin, se cumple lo prometido en el 'Prólogo en el cielo.' Es decir, que de algún modo llegamos a conocer detalles de la vida y muerte del Héroe, y la razón por la cual éste se confiesa asesino ante Dios. Pero estos detalles los narra otra persona. Como sugerí antes, hay algo de improvisación en el plan narrativo de este ciclo, plan que es constantemente modificado sobre la marcha para que el desarrollo del argumento pueda obtener coherencia. Nos encontramos, entonces, ante una paradoja: Doña Emilia es incoherente en el desarrollo de su plan novelístico para ser coherente en el desarrollo de su argumento. Y su argumento es decididamente feminista, razón por la cual este ciclo de novelas fue poco comentado en su momento y obtuvo una reacción adversa de parte del público.

He insistido en el aspecto de improvisación que presenta el plan narrativo adoptado por doña Emilia para estas novelas. Ella debió notarlo, naturalmente, pero lo dejó sin rectificar. Hubiese bastado para corregirlo la eliminación del 'Prólogo en el cielo.' Hay dos cosas que saltan a la vista sobre este defecto estructural. La primera y más obvia es que el arte narrativo de doña Emilia logra que suspendamos nuestra incredulidad y leamos estas dos novelas sin fijarnos en las incongruencias narrativas mencionadas en las que sólo reparamos *a posteriori*, después de haber gozado de nuestra lectura; la segunda es que, con el tiempo, las incongruencias apuntadas le han añadido a estas novelas un aire de modernidad. Leyéndolas ahora, a cien años de su publicación (la primera es de 1894 y la segunda de 1896), encontramos en estas incongruencias una especie de juego de la autora con el lector que nos obliga a formular preguntas que, a su vez, nos llevan al meollo del asunto.

Doña Emilia inició, en 1894, un ciclo de novelas al que dio el título de 'Adán y Eva.' Sólo dos novelas aparecieron bajo ese título, por lo cual muchos críticos han pronunciado este ciclo como inconcluso ya que después de éstas ninguna otra novela apareció ostentando esa rúbrica. El ciclo de estas dos novelas presenta la vida de don Benicio Neira vista desde dentro y desde fuera; es decir, desde dos perspectivas distintas. Las dos novelas no sólo completan el círculo que torna en derredor de Neira y su familia, sino que, además, contienen el desenlace de otra novela muy anterior, *La Tribuna*, de 1882. Es decir, que el ciclo cumple con la premisa de que 'cierto número de personajes —que siendo protagonistas en algunas de [las novelas], figurarán como comparsas en las demás— y el ambiente, ya que el escenario de su conjunto sería la ciudad de Marineda[...],' para citar las palabras de Federico Sáinz de Robles en su 'Prólogo' al 'Ciclo Adán y Eva' (ver Emila Pardo Bazán, *Obras completas*, II, Madrid, 1956, p. 351; todas las citas de estas dos novelas han sido tomadas de esta edición). Posiblemente el título del ciclo da a entender algo mucho más extenso que las dos novelas en cuestión. Pero, creo, el título se encuentra justificado en *Doña Milagros* cuando la protagonista le explica a don Benicio su teoría de que 'en el mundo todo lo hace Adán por Eva y Eva por Adán':

> Siempre que vea usté una mujer o un hombre con fatigas de muerte, no se derrita los sesos cavilando; es por la otra cara de la luna... ¿Está usté? Es por un Adán o una Eva, y digasté que yo lo digo. Cuanto zafarrancho se arma por ahí; cuanto inventan los hombres con esos discursos endemoniaos de mecánicas y de construcciones y de embarcaciones; cuantas trifulcas arman de teatros, y bailes, comersios y fábricas, y diablos coronaos..., todito es por la pingorrona de Eva, por eya nada más. Y cuanto nosotras no componemos, y no asicalamos, y no despepitamos, y no ponemos tristes, y no reimos a carcajá, y murmuramo y chillamo, y arañamo y reñimo... y no tragamos a la gente..., como le susedía a su difunta de usté, señó Neira..., too es por el perdío de Adán, ni ma ni meno. (p. 402a)

Pero si a doña Emilia se le ocurre ahora exteriorizar, por boca de doña Milagros, esta teoría, debemos reconocer que toda su obra, con poquísimas excepciones, está basada en ella. De modo que el título 'Ciclo Adán y Eva,' aunque aplicable a las dos novelas de Neira, donde se expone la teoría, rebasa esa aplicación y se extiende a muchas novelas más que no llevan esa apelación. Es decir, que otra vez nos encontramos con un detalle arbitrario que debemos dejar a un lado y simplemente aceptarlo como aplicable a las novelas que nos ocupan que es donde ocurre; pero, me parece, no debemos hablar propiamente de un ciclo inconcluso.

Pasando por fin de la periferia al núcleo, deseo ahora concentrar mi atención en lo que sucede en estas dos novelas y su significación.

En ninguna de sus otras novelas se manifiesta el feminismo militante de la condesa de Pardo Bazán como en las del 'Ciclo Adán y

Eva.' Para empezar, el Héroe (y lo llamo así porque es el nombre con que aparece don Benicio en el 'Prólogo en el cielo') de la primera novela y el protagonista-narrador de la segunda, Mauro Pareja, son hombres perfectamente ordinarios; de héroes no tienen nada. Y si repasamos atentamente las figuras masculinas que aparecen en *Doña Milagros* y en *Memorias de un solterón*, de todos ellos no se hace uno. Don Benicio es un 'zanguango' de carácter tan débil, que siempre se ha dejado dominar por otros —o, mejor dicho, por otras—: su madre, su hermana, su esposa, sus hijas (después de la muerte de ésta), y sí, aunque de un modo distinto, por Doña Milagros. El único acto varonil de su vida es el que le redime, al final de la segunda novela, y es el que precede a su muerte. Si en el 'Prólogo en el cielo' se le da la esperanza de entrar ahí es, paradójicamente, por esa única demostración de energía que ha tenido en toda su vida: el asesinato del gobernador civil Mejía, el seductor de su hija *Argos divina*, el mote que la familia ha puesto a María Ramona. Dios perdona a Neira porque, como le dice, 'Has amado mucho. Recuerda que quien mucho ama, mucho se le perdona.' Estas palabras no dejan de contener una doble ironía: don Benicio es padre de dieciocho hijos, doce de los cuales vivieron; además, entre paréntesis, es como un 'curarse en salud' que la novelista se aplica a sí misma. Esta última ironía es externa al texto, naturalmente, y se reserva para 'los iniciados.' Hay que tener en cuenta que Dios también pasa por alto el grave caso del asesinato diciéndole, 'He medido y pesado *los móviles* de tu falta. Ya has expiado viviendo. El que mata y vive, expía.' Es decir que Neira, al matar a Mejía lo hizo impulsado por su amor paterno y en defensa legítima de la reputación de su hija. Además, su arrepentimiento y el sufrimiento que siguen a ese único acto enérgico de su vida, le redimen. Fuera de esta acción suya, su vida es un fracaso gris, sin drama (en el sentido unamuniano de lucha). Por otro lado, el héroe de las *Memorias,* aunque no tan un cero a la izquierda como don Benicio, es un soltero comodón, egoísta, cuya vida torna alrededor de una rutina especialmente diseñada por él para huir de molestias, compromisos y todo aquello que pueda afectar el sibaritismo de su estéril existencia. Al único hijo varón de don Benicio, Froilancito, ni siquiera le vemos actuar ni hablar directamente. Se le hace a un lado como la nulidad que es y basta. La Sociedad de Amigos está constituida por un círculo de hombres chismosos sin proyecto alguno de vida excepto jugar al tresillo y murmurar de la gente. Entre ellos se destacan un poco: Primo Coba, por sus 'donosísimas humoradas' que, por cierto, nunca salen a relucir, y por ser el centro nervioso de los chismes que se esparcen por Marineda; don Tomás Llanes, el comandante de Otumba, por ser el marido de doña Milagros; y Baltasar Sobrado, a quien ya conocíamos por haber sido el seductor de Amparo, *la Tribuna*, en la novela de ese título. La única excepción que prueba la regla en este conjunto de nulidades es el doctor Moragas, médico de la familia Neira, cuya vida está dedicada al servicio altruista de sus semejantes, pobres o ricos, y cuya ilustración le permite comprender y apoyar los proyectos de Feíta, una de las hijas menores de don Benicio, en quien el médico reconoce aptitudes excepcionales. Otra figura masculina que pudo haberse destacado de esta mediocridad, *el compañero* Sobrado (hijo bastardo de Baltasar y *la Tribuna*), apenas logra hacer efectivo su plan de casar a sus padres a la fuerza, adquiriendo así posición y riqueza, pierde toda su energía vital y se convierte en un pequeño burgués. En palabras de Feíta,

> Francamente, quizá me hacía gracia cuando gastaba blusa; ahora me parece un tipo de lo más vulgar. Ese no tenía fe... Buscaba lo que hoy posee: dinero, comodidades, holganza... (p. 527)

Quedan entonces las mujeres. Las novelas de este ciclo se salvan gracias a la presencia de dos mujeres: doña Milagros en la primera, y Feíta en la segunda. Doña Ilduara, la esposa de Neira, muere muy pronto y, además, no pasa de ser una caricatura de la mujer enérgica, celosa e inmensamente fértil.

Doña Milagros es el prototipo del amor maternal frustrado por la infertilidad, como la Jacinta de Galdós. Aquí tampoco se sabe si esa infertilidad es culpa de ella o de su marido, pero no hace falta indagarlo pues son sus efectos lo que interesa. Por esta razón adopta a las hijas de Neira, especialmente a las mellizas que llegaron tan a deshora, cuando su madre estaba ya bastante enferma. Las continuas visitas de la comandanta a sus vecinos apuran el natural celoso de doña Ilduara y precipitan su muerte, causada por un exceso de cólera del que hablaremos más tarde. Resulta que sus celos no eran del todo infundados ya que don Benicio siente una secreta admiración por la andaluza. Más tarde, la viudez de Neira facilita no sólo la tendencia natural de doña Milagros a hacerse útil —sobre todo en lo que toca a las recién nacidas— sino también, dada su continua presencia en el hogar de las huérfanas, el encaprichamiento de don Benicio por ella. Doña Milagros se convierte en su paño de lágrimas y, poco a poco, su natural atractivo empieza a ejercer sobre Neira algo más que una desinteresada amistad. Llega un momento en que, consciente de los efectos que ella ejerce sobre su libido, don Benicio acude horrorizado al confesor, el padre Incienso, un jesuita de quien, según se entera luego, su hija Argos está prendada. El jesuita le aconseja una sana separación, pero las circunstancias de su proximidad, ya que son vecinos, no le ayudan. Además, la idea de una mudanza se le dificulta también ya que al intentarlo, hablando con su casero Baltasar Sobrado, éste no sólo le rebaja el alquilar sino que le ofrece prestar dinero sobre sus propiedades. La presencia casi constante de doña Milagros en su casa da que hablar entre los chismosos de la Sociedad de Amigos. Es, sin embargo, la llegada de un nuevo asistente en casa del Comandante, lo que precipita la situación. La presencia del buen mozo y la satisfacción expresada por doña Milagros sobre la eficiencia de éste en los trabajos domésticos, empieza una nueva ronda de maledicencias incriminatorias para la comandanta. Neira se constituye en su quijotesco defensor. Pero la situación se hace tan tensa y el encaprichamiento del asistente con la comandanta tan evidente, que por fin dan patente de veracidad a los chismes, y hasta don Benicio llega a aceptarlos como verdaderos. Haciendo un esfuerzo casi sobrehumano para él, Neira le prohibe a doña Milagros la entrada en su casa y el trato con sus hijas. Al darse cuenta de lo insostenible de su situación, la comandanta exige a su marido que despida al asistente. Antes de su partida hay un violento encuentro con doña Milagros que termina con la agresión con intento, dichosamente frustrado, de matarla y con el suicidio del mozo. El escándalo obliga al comandante a pedir el traslado y, al final, parte doña Milagros hacia Barcelona no sin antes recibir de manos de don Benicio, como penitencia por su falta de fe en su inocencia, el regalo de las adoradas mellizas. En este momento de reconciliación final se llega a una cuasi revelación del mutuo afecto que existía entre Neira y su vecina. Es posible que Valle-Inclán se haya inspirado en este episodio para su esperpento *Los cuernos de Don Friolera*.

Aunque el argumento de la primera novela del Ciclo está claramente dominado por doña Milagros, lo que justifica plenamente su título, hay otro personaje femenino que, poco a poco, empieza a destacarse por su originalidad. Se trata de Feíta quien, por su natural inteligencia se convierte en consejera de su padre a quien continuamente asusta por sus avanzadas ideas. De las nueve hijas de Neira que durante el tiempo de la narración han alcanzado 'uso de razón,' Feíta es la única que adquiere un papel destacado. Tula, la hija mayor y la heredera del carácter de su madre, por su horror a quedarse para vestir santos se casa con un pintor de brocha gorda muy en contra de los deseos de su padre. Clara, la hija segunda, comprendiendo que no va a encontrar un pretendiente a la altura de su posición social de nobles aunque arruinados, decide meterse en un convento. Ninguna de las dos tiene un papel destacado en la novela. De las dos siguientes, Rosa y *Argos divina*, esta última adquiere algunos capítulos de protagonismo al narrarse sus impulsos místicos, resultado de su encaprichamiento por el padre Incienso, que desembocan en un ataque de histerismo cuando el Jesuita parte de Marineda para huir de ese posible escándalo en el que él no ha tenido parte. De Rosa sabemos que es muy bella y que su principal interés es el hacer destacar su natural atractivo por medio de los trapos. El resto de las hijas apenas se mencionan. A la única que escuchamos en diálogos íntimos con su padre y, por consiguiente, a la única que llegamos a conocer directamente y no sólo a través de la narración autobiográfica de éste, es a Feíta. En ella notamos, desde los primeros instantes, iniciativa, disposición para hacer las cosas bien, inteligencia para discernir lo que está ocurriendo, e independencia de criterio para juzgar lo que sucede en su entorno. Todo esto la convierte en un fenómeno dentro del mundo social en que vive. Es la mujer que dominará la segunda novela del Ciclo al convertirse en el catalizador que logra poner patas arriba la ordenada existencia de Mauro Pareja, alias *el Abad*.

Si en *Doña Milagros* empezamos a vislumbrar el discurso feminista en las 'genialidades' de Feíta —que se manifiestan en las conversaciones con su padre— , en *Memorias de un solterón* este discurso adquiere características directrices en el planteamiento que se hace la muchacha de su situación personal como mujer en un hogar que se derrumba por el mal gobierno y falta de carácter de don Benicio. La lógica inapelable de sus argumentos no sólo conquista a Primo Coba, ganándose así al más importante aliado que le permitirá poner en práctica sus planes sin el peligro de que se la coman viva, sino que, y a pesar suyo, enamora a *el Abad*, quien como amigo y confidente del padre, se ha convertido también en confidente de la hija. Todo esto es muy conveniente para efectos del método narrativo adoptado por doña Emilia, puesto que en *Memorias* Mauro Pareja es el narrador.

Con Feíta doña Emilia puede avanzar su planteamiento de la situación de la mujer en la última década del siglo pasado. Ya Galdós, por medio de las Troyas, de las Sánchez Emperador, y de Tristana, entre otras, había pintado claramente la triste situación de una joven quien, habiendo pertenecido a la clase media, pierde, con la muerte de sus padres, la situación social que hasta entonces había gozado. El quid del asunto es que estas jóvenes deben continuar guardando las apariencias pero sin los medios necesarios para hacerlo. Es la clásica situación del 'quiero y no puedo.' Hay sólo tres avenidas para solucionar esta situación: el claustro, coser en casa para mal vivir, o aceptar un 'protector.' Incluso en los casos que terminan mejor, el de Amparo en *Tormento*, la solución es humillante. En el caso de Tristana, el matrimonio con su seductor es tardío y se convierte, en sus manos, en instrumento de venganza. Por eso se ha considerado esta novela una de las más feministas de Galdós, aunque para doña Emilia, como lo expresó en su reseña, no lo fue suficientemente. El caso de las hijas de Neira es, entonces, ejemplar. Ya hemos visto la solución encontrada por las dos hermanas mayores: malcasarse y entrar en un convento. Feíta considera la situación de sus otras dos hermanas mayores, Rosa y *Argos*. Las entradas de su padre no alcanzan para seguir aparentando, a pesar de los préstamos que recibe periódicamente de Baltasar Sobrado por medio de la hipoteca de sus propiedades. Sus hermanas no cuentan con una dote que sirva de tentación a posibles pretendientes. Su hermosura natural no es suficiente para garantizarles el matrimonio. ¿A quiénes pueden ellas pretender en un medio provinciano como el de Marineda donde todos se conocen? En el Capítulo III de sus *Memorias*, Mauro Pareja describe con lujo de detalles la situación de las jóvenes de Marineda que buscan marido. Son víctimas pasivas de los caprichos de sus pretendidos. La sociedad les prohibe cualquier tipo de acción. En una conversación con *el Abad*, don Benicio comenta el caso de su hija Clara:

> Nada; ella comprendió que una señorita o se casa con arreglo a su clase... o no se casa, y decidió tomar el velo, conservando su dignidad, su posición, su señorío... (Cap. V, p. 461a)

Desde el capítulo VI se empiezan a escuchar los rumores de que 'el lujo asiático' que gasta Rosa se debe a que Baltasar Sobrado le ha dado carta blanca para que adquiera sus trapos en 'La Ciudad de Londres,' la tienda más elegante de Marineda. Este rumor, a la larga, resulta ser verdad, con las peores consecuencias posibles para la joven, como se verá. Y *Argos*, una vez superada su crisis mística y su capricho por el padre Incienso, se ha dedicado con gran empeño a desarrollar su talento musical y en las tertulias de las Neira *el Abad* la observa muy entusiasmada con León Cabello, su maestro de piano. Pero este amartelamiento, como también se verá, resulta ser otra afición pasajera. Mientras tanto Feíta, de la que nadie se ocupa debido en parte a sus 'extravagancias,' se sincera con Mauro Pareja:

> ¿No ve usted que a mí, como enseñar, no me han enseñado ni esto? Coser, bordar, rezar y barrer, dice mi padre que le basta a una señorita.

Y cuando, de rodillas, le ha pedido que la envíe al Instituto a estudiar como a su hermano Froilán, su padre la ha amenazado con azotes; aunque, como ella dice,

> No me asustan los azotes, ni mi padre es capaz de azotarnos con un hilo de seda; pero ni tenía dinero para las matrículas, ni los catedráticos me recibirían contra el gusto de papá [...]pero hoy ya estudio, yo sola, lo mismo que en el Instituto. ¡O más si se me antoja, hombre! (p. 470a)

Cuando Pareja le advierte que no debe preocuparse porque como no es hombre no necesita hacer carrera, como su hermano, pues vivirá de lo que gane su maridito, Feíta le replica indignada:

> ¡Maridito! Si que andan los mariditos mantenedores de sus mujeres por ahí a patadas. [...] Además, ¿de dónde saca usted que quiero recibir de nadie lo que pueda agenciarme yo misma?

Feíta se declara sin ambages en contra del matrimonio, por lo menos para ella, como solución para la vida. Declara su vocación por la soltería:

> Sí, amiguito *Abad*: esta joven se ha de quedar para vestir imágenes, aunque se me presenten partidos que no se me presentarán. Y sentiré

que no se me presenten, sólo por el gusto de que vean que no les admito. (p. 470b)

Y añade luego: 'En algo me he de distinguir de esas otras— y diciendo así señalaba a sus hermanas y a las demás niñas casaderas de la tertulia.'

Para escándalo de sus lectores doña Emilia pone en boca de su heroína la siguiente proposición:

Ustedes son, bien mirado, más inocentes que nosotras, porque ustedes ¿para qué quieren casarse? Mejor dicho, ¿hay entre ustedes ninguno que no pueda disfrutar las ventajas del matrimonio sin arrostrar sus inconvenientes? (pp. 470b–471a)

Ya podemos imaginar la reacción de Pereda ante semejante declaración de la existencia de una doble norma de conducta. Decididamente, doña Emilia no se para en barras y expresa exactamente lo que siente en esta novela.

Pero, el hecho es que Rosa y *Argos divina*, quienes se comportan con la libertad de un hombre para, en palabras de Feíta, 'disfrutar las ventajas del matrimonio sin arrostrar sus inconvenientes,' se encuentran con la inconveniencia de ser censuradas por su comportamiento aún por Feíta. A ésta, lo que más la afecta es que se da cuenta de que Rosa, como la de Bringas, se ha vendido a Sobrado a causa de su amor a los trapos y, como en el caso de la heroína de Galdós, sale defraudada porque la trama secundaria le impide el matrimonio con Sobrado, la solución soñada por su padre. Resulta que el hijo bastardo, *el compañero* Sobrado, obliga a su padre a reparar la deshonra de *la Tribuna,* su madre, casándose con ella y consiguiendo así un desenlace feliz, aunque tardío, para la novela de ese título, tan anterior en la fecha a las que nos ocupan. En todo caso, doña Emilia establece muy claramente que en cuestiones sexuales, como en casi todas, la mujer está siempre en posición de desventaja. Y es la situación de Rosa y de *Argos* la que precipita el desenlace para las *Memorias de un solterón* y para la vida de don Benicio Neira.

Ante la bochornosa situación de sus hermanas, Feíta decide abandonar Marineda e irse a Madrid a buscarse la vida dando clases particulares, como hasta ahora ha estado haciendo en su pueblo. Acude a Mauro Pareja para que éste le preste unos pocos duros que le permitirán su viaje e instalación en la Corte. La idea de que no verá más a la joven le hace realizar al solterón que no podrá vivir sin ella. Decide entonces declarársele y pedirle su mano. Feíta, fiel a sus ideas, le rechaza. Pero, otra vez, la trama le frustra sus planes. La deshonra de sus hijas y, sobre todo la de *Argos* por el gobernador civil, lanza a don Benicio al único acto enérgico de su vida: una confrontación con el causante de su deshonra para exigirle que se case con su hija. Ante la actitud cínica de Mejía, quien resulta ser hombre casado, Neira se enfurece y le atraviesa con una espada que colgaba del despacho del gobernador en una panoplia. Mauro Pareja, que esperaba en la antesala para una cita con Mejía, al escuchar los ruidos en el cuarto vecino, se precipita y al entrar encuentra a éste muerto en el suelo. Sin dudarlo un instante toma la otra espada de la panoplia y la pone en la mano del gobernador para que parezca que ha habido un duelo. Neira se salva de la cárcel y su acción le priva de la maledicencia de sus amigos. Sin embargo, esta descarga de energía además del arrepentimiento de haber asesinado a un hombre, le hace caer gravemente enfermo y muere. Ante tal situación Feíta no tiene más remedio que tomar las riendas del hogar. Para evitar más escándalo envía a *Argos* a Barcelona a casa de doña Milagros, donde podrá desarrollar una carrera musical. Aprovecha el talento de Rosa para los trapos y monta un taller de alta costura donde podrá utilizarlo y ganarse la vida. A Froilancito, una nulidad para el estudio, lo coloca de hortera en 'La Ciudad de Londres' donde con su sueldo podrá cancelar la gran deuda que Rosa había incurrido bajo la protección de Sobrado. En cuanto a ella, se sincera con Pareja diciéndole:

> No quería casarme. A usted le consta. Soñaba con la libertad y con algo que me parecía el ideal. Las cosas se me han arreglado de muy diferente manera. El Deber y la Familia —con mayúscula, amigo Mauro— han caído sobre mi... y ¡cuánto pesan! Me declaro rendida... Necesito un Cirineo...

Y las *Memorias de un solterón* terminan cuando éste deja de serlo. ¿Tenemos un final feliz o un final frustrado? Doña Emilia deja esa decisión en nuestras manos y esta depende del temple del lector o lectora de la novela.

Es evidente que en el 'Ciclo Adán y Eva' la condesa de Pardo Bazán deseaba poner de manifiesto su planteamiento de la situación de la mujer en la ecuación que coloca a ésta frente al hombre. Las dos novelas del ciclo son, entonces, novelas ejemplares en el sentido unamuniano de este término. En *Doña Milagros* nos presenta una situación: la de la mujer maternal cuya vida se ve frustrada por un matrimonio estéril, teniendo que sublimar sus instintos por medio del altruismo. Es evidente, aunque no se exprese en forma directa, que su matrimonio con un hombre tan ordinario como don Tomás Llanes, el comandante de Otumba, no puede ser feliz. Sin embargo, doña Milagros es modelo de fidelidad y nunca se le oye una queja en contra de su marido y en ningún momento deja que su posible afecto por el buenazo de don Benicio se deje traslucir. Es posible que en su prolífico vecino vea ella el que pudiera haberle colmado sus ansias de maternidad. Aunque su difunta esposa, en sus últimos momentos de delirio, renegara de su maternidad y maldijera 'la tarea que la dignificaba a mis ojos,' en palabras de Neira. Pero éste es otro de los argumentos feministas que doña Emilia intercala en su narración de vez en cuando. De todas formas, doña Milagros entra y sale incólume del espacio narrativo que le corresponde en este ciclo y representa un ejemplo; desde el punto de vista feminista, un ejemplo *negativo*. Es decir que ella representa el papel de víctima sacrificada pero heroica: una Jacinta. E Ildaura, la esposa muerta, representa, a pesar de su mal genio, otra víctima del matrimonio y del 'calzonazos y pelele' de su marido, para citar sus últimas palabras.

Feíta, por el contrario, representa un ejemplo *positivo* del ideal feminista, porque ella logra llevar a cabo, por lo menos en parte, su programa de independencia, hasta que las circunstancias le impiden llevarlo a su lógica conclusión. Por eso, su matrimonio con Mauro Pareja no se puede considerar tampoco como un final feliz. El matrimonio, tradicionalmente, constituye el final feliz del género comedia (y ésta novela *es* una comedia de costumbres). Pero, paradójicamente, aquí el matrimonio constituye un final frustrado y, otra vez, encontramos a una mujer víctima de las circunstancias de su medio. Es posible que en su matrimonio haya encontrado felicidad ya que Mauro Pareja parece comprenderla y admirarla. Pero también sabemos que dentro de él le será imposible a Feíta completar el pleno desarrollo de su potencial humano.

De todas formas, resulta clarísimo que doña Emilia quiso avanzar con las novelas de este Ciclo un argumento en pro de la mujer, dando ejemplos negativos y positivos, aunque frustrados estos últimos, de su situación en la España de su momento, a finales del siglo. Si la novelista añadió, en mi opinión *a posteriori*, un 'Prólogo en el cielo' y utilizó el título *Memorias de un solterón* para la segunda novela, fue sólo para despistar a sus lectores haciéndoles creer que estaban leyendo las vidas de dos hombres, Benicio Neira y Mauro Pareja. Es por eso que surgen tantas preguntas e incongruencias como apunté en la introducción de este trabajo. Las preguntas, como ya había observado, nos obligan a hacer una lectura más atenta de los textos, después de la cual nos damos cuenta de que todo ese tinglado ha sido un juego narrativo para encubrir un planteamiento muy serio.

4

Emilia Pardo Bazán
Los preludios de una *Insolación*
(junio de 1887–marzo de 1889)

José Manuel González Herrán

En los primeros días de la primavera de 1889 aparecía en las librerías de Madrid una novela de doña Emilia Pardo Bazán, primorosamente editada, *Insolación*, en cuya primera página podía leerse esta dedicatoria: 'A José Lázaro Galdiano /en prenda de amistad'. Los dimes y diretes —no del todo benévolos— que tal declaración suscitaría en determinados círculos han venido propiciando desde entonces una *lectura* de la novela en clave autobiográfica, que considero equivocada. Así espero demostrarlo en las páginas que siguen, en las que me propongo reconstruir su largo proceso (de redacción, impresión y edición), entre junio de 1887 y marzo de 1889.

Según aquella *lectura*, en la anécdota de *Insolación* doña Emilia habría recreado literariamente una experiencia propia, su aventura amorosa, en la primavera de 1888 en Arenys de Mar, con el dedicatario de la novela. Aunque es muy posible que tal especie hubiese empezado a propalarse con la aparición del libro (cuya inequívoca ofrenda estimulaba la sospecha), fue Narcís Oller el primero en ponerla por escrito en el capítulo VII de sus *Memòries literáries. Història dels meus llibres* [1918]:

> [...] l'endemà no em vig atansar a l'hotel on posava la Sra. Pardo, fins al vespre; però ella no hi era. Vaig tornar-hi el migdia següent i tampoc. A la nit va dir-me que amb En Lázaro havien fet una excursió a Arenys de Mar d'on tornava encisada. (Alguns volgueren suposar després que Insolación n'és un reflex). (Oller, 1962: 108)[1]

75

Lo novelesco de tal suposición ha llegado a convertirla en certeza, admitida y reiterada por algunos críticos e investigadores: Carmen Bravo-Villasante,[2] Nelly Clémessy,[3] Marina Mayoral,[4] Daniel S. Whitaker,[5] Pedro Ortiz Armengol,[6] entre otros.[7] Como enseguida demostraré y en contra de tan coincidentes suposiciones, los datos cronológicos no parecen confirmar tan sugestiva hipótesis, ni —en consecuencia— las no menos sugestivas interpretaciones que de la novela se han hecho. Como la de Whitaker, que resume así su explicación del cierre de la novela:

> Pardo Bazán reflects in the novel the general experience she herself had with Galdiano, excluding the proposed matrimony in the epilogue. In real life Doña Emilia broke off with her companion before any consideration to marriage was given, for by this time the Countess had been married for many years. Thus, the closure of *Insolación* allots to Asís what Emilia Pardo Bazán lacked in her friendship with Lázaro and others: an ordering of the chaos of life's experience. (Whitaker, 1988: 364)

Pues bien: *Insolación* comenzó a escribirse bastante antes de que su autora y José Lázaro Galdiano se conociesen; más aún: su redacción —también probablemente su impresión— estaba bastante avanzada cuando ocurrió el *episodio de Arenys*. Y lo más sorprendente es que algunos de los datos que aquí aduciré en apoyo de mi propuesta proceden de documentos ya conocidos (aunque tal vez no suficientemente atendidos).

El más importante es una carta (por ahora inédita y conservada en la Casa-Museo Galdós de Las Palmas de Gran Canaria) de la escritora coruñesa a su colega canario; la fecha que consta en su encabezamiento es '16 de junio', debajo de la cual —a lápiz y acaso de mano de Galdós— está anotado '87'[8] y en ella le informa que ha comenzado a escribir una novela: como será breve, espera poder despacharla en el mes de julio en su residencia veraniega de *la Granja de Meirás*; la idea se le ocurrió en el tren y ya tiene título: *Insolación*.[9]

Según creo, la primera referencia (publicada) a esa carta corresponde a Francisca González-Arias (1992: 121), quien, comentando las relaciones intertextuales de *Insolación* y *Fortunata y Jacinta*, aduce cartas de doña Emilia a don Benito escritas en 1887, entre ellas la que ahora nos importa: 'In the letter dated June 16th Emilia revealed that on the train returning from Madrid to Galicia, she had the idea for a novel. Though she did not specify what the novel was to be about, she had a clear idea of the title: *Insolación*'.[10]

Aun reconociendo su primicia a esta colega, he de señalar que, antes de la aparición de su libro,[11] tuve noticia de la citada carta en una conversación con Maurice Hemingway (en septiembre de 1989); dato que —según me indicó— tenía intención de recoger y comentar en un estudio que entonces preparaba, 'La obra novelística de Emilia Pardo Bazán' (y que entregó dos años más tarde); Maurice falleció en junio de 1994, sin ver impreso ese trabajo, que al fin ha visto la luz en el verano de 1998; su nota 14 dice:

> Siguiendo el testimonio de Narciso Oller [...] varios críticos han asegurado que la historia amorosa de *Insolación* está basada en una aventura que se supone tuvo doña Emilia con Álvaro [sic, por José] Lázaro Galdiano. Pero en una carta escrita a Galdós el 16 de junio de 1887 (y conservada en la Casa-Museo Galdós en Las Palmas) dice la autora que ya tiene empezada una novela titulada *Insolación*, es decir, un años antes de conocer a Lázaro en mayo de 1888. Por tanto, parece poco probable que la intriga de *Insolación* refleje la supuesta aventura amorosa entre doña Emilia y Lázaro. (Hemingway, 1998: 670)

Fue pues el llorado colega que aquí homenajeamos uno de los primeros en llamar la atención sobre esa noticia que, conocida por varios pardobazanistas, parece haber pasado inadvertida: si *Insolación* comenzó a redactarse en junio de 1887, ¿cómo podría basar el lance principal de su argumento en un suceso que aún tardaría en producirse casi un año, en mayo de 1888?

Apoyándose en el testimonio señalado por Hemingway (cuyo trabajo inédito tuvo ocasión de consultar), pero también en sus propias pesquisas y deducciones, Cristina Patiño Eirín ha discutido con razonamientos muy convincentes el problema que nos ocupa en los párrafos iniciales de su comunicación 'La aventura catalana de Pardo Bazán', presentada en el Primer Coloquio de la Sociedad de Literatura Española del Siglo XIX (Barcelona, octubre de 1996) y que se publicará en las *Actas* correspondientes: 'Además de la propia transitividad novelística —afirma—, existen otras razones que parecen no justificar la simplista equivalencia autora = protagonista de la peripecia amorosa de *Insolación*'; y alude a 'circunstancias [...] que parecen conceder a la invención novelesca una prelación cronológica con respecto a su aventura mediterránea con Lázaro Galdiano' (Patiño Eirín, 1998 [en prensa]). Aduzco aquí la aportación de mi apreciada discípula y colega[12] porque, si bien nuestras argumentaciones coinciden en algunos puntos, en otros se complementan (o discrepan).

Podría argüirse, en favor de la hipótesis apuntada por Oller —y tan precipitadamente repetida—, que la información de aquella carta a Galdós es muy imprecisa: sólo un título y una *idea* (que, por otra parte, no se especifica);[13] cabría suponer, pues, que acaso la redacción no fue tan rápida como la autora esperaba, de modo que ni en julio ni en los meses siguientes se concluyó; y la aventura de Arenys de Mar, en la primavera siguiente, habría actuado así como catalizador de aquel proyecto atascado. Mas, por convincente que pueda parecer esta conjetura, otros datos proporcionados por los epistolarios impiden que pueda aceptarse.

En este caso se trata de otra carta de doña Emilia, ahora al dedicatario de la novela, José Lázaro Galdiano, fechada en 10 de julio de 1888 (y publicada en 1988 por Enrique Pardo Canalís). Escrita al regreso de doña Emilia a su ciudad natal, tras ese viaje a Cataluña en el que ambos se han conocido, la misiva dedica su mayor parte a evocar tan grata excursión; y, entre otras consultas y encargos a su corresponsal, doña Emilia le pregunta 'si ha visto ya alguna galerada de *Insolación*, por cuya salud debe V. interesarse a fuer de padrino [esto es, como dedicatario y acaso recomendante ante sus editores].' (Pardo Canalís, 1988: 522).[14]

El testimonio parece irrefutable: en el verano de 1888 aquella novela —cuya idea matriz había surgido en el tren de Madrid a Galicia justamente un año antes— estaba ya en prensa, y lo suficientemente adelantada como para que a comienzos de julio pueda haber ya galeradas; por lo tanto, de nuevo resulta imposible aceptar su relación con la que vengo llamando *aventura de Arenys de Mar*. Si ésta tuvo lugar en mayo de 1888, no parece fácil suponer que en poco más de un mes —y en plena excursión— doña Emilia redactase la novela, la pasase a limpio y la entregase a los editores. En consecuencia, creo que no puede mantenerse ya la afirmación (ni siquiera la conjetura) de que *Insolación* recrea un episodio vivido por su autora, pues los datos demuestran que la novela había comenzado a redactarse (más aún, posiblemente estaba ya concluida) antes de aquella *flirtation*.[15] Lo que no impide que tal experiencia real pueda relacionarse con la ficticia, aunque en un sentido inverso.

En efecto: para quienes se sientan decepcionados por mi demostración, que destruye una hipótesis muy atractiva, propongo otra, acaso más interesante: por esta vez el arte no refleja la realidad, sino que es la vida quien imita al arte. La imaginación novelesca de doña Emilia habría inventado primero la anécdota de una mujer independiente que, en uso de su libertad y estimulada por un ambiente propicio, se entrega a un hombre atractivo; y luego —acaso para verificar el supuesto, como postulaba el método *experimental*— lo quiso poner en práctica con la involuntaria ayuda de José Lázaro Galdiano, que merecería aquella dedicatoria en pago por su más o menos involuntaria 'colaboración'. Hipótesis que, lejos de contradecirla, confirma la sagaz explicación que ha sugerido Marina Mayoral:

[...] la novela está dedicada a José Lázaro Galdiano 'en prenda de amistad'. El gesto de doña Emilia de dedicar la novela a su amigo siempre me ha recordado el gesto del personaje de la novela, de Asís Taboada cuando abre la ventana de su dormitorio y se asoma con su amante para que todos puedan verlos juntos. Es un gesto similar, pero mucho más arriesgado y valiente, porque en la marquesa literaria es preámbulo de matrimonio y en la Pardo Bazán no tiene esa cobertura legal, sólo puede interpretarse como un gesto de independencia y de desafío a la hipocresía de la sociedad. (Mayoral, 1987: 12–13)

Una pregunta ha podido quedar en el aire tras las explicaciones precedentes: si *Insolación* se redactó —como esperaba hacer su autora— en el verano de 1887, ¿por qué tardó casi dos años en publicarse? Según la citada carta de doña Emilia a José Lázaro, ya estaba en prensa en julio de 1888, lo que confirma que el retraso no fue de redacción sino de publicación; o —para ser más precisos— de impresión, corrección, ilustración y edición. Sabíamos algo de ese laborioso proceso por las cartas de doña Emilia a Josep Yxart (en Torres, 1977); el reciente descubrimiento —cuya primicia doy aquí— de unas galeradas corregidas de *Insolación*, aparte de su valor para el estudio *genético* de ese texto, nos proporciona valiosos datos que pueden ayudarnos a resolver aquella pregunta.

Aunque en la citada carta de julio de 1888 doña Emilia encargaba a su amigo que vigilase la edición de la novela (y acaso que corrigiese sus primeras pruebas), fue ella misma quien lo hizo, según muestran las galeradas conservadas en el archivo de la Real Academia Galega en la casa coruñesa de la escritora,[16] minuciosa y abundantemente corregidas por su propia mano. Ello ayuda a explicar también las razones del retraso en la publicación: más que enmienda de erratas —muy escasas, por cierto[17]—, en el texto inicialmente compuesto se introducen bastantes cambios, crecientes según avanza la lectura: poco abundantes en los primeros capítulos, se incrementan a partir del XIII, y son ya muchos en el XVI y siguientes; especialmente en los dos últimos, algunas de cuyas páginas llegan a tener en sus 47 líneas de texto más de 40 correcciones (que a veces suponen una reescritura de ciertos párrafos). Veamos algunas muestras:

Así, en el capítulo XXI, las frases '¡Ay infeliz de la mujer que se fiase de sus exageraciones y locuras! ¡Requebrar a las cigarreras así, delante de...' (página 297 de la primera edición) sustituyen a la inicialmente escrita, tachada pero legible: 'No le arrendaba la ganancia Asís a la desgraciada que tomase al pie de la letra ciertas exageraciones'. Poco más adelante, el texto '¡Qué tontera! Lo probable es que a Pacheco no volviese a verle nunca más... Y esta punzada del corazón ¿qué será? Será enfermedad, o... Parece que lo aprieta un aro de hierro... ¡Jesús, qué cavilaciones más simples!' (p. 298) sustituye a este otro, muy diferente: '*In Memoriam*, que es lo que ponen los ingleses para recordar a un muerto. Vaya unas emociones... ¡Qué quebrantados tenía los huesos!... La alcoba... estaba fresquita'. Lo mismo sucede con '¡Ya pareció aquello! ¡Se despejó la incógnita! ¡Y decir que no hará dos semanas que se conocieron en casa de Sahagún! ¡Mujeres...!' (p. 304), que en la primera redacción decía: '¡Esto era! pensó para sí, con la desaprobación y la censura que invariablemente acompaña a descubrimientos semejantes'. Y todo el final del capítulo (desde 'Miró al comandante, que se hacía el sueco') es de nueva redacción: 84 líneas que ocupan casi íntegramente las páginas 305 a 308, en lugar de esta primera versión, muy diferente y más breve:

> Naturalmente que a don Gabriel le pinchaba ya el asiento de la silla: no veía el minuto de echar escalera abajo. Aprovechó cualquier pretexto, y sólo se detuvo en la esquina de la calle.— ¡Cómo escogen las

mujeres!... En llegando el cuarto de hora... En fin..., indulgencia, pensador, indulgencia... La severidad no le sienta bien ni aun al justo... Gabriel, se prohibe el mal humor... Se parece tanto, en estos casos, a la... ¿Envidioso tú? No, hijo, eso no. Lo que te sucede es que, buen amigo de esa dama, ves claramente lo que ella no puede ver... Ese amante que ha escogido es una de las más caracterizadas formas de la decadencia de la raza hispana, o si se quiere, del influjo que sigue ejerciendo sobre nosotros el Africa, nuestra eterna conquistadora... Perezoso, débil, ignorante, sensual, indefenso contra las pasiones, incapaz del honroso trabajo y de la fecunda lucha; enamoradizo, pendenciero, escéptico en fuerza de su propia indolencia y egoísmo, ese hombre no puede ni fundar una familia seria que ayude a la reconstrucción social como la humilde célula a la del organismo, ni lleva en sí la firmeza que da valor a los juramentos de constancia y los consagra para el porvenir... Pero, ¡bah! ¡Qué tonterías!...— añadió para sí el Comandante. —Cualquiera pensaría que Paquita acaba de darme parte de boda... ¡Esto no pasa de un devaneo... por fortuna para ella! Como aventura... quizá tendrá su poesía..., poesía de romance morisco... Después dirán que no hay casualidades. Tarjetero, tarjetero... — El Comandante se caló los lentes, se retorció la barba, se encogió de hombros... El que en ello tenga empeño, que le siga al Círculo Militar, siquiera por oírle explicar la teoría de la guerra según el Conde Tolstoy.

En el capítulo XXII, 'Epílogo', hay también importantes enmiendas: la mitad de su segundo párrafo (desde 'Y ahora también piensas en cosas así, muy tristes', p. 310) era inicialmente: '¡Y ese cariñito que te está entrando ahora y que te lo veo en los ojos..., hermosa, ¡te lo veo!... es también porque tú dices —A éste, ¡quién sabe si no lo vuelvo a ver en el mundo! ¡Ay! Yo no seré tan sabio como ese amigo tuyo, ese comandante...; pero de tonto, no tengo un pelo..., y a las mujeres, las leo de corrío... ¡Vaya si las leo, prenda!' En el párrafo siguiente, el texto: 'Sus pupilas se humedecieron, su respiración se apresuró, y corrió por sus vértebras misterioso escalofrío, corriente de aire agitado por las alas del Ideal' (pp. 311–12), era en la primera versión: 'Sus ojos se humedecían, su respiración se apresuraba, y la noción del tiempo se le había borrado, así como en alta mar se borra la idea de la orilla'. Pero la modificación más notable se produce en las páginas 313 y 314 (desde 'Pacheco exhaló un suspiro', hasta '—Quédate.'), cuyo diálogo desarrolla lo apuntado en una redacción inicial más sintética y suprime las importunas reflexiones de la voz narradora:

> Pacheco no necesitaba tanto para decir mil desatinos, todavía más románticos que los anteriores. El que dominó fue el de asegurar que no podía resistir más la pena y que se retiraba. No tenía fuerzas para tanto. De despedirse valía más entonces. Asís se le colgó del cuello.
>
> —No te vas...
>
> —Míralo bien... Si me quedo ahora..., me quedo toda la noche. Piénsalo... No digas después que los criados...
>
> Sociedad, peligros, murmuraciones, respetos humanos, ¿qué sois ante esos torrentes que se desatan a veces en el alma humana, rompiendo todos los diques de la razón?

Es de suponer que tantos y tan sustanciales cambios hubieron de ocasionar un considerable trabajo tipográfico, con las consiguientes demoras. Pero es que, además, del cotejo entre el texto de esas galeradas y el finalmente impreso se deducen tantas variantes que es forzoso suponer otra corrección de pruebas posterior. Dado que el libro se imprimía en Barcelona, no le era posible a la autora hacerlo directamente *en prensa* (como Galdós),[18] por lo que aquellas segundas pruebas tuvieron que viajar —en ida y vuelta— desde la Imprenta de los Sucesores de N. Ramírez y Compañía (en el barcelonés Pasaje de Escudillers, número 4) hasta la residencia de la escritora, en Galicia o en Madrid. Por eso doña Emilia pudo conservar entre sus papeles un juego de pruebas —acaso las primeras—, pero no las definitivas, que quedarían en la imprenta.

Hay todavía otro factor que pudo complicar —y retrasar— el proceso: los grabados de J. Cuchy que ilustraban la edición, no sólo en los márgenes sino dentro del texto, lo que sin duda obligó a recomponer el preparado para las galeradas que conocemos. Las cartas de doña Emilia a Josep Yxart aluden repetidamente a estos y otros pormenores interesantes en la *fabricación* del libro; lamentablemente, el editor de este epistolario no fecha con exactitud todas las cartas, lo que impide reconstruir con la precisión que quisiéramos esta última fase del proceso.

La primera carta que nos importa, número XII de este epistolario, está fechada en Madrid el 24 enero de 1889 y en ella se tratan asuntos de índole editorial, pues Yxart acaba de ingresar en la casa que publicará *Insolación*: la escritora corrige sus primeras impresiones, no muy favorables, acerca del dibujante:

La ilustración, sin ser una obra de arte de esas que sorprenden, resulta muy aceptable, bastante graciosa y fina. Y como así lo creo, así lo dije. Mi mala impresión era natural, toda vez que me aseguraron no había hecho el Sr. Cuchey [*sic*] más que caricaturas.

Yo al tratarse de la ilustración de un libro mío, no la miro como autora, sino como lectora solamente. (Torres, 1977: 400)

En la siguiente, del 4 de febrero, hay un comentario de doña Emilia que permite deducir algo de lo que no había noticia en la bibliografía pardobazaniana: ¿hubo una tirada de *Insolación* que se vendió por entregas o como parte de alguna de las revistas editadas por aquella misma casa? 'Me satisface mucho su dictamen favorable a *Insolación* (de la cual, entre paréntesis, me gustaron más los primeros pliegos que los que se van *vendiendo* [cursiva mía]:[19] tengo para mí que la tirada de la ilustración decae)' (Torres, 1977: 401). La deficiencia se subsanó con prontitud, pues semanas más tarde, el 2 de marzo (en la carta, número XIV, no consta el año, pero su editor supone razonablemente que es también de 1889), doña Emilia escribe: 'Veo con mucha satisfacción que se ha arreglado lo de las ilustraciones de *Insolación*. Dé usted gracias a los Sres. Henrich';[20] y añade una apostilla que parece aludir a la intervención de Yxart como corrector del texto (en una lectura posterior a la hecha por ella en las galeradas antes comentadas): 'No me tomo el trabajo de examinar la palabra que usted haya añadido, porque sé que estará perfectamente y lo estaría aun tratándose de adiciones más importantes' (Torres, 1977: 403).

La carta XV está fechada en Madrid el día 21 de un mes que no se indica (su editor la coloca antes de la del 19 de abril) y que sin duda corresponde a marzo: la autora ha recibido ya ejemplares del libro (por cierto, en dos encuadernaciones diferentes, dato que tampoco mencionan las bibliografías: 'Diga usted a los Sres. Ramírez que [...] he recibido el primer ejemplar encuadernado y [...] otros nueve en rústica'; Torres, 1977: 403), pero todavía no los hay en las librerías.[21] No tardarían mucho, puesto que aparecen reseñas de la novela el 24 de marzo (de Mariano de Cavia, en *El Liberal*) y el 3 de abril (de Luis Alfonso, en *La Época*).[22]

En conclusión: según los datos y documentos aquí comentados, con las hipótesis que de ellos cabe deducir, la cronología de escritura de *Insolación* puede resumirse así: a fines de junio de 1887 Emilia Pardo Bazán comienza a escribir en su residencia veraniega de Meirás una novela cuya *idea* se le ha ocurrido viajando en tren de Madrid a Galicia; en mayo del año siguiente (posiblemente con la novela ya redactada), una excursión a Arenys de Mar con José Lázaro Galdiano le pone en situación de vivir una experiencia erótica muy similar a la ficticia protagonizada por la heroína de su novela; dos meses más tarde, en julio de 1888, el libro está ya en prensa, pues encarga a su ocasional amante que vea en la imprenta barcelonesa las galeradas de aquella novela a él dedicada; las abundantes correcciones hechas por la autora a las primeras pruebas del texto obligarán a demorar el trabajo de impresión a lo largo del otoño e invierno de 1888–1889; de modo que el libro, primorosamente ilustrado y lujosamente encuadernado, no verá la luz hasta marzo de 1889: habían transcurrido 21 meses desde aquella idea germinal.[23]

Referencias Bibliográficas

ÁVILA ARELLANO, Julián, 'Doña Emilia Pardo Bazán y Benito Pérez Galdós en 1889. Fecunda compenetración espiritual y literaria', *IV Congreso Galdosiano*, Las Palmas de Gran Canaria: Ediciones del Cabildo Insular, 1993, pp. 305–24.

BOTREL, Jean-François y Josette BLANQUAT (eds.), *Clarín y sus editores*, 1884–1893, Rennes: Université de Haute Bretagne, 1981.

BRAVO-VILLASANTE, Carmen, *Vida y obra de Emilia Pardo Bazán*, Madrid: Ediciones de la Revista de Occidente, 1962; 2ª edición, corregida y aumentada, Madrid: Magisterio Español, 1973.

— (ed.), E. Pardo Bazán, *Cartas a Benito Pérez Galdós* (1889–1890), Madrid: Turner, 1975.

— , 'Aspectos inéditos de Emilia Pardo Bazán (Epistolario con Galdós)', *Actas del Cuarto Congreso Internacional de Hispanistas* [1971], Salamanca: Asociación Internacional de Hispanistas–Consejo General de Castilla y León-Universidad de Salamanca, 1982, pp. 199–204.

CLÉMESSY, Nelly, *Emilia Pardo Bazán, romancière* (*La critique, la théorie, la pratique*), Paris: Centre de Recherches Hispaniques, 1973.

DeCOSTER, Cyrus, 'Pardo Bazán and her Contemporaries', *Anales Galdosianos*, 19 (1984), pp. 121–31.

GONZÁLEZ-ARIAS, Francisca, *A Voice, not an Echo: Emilia Pardo Bazán and the Modern Novel in Spain and France*, [tesis doctoral presentada en Harvard University, 1985]; Ann Arbor: University Microfilms International, 1986.

—, *Portrait of a Woman as Artist. Emilia Pardo Bazán and the Modern Novel in France and Spain*, New York: Garland, 1992.

—, 'Diario de un viaje: las cartas de Emilia Pardo Bazán a Benito Pérez Galdós', en J. Kronik y H. Turner (eds), *Textos y contextos de Galdós*, Madrid: Castalia, 1994, pp. 169–75.

—, 'La Condesa, la Revolución y la novela en Rusia', *Bulletin Hispanique*, 96 (1994), pp. 167–88.

—, 'La poética de Galicia en los cuentos de Emilia Pardo Bazán', en J. M. González Herrán (ed.), *Estudios sobre Emilia Pardo Bazán. In Memoriam Maurice Hemingway*, Santiago de Compostela: Universidade-Consorcio de Santiago, 1997, pp. 147–69.

GONZÁLEZ HERRÁN, José Manuel, *La obra de Pereda ante la crítica literaria de su tiempo*, Santander: Ayuntamiento de Santander-Ediciones de Librería Estudio, 1983.

—, 'Un texto inédito de Pardo Bazán: ¿El cuento *La mina*?', en J. M. González Herrán (ed.), *Estudios sobre Emilia Pardo Bazán. In Memoriam Maurice Hemingway*, Santiago de Compostela: Universidade-Consorcio de Santiago, 1997, pp. 171–80.

HEMINGWAY, Maurice, 'La obra novelística de Emilia Pardo Bazán', en V. García de la Concha (dir.), *Historia de la Literatura española*, 9. L. Romero Tobar (coord.). *Siglo XIX (II)*, Madrid: Espasa-Calpe, 1998, pp. 661–81.

MAYORAL, Marina, 'Introducción' a su ed. de E. Pardo Bazán, *Insolación*, Madrid: Espasa Calpe, 1987.

OLLER, Narcís, *Memòries literàries. Història dels meus llibres*, [1918], Barcelona: Aedos, 1962.

ORTIZ ARMENGOL, Pedro, *Apuntaciones para 'Fortunata y Jacinta'*, Madrid: Edit. Universidad Complutense, 1987.

—, 'Entrando en *La Fontana de Oro*', estudio introductorio a la edición facsímil del Manuscrito de 1868 de B. Pérez Galdós, *La Fontana de Oro*, Madrid: Editorial Hernando, 1990.

—, *Vida de Galdós*, Barcelona: Crítica, 1996.

PARDO BAZÁN, Emilia, *La Madre Naturaleza*, Barcelona: Cortezo y Cía, 1887.

—, *Insolación*, Barcelona: Sucesores de N. Ramírez y Cía, 1889.

PARDO CANALÍS, Enrique, 'Una carta de Doña Emilia Pardo Bazán a Don José Lázaro Galdiano', *Varia Bibliographica. Homenaje a José Simón Díaz*, Kassel: Reichenberger, 1988, pp. 521–4.

PATIÑO EIRÍN, Cristina, 'La aventura catalana de Pardo Bazán', *Del Romanticismo al Realismo. Actas del Primer Coloquio de la Sociedad de Literatura Española del Siglo XIX*, Barcelona: S.L.E.S. XIX [1998; en prensa].

PATTISON, Walter T., *Emilia Pardo Bazán*, New York: Twayne Publishers, 1971.

PENAS, E., '*Insolación* de Emilia Pardo Bazán y la crisis del naturalismo', *Letras Peninsulares*, 6 (1993–1994), pp. 331–43.

SANTIÁÑEZ-TIÓ, N., 'Una marquesita 'sandunguera', o el mito del naturalismo en *Insolación*', *Revista de Estudios Hispánicos*, 23 (1989), pp. 119–34.

SHOEMAKER, William H., *Las cartas desconocidas de Galdós en 'La Prensa' de Buenos Aires'*, Madrid: Ediciones de Cultura Hispánica, 1973.

TORRES, David, 'Veinte cartas inéditas de Emilia Pardo Bazán a José Yxart

(1883–1890)', *Boletín de la Biblioteca de Menéndez Pelayo*, LIII (1977), pp. 383–409.

—, 'Trece cartas inéditas de Pereda', *Boletín de la Biblioteca de Menéndez Pelayo*, LVI (1980), pp. 294–314.

WHITAKER, Daniel S., 'Artificial Order: Closure in Pardo Bazán's *Insolación*', *Romance Quarterly*, 35 (1988), pp. 359–65.

Genre and Uncertainty in *La dama joven*

Julia Biggane

Most of Emilia Pardo Bazan's twenty-one *novelas breves* have received no critical attention. *La dama joven*, published in 1885, is an exception, perhaps because some critics feel it lends itself to a feminist reading. Carmen Bravo-Villasante boldly posits a link between Pardo's personal circumstances in the early 1880s and the thesis of *La dama joven*. She ascribes Pardo Bazán's recent marital separation to the author's feeling that her husband was stifling her independence as a writer and critic, and says of the text:

> La breve novela resulta autobiográfica. Emilia, como la dama joven, quería un destino ancho, grande, hermoso [...] y, como la protagonista, tiene que escoger entre un destino brillante, aunque, al parecer, peligroso, y una vida oscura. [...] En la novelita hay una intención feminista.[1]

Nelly Clémessy also sees *La dama joven* as a feminist text, and says that Pardo Bazán had made the subject matter:

> ... l'une des revendications de ses campagnes féministes. Dans son étude critique de 1889, elle se plaignait même de ce que les actrices, une fois mariées, abandonnassent souvent la profession. L'une des premières nouvelles qu'elle écrivit, *La dama joven*, aborde déjà le thème.[2]

David Henn, though, takes a different approach, and treats *La dama joven* as an example of the social stasis that he sees in much of Pardo Bazán's early prose fiction. Although not explicitly accounted for in works such as *La Tribuna*, *El Cisne de Vilamorta* and *La dama joven*, this stasis is subsequently explained, he suggests, by the partial environmental determinism visible in *Los pazos de Ulloa and La madre naturaleza*.[3] Lou Charnon-Deutsch agrees: 'Outside of *Viaje de novios* [...] *La dama joven* may be Pardo Bazán's most representative example of environmental determinism'.[4]

The novella describes how Concha, a young dressmaker living in modest circumstances, is given a chance to exchange her job, and pursue her interest in amateur dramatics, by taking employment as an *ingénue* with a professional theatre company. The opportunity is strongly opposed both by Dolores, Concha's older sister and surrogate mother since the two were orphaned, who feels that her sister would be in moral danger within what she sees as the louche profession of acting, and by Ramón, Concha's fiancé. Eventually, Concha opts for marriage and renounces a career in acting. With the exception of David Henn, who says that judgement is left to the reader, all the critics claim that Concha's decision is portrayed by the narrator as misguided, and although they disagree about whether *La dama joven* is principally a feminist or a deterministic text, none of them attributes any thematic complexity to the novella. Lou Charnon-Deutsch is alone in raising the question of genre, yet she reaches no conclusions specifically about *La dama joven,* and in fact conflates the *novela breve* with Pardo's short stories. In this article, I argue that addressing *La dama joven*'s generic status is vital, and that its complex liminal generic structure produces a correspondingly complex and problematic thematic structure which neither lends itself to a naturalistic nor a feminist reading.

The novella's liminal generic status is immediately apparent in the interchangeable Spanish terms for it—*cuento largo* and *novela breve*. It stands both outside and within the conventional binary division of prose fiction into short story and novel. *La dama joven* meshes narratological, characterizational, diegetic and structural conventions from the novel and the short story. Given that, as a trope, liminality signifies in-betweenness, undecidability and the blurring of differences, it is not surprising that *La dama joven*'s generic liminality provides an apt matrix for the occupation of liminal and uncertain thematic and narratological space as well. By using Pardo's own novels and short stories as counter-examples to the *novela breve*, I hope to avoid becoming mired in inaccurate and reductive totalizing definitions which seek to reify 'the short story', 'the novel' and any supposed attendant properties.

As the plot summary above indicates, the diegetic structure of *La dama joven* is simple: the number of characters is very small, action is limited to one *barrio* of the imaginary Galician town of Marineda, and takes place within four days. The characterization, like the diegetic structure, could be accommodated comfortably within the generic confines of the short story. The minor characters in particular are easily recognizable types: Gormaz, the actor-manager in charge of the amateur production in which Concha stars, Estrella, the well-known actor who offers her a job, and Dolores's confessor are all associated with one salient physical characteristic that acts as a concise synecdoche for their personality. The near-constant asthmatic coughing and compulsive throat-clearing that punctuates Gormaz's speech connotes his nervous, exhausted frailty (I, 912 a, b).[5] Both the priest and Estrella are characterized by their noses. Estrella's is described as 'borbónica' (I, 914b) signifying his grand, imposing manner; the confessor's is a 'nariz afilada y ascética' (I, 923a). This synecdochal shorthand is, of course, ideally suited to the short story, as are generalizing constructions such as

> Gormaz pertenecía *a aquella falange de* actores, ya casi extinguida, *que* amaba el arte y se preciaba de entender de letras. (I, 912a)
>
> [Tenía Estrella]... *una de esas* caras inteligentes y castizas de pelucona rancia que aún hoy se ven en aldeanos del cerro de Castilla. (I, 914b; my italics)

The protagonists of *La dama joven*, Dolores and Concha, are not so very much more complex than the minor figures. The main points of Dolores's character are established, explained and fixed in the very first paragraphs of the text. Her over-zealous protectiveness towards Concha is succinctly explained by the narrator as resulting from the loss of both parents, and from the shame she herself suffered after being seduced and abandoned—a shame that she is determined to save Concha from. This protective zeal, together with a deferential awe towards the Church (which gave her alms and support after she had been abandoned and was trying to bring Concha up in wretched conditions), accounts entirely for Dolores's behaviour throughout *La dama joven*. Concha's character is no more complex than Dolores's, but may appear to be so as it is determined only gradually and partially, and because the narrator makes few explicit statements

about Concha's personality, relying instead on more indirect techniques. I discuss Concha's character in more detail below, but
together the two sisters are, unsurprisingly, more akin to the one-
dimensional, quickly-defined characters found in Pardo's contemporaneous short stories than the protagonists of, say, *La Tribuna*, *Los
pazos de Ulloa* or *La madre naturaleza*, who display the contra-
dictions, evolution and subtleties demanded of the conventional
mimetic novelistic character.

But if the simple diegetic structure and characterization belong
more within the arena of Pardo's short stories, the ambiguity of the
narratorial perspective, and the presentation of discourse are more
akin to Pardo's novelistic output. *La dama joven* is narrated in the
third person by an anonymous, ostensibly uncomplicated figure.
However, the narrator's perspective is not fixed or identifiable, and
shifts constantly from the most intimate omniscience or empathy
with characters to the most resolutely non-judgemental distance
from them. In the opening paragraphs of the text, for instance, which
recount the sisters' frenetic preparations for the following night's
theatrical production while their lamp is running out of oil, the
narrator works hard to efface her own presence and positionality.[6]
There are several speech-acts that might be free-indirect-speech
transcriptions of the sisters' utterances, might be interjections from
the spectating narrator, or might be a combination of the two:

> Aún ardía el quinqué de petróleo, pero ¡con qué tufo tan apestoso y
> negro! (I, 903a)
>
> Se oía [...] el crujido de la tela a cada movimiento de la mano. ¡Qué
> lástima que se apagase el quinqué! (I, 903a)

There is also more immediately recognizable use of free indirect
speech:

> Al quedar en tinieblas, el primer movimiento de las dos muchachas
> fue soltar la risa. ¿Acertarían con la cama? (I, 903b)
>
> Concha [...] dio varias vueltas en la cama, lo mismo que si alguna
> inquietud la desvelase. Volvió su hermana a interrogarla.
>
> ¿Qué tenía? (I, 903b)

When the lamp-light that Concha and Dolores are sewing by finally
fails, the narrator's appeals to the visual sensibility of the reader also
stop. Only aural descriptions of the sisters' actions are given until

dawn breaks, as if the narrator is also plunged into darkness when the characters are (I, 903–907a). In all cases, the presentation of discourse, and the narratorial position it supposes, eithers blurs the distinction between the characters and the narrator, or ostensibly erases the narrator's position. A similar intimacy and narratorial empathy is present when Dolores asks her confessor's advice on how to dissuade Concha from becoming a professional actress. Although in the third person, the passage is narrated largely from Dolores's perspective. Only the priest's voice and nose are described in the scene (I, 922 b–924a) because Dolores is unable to perceive anything else through the grille of the confessional: here the narrator once again reduces the distance between herself and the characters she is describing by seemingly reporting on events from a position apparently alongside, or even on behalf of them.

However, such intimate, sympathetic immediacy is selective, as the portrayal of Estrella reveals. The narrator seems to distance herself from him: no judgement is offered on his motivations or character. This ambiguous presentation of Estrella is most evident when the narrator describes his watching Concha perform on stage. The description is introduced by an account of how a rather bored audience begins to notice the movements and expressions of Estrella, who is straining to get a better view of the stage:

> No cabía duda: lo que le llamaba la atención en la escena era la chica encargada del papel principal: Bien, ¿y por qué? ¿Por lo guapa? Estrella había sido un gran conquistador en otro tiempo: puede que aún le durase el humor ... ¿Tan viejo? ¡Quién sabe! Sin embargo, los gestos aprobadores de Estrella desmentían la presunción de un flechazo súbito. Más bien parecía —cosa inverosímil— que le agradaba el modo de representar de la chica. ¡Bah! Imposible.
>
> ¡Gustarle a un actor de tanto mérito una aficionadilla de tres al cuarto! Y con todo [...]El caso es que lo hacía mejor que las otras: A ella se le oía y entendía todo ... Y no decía mal, no, señor. (I, 915b, 916a)

This equivocal view from afar, relying heavily on the free-indirect-style interjections from the audience, suggests that the narrator has no more privileged information than the audience, who can only conjecture about Estrella's interest in Concha. And what information the reader does receive is contradictory and uncertain: although the narrator states that his gestures discount the theory that he might have an amorous interest in Concha, this view is immediately challenged in the transcription of anonymous free indirect discourse from the audience (¡Bah! ¡Imposible! ¡Gustarle a un actor de tanto mérito...). This view in turn is then questioned, perhaps by another member of the audience, further clouding the issue. It is at no subsequent point revealed whether Estrella's interest in Concha is professional and benevolent or not. Furthermore, the apparent empathy with the audience that the use of free indirect discourse seems to indicate is only fleeting. Shortly afterwards, the narrator distances herself from them with naked condescension:

> ... la gente aburrida [...] se dedicó a observar, pacientemente, como se observa en provincias donde la telaraña de la curiosidad teje y desteje cada día las mismas mallas menudas. (I, 915b)

This shifting in the narratorial focus and attitude means that the reader has no access to a consistent anchoring viewpoint. The narratorial voice is not uniformly non-judgemental and impassive (in which case the reader would presumably use other aspects of the text's narrative structure to form her own judgement), but neither is it obviously consistently judgemental or partisan towards one character or course of events in La dama joven. Such narratorial slipperiness is more usually associated with Pardo's novels than with her short stories (Insolación, La quimera and Los pazos de Ulloa are three notable examples). Because of the severe length restrictions inherent in the genre, the narrator of the short stories is necessarily usually an uncomplex figure, as one-dimensional as the characters, either apparently impartial and self-effacing or an openly obtrusive figure. Certainly this is the case in Pardo's short stories of the 1880s.[7]

Overall, the presentation of discourse within the novella is more novelistic than short-story-like. Approximately thirty per cent of La dama joven is presented in the form of dialogue, and just under ten per cent of the text is presented in free indirect speech or thought, both large ratios for a text of around sixteen thousand words. The representation of dialogue is, after all, a relatively lengthy way of representing discourse, characterizing and developing the plot, particularly when, as is the case here, the narrator is an elusive figure who does not often explicitly direct the reader's judgement with obtrusive comment. Three of the characters, Concha, Ramón and Estrella, are presented largely through their speech or transcriptions of their thoughts. Such an approach necessarily demands more length than the understandably common short-story method, where narrative report or summary of thought and speech acts, supplemented by pithy definition or indication of character, is the norm. In *La dama joven*, dialogue is used in two main instances to heighten thematic uncertainty. The first in the characterization of Concha's fiancé, Ramón.[8] There is no judgemental comment from the narrator about Ramón's personality or motivations; he characterizes himself through his own speech-acts, and it is left for the reader to decide whether the statement below is indicative of a touchingly possessive, jealous love for Concha, or of boorish chauvinism:

> —Cuando nos casemos yo no consiento que vuelvas a representar [...] En fin, ve acostumbrándote a la idea ... No me gusta a mí, ni a ningún hombre blanco queriendo a una mujer como te quiero a ti, oír que dicen en las butacas estupideces y barbaridades ... (I, 909b)

Estrella, too, is largely characterized by dialogue, and his utterances, like Ramón's, are not glossed or judged by the narrator. They offer no more clue about his motivations or personality than the first few direct narratorial descriptions. For example, it may be telling that, immediately after he is introduced, Estrella misinterprets a glance from Gormaz during Concha's performance:

> ¿Qué? —pronunció— ¿Qué, hay algo bueno que ver, eh? ¿Una chica guapa? (I, 915a)

Equally, his jumping to a wrong conclusion may not be significant, and it may be that his subsequent protestations to Gormaz that he is no longer a Lothario are sincere: (I, 915a). This protest is mocked in turn by an acquaintance, but in the continued absence of any comment from the narrator, it is impossible to be certain about Estrella's motives.

Now, it is of course necessary for the reader to know whether or not Ramón and Estrella are good, trustworthy characters in order to be able to interpret the closure of *La dama joven* in an unequivocal way. Does the narrator think Concha is right to reject a possibly glamorous but highly precarious career in the theatre, or does she think that Concha has condemned herself to a life of petit-bourgeois stultification with a boorishly possessive husband? The use of un-glossed dialogue to characterize the two figures and the lack of explicit narratorial judgement of their characters makes it impossible for the reader to decide. To make matters even more uncertain, dialogue unglossed by the narrator is also used at the most pivotal parts of the text, when Concha's decision about her future is being mooted. For example, at the very end of the novella, when Concha has just told Gormaz and Estrella of her decision to marry Ramón, the two men speculate on her destiny as they trudge disappointedly down the stairs from the sisters' attic. Gormaz says generously:

> ... A veces en la obscuridad se vive más sosegado ... Acaso ese novio, que parece un buen muchacho, le dará una felicidad que la gloria no le daría ...

Estrella, though, is less disposed to be gracious:

> ¿ Ese? ... Lo que le dará ese bárbaro será un chiquillo por año y si se descuida un pie de paliza. (I,927a,b)

As these are the closing lines of the text, the reader has no way of knowing whether Estrella's comments stem from a sincere belief that Concha will be ill-served by marriage or whether he has been made petulant by jealous pique, just as the reader has no way of knowing whether Concha's decision will turn out to be correct.

If dialogue in *La dama joven* is used to contribute to the ambiguity of the text and ostensibly efface the narrator and her judgement of its characters and situations, is the role of free indirect speech used for a similar purpose? It is principally used to define Dolores's and Concha's characters in an unobtrusive manner, but its use is not wholly straightforward. First, there is a large imbalance between the amount of free indirect speech used to report Dolores's speech and thought-acts, and that used to report Concha's. Examples of the extensive free indirect speech used to explain and fix Dolores's character may be found throughout the text (I, 905a, 906a, 921a,). As I noted above, Dolores is an uncomplicated figure; Concha is not necessarily any more complex. However, the reader is not given the same amount of access to Concha's thoughts as to Dolores's: there are only a couple of passages in which free indirect speech is used to transcribe her thoughts. There is a second complication: these passages reveal that she feels genuine ambivalence about the respective merits of marriage or a career in the theatre. At the beginning of the text, when free indirect speech is first partly used to characterise Concha, to whom the reader has only just been introduced, Concha is unworried about any possible conflict between marriage and acting:

> ¡Casarse! ¡Bah! Claro que se casaría; pero ¿qué prisa corría eso? (I, 906b)

She is seduced by the glamour of the stage:

> ¡Artista! Ser «artista» era pertenecer a una clase aristocrática, superior a la humilde condición de costurera ... (I, 906b)

But also recognizes it as a daunting and arduous occupation:

> ¿Como saldría ella de aquel apuro? ¿Se cortaría? ¿Se le olvidarían los versos? ... tratábase de una comedia en tres actos [...] En fin un compromiso gravísimo. (I, 906b, 907a)
>
> ... ¡Qué de mañas, ardides y cálculos representaba la conquista de [los] trajes! [...] ¡Imposible que alcanzase el tiempo para todo!
>
> [...] ¡Cuánto iban a apretar las uñas al día siguiente! (1, 907a)

Another brief passage shortly afterwards demonstrates that Concha is entirely consumed by her approaching performance, and the narrator seems gently to mock her ingenuousness:

> ¡Bastante pensaba Concha en Ramón! Todo el día en el taller, estuvo repasando su papel mentalmente. ¡Don Manuel Gormaz le había encargado tanto que «se fijase» y que «tuviese alma» en algunas escenas! Tener alma ... ¿ sería gritar mucho? (1, 908b)

However, later on in the text, after Concha has had an argument with Ramón, she is more cautious and serious about her future:

> Ella podría ser actriz ... es decir, dominar aquel arte, apenas entrevisto [...] Un destino ancho, grande, hermoso ... (I, 922a)

Almost immediately afterwards, in prefacing comments to a free indirect transcription of Concha's thoughts, the narrator notes the fear that a career on the stage inspires in Concha:

> Aquel destino desconocido le infundía, a la verdad, algún pavor. Hasta el día de hoy, gracias a Dios, aunque pobres, nunca les había faltado el pan. Ella había oído decir que los cómicos a veces pasan hambre, que

tienen días de apuro terrible. [...] Una noche, recordaba haber
encontrado a las cómicas y cómicos que salían del ensayo. Ellas iban
hechas unas brujas [...] y todos mezclados, hombres y mujeres ... ¿Si
tendría razón Dolores ? (I, 922a)

So the passages that transcribe Concha's thoughts in free indirect
style are inconclusive, and this uncertainty only makes the closure
of the text more ambiguous. Now, there are hints that Concha's
apparent inability to decide about her future is not so much due to
ambivalence alone but is instead evidence of a general passivity and
complaisance. Several passing references are made by the narrator
that might indicate that Concha is rather suggestible and easily
persuaded. For instance, despite Dolores's orders to the contrary,
Concha allows Ramón to escort her home after he makes an angry
criticism of her firm attempts to dissuade him:

Díjolo con tal rabia, que Concha, cediendo a un movimiento
compasivo, le llamó.
—Bueno, ven ... (I,909a)

A similar deference to others' wishes is visible when Concha at first
refuses her fiancé a kiss, but then relents when she sees his
crestfallen reaction (I,910b). The narrator does also state that
Concha is partly motivated by curiosity at this point, but even so she
seems to be driven primarily by a desire not to upset Ramón. The
most obvious example of Concha's passivity occurs when, surrounded
by Estrella, Gormaz, Ramón and Dolores, she is asked whether she is
going to opt for marriage, or a career on the stage. Concha replies:
'Qué sé yo... Lo que quiera mi hermana' (I, 926b). Then, urged by
both Dolores and Gormaz to state her own preference, she opts for
marriage, the decision that Dolores wanted anyway. But although
hinted at briefly by the narrator, the extent of Concha's self-
sacrificing complaisance and accompanying passivity is not examined
in any detail. Certainly it is not made clear whether this aspect of
Concha's personality is wholly, or even partly, responsible for her
choosing a future with which she will not be happy.

If the narratorial perspective and presentation of discourse both
make La dama joven's closure apparently insolubly ambiguous, do
other aspects of the text provide a clue to the narrator's views or as

to how the reader should interpret the closure? Charnon-Deutsch refers to a 'subtle coding' within the text, although she sees this coding as being present only within the characterization and as reinforcing what she sees as the deterministic thesis of the text. She cites only one example of this coding: the characterization of Dolores's confessor by portrayal only of his nose. Charnon-Deutsch thinks that this portrayal indicates the 'sinister nature of his function and the probity of his advice', and sees the priest as a synecdoche for the Church, which she describes as a 'cunning and experienced force at work to shape Concha's future':

> He is always described as an extension of his black confessional, a 'jesuita sagaz' whose pious words cloak the plan that may or may not be leading to Concha's happiness ... he is anxious to play a role in Concha's future. It is only the tip of the nose that Dolores sees through the grate; he is perceived as a non-person, whose feelings and thoughts are translated through his nose.[9]

But Charnon-Deutsch's portrayal of the priest as a menacing figure, whose dark ambitions and machinations include manipulating Concha's future, is inaccurate. There is nothing in the text to suggest that he is sinister or malevolent. Description of him is confined to his nose because that is the only part of him that Dolores can see through the grille. Charnon-Deutsch quotes the priest's being a 'jesuita sagaz' as if this were somehow further evidence of his being Machiavellian; it is, rather, surely a simple indication of his experience and intelligence, and there is nothing to indicate that the description is ironic. Moreover, there are several instances in the passage which directly belie Charnon-Deutsch's attempts to depict the confessor as an inhuman, untrustworthy and meddling figure:

> El confesor ... [tenía] ... una punta de nariz afilada y ascética, y el cóncavo de una oreja inteligente, *abierta para escuchar y entenderlo todo.*
>
> La punta de la nariz [...] se contrajo con severidad. Pero dilatóse al punto, *como si la llenase el aura de una idea bienhechora.*
>
> Dolores miraba atónita aquella nariz, severa por costumbre, y la desconocía viéndola tan *tolerante, tan benignamente entreabierta. Sin embargo, no dudó: no había recibido allí jamás consejo alguno que no le probase bien seguir.* (I, 923a, b and 924a; my italics)

Furthermore, the Church itself is portrayed as a benevolent force, as its charity rescued Dolores and Concha from the lethally squalid poverty in which the two were previously living (I, 904a,b) The narrator further notes that when Dolores goes to the church to see her confessor:

> ... experimentó algún alivio y su cólera amainó instantáneamente. No hay cosa más calmante que el reposado y aromático ambiente de los templos. El agua bendita [...] le sosegó las hirvientes ideas. (I, 922b)

Charnon-Deutsch's deterministic thesis relies on the portrayal of the Church as a malign influence, preventing Concha and Dolores from bettering their lot. Given that the evidence she provides is flawed, I think Charnon-Deutsch's naturalistic interpretation should be treated with caution.

Is there any other coding in *La dama joven*? Possibly that most hackneyed of tropes, the interplay of light and darkness. But even this aspect of the text is inconclusive. At first, darkness in *La dama joven* seems to symbolize the poor, shabby conditions in which the two sisters live: in the opening lines they have not even enough oil to keep the lamp they are sewing by lit in their 'cuartito abuhardillado', with its broken furniture and clutter of clothes and materials (I, 907b). When Concha is inveigled into the public gardens by Ramón, the narrator describes the lights of the *casino* shining out against the cold park where:

> ... la oscuridad era mayor, y completa la soledad y el silencio, a menos que una ráfaga de vientecillo marino sacudiese los siempre verdes evónimos, haciéndoles murmurar cosas tristes. (I, 910a)

The *casino,* where the performance is staged, is thus initially portrayed as an attractive shining beacon of glamour (I, 910b). But as the novella progresses, the respective roles of light and darkness seem to be reversed. When Concha actually reaches the *casino* it seems quite different:

> El recinto del teatro se hallaba todavía a oscuras, y el conserje barría con afán las puntas de los cigarros y los fragmentos de papel. En el escenario ardía un quinqué puesto sobre una consola, y dos o tres candilejas ... (I, 911a)

Clearly quite a prosaic antithesis to its resplendent façade. Perhaps this is meant unsubtly to signify that the theatre, although superficially attractive, is not really very glamorous. And at the end of the tale, it is the theatre, represented by Gormaz and Estrella, that is in darkness: the two struggle painfully up the unlit stairs to the sisters' attic, which, unlike the gloomy dilapidated room of the beginning of the novella, is now described by the narrator as a:

> ... palacio modistil.
>
> El quinqué, bien despabilado, ardía con clara luz sobre la mesilla de la máquina: la habitación, arregladita, con sus dos camas limpias, revelaba cierto bienestar humilde; y en el sofá, libre a la sazón de todo estorbo de trajes, una pareja se hablaba muy de cerca ... (I, 926a)

The gentle condescension of the narrator's referring to it as a 'palacio modistil' does not detract from the cosy, clean, inviting nature of the room, and it may be—lightheartedly—significant that the light comes from a lamp placed on the plate of the sewing machine, the source of Dolores's and Concha's livelihood, against which a career in the theatre is trying to compete.

The significance of light and darkness in *La dama joven* is hard to gauge. There *is* a conspicuous contrast between the opening and closing passages of the text, and both light and darkness *are* prominent in the text, if only because of the number of times the reader's attention is called to them (I, 903a, b, 904a, 906a, 908b, 909a, 910a, b, 911a, b, 912a, 919b, 922b, 924a, 925b, 926a, b). Their metaphorical use would seem to indicate that Concha was right to value marriage and domestic stability over a glamorous but unreliable career. On the face of it, such an interpretation would seem to be supported by a single, casual, but directly obtrusive remark that the narrator makes towards the beginning of the text. In a long passage summarizing Dolores's past, and accounting for her zealous protectiveness towards Concha, written partly in free indirect style, the narrator describes how:

> Concha era fácil a guardar: no quería salir sola: a los bailes, a los temibles bailes, prefería el teatro, su única afición [...]Semejante gusto no parecía peligroso: mas el diablo la enreda, y he aquí cómo vino a resultar alarmante. (I, 905b)

At first glance, the narrator seems explicitly to be vindicating Dolores's fears about the acting profession and signalling that Concha's interest in it is misguided and unwise. Presumably, Concha is right finally to reject it in favour of marriage. But the adjective 'temible' and the verb 'guardar' in the first sentence are terms that Dolores herself would have used. Part of the diction, although not the syntax, of this first sentence then belongs to the format of free indirect speech or thought: the narrator's own views seem to be merged once again with Dolores's. Is this quasi-indirect style also present in the following sentence? Given the extensive blurring of the narratorial voice with characters' speech and thought-acts throughout the text, it is certainly possible. But given that the narrator later distances herself from the naive provincialism of the inhabitants of Marineda, it is not unlikely that the narrator is gently mocking Dolores's protectiveness: an innocent infatuation with the theatre seems unlikely to attract diabolical interest. And even if the second sentence were a direct, unironic statement of the narrator's own views, could this single comment (the *only* such explicit comment), together with a supposed metaphorical patterning, really constitute the entire thesis of *La dama joven*? If the text were tendentious and didactic as the narrator's comment apparently implies, its thesis would surely be more forcefully and more obviously stated.

In conclusion, it is simply not possible to be unequivocal about the closure of *La dama joven*. David Henn says that judgement about the ending of the text is left to the reader. I disagree: because of the imbalance in the portrayal of the respective feelings of the sisters, and the shifting narratorial perspectives, the reader simply does not have enough information even to reach a judgement. It is the generic hybridity that generates the thematic ambiguity: the combination of novelistic presentation of discourse with conventionally short-story-like concise and limited characterization in *La dama joven* means that characters' motivations and private feelings cannot be gauged easily, in this case making the text's thesis unclear. Furthermore, the shifting perspectives and selective elusiveness of the narrator, again properties found more commonly in Pardo's novels (which have greater scope to accommodate complexities of narratorial perspective), when combined with the conventionally short-story-like limited diegetic structure, also cloud the thesis of the text. *La dama joven* then resists thematic containment because it cannot be generically contained by binary divisions between short story and novel. This is also true of Pardo's early *novelas breves* as a whole, which deserve greater critical attention.

6

Galicia in English Books on Spain in the Lifetime of Emilia Pardo Bazán

Richard Hitchcock

The step towards establishing a corpus of material in the above category entailed trawling through upwards of seventy works which, by their titles or other indicators, suggested that they might contain relevant information. However, barely a quarter mentioned Galicia and, of those that did, the treatment was sometimes rather scanty. This fact in itself is not a surprising one, as the pattern of travel in the Peninsula during the second half of the nineteenth century shows that the north-west corner was very much off the beaten track. The attraction for many who did venture away from the well-trodden paths that led down to the magnetic south, would have been the Cathedral of Santiago de Compostela. This shrine was not, however, on the railway line which went from Lugo through to La Coruña, the access to Santiago being via diligence. There was a small branch-line which ran from Carril on the west coast to Santiago, but it was mainly used for access for those travelling from the north of Portugal. In practice, there are few instances of travellers in the time-span concerned entering Galicia by this route.

The travel guides give an uneven picture. The inveterate travellers to Europe who turned to Murray's Guides would have found the varying editions of Richard Ford's *Hand-book for Travellers in Spain*, originally published in 1846, attentive to the changes in the Peninsula.[1] The fourth edition, published in 1869, was the first one to have been written by someone other than Ford, who had died in 1858. Murray's new editor for the fourth edition was Dr Henry Ecroyd, not a specialist on Spain, but some of the text was written by the Irishman, John Ormsby, celebrated translator of the *Poem of the Cid* and of *Don*

Quixote, and somebody who, additionally, knew the Peninsula well through various visits there.[2] The old Etonian lawyer, Charles Packe, and fellow-member of the British Alpine Club with Ormsby, was also paid for his contribution, but minimally, as his expertise lay in climbing, mountain flora and the Pyrenees, the subject of several of his books.[3] Another contributor was the Trinity College, Dublin-educated barrister Ulick Ralph Burke, distinguished as the author of one of the most respected histories of Spain, published in the year of his death through sudden illness shortly after leaving England en route for an official appointment in Peru. He had been visiting Spain regularly since taking a brief holiday there in 1871.[4] It was this team that set the tone for subsequent editions of the *Hand-book*, the last of which, the ninth, was published in 1898. Ford's discursive intro- duction to Galicia, ranging over the history of the kingdom, the character of the Galicians and the language, is largely dispensed with in the 1869 edition, although in an interesting footnote the editor states that among the works 'about to be published (September, 1868)' is the book entitled '*Cantares Gallegos* by Doña Rosalía Castro de Murguía, Lugo' (vol. I, p. 184 n.). This work is acknow- ledged, in the eighth edition of 1892, to have been published in 1868.[5] Richard Ford's denunciation of the Galician character, based rather on Classical sources than on personal observation, is prudently excised from the later editions, although snippets of his orotund prose survive. There appears to be no consistent pattern in later editorial pruning. For example, whereas Ford wrote of the Galician men that they were 'boorish and rude, seldom giving a direct answer; seen in their wretched huts, they are scarcely better than their ancestors', the identical entries in the fourth and eighth editions read; 'The men, however, are fine fellows, although, when seen in ther wretched huts, they seem scarcely more intelligent than their Iberian ancestors'.[6] Neither the earlier free-ranging commentary of Ford, nor the by and large emasculated versions of subsequent editors, seem to have incited travellers to swarm towards Galicia in any appreciable numbers before the turn of the twentieth century. *The Hand-book*, however, in whatever its edition, is more thorough in its coverage of Galicia than, for instance, Baedeker's *Spain and Portugal*, which nonetheless paints a strikingly divergent picture of the Galicians: 'Almost devoid of all independent spirit, they ... are docile and good- natured, temperate and frugal, ready for any task, full of piety and

under the thumb of the priesthood.'[7] Baedeker's guide, supplemented by an extensive and informative 'Historical Sketch of Spanish
Art', by Professor Carl Justi of Bonn (pp. xxxix–lxxxvi), provides quite
a thorough treatment, for the culturally and historically minded
tourist, of the cities of Galicia.[8]

O'Shea's readable guide, first published in 1865 and kept up-to-
date by informed authorities such as John Lomas, pulls no punches
about the Galicians, but is less scornful than Murray's *Handbook*. It
is also more informed, particularly concerning emigration: 'love of
home, *la tierra*, sickens the emigrant Gallego a year or two after he
has quitted it'.[9] Perhaps because O'Shea, although of Irish origin, was
born in Madrid and was a member of the Spanish diplomatic corps
before moving to Biarritz and adopting French nationality, the
discussion of Galicians is seen from a centralist perspective: 'They are
very honest, and may be depended upon ... Their customs are plain,
patriarchal; they are given entirely to rearing fine cattle and cultivating their too much divided properties.' In the 1892 edition, the
reader is given the following recommendation: 'For a description of
student life at Santiago read "Pascual Lopez", by Pardo Bazan',
Pascual Lopez being the author's first novel, published in 1879.[10]

Bradshaw's *Illustrated Hand-book to Spain and Portugal* was
expressly designed to fulfil the need for 'a convenient guide book'.
Accordingly, this one contains, amongst other things, 'the best
routes, a glossary, and a vocabulary in English and Spanish'.[11] The
first edition was brought out in 1865; it was edited by Charnock in
1870. The treatment of cities in Galicia is brief, but not dismissive,
concentrating as one might expect, on access to the places by the
most convenient routes. In the descriptions, evaluative judgements
are absent, with an emphasis on factual and historical data.[12] It is
noteworthy that Orense has a more extensive coverage than Santiago,
La Coruña or Lugo together.[13] The comments on literature, however,
are idiosyncratic, mentioning Zorrilla, Tassara and Bretón de los
Herreros but not Pardo Bazán or Galdós.[14]

When the *Handbook for Spain* was added to Thomas Cook's series
in 1912, it was perhaps natural that the writing of it should have
been entrusted to Albert Calvert. He was already the author of over
thirty books on Spain, including seventeen volumes of the nineteen
in the Spanish series, and was regarded as 'one of the best known
authorities on Spain and its people'.[15] Calvert (1872–1946) was

noted as a traveller, mining consultant and writer on Australia, before turning to Spain in the late 1890s.[16] His first work on the Iberian Peninsula, *Impressions of Spain,* was published in 1903 and is described self-effacingly as 'the first fruits of fugitive note-book jottings collected over a period of several years'.[17] The section on Galicia is very brief compared with the coverage of other areas of Spain. Calvert may have visited the region but it is significant that *Galicia. The Land and the People, a Historical and Descriptive Account,* announced as being in preparation in 1921, never in fact materialized. In his *Impressions,* Calvert gives relatively short shrift to Galicia, 'where the scenery is exquisite, the hotels are famously bad, and devotion is the chief recreation of the community'.[18] He adds that 'muleteers and commercial travellers constitute the principal vistors to Galicia—for those who have a soul above scenery, and an ambition above fishing, the country is practically without attraction'. He is more sympathetic in his discussion of the cities, but Santiago is accorded only a paragraph, as are Orense and Lugo.[19]

If one compares Calvert's later comments in Cook's *Handbook for Spain,* it is apparent that his views have mellowed. Far from having 'the hand of death on its crooked, branching streets, and its crazy, deformed squares, which echo the pilgrims' footfalls to the deaf ears of the dead', Santiago 'the goal of fanatics from every corner of Europe', is now described, more neutrally, as a 'favourite resort of pilgrims to the shrine of St. James ... picturesquely situated on a plateau surrounded by mountains'.[20] The single page devoted to the Cathedral itself suggests that Calvert had not been there, as the brief comments are derivative and drawn from secondary sources, including Street's memorable observation that 'the plan is a curiously exact repetition of the church of St. Sernin at Toulouse'.[21]

The reference to Street serves as an introduction to the scholarly area of architectural studies and, in this particular example, demonstrates the interaction between scholarly and popular, albeit seriously popular, literature. George Street (1824–1881) has been described as one of the 'greatest Gothic architects in Europe', and received major commissions throughout Europe, including the New Law Courts in London, many churches, schools and official buildings. He had visited north Italy and north Germany in the 1850s, and he made three tours of Spain in successive years from 1861. He drew the buildings himself, and the illustrations in his book are from his own designs.

He acknowledges an initial debt to Richard Ford's *Hand-book of Spain*, because 'it had the rare excellence (in a Guide-book) of constantly referring to local guides and authorities, and so enabling me to turn at once to the books most likely to aid me in my work'.[22]

When he is not describing the intricate details of an ecclesiastical building, Street is an observant and unsensational reporter of what he encounters. He was struck by the poverty of what he saw, being moved to observe that 'the poorish Irish would have some difficulty in showing that their misery is greater than that of these poor Gallegans'.[23] He was also surprised by the lack of pilgrims : 'There is none of the evidence of the presence of pilgrims which might be expected, and I suspect a genuine pilgrim is a very rare article indeed. I never saw more than one...'[24] A knowledgeable writer, Street is as good as his word, for he quotes not only from Spanish historical and documentary sources, but also from Ford's *Hand-book*. From henceforward, those wishing for an authoritative account of the principal Gothic buildings in Galicia, and in other parts of Spain, now had a reliable work of reference to consult.

A less well-known, but nonetheless worthy successor to Street was A. N. Prentice (1866–1944), who published his study of the Plateresque in 1893.[25] Prentice, a Scot who was articled to a Glasgow architect before embarking on European travel, particularly in Spain, was noted as a designer of country-houses and the interiors of steamships. His book comprises primarily his own drawings 'in all cases laid down on the spot, those in pencil being completed at the buildings themselves'. His Plateresque tour starts at Santiago, with a brief commentary to complement the excellent architectural drawings, and moves through León to the interior of the Peninsula.[26]

A Guide Book to Books, published in 1891, designed 'to give sound advice as to the books which are of value in each department of knowledge', provides an indication of those works considered to be recommended reading in the realm of Hispanic studies.[27] Amongst these there figures H. J. Rose's *Untrodden Spain*, a much respected work, according to the references made to it.[28] The Reverend Rose (1841–1878), MA, of Oriel College, was Chaplain to the mining companies at Linares from 1873 to 1874, and at Jerez and Cádiz between 1874 and 1876. He was a correspondent of *The Times* and a writer of articles on social subjects in Spain. *Untrodden Spain* is full of points of interest, which mainly reflect life in the South of the

Peninsula. There is an interlude in Galicia, describing 'a week's shooting in the mountains', with the village of Brañuelas being used as the base. This is a cameo of a fairly modest hunting expedition.[29] A book entirely devoted to the sport is the first of two jointly written by Abel Chapman and Walter J. Buck.[30] Abel Chapman (1851–1929) MA, JP, was a company director in Northumberland and big-game hunter who composed and published his own *Reminiscences of a Hunter-Naturalist* under the title of *Retrospect* in 1928. Walter Buck was Vice-Consul at Jerez and the works for which he was responsible jointly with Chapman achieved considerable renown amongst naturalists. They are interesting for their detailed accounts of out-of-the-way places in the remote Spanish sierras. The scant mention of Galicia is confined to generally sympathetic comments on the Galicians as a race.[31]

The first of the travel books *per se* in the period after the 1860s that contains a Galician itinerary, is Jane Leck's *Iberian Sketches*.[32] Little is known of the author, apart from a book of poems, published in 1894, also in Glasgow, and at her own expense. Her journey was undertaken in the spring of 1883 with a twofold objective: 'to fix in the writer's own memory the varied beauties of nature and art which it was then her privilege to survey, and to awaken or strengthen in others a desire to visit that too little known part of Spain comprised in the provinces of Leon and Galicia.' In effect, only one and a half of the thirteen chapters deal with Galicia; more concern Portugal, but more still, despite the title of the book, relate to Madrid (the Museo Real), and to Castilla. She travelled on the 25-mile rail journey from Carril to Santiago, and she provides a pleasing but unexceptional description of the cathedral and her minimal social commentary is confined to some deprecatory phrases about the beggars in Santiago.[33] A feature of the work are the references to birds and flowers, for which the author acknowledges the assistance of Robert Gray, also responsible for the atmospheric sketches. This may be a slight book, and it may hardly be said to fulfil the promise implicit in the title, but it is nonetheless a pleasant and undemanding account of her experiences, supplemented by the home reading of major historical writers, such as W. H. Prescott.

John Lomas (1846–1927), who edited a later edition of O'Shea's *Guide*, was educated in Manchester Grammar School, and was a prominent Anglican churchman, being the editor of the *Anglican*

Church Magazine between 1886 and 1912. He presided over a number of charitable and educational organizations, and had his permanent address in Switzerland, where he owned estates. He was noted as a writer on Spain, and his *Sketches* were first published in 1884.[34] He was a careful and well-prepared traveller, whose route embraced much of the Peninsula, excluding Extremadura. In Galicia his ports of call were the main cities, and he admitted to Santiago being 'terribly disappointing at a first visit ... the place is oddly like a north of England manufacturing town, stone-built and gray, busy and yet dull'. With a knowledge of the city, however, came an appreciation of its 'infinite variety of picturesqueness', and Lomas declared that 'the glory of Santiago is her cathedral', ranking 'among the noblest legacies of the Golden Age of Church architecture'.[35] Despite his own reserve on religious grounds, Lomas is nevertheless fulsome in his praise of the architectural merits of the building. As the visit to Santiago is the concluding chapter of a long book, one gets the impression that Galicia has been tagged on to the description of the rest of Spain, a *de rigueur* inclusion for anyone aiming, as Lomas was, for a thorough coverage.

Hans Friedrich Gadow's *In Northern Spain*, the fruit of two pro-longed journeys, one of them undertaken in 1892, the other in 1895 together with other ventures into the Peninsula, is a scholarly work.[36] Gadow was born in Pomerania in 1855 and, after studying at Berlin and Heidelberg, went to live in England, where he studied in the Natural History Department of the British Museum between 1880 and 1882. He was a distinguished naturalist who became Strickland Curator in Cambridge in 1884. In 1902 and 1904, he spent eight months in Mexico which led to the production of his second major work.[37] The critical apparatus of *In Northern Spain* is impressive: 'A condensed account of the history of the Northern Provinces, (pp. 302–345); notes on the fauna of northern Spain, some of which had been published previously in article form (pp. 346–382), and on the flora (pp. 383–397, with a detailed glossary), and appendices incor-porating etymological notes and a full bibliography. This latter includes an article by Unamuno.[38] When in Santiago, Dr Gadow met the eminent Galician historian, Antonio López Ferreiro, who con-ducted him and his wife into the Reliquary. However, his description of the cathedral is only just more extensive than his account of the journey by mail-coach that transported him from La Coruña to

Santiago.[39] Where he does mention Galicians, he is not complimentary about them: 'There is no race who will stand a rebuke so well, and who can be cowed so completely, as the Gallegos.' He is less inclined to describe them as *melancólicos*, as they were described to him by a Gallego, as *poco simpáticos*.[40] The snippets of information about Galicia, nonetheless, provided over the course of four hundred or so pages are interesting; the river Tambre is identified with the river Tamar in Devonshire (p. 407); *berzo* in Galician is equated with English *berth* (p. 411); speaking of oak-trees, the '*quercus occidentalis*, which gives an inferior sort of cork, is rather common in Eastern Galicia', whereas the *quercus ilex,* the evergreen oak, is not to be found in Galicia (p. 389);[41] the University collection (of fauna) at Santiago 'is extremely well kept, and, what is rarer still, the specimens are correctly named. Unfortunately the authorities... prefer to spend a great deal of the little money available on sensational specimens, as for instance a tiger' (p. 346); the badger, otter and hedgehog are common in Galicia, and although a stuffed marmot is to be found in the Museum at Santiago, the author never saw or heard of one in the wild (pp. 364–65, and 368). Gadow also contributed a lengthy study of dolmen, concentrating on the dolmen of Álava, and supplying a map of dolmen in Spain and Portugal (p. 299). The only entry for Galicia is at Betanzos, where there are several dolmen, and 'probably more in various parts of Western and Northern Galicia'.

Gadow evidently approached the Peninsula with an anthropologist's and naturalist's eye, and his narrative is a leisurely and discursive one, in which he shows a readiness for an anecdotal interpolation. However, the region of Galicia was not *per se* his primary interest, and it does not form a predominant part of the book.

Katharine Lee Bates (1859–1929) was an American tourist, who published her account of her travels in 1900.[42] These achieved some popularity among the reading public, and were republished half a dozen times up to 1920. She was a copious writer, with around one hundred and thirty titles to her credit, although not on Spanish themes. In the company of a young compatriot, she started her journey into the Peninsula from Biarritz in February 1899. She is an enthusiastic recorder of traditional Spanish attractions, and shows a particular partiality to popular songs, fragments of which she reproduces liberally in quaint English versions. Following the pattern set by her predecessors, the chapters on Galicia, here the final four out of twenty-seven, come at the end of the book. The author revels in the adventures of her journey to Santiago, which are amusingly recounted. After Gadow, it is refreshing to come across someone who does not seem to take herself too seriously, for she subtitles her twenty-fifth chapter ('The Building of a Shrine'), 'a historical chapter, which should be skipped'.[43] The familiar story is, nevertheless, told in a sprightly manner. The arrival of Katharine Bates into Santiago coincided with the twenty-fifth of July. Her intensely evocative descriptions bring alive the celebrations of the Santiago festivities; on the previous day, she conveys the feeling that she and her companion experienced, that of being 'precipitated out of the Middle Ages into an exaggerated Fourth of July' (p. 431). She qualifies Spain as mediaeval, and Galicia as being characterized by 'debasing ignorance and superstition', yet she still appreciates 'wild Galician lore that lives on the lips of the people', and sees in Spain 'that mediaeval grace for which happier countries may be searched in vain' (p. 442). This lively account is more substantial than many contemporary ones. The graphic descriptions, the knowledge of Spanish culture on display, the literary allusions, the frequent songs, and the easy combination of the anecdotal and the learned, ensured the continuing appeal of this book during the first two decades of the twentieth century.

The earliest, in chronological order, of those works which deal, to a greater or lesser extent, with Galicia after the turn of the century, is Edgar Wigram's *Northern Spain*.[44] Sir Edgar Thomas Ainger Wigram (1864–1935), 6th Bart., MA, ARIBA, educated at King's School, Canterbury, and Trinity Hall, Cambridge, was Mayor of St Albans, 1926–1927. The notes and sketches that constitute his book on Spain, are 'the fruit of four successive bicycle tours', some of them in the company of W[illiam] A. W[igram], in collaboration with whom he later wrote a travel book of the East, entitled *The Cradle of Mankind*, first published in 1914. The finely executed, picturesque watercolours of town and country scenes that illustrate the volume are a distinguishing feature, and have ensured that this work has not been lost from the public eye. His route took him along the pilgrim's way from León, via Lugo to Santiago. As seems to have been the case with a number of the travellers, the expectation of arriving at

Santiago provided more excitement than the city itself. Wigram found the interior of the cathedral disappointing, but he admired the exterior, calling the west front Churriguera's masterpiece.[45] Vigo is given lengthier coverage than Santiago, but the descriptions of Wigram's sojourn in Galicia are not penetrative, neither are they intended to be. The charm of the volume as a whole lies in the richness of the plates, for which the text provides an appropriately undemanding commentary.

A brief mention may be made here of a similar work devoted to the cathedral cities of Spain by W. W. Collins.[46] William Wiehe Collins (1862–1951), author of two other *Cathedral Cities* volumes, *England* (1907), and *Italy* (1911), was a successful aquarellist and landscape painter. A Westcountryman, he lived in Bridgwater and had a very large number of paintings exhibited over the years, including no fewer than 158 at the Royal Institute of Painters and Watercolourists. His paintings are every bit as colourful as those of Wigram, and his command of light and colour is exquisite. His commentary is more extensive, however, and one receives the sensation that Collins was keen to absorb the context of the place, before recording it for posterity in his sketchbook. Like Wigram, Collins is struck by the perceived mediaeval quality of Santiago, notably an ox-cart, and his description suggests the setting for a Gothic novel.[47] His observations on the cathedral itself are bolstered by appropriate historical references, but throughout the book, one gets the impression that Collins is creating illusions which become reality in his illustrations. His brief commentary on the Gallegan character treads a familiar path. The Galician is 'an ardent advocate of small holdings', 'knows the value of a peseta', 'is looked down upon by the Castilian', and is 'driven to emigration by the subdivision of land which cannot support more than those who own and work it now' (p. 181). Collins also visited Tuy and Orense.

A book familiar to students of Galicia is Annette Meakin's *Galicia*, published in 1909.[48] The author has fifteen entries in the British Library Catalogue for the years between 1901 and 1932, including translations from the French and German, and several travel books on Russia. Prior to her study on Galicia, she had brought out her account of the trans-Siberian railway: *A Ribbon of Iron*, in 1901. *Galicia* starts out with the not unreasonable premise that 'Galicia is the least known and the least written about of all the little kingdoms that go to the making of Spain'. Annette Meakin embarks on the task of making good this lapse in an overarching treatment of all aspects Galician: history, geography, language, architecture, society, literature, religion, flora and fauna. She appends a three-page bibliography, revealing that she had clearly read widely into the background of her subject. She had no problem in finding material for her twenty-seven chapters, and notes that she was 'obliged, from lack of space, to omit two chapters describing the monasteries of *San Martin Pinario, San Lorenzo, San Francisco,* and *Santo Domingo*—four remarkable relics of the Middle Ages which no visitor to Santiago should fail to see'.[49] In the chapter treating 'The Great Monasteries of Galicia' (XXV), Annette Meakin shows herself well versed in their historical background, and she even goes to the trouble of making excursions to the tiny *Eremita de San Miguel* at Celanova, and to Santa Comba de Bande, a two hours' drive further on. She debates the antiquity of both, quoting the appropriate authorities (pp. 328–33). Rosalía de Castro merits a chapter to herself (XV, pp. 182–9), which includes the author's own translation of 'Un-ha vez tiven un cravo', and a favourable critique of her work; 'So far no other Gallegan poet of the nineteenth or twentieth centuries has approached Rosalía in individuality' (p. 189). Translating a passage from the Marqués de Figueroa's 'De la poesía gallega' (1889), Annette Meakin reproduces Emilia Pardo Bazán's judgement on Rosalía de Castro: 'If her tears are softened by smiles, her smiles in their turn are tempered by tears, and the one and the other are mingled to the sound of the *gaita*' (p. 188). It is perhaps surprising that Doña Emilia's works are not accorded a critical survey to themselves, but a special accolade is reserved for her. James Fitzmaurice-Kelly's comment that she was 'the best authoress that Spain has produced during the present century' is duly acknowledged, and Annette Meakin adds that 'Doña Emilia Pardo Bazán is Galicia's daughter. So much for the stupidity of the Gallegans'.[50] Overall, this book gives the impression of being accessibly encyclopaedic, more complete if less specialized than Gadow's. Annette Meakin is at home with the history of Galicia , but her prolonged studies have led her to an affection that is expressed in a concluding paean of praise, in archaic language, addressed to Galicia herself. Amongst the valedictory comments are the following phrases : 'not only art thou practically unknown to the rest of the world, but thou art forgotten even by Spain: thy own Peninsula is almost unconscious of thy existence'.[51] Annette Meakin's work does remedy this situation for the English-speaking readership.

The concise but informative comments that E. Boyle O'Reilly in *Heroic Spain* makes about Doña Emilia have not gone unnoticed, but they do, nonetheless, represent a growing awareness of her, and indeed of other Spanish writers, in America.[52] Elizabeth Boyle O'Reilly was born in 1874, possibly one of the four daughters of the novelist, John Boyle O'Reilly, who had settled in Boston in 1872. She was also the author of a book of poems, and of *How France Built her Cathedrals*, which was published in New York in 1921. She spent eight months in Spain in 1908, and prior to leaving had visited the Bodleian Library in order to read 'certain accounts of St. Teresa' (p. 10). As a preparation for the traveller, she recommends Baedeker as a guide book, 'as good as any'. She concedes that Murray's *Handbook* 'is more entertaining, but is rather to be kept as amusing literature ..., much of it being the personal opinions and prejudices of Richard Ford, and bristling all over with slurs at Spain's religion' (p. 8), thus providing a fair indication as to where she stands in these matters. Her journey took her through the north of Spain to Galicia, via Lugo and La Coruña to Santiago. which she found 'very solemn, very gray, very stately and aloof'. She was by no means entranced by the baroque West Front, but considered the *Pórtico de la Gloria* to be matchless.[53] Taking a break from her itinerary, the author devotes a chapter to 'A Few Modern Novels' (pp. 326–50), wherein are incorporated her observations on the Condesa 'who has been called the most notable woman of letters in Europe', and 'the boast of every Gallego'. Two novels are mentioned, *Los pazos de Ulloa* and *La madre naturaleza*, of which it is jointly said that 'work such as this is exquisite and sure to last'. Although E. Boyle O'Reilly says that 'Madam Pardo Bazán edits one of the best reviews in Madrid', she concludes by remarking that 'it is in the novels of her beloved *paisanos* she will live'.[54]

Walter Wood (1866–c.1935), a writer credited with over forty volumes on subjects as diverse as battles, fishermen and Germany, contributed a modest work entirely devoted to Galicia, published in 1910, the only one of his works to have been concerned with the Peninsula.[55] It has achieved some prominence on account of the expertly accomplished illustrations by Frank H. Mason, and for the introductory essay by Martin Hume (pp. 3–21). Not one to let an opportunity pass by, Major Hume (1847–1910), lecturer in Spanish

History in Pembroke College, Cambridge, author of many well-known books on Spanish topics, and a respected authority on Spanish affairs, advertises the new London branch of the Association of Galicia, of which he is the Chairman, 'for the purpose of rendering the province agreeable to English visitors' (pp. 20–1). Hume's essay is instructive as representing the revised view of Galicians. The dismissive tone of some of the guidebooks is replaced by a more realistic appraisal of Gallegos as 'brother Celts indented by the sea' with a 'Celtic instinct and need to wander in search of work in order to render less hard the lot of the weaker ones left behind', and 'hard, frugal, and honest, yearning like a true Celt for his own home and his own kin again (pp. 6–7). Hume comments on the 'present poverty and backwardness' but also outlines steps being taken to check 'the terrible exodus of the able-bodied male population', such as 'investment of capital in native enterprises and factories', and looks forward to a time when 'Galicia should be one of the most prosperous regions in Europe'(pp. 15–16). He also finds space to praise 'the greatest of living Spanish women, the Countess of Pardo Bazán, whose books on her native land of Galicia are redolent of the soil' (p. 17). Hume 'has little to add to Mr Wood's glowing descriptions of many of the places he visited, except to confirm them fully and completely from long and intimate local knowledge' (p. 5). This somewhat paternal seal of approval turns out to be justified as Walter Wood provides an informative, entertaining and readable account of the areas he visited with a concluding chapter on Sir John Moore in La Coruña. He emphasizes the changes taking place in Galicia, and one suspects that Martin Hume recognized the proselytizing potential of Wood's accounts of the 'energetic measures for development being taken by the "Asociación para el fomento del Turismo en Galicia", the Grand Hotel at La Toja, and the hotel at Mondáriz (the Mondáriz Hydro), opened in 1897, 'that can accommodate six hundred people'.[56]

Wood's tendency to present a picture of what he sees through rose-tinted spectacles is exemplified by his enthusiastic description of the sardine trade at Cangas and around Vigo Bay: 'no visitor to Galicia should fail to visit one of these [sardine] factories' (pp. 62–3). One further imagines that Wood's book may have been subsidized by or written on behalf of Booth's Steamship Company Limited, 'whose powerful and splendid modern vessels have the reputation of being the most comfortable of all that cross the Bay of Biscay' (p. 45). 'In

1909, for the first time in nearly four centuries, an English band of pilgrims, headed by the Archbishop of Westminster, visited Galicia, by the Booth Line, under the guidance of the Catholic Association' (p. 91), and, finally, English tourists, when travelling by train in Galicia should go in the first-class compartments 'by which alone the Booth Steamship Company's tourists travel', and which are 'excellently adapted to the country's needs' (p. 130). When Wood observes, in his brief Preface, that his purpose is 'to deal with things seen and done by the visitor who travels under competent and comfortable guidance', it should be understood that there is little doubt that this guidance is to be supplied by Booth's Steamship Company. A feature of Wood's approach is the unfavourable comparison made with England: 'In England, when the streets are fog-bound, and the navvies are content ... while eating and drinking, with a warm ray or two from a neighbouring watchman's fire, the Galician worker is taking a midday meal on the shore of some glorious bay or river, ... in almost constant sunshine' (p. 29). Elsewhere, talking about the loads Galician women carry on their heads, Wood implies that these were of such weight that 'a Billingsgate or Covent Garden porter would refuse to have planted on his crown' (p. 156). Again, on a Sunday in a Galician village, Wood noticed 'young men and young women, laughing and chatting gaily, and some of them singing sweet Gallegan songs', whereas their counterparts in England 'even in the villages ... would have been bellowing banalities from music-halls' (p.102). Wood does strive to create an objective picture of what he experienced, however, in his unpretentious work, which shows traces of having been written with the account that George Borrow had given of his travails in Galicia some eighty years earlier uppermost in his mind.

In drawing a halt at this stage, I am aware that my task has to remain incomplete. The works of C. Gasquoine Hartley (Mrs Walter M. Gallichan), for example, must be reserved for consideration on a later occasion.[57] There are other works that merit a mention, whose omission from this account should not be considered in any way as an indication of lack of interest or esteem. In fact, the exercise undertaken here could be repeated with a different emphasis, and would reveal many other writers whose works took in Galicia. It is also apparent that this attempted coverage of writings on Galicia in the lifetime of Doña Emilia, mainly comprises the years between 1880 and 1910. This thirty-year period marks a changing of attitudes towards Galicia. In the latter part of the Victorian era, the condescending and condemnatory comments of a number of the then available guidebooks held sway. As travellers went to Galicia to see for themselves, and to express their own opinions of what they saw and experienced, so the public perception gradually underwent a change. By the end of the first decade of the twentieth century, commercial enterprises began to have a role to play. Whilst the quaintness and the charm of the region should not be compromised, because this would have an adverse effect, at the same time the modern amenities are given prominence. The message appears to be that Galicia is no longer a backwater, to which traditional and oft-repeated dismissive commonplaces apply; it is vibrant, modernizing and distinctive. This quality of distinctiveness is one that is shared with Emilia Pardo Bazán, whose appearance on the world stage of literature matches the gradual awareness and increased understanding of Galicia itself.

7

P.A. and *P.B.*
(*Peñas arriba* and Pardo Bazán)

Anthony H. Clarke

'...la aldea...envilece, empobrece y embrutece...'
(Pardo Bazán, *Los pazos de Ulloa*)

'C'est la Nature' (Zola, *La Terre*)

'Great things are done when men and mountains meet'
(Blake)

Some preliminary explanation of what lies behind my title may be helpful. For twenty years or more I have been amassing material on José María de Pereda's novel *Peñas arriba*, partly with a view to bringing out an edition[1] and partly because of a certain fascination exercised by this, his finest novel. Eventually the collection of 'apuntes' may see the light of day in the interest of collaborative scholarship; in the meantime it has grown to vast proportions, sprouting some three years ago a subsection headed '*P.A.* and *P.B.*' as a consequence of work I engaged in on the parallels and points of contact between the journey and arrival of Julián in Pardo Bazán's *Los pazos de Ulloa* and other similar journeys and arrivals in both Spanish and European novels of the period. Unable to fit consideration of *Peñas arriba* within the constraints of the resultant paper and article,[2] I envisaged a separate treatment wherein a specific comparison of the arrival/journey in *Peñas arriba* and *Los pazos de Ulloa* would be made. Since then I have been able to consult two related articles, both by Laureano Bonet,[3] which have caused me to further rethink my views on *Peñas arriba* insofar as it stands in any relationship at all to Pardo Bazán and her two linked novels *Los pazos de Ulloa* and *La madre naturaleza*. In working on this article I have been aware that there is a lack of data which would show conclusively that *Los pazos de Ulloa* constituted an influence on *Peñas arriba* or that *Peñas arriba* could have been written—to some extent at least—with the intention of refuting Pardo Bazán's contention and demonstration in *Los pazos de Ulloa* that '...la aldea ...envilece, empobrece y embrutece...'.[4] It is, however, unlikely that further evidence on this subject will come to light at this stage; thus I feel justified in presenting the case, as I see it, and in some measure as a coda to the previous article on journeys and arrivals. The knowledge that Maurice Hemingway enjoyed—and perhaps deliberately culti-vated—the 'on-balance' article rather than the one which presented a completely cut and dried case, serves as some encouragement in what seems, on the face of it, an uphill task.

The work of José María de Pereda and Emilia Pardo Bazán is sufficiently well known for me to dispense with a mass of background material. Similarly, the genesis and thesis of the novels in question scarcely require elaboration, given the critical attention paid to these novels over the past twenty years or so. Nevertheless, some aspects of recent and not-so-recent assessments will be considered in an effort to place the principal contentions of this article in some sort of perspective.

A number of major Spanish novelists writing in the last third of of the nineteenth century came to be seen and known as regional novelists; even in the cases where the regional or regionalist factor was in large measure transcended in their middle or later period, the label and convention continued to stick. Thus José María de Pereda, Emilia Pardo Bazán, Armando Palacio Valdés, Pedro Antonio de Alarcón, Vicente Blasco Ibáñez, etc. It is not germane to our purpose here to debate why the regional label or association tended to identify and define these novelists long after its critical precision had ceased to obtain, but it is crucial to our purpose to establish that strong tensions and highly differing perceptions existed between the regions and the capital or large towns and that the consideration of these factors provided much of the staple material of the nineteenth-century realist novel. Whether one thinks of the predominantly urban novelist—a Galdós for example—handling aspects of the capital versus provinces debate, or a Pardo Bazán or a Pereda viewing the nation and its problems from the periphery—Galicia and Cantabria

(Santander or the Montaña as it was known then)—it is nevertheless true that a vast proportion of their material related to the dialectic of town and country (*corte* and *aldea*) and to characters and situations which embodied and reflected the tensions between the capital and the regions. The question of the rise and the nature of the regionalist impulse in Spain has been the subject of much scholarly investigation over recent years. Behind this or that provincial novel may lurk a strong regionalist thesis, occasionally with overt political intentions. All of this is well known and well documented, but perhaps more so with regard to certain novels —e.g. Galdós' *Doña Perfecta* (1876)—than to others. It is generally accepted that the perceived ingredients of the capital/provinces or town/country debate varied considerably from author to author and from novel to novel; I shall seek to show that in the case of one of the two novelists covered by my title, other interpretations of their handling of these ingredients may be entertained; indeed, it will be my contention that the reasons for the writing of Pereda's *Peñas arriba* may well lie broadly within the framework of the regionalist debate but at the same time specifically within the Pereda/Pardo Bazán relationship.

To return, firstly, to the paper and article I mentioned earlier: 'Viaje y llegada de Julián a los Pazos y otros viajes y llegadas afines'. This was an attempt to demonstrate certain affinities within a group of Spanish novels published between 1876 and 1895, taking in Galdós' *Doña Perfecta*, Pardo Bazán's *Los pazos de Ulloa*, and referring briefly to Pereda's *Peñas arriba* (with the intention of devoting a separate article later to the last-named novel and its links with Pardo Bazán). The wider European implications of journey and arrival at a rambling, gloomy house entered into consideration through reference to such well-known precedents as *Wuthering Heights*, *Bleak House*, *Great Expectations*, etc., while both Poe's *The Fall of the House of Usher* and Hawthorne's *The House with Seven Gables*—mainly the former—represented the American connection. Broadly speaking, the Spanish novels were seen as prolonging a tradition of European and American novels or stories in which both journey and arrival[5] prefigured and set the mood for the subsequent immersion of the protagonist in a scenario involving some, if not all, of the following ingredients: mystery, gloom, sinister happenings, decadence, violence, the neo-Gothic, etc.

While the points of similarity between the first chapters of *Los pazos de Ulloa* and the early paragraphs of *The Fall of the House of Usher* are sufficient—and sufficiently relevant and telling—to give credence to the idea of a deliberate use by Pardo Bazán of elements of Poe's tale,[6] the other instances of initial descriptive sequences of journey and arrival are such as to lend support to the idea of a generic mutuality of approach, somewhat in the line of Faulkner's 'pollen of ideas' as recently reformulated by Darío Villanueva.[7] Within a span of some fifty years, a number of what will become key novels in the western European canon chart the confrontation of two widely differing worlds—usually town and country, but with crucial 'matizaciones'—and offer as both concrete and symbolical prologue to this study a journey/arrival involving the protagonist, who may also be the first-person narrator. The reader is referred to the above-mentioned article with the qualification that the coverage did not purport to be complete; many other examples could no doubt be adduced, but it was important at that stage to focus on novels well known to potential readers. The present article attempts to take the argument further, filling in the serious gap of of the comparison of journey/arrival in *Los pazos de Ulloa* and *Peñas arriba*. Since the latter novel comes at the tail-end of the period mentioned—and, in Spain at least, at the tail-end of a particular approach to the novel form—it is perfectly possible that the tradition perceived as characterizing certain novels of this period effectively ends here. Certainly there are very few examples of a similar prologue-like use of journey and arrival in Spanish prose fiction of the next twenty years or so. Additionally, it should be made clear that *Peñas arriba* is in many ways an anachronism.[8] Despite the regenerational implications and the *fin de siglo* sense of doom, ending, completion, new beginnings, etc., the overall novelistic mode and tone are predominantly characteristic of an earlier age. The novel has the patina of the 1870s or early 1880s rather than of the mid-1890s.

Pardo Bazán's protagonist—who is not the narrator and who is handled with a certain detached, occasionally humorous, irony—is a young unworldly priest. At the beginning of *Los pazos de Ulloa* he is travelling on horseback towards los Pazos, on the Santiago–Orense road in Galicia. He is no great shakes as a horseman, but Nature seems to conspire against him as he loses his way. Julián's urgent desire to get to his destination modulates into awareness of the hostility of his surroundings—the fading light, his sense of disorientation, the threatening nature of the 'pinar' and the peasant's answer to his question as to how far it is ('la carrerita de un can')—and the reader is drawn skilfully into both the sense of Julián's tender unpreparedness and the notion of an inimical natural environment. The unpleasant associations of the 'cruz de madera' (marking the spot where years before a violent death had occurred) lead into a new sequence in which his horse bolts at the sound of shots. Suddenly we are introduced to three riders/huntsmen who turn out to be key characters in the new world he is going to inhabit. Thus, before his arrival at los Pazos, Julian has experienced sheer terror at the hands of Mother Nature, has had premonitions of violent death, and made the acquaintance of three characters in the subsequent narrative whose attitudes and conduct are more calculated to inspire fear and loathing than anything he has experienced from Nature. It is worth noting that Julián's terror and plight stem in part from his unpreparedness for the rough terrain and from his 'escasa maestría hípica'. The innocent young priest passes rapidly from soft, civilized ways to the uncouth, rough and outlandish world of Spain's provincial periphery—the Spanish 'badlands' at their most hostile —but all the time the narrative suggests that Julián may be as much to blame for this resultant effect as the terrain and the conditions. Whatever criticism is being ironically suggested here is not wholly directed at the environment.[9]

The arrival of Julián at los Pazos and the subsequent points of contact between this description and other elements and sequences in the narrative, form a set of guidelines towards interpretation of the novel's key preoccupations. As such, they have been widely commented on and it will be sufficient for me to pick out those features which are relevant to the thrust of this article.

Era noche cerrada, sin luna, cuando desembocaron en el soto, tras del cual se elevaba la ancha mole de los Pazos de Ulloa. No consentía la oscuridad distinguir más que sus imponentes proporciones, escondiéndose las líneas y detalles en la negrura del ambiente. Ninguna luz brillaba en el vasto edificio, y la gran puerta central parecía cerrada a piedra y lodo. Dirigióse el marqués a un postigo lateral muy bajo, donde al punto apareció una mujer corpulenta alumbrada con un candil.

Después de haber cruzado varios corredores sombríos, penetraron todos en una especie de sótano con piso terrizo y bóveda de piedra... y desde allí llegaron presto a la espaciosa cocina, alumbrada por la claridad del fuego que ardía en el hogar, consumiendo lo que se llama arcaicamente un mediano monte de leña, y no es sino varios gruesos cepos de roble, avivados de tiempo en tiempo, con rama menuda.

Adornaban la elevada campana de la chimenea ristras de chorizos y morcillas, con algún jamón de añadidura, y a un lado y otro sendos bancos brindaban asiento cómodo para calentarse, oyendo hervir el negro pote, que, pendiente de los llares, ofrecía a los ósculos de la llama su insensible vientre de hierro. (*Los pazos de Ulloa*, pp. 15–16)

With the addition of the elements which round out the scene moments later—the dead game, the 'potes y vasijos', the hunting dogs—it is hardly surprising that Ricardo Gullón should have described the picture as 'casi de bodegón'.[10] This should not cause us to undervalue the deliberate allusions earlier, as Julián arrives, which evoke a castle-like structure—'ancha mole, sus imponentes proporciones' (the darkness suggesting even greater size), 'gran puerta central...cerrada a piedra y lodo, postigo lateral, varios corredores sombríos, especie de sótano con piso terrizo y bóveda de piedra' —since these hint at castle-like features which will link up with, and indeed prefigure, the dream sequence (Chapter XIX) in which Julián's fevered mind creates a castle with virtually *all* of such a building's attributes: 'ancho y profundo foso; macizas murallas; saeteras; almenas; puente levadizo con cadenas rechinantes; en suma, era un castillote feudal hecho y derecho...indudablemente, Julián había visto alguna pintura o leído alguna medrosa descripción de esos espantajos del pasado...' (pp. 188–9).[11]

Immediately prior to the dream sequence Julián has rescued a damsel in distress, who on one level is the Marqués' wife, Nucha, frightened by a huge spider which the Marqués is about to dispatch, and on another level a young woman in dire need of Julián's protection, since Don Pedro, the Marqués, has his sword raised. The scene is set, perhaps rather heavy-handedly, for the dream sequence not merely by the spider/monster effect and the references to Julián's 'temperamento linfático' and his 'valor temblón...el breve arranque nervioso de las mujeres' but more pertinently by the final words of the Marqués before Julián goes back to his room: '¡Valiente

122

cosa para tanto alboroto!... ¡Os crían con más mimo! En mi vida he visto tal. Don Julián, *¿usted creería que la casa se venía abajo?'* (p. 188, my italics).

Thus the imminent dream sequence—in which Julián's 'temperamento linfático' and impressionable mind, brought to fever pitch by an accumulation of external factors, converts the Pazos into a fully-fledged castle whose only clear identifying link with the real Pazos is the family shield and coat of arms—is ushered in by the words '¿usted creería que la casa se venía abajo?'

One further allusion connected with Julián's journey and arrival needs comment. At the end of chapter II, having come successfully — though not unmarked—through the 'prueba' of the journey and having witnessed the uncouth behaviour of the Marqués, Primitivo and the abad de Ulloa, etc., he recalls the words of 'el señor de la Lage', who had recommended him to the Marqués: 'Encontrará usted a mi sobrino bastante adocenado...*La aldea, cuando se cría uno en ella y no sale de ella jamás, envilece, empobrece y embrutece*' (p. 24, my italics).

Marcelo, the first-person narrator/protagonist of *Peñas arriba*, is also called to the periphery. The 'calling' is far removed from Julián's priestly vocation. He responds to the *cri de coeur* of his uncle, Don Celso, who writes him a letter from his mountain fastness, advising Marcelo of his awareness of the advancing years and of the need for him to step aside as patriarch of his village and valley. The first chapter, containing ample quotation from Don Celso's letter and explaining something of Marcelo's own condition and temperament, has been described as 'la llamada'.[12] The second chapter covers the journey on horseback and on foot from Reinosa to Tablanca (Tudanca) and the third chapter the arrival at the *Casona*, Don Celso's home. As with the first two chapters of *Los pazos de Ulloa*, I shall refer solely to features which are relevant to the argument of this article.

Marcelo's journey is made in the company of Chisco, of Don Celso's household, an 'espolique' or guide, versed in the ways of Nature, the weather, etc., and familiar with the tracks they have to follow. Thus Marcelo's introduction to the Montaña, through Chisco, does not carry the dangers attendant on Julián's journey towards los Pazos. However, although Marcelo is not placed in circumstances which might—as with Julián—cause him to panic, he nevertheless is subjected to a series of 'pruebas' at the hands of Nature:[13] the difficulties of the terrain, the hostility of certain plants and bushes, the overpowering dehumanizing effect of scant vegetation and vastnesses of forbidding rock. A few brief quotations will suffice:

> ...y me presentaba toda la superficie del Puerto bajo un aspecto feroz y repulsivo. Yo no veía más que una llanura infinita plagada de costras y tumores; y los monolitos solitarios y dispersos se me antojaban erupciones de verrugas asquerosas sobre una piel inmensa de leproso.

> ...hubiera jurado yo que circulaban por mis venas líquidos pedernales, y era mi cuerpo una estatua de granito coronada con manojos de *loberas* y acebuches.

> A todo esto, la noche se aproximaba; el tinte amarillento del follaje que se moría, destacando sobre el plomizo oscuro de los montes, daba a los términos más cercanos una lividez cadavérica; y del fondo de los precipicios donde se pudría la vegetación que ya había muerto, subía un olor acre, un vaho de tanino que me crispaba los nervios.

> Metido ya en la grieta como una lagartija, apenas daba el camino, *usgoso* y desconcertado, para sentar sus pies, con grandes precauciones, mi jamelgo. A lo mejor, grandes doseles de granito con lambrequines de zarzas y escaramujos raspándome la cabeza, mientras que por el lado derecho me punzaban las espinas de los escajos, y el más ligero resbalón de mi cabalgadura podía lanzarme a las simas de la izquierda. Y mirando hacia arriba en busca de luz, que ya nos faltaba abajo, montes erizados de crestas blanquecinas y conos encapuchados de espesa niebla, y gárgolas de tajada roca amenazando desplomarse sobre nosotros; y a todo esto, el camino estrechando y retorciéndose cada vez más...[14]

Two further features require comment before we move on to the arrival. The high dramatic point of Marcelo's journey is obviously the near encounter with the bear. The horses sense the bear's presence, Marcelo's 'enderezando las orejitas y mirando recelosa a la izquierda...'. The moment of danger passes, but the narrative has established a reference which will later link up with the bear hunt (Chapter XX) and Marcelo's first dream (Chapter V). The moment of near panic, certainly of danger, parallels Julián's moments of panic in the 'pinar', when Nature seems to threaten him, and also the final sequence of his journey involving the shots and the Marqués' hunting party.[15]

Secondly, Marcelo's imagination runs riot on the idea of Chisco as a 'cántabro primitivo': 'Aquel cuerpo fornido e incansable...aquel palo pinto, que en la diestra remedaba un venablo...aquella mandíbula saliente; aquel mirar poderoso e imperturbable; aquella faz montuna y atezada...' (p. 41), leading into tales of the resistance of the 'cántabros' against the Roman legions. In turn, this will link up with Marcelo's dream at the beginning of Chapter V—in which the bear(s) and the moving of mountains play a role—and also with his second, and much more extensive, dream (Chapter XV) in which he imagines scenes typical of 'Laro el cántabro'. Marcelo's dream sequences hark back to elements of his journey, just as Julián's dream sequence harks back to his initial impressions of an outlandish region (as perceived in the journey) and to his first awareness of los Pazos in terms of a quasi-castle.

Marcelo's arrival, like Julián's, takes place in pitch darkness. A number of scholars have commented on the special role of other sensorial channels than sight in Marcelo's first impressions of the *Casona* and the approach to it. The sense of vague outlines that was present in Julián's imprecise assimilation of los Pazos in the dark is accentuated to such an extent in Marcelo's confused account of his arrival (end of Chapter II and beginning of Chapter III) that hearing, smell and touch become the principal channels whereby he apprehends the scene. Marcelo's first contact with the 'solar de sus mayores', then, is restricted mainly to these three senses, with vision coming a poor fourth. Thus we have a striking contrast between the tentative and tenebrous first contact with the *Casona* and the role of sight as Marcelo subsequently takes in the Montaña in its multiple aspects. Needless to say, that first overall impression of the 'solar de sus mayores' prefigures the early role of *Casona*, village and valley as imprisoning, stifling force.

A further influence is at work in the framing and individual detail of Marcelo's journey and arrival, especially in the later stages. It is known that certain aspects of *Peñas arriba* represent a throwback to, and a recycling of, passages written many years earlier in *Los hombres de pro* (first published in 1872). Most notable are the parallels, firstly, between other senses than sight in the latter stages of the journey and the arrivals—again darkness is a shared factor—

and, secondly, the key similarities between Don Celso's kitchen and contents and Don Recaredo's in *Los hombres de pro*.[16] It is not to our purpose here to pursue these points of contact any further, save to note that this early novelette by Pereda, so plundered by the novelist for his masterpiece, was familiar to Pardo Bazán.[17]

The actual arrival at los Pazos and the *Casona*, consisting of approach to the building in the dark, perception of vague outlines, intuition of bulk, massiveness, etc., with suggestions of limitless possibilities through doors, passageways, up steps and so on, then gives way to the precise description of the kitchen, with attributes of 'bodegón' in both cases. The key role of the journey and the first impressions of the building—linking up with and prefiguring aspects of the later narrative such as dream, weather, oppressiveness, 'tosquedad', the protagonists' tenderfoot status, etc.—gives way to the simple *costumbrismo* of the presentation of the kitchen in Pereda's case and to a substantially more active scene in the case of Pardo Bazán (namely the stowing of the hunting booty, preparations for the meal, the scavenging of the dogs and the confusion in Julián's mind over Perucho, i.e. whether he is human or dog). In both novels the subsequent meal and conversation provides, logically enough, points of contact with the ensuing narrative and with aspects of the protagonist's story and predicament. As with almost any *Casona* or *Pazos* at that period, and more especially in winter, the kitchen is the central meeting-point, focus of warmth and of communication. It will be the one exception to Marcelo's overall early impression of the *Casona* and the valley as sombre and oppressive. Its equivalent in los Pazos will be the one room where Julián can find some sort of domestic comfort; outside the kitchen and its charmed confines he is a prey to the individual hang-ups of the inmates—the Marqués, Sabel, Primitivo, even Nucha. Thus the symbolical and figurative lines of connection between journey/arrival, on the one hand, and the later thrust of the narrative and presentation of the protagonist's conversion or dilemma on the other, are conditioned and back-grounded to some extent by the comforting social role of the kitchen.Where there is communication there are fewer grounds for apprehension, within the sinister or potentially sinister developments of the two narratives.

The sequence up to the moment when Julián and Marcelo bid their hosts goodnight and retire follows, as we have seen, a markedly similar pattern: a journey on horseback with attendant difficulties from the roughness of the terrain and/or lack of 'maestría hípica'; a scare (losing one's way, hostility of Nature, the bear episode, the 'crucero', the huntsmen and the shots); arrival in pitch darkness and the resultant sombre and imprecise evocation of the building and its setting, with suggestions of castle-like features; roughness of terrain in conjunction with uncouthness of persons conditioning the protagonist; comforting role of the kitchen prior to the mini-dream of Julián ('empezaron a danzar en su fantasía los sucesos todos de la jornada' p. 24) and Marcelo's dream-like thoughts about the day's events and the real dream of that same night (beginning of Chapter V).

Whether or not one can reasonably argue the case for either a specific influence of the journey/arrival in *Los pazos de Ulloa* on those of *Peñas arriba*, or for points of similarity, or for a generic presence of the journey/arrival tradition (with subsequent symbolical resonances) as outlined earlier, it would seem to be necessary to take account of two other possible factors: firstly, the relationship between Pereda and Pardo Bazán during the 1880s and first few years of the 1890s; and secondly, the nature of Pereda's motivation to write *Peñas arriba*.

The Pereda/Pardo Bazán relationship has exercised scholars over the years, partly because what is known is in itself fascinating—given the extent to which Pereda's attitude changed according to whether he was writing to Pardo Bazán or writing about her to somebody else—but not least because the gaps (what is not known or only imprecisely known) are no longer likely to be filled in, since the letters which would almost certainly have helped to round out the picture have not come to light and are now unlikely ever to come to light.[18] It is not necessary here to rehearse the whole story, merely those parts of it which may have some bearing on the considerations of the present article.

As has been noted frequently in Pereda scholarship,[19] the starting point for any discussion of the Pereda/Pardo Bazán saga is the famous passage about the older novelist in Pardo Bazán's *La cuestión palpitante*:

Puédese comparar el talento de Pereda a un huerto hermoso, bien regado, bien cultivado, oreado por aromáticas y salubres auras campestres, pero de limitados horizontes... Descuella como pintor de un país determinado, como poeta bucólico de una campiña siempre igual, y jamás intentó estudiar a fondo los medios civilizados, la vida moderna en las grandes capitales, vida que le es antipática y de la cual abomina...Si algún día concluyen por agotársele los temas de la *tierruca*...por fuerza habrá de salir de sus favoritos cuadros regionales y buscar nuevos rumbos.[20]

It is important to note that Pardo Bazán's strictures are served up with an abundance of praise—though praise of a highly perceptive sort—and that she is aware of possible dangers if/when Pereda abandons his *tierruca*:

No falta, entre los numerosos y apasionados admiradores de Pereda, quien desea ardientemente que varíe la tocata: yo no ignoro si el hacerlo sería ventajoso para el gran escritor; siempre reina cierta misteriosa armonía entre el estilo y facultades de un autor y los asuntos que elige; esta concordia procede de causas íntimas; además el realismo perdería mucho si Pereda saliese de la montaña.(sic)[21]

It has been generally accepted in pre-1980s Pereda criticism that his novel *Pedro Sánchez* (1883) represents a direct reaction, in novelistic terms, to Pardo Bazán's reservations about the narrowness of his world of fiction. However, González Herrán has pointed out in his Introduction to *Pedro Sánchez* (*cit.*) that the date of first publication of the relevant section of *La cuestión palpitante* renders impossible the idea of *Pedro Sánchez* being a 'reply' to Pardo Bazán's 'huerto' comments and it is interesting that one recent critic, Francisco Pérez Gutiérrez, has made a convincing case for *Pedro Sánchez* being in one respect a 'salida hacia dentro', as well as the obvious 'salida hacia fuera'.[22] The question of the role of *Pedro Sánchez* as a reply to Pardo Bazán's remarks in *La cuestión palpitante* will necessarily enter into consideration at a later stage. For the moment we stay with the developing relationship between the two writers.

Between 1883 and 1892, in addition to a favourable review of *Pedro Sánchez*, Pardo Bazán also wrote on *La Montálvez*, *Nubes de estío* and *Al primer vuelo*. Her article 'Pereda y su último libro', gives an overview of Pereda's prose fiction from *Los hombres de pro* ('mezquina historieta de campanario') to *Nubes de estío*, which is the 'último libro' of the title. There is hardly a phrase here that is critically out of place; Pereda himself could not complain that she had treated his novels unfairly, and yet during this period their relationship deteriorates to such an extent that there was little or no possibility of mutual friends—Galdós for example—repairing the damage. The letters of Pereda to Menéndez Pelayo, Laverde and others bear witness to a certain twofacedness on Pereda's part, especially when compared with both comments and general tone in his extant and reconstructed letters to Pardo Bazán herself. After the publication of *Pedro Sánchez* it may be said that Pereda maintained appearances as far as the public awareness of his attitude to Pardo Bazán was concerned, but in private letters he was content to be far less polite. The 'ruptura' proper comes with the publication of 'Los resquemores de Pereda' by Pardo Bazán (*El Imparcial*, 31 January 1891) and Pereda's reply twelve days later in the same paper, 'Las comezones de la señora Pardo Bazán'. After this exchange, as Concepción Fernández-Cordero notes, there was no way back; they had 'sobrepasado los límites de la cortesía'.[23]

And yet, there was a later attempt—solely on Pardo Bazán's part —to put things on a better footing. In the early summer of 1894 Pardo Bazán had spent a period of four or five days in the Montaña with a view to making contact with Galdós and other friends and collecting material for a travel book which would subsequently be given the title *Desde la Montaña*. The details of her visit and the reasons for the general lack of critical awareness of the existence of this little book are expertly covered in the recent edition by J.M. González Herrán and J.R. Saiz Viadero.[24] With reference to the relationship between Pardo Bazán and Pereda—then at an all-time low—it is fascinating to discover that on the one occasion when the Galician novelist came to the Montaña—after comments in numerous letters to the effect that she wanted to see for herself the setting of *Sotileza*, etc.—the Montaña was not willing to come to her, or even make himself available. González Herrán adduces various other reasons for Pereda's unwillingness to meet Pardo Bazán at this time—the Cabo Machichaco disaster, the death by suicide of Pereda's eldest son[25]—but it seems clear that the now-ageing novelist was simply against the idea of a possible reconciliation. Things had gone too far.

A literary relationship which, in its best moments, saw cordial invitations from one party to the other and sincere professions of admiration, degenerated into permanent pique on Pereda's part and a dignified indifference on Pardo Bazán's. Outside the chronological framework imposed on this article, and not affecting its conclusions in any way, although symptomatic of Pardo Bazán's attitude, one might refer to her eminently discreet and proper handling of the matter of the 'velada académica' in memory and honour of Pereda when she was presiding over the Literature section of the Madrid Ateneo.[26]

In the case of Pereda's finest novel, *Peñas arriba* (1895) it has been generally supposed that there were a number of reasons which explain how and why it came about. It may not be critically fashionable to ask oneself why this or that writer wrote this or that novel, but we know fairly well why Dickens wrote *Little Dorrit* and why Galdós wrote *Fortunata y Jacinta*, though answers might vary a little. In the first place, Pereda wrote *Peñas arriba* because it was there, waiting to be written.[27] Secondly, because his championship of the Montaña in some of his earlier novels—*Don Gonzalo...*, *El sabor de la tierruca*, *Sotileza*, *La puchera* (despite the latter's grim picture of rural poverty)—led him on logically to a final novel which would bring together in one definitive statement and synthesis his most pressing preoccupations. Thirdly, because *Peñas arriba* would allow him to use a setting which had interested him since his own electoral journey of 1871 and which he had been unable to cover more than summarily in his previous novels (*Los hombres de pro*). And fourthly, perhaps, because such a novel fitted in with his increasing concern with old age and the idea of death. There is, of course, another reason, which impinges on and takes part of its impulse from the ones already given. It has been said that, with one or two minor exceptions, Pereda wrote just one novel. *Peñas arriba* may reasonably be seen as the compendium and recycling or cannibalizing of much of his major fiction and of a considerable number of his novellas and sketches. If the *raison d'être* of *Peñas arriba* lies in part in the earlier novels, it may also validly be held that these novels and sketches paved the way in some measure for the *magnum opus*, not in the sense of rehearsals so much as in a subconscious grappling with themes and topics which would later receive much fuller treatment.

Of all the possible motives for writing *Peñas arriba* the one which should concern us here is the second, because it links up with Pereda's use of the *corte/aldea* thesis, and because it may be seen as part of a wider European tradition of a return to Nature.[28] Coinciding, then, in *Peñas arriba* we have a regionalist impulse—this latter well evaluated by Enrique Miralles in a recent article[29]—an exaltation of *aldea* over *corte*, and, crucially, a desire to rise to actual physical, symbolic and religious heights which would potentially transcend the more mundane aspects of the narrative. Constraints of space do not permit further elaboration of the regionalist thrust and debate behind Pereda's major fiction, thus references are given below to recent critical coverage of this area.[30] It may well be that Pereda planned and embarked on the writing of *Peñas arriba* impelled initially by his involvement with the regionalist debate, and in the course of his work on the novel gave himself up to other aspects— symbolism, myth, the complicated range of allusion to stony hardness and yielding liquidity, the all-pervading influence and presence of the *Book of Job*—which may eventually have usurped and overshadowed the original regionalist thrust. Be that as it may, scholars are forced to acknowledge the multifaceted nature of the *raison d'être* of *Peñas arriba*.

Bonet has written a suggestive article on the *madre/madrastra* motif as used by Pardo Bazán in *Los pazos de Ulloa* and *La madre naturaleza*, in conjunction with an apparent echoing or coincidental use of that motif by Pereda in *Peñas arriba*.[31] The relevant passages are well known, though no one, apparently, had previously thought to link them together to postulate a possible influence or coincidence. At the end of *La madre naturaleza*, Gabriel Pardo de la Lage looks back at the valley which has been the setting of the two novels, with an 'extraña mezcla de atracción y rencor' and says to himself: 'Naturaleza, te llaman madre... Deberían llamarte madrastra'.[32] In *Peñas arriba*, Chapter V, the protagonist, Marcelo, affected by the sombreness, oppressiveness, 'estrechez' and cold of his Montaña environment and by the thought that the Montaña winter was yet to come, thinks to himself the following:

> ... y por lo tocante a la señora Naturaleza, la de los montes altivos y los valles meláncolicos y los umbríos bosques y las nieblas diáfanas, y las sinfonías del favonio blando entre el pelado ramaje, y los rugidos del huracán en las esquivas revueltas de los hondos callejones, vista de cerca, mejor que madre, me parecía madrastra, carcelera cruel, por el miedo y el escalofrío que me daban su faz adusta, el encierro en que me tenía y los entretenimientos con que me brindaba... (pp. 87–8)

Although Marcelo does not use the precise phrase at the end of this, his most searing diatribe against Nature in the raw, the implicit unspoken words are those used by Julián when at the lowest point of his journey and his own experience of Nature's rougher face: '¡Qué país de lobos!'

With laudable scholarly caution Bonet refrains from postulating a direct influence of Pardo Bazán's *madre/madrastra* ending on the similar sequence placed in Marcelo's mind. Instead, he explores with great insight and sense of proportion the uses (and the contexts of the uses) of 'madre' and 'madrastra' and all the variants, pre-figurations and repercussions of such uses throughout the text of *Peñas arriba* and elsewhere in Pereda's work, with full references to related sources. However, in my opinion, the thoroughness and obvious commitment and enthusiasm with which he sees through such a daunting task cause him to miss one of the main points, if not the most important point, relating to the *madre/madrastra* parallel. If we look at the three novels closely, it quickly becomes obvious that while the 'madrastra' image is intermittently predominant in *Los pazos de Ulloa* and *La madre naturaleza*, it only applies in *Peñas arriba* up to a certain stage of the narrative, which is the one quoted above. While Marcelo may have further low moments *vis à vis* Nature, they are not pointed up by suggestions of the 'madrastra' in Nature. On the contrary, what Pereda seems to have contrived is a deliberate introduction of the concept *madre/madrastra* into his narrative—whether or not this is a direct borrowing from Pardo Bazán—precisely in order to turn it on its head. Marcelo is viewed at this crucial low point in terms of the *madre/madrastra* concept in order to give added dramatic effect and contrast to his gradual conversion in which he will perceive the great scheme of things, read in Nature's book with Don Sabas and Chisco and come to accept Nature as Mother, as naturing Nature,[33] without any further intrusion of the *madre/madrastra* image. This simple proposition—a patent fact within the narrative of *Peñas arriba* but nebulously speculative with regard to its connection with Pardo Bazán's prior use of the concept—takes on another dimension and purport, I believe, in the light of the conclusions which follow.

It will be apparent by now that I hold that there may be a case for Pereda having written *Peñas arriba* in some measure as a reaction and a reply to Pardo Bazán. The available letters of the period provide evidence that he had read *Los pazos*, although there is no suggestion that the novel might have influenced him in any way. Writing to Gumersindo Laverde (28 December 1886) Pereda asks: '¿Ha leido V. *Los Pazos de Ulloa*? Con excepción de lo del parto de la compostelana, que es de un naturalismo sucio y de escuela, y el prólogo, que es pedantesco y ridículo, aquella novela es *la que más me gusta de todas las de la misma escritora*. Así se la digo hoy a ella.'[34] The intended letter was presumably one of those from Pereda to Pardo Bazán which neither survived to recent times nor was reconstructable on the basis of the 'borradores' mentioned by González Herrán. However, Pereda voices substantially the same opinion on *Los pazos* in other letters and it seems reasonable to assume from these comments that he knew the novel well. Not so *La madre naturaleza*. The only references available to us now indicate that he was not sent a copy of the sequel to *Los pazos* and that he did not in fact read the novel, surprising as this may be in the context of the subject matter of the first novel and Pereda's awareness that a sequel existed. Much later than the date when Pereda had announced his intention of writing favourably to Pardo Bazán about *Los pazos* he refers incidentally to this novel when he writes to her about *Una cristiana —La prueba* (25 or 29 September, 1890): 'Leidos los dos tomos de *Una Cristiana* ...en mi pobre [ilegible] esta novela es la mejor que V. ha escrito, después de *Los Pazos de Ulloa*, que es lo mejor que V. ha hecho y de lo mejor que se ha hecho en España en su género, muchos años ha.'[35] High praise indeed, coming from this source!

If, as seems certain, Pereda has not read *La madre naturaleza*, despite the fact that he thought so highly of *Los pazos*, it might logically be inferred that his use, in Chapter V of *Peñas arriba*, of the *madre/madrastra* image did not therefore derive from nor have any connection with the sequel novel. As we have seen, Laureano Bonet assumes either points of contact or a mutual use of earlier traditions re *madre/madrastra* but does not postulate an influence. However, if we survey the dominant trend of *Los pazos de Ulloa* with regard to its handling of Nature and of Nature's attitude to Man, the conclusion must inevitably be that, without spelling out in this novel the *madre/madrastra* equation—as she does at the end of *La madre naturaleza* —Pardo Bazán was already developing a view of Nature which would make such an image or concept appropriate and even expected. Had Gabriel Pardo de la Lage's words appeared towards the end of *Los pazos* instead of at the very end of *La madre naturaleza*, few readers would have been surprised in terms of the underlying assumptions. Julián's journey, the representation of the world of Nature in *Los pazos* and the conduct of many of the characters in the novel, would lend credence to the idea of a developing sense of the *madre/madrastra* image. More telling, however, are the words of Gabriel Pardo de la Lage remembered by Julián at the end of chapter II of *Los pazos*: 'Encontrará usted a mi sobrino bastante adocenado... La aldea, cuando se cría uno en ella y no sale de ella jamás, *envilece, empobrece y embrutece*' (my italics). Intentionally, Pardo Bazán ends the sequel with further words of Gabriel Pardo de la Lage—this time his own thoughts directly expressed—'Naturaleza, te llaman madre... Deberían llamarte madrastra'. We are invited to conclude, surely, that a considerable part of the final *madre/madrastra* image springs from the belief on his part that 'la aldea...envilece, empobrece y embrutece'.

It would be perfectly possible to argue that *Peñas arriba*, bringing together as it does a number of the key preoccupations of the period, preoccupations given all the more force and poignancy because of the novelist's acute awareness of personal tragedy and approaching old age, had no need of either crutch or inspiration from Pardo Bazán. The richness of the symbolism and the attraction of the familiar themes from earlier works would have given the author scope enough. But if we consider the evidence presented here and then turn to the crucial connection in Pereda's mind between *Peñas arriba* and *Pedro Sánchez*[36]—in so many ways, despite all the differences, two sides of the same coin—and consider for a moment that *Pedro Sánchez* may not have been the whole—or even the main —story with regard to Pereda's reaction to Pardo Bazán's criticism in *La cuestión palpitante*; if we suppose that he was left with a burning desire to show the Galician novelist that he could not only successfully set a novel in Madrid, but that he could write a novel of universal implications with the Montaña as setting—and not just the Montaña as previously presented, but a remote mountain valley and village—and then we look at that hypothesis in the light of the material outlined in this article, and most crucially the likelihood that Pereda had taken account of and assimilated Pardo Bazán's slanted presentation of rural Galicia in terms of 'la aldea...envilece, empobrece y embrutece', along with the implicit *madre/madrastra* image, then it becomes difficult to view Pereda's novel as not indebted in some measure to the precedent of *Los pazos de Ulloa*.

A moment's reflection on the subject of the handling of village and rural life in the Spanish regional novel between 1875 and 1895 will lead us to infer that the regional novelists of the period must have been regularly looking over their respective shoulders at what their fellow-novelists were up to. The letters of the period reveal a considerable awareness of what was going on in the relatively narrow confines of the Spanish provincial novel. Pereda, Pardo Bazán, Palacio Valdés, Narcís Oller, etc., knew what their peers were doing. While it is surprising to discover that Pereda may well not have read *La madre naturaleza*, it seems unlikely that *Peñas arriba* could have been written without some conscious or subconscious echoing of, or reaction to, *Los pazos de Ulloa* on Pereda's part. Pardo Bazán's novelistic picture of rural Galicia must have impressed Pereda as essentially distorted, despite his presentation of rural poverty and squalor in earlier novels of his own such as *La puchera*. He countered it with a rural vision of the Montaña, in *Peñas arriba*, which was perhaps equally distorted in a different way, showing—with characteristic catholic idealism within his personal pessimism—that 'Great things are done when men and mountains meet'.[37]

While one must acknowledge that it is well nigh impossible at present to demonstrate beyond reasonable doubt that *Peñas arriba* was in some measure a reaction and reply to Pardo Bazán's vision of rural Spain in *Los pazos de Ulloa*, it would seem fair to assume, on the basis of the evidence here presented, that Pereda was irked by this vision and that some portion of his anger and indignation over her *huerto* comments still remained to be vented. We know from other examples that Pereda was a past master at keeping quiet on certain contentious issues, particularly of—in his view—a private nature. The concealment of identities and situations in *El sabor de la tierruca*, *Nubes de estío* and *Peñas arriba* reveals an author who enjoyed teasing his readers. That he should have written *Peñas arriba* in part as a reply to Pardo Bazán's criticism and to the picture of rural Galicia contained in *Los pazos* would not be in any way out of character.

The ideal coda to the argument as presented here might have been to quote at length from a damning and piqued review of *Peñas arriba* by Pardo Bazán in 1895. That it is impossible to do this because no such review exists may, on the other hand, be seen to be at least as eloquent in its implicit comment on the situation.

8

Unas cartas de Emilia Pardo Bazán a Benito Pérez Galdós

Nelly Clémessy

La publicación hace años de treinta y dos cartas de Emilia Pardo Bazán a Benito Pérez Galdós constituyó notable aporte para mejor biografía de ambos escritores e incluso conocimiento más exacto de la génesis de algunas de sus obras. Como lo puso de manifiesto Carmen Bravo-Villasante en *Vida y obra de Emilia Pardo Bazán*, el análisis de esta correspondencia íntima se presta a múltiples consideraciones psicológicas, sociológicas y de crítica literaria.[1] De sumo atractivo son esas cartas que van perfilando las respectivas personalidades de la Pardo Bazán y de Galdós al tiempo que revelan su estrecha amistad literaria. A modo de coletilla a este sustancioso epistolario no creo superfluo presentar aquí cinco cartas más, conservadas en la Biblioteca Nacional de Madrid.[2]

Trátase de unas cuartillas manuscritas que corresponden a épocas distintas. Están firmadas: Emilia Pardo Bazán, las dos primeras. Menciona el corto billete una dirección pasajera en Madrid. En cuanto a la carta I fue remitida desde París donde su autora, por segunda vez, pasaba una temporada invernal estudiosa en un hotel vecino a la Biblioteca Nacional que solía frecuentar. Puede fecharse esta carta en marzo de 1887 puesto que en ella se alude a una próxima salida para Galicia sin pasar por la capital española a principios de abril. En 1887, la amistad literaria entre los dos escritores se remontaba a algunos años atrás. Era conocida ya hacia 1881. Debió empezar por relaciones de discípula a maestro. En aquel entonces, estaba el novelista en el apogeo de su gloria a raíz de la publicación de *La desheredada* y Dª Emilia salía a la palestra con *La cuestión palpitante*. Una mutua simpatía y admiración nacida al calor de afinidades literarias no tardaría en cimentar la amistad entre los dos escritores.

Con el encabezamiento de su carta: 'al ilustre maestro', Dª Emilia sigue marcando su respeto, pero la sencillez y soltura de su prosa denotan familiaridad y confianza en el trato: habla de su hijo Jaime, evoca a los comunes amigos parisinos, informa sobre su actividad literaria no sin interrogar a Galdós sobre la suya. Da sin rodeos su parecer sobre una novela de Luis Alfonso, persuadida de que coincide con el de su correspondiente. En esta carta, se nos aparece la escritora toda entregada a la labor intelectual que le impone firme disciplina: No bien acabada su gran novela de *Los pazos de Ulloa* cuya próxima edición anuncia, está proyectando ya el aislamiento en Galicia más propicio a la lectura y a la creación que la bulliciosa vida madrileña. Por fin, en el billete como en la carta, es notable la amistosa solicitud para con Galdós a quien manifiesta cuán gustosa espera sus entrevistas.

Pertenecen a una época posterior las tres cartas siguientes que presentan particular interés desde el punto de vista de la historia literaria porque revelan como intervino su autora en la adaptación teatral de *Realidad* y su representación en las tablas madrileñas. Escritas en el otoño de 1891, estas cartas quedaron separadas del epistolario publicado por Carmen Bravo-Villasante y que atañe a los años 1889–1890.[3]

Conocida es la larga intimidad amorosa de Galdós y la Pardo Bazán, que parece datar de principios de 1889. Da fe el mencionado epistolario de la profunda crisis sentimental provocada algunos meses después por la infidelidad de Dª Emilia. Sabido es que ambos novelistas, cada uno a su modo, reflejaron su experiencia personal en forma literaria. Para ella, el episodio nefando no pasa de historia galante, sin trascendencia, es *Insolación*. Para Galdós, herido en lo hondo de una sensibilidad delicada, es *La incógnita* y *Realidad*, un conflicto dramático, atormentador, resuelto en un esfuerzo de generosa comprensión.

Muy poco tardó en perdonar el bondadoso escritor, reanudándose pronto la tierna relación y el fecundo diálogo literario. Solían los dos amantes intercambiar sus ideas e impresiones, comunicarse sus proyectos, relatarse el argumento de sus obras y comentarlas. Conmovida y desasosegada aún, la Pardo Bazán evoca con absoluta sinceridad el afecto que siente por Galdós y esa pasión del alma que por culpa suya estuvo a punto de malograrse:

Lo imposible y lo terrible era que no nos viésemos, que suprimiésemos
la comunicación, cuando nuestras almas se necesitan y se completan,
y cuando nadie puede sustituir en ese punto a tu Porcia. No deseo
ciertamente que me hagas una infidelidad, no; pero aún concibo
menos que te eches una amiga espiritual, a quien le cuentes tus
argumentos de novelas. A bien que esto es imposible; verdá, mi alma,
¿que es imposible?[4]

Durante aquel verano y principios de otoño de 1889, aunque ocupada
en la Exposición de París y luego atareadísima con la redacción
apremiante de sus crónicas, Dª Emilia no deja de interesarse de cerca
a lo escrito por Galdós, ayudándole incluso en su labor. Desde La
Coruña, le escribe : 'Ya me quedaré más libre la semana próxima, y te
diré la gratísima impresión que me produjo la Jornada I de *Realidad*:
muy superior ella sola (en mi concepto) al primer tomo enterito, sin
que este deje de gustarme bastante'. Y en otra ocasión, en Madrid,
llena de solicitud: 'Si me voy, me contestas a Marineda largo y
tendido y allí me envías todo lo que quieras de pruebas de *Realidad*.
Si antes de esta fecha he recibido algunas (pruebas digo) se corregirán
y restituirán a tiempo'.[5]

¿En qué medida se sentiría implicada la Pardo Bazán en el caso de
Realidad? Pocas dudas le quedarían sobre las bases reales de la
inspiración galdosiana después de leída *La incógnita*. Le mandó el
novelista parte de la obra a fines del verano y ella le comunicó su
interés : 'Espero con impaciencia las cuartillas de *La incógnita*, que
me ha dejado a media miel'.[6] Ahora bien, algunas semanas después,
se sincera con su correspondiente al evocar la puesta en venta de
Morriña y de *La incógnita*: 'el mismito día, a la propia hora. ¡El hado!
¡El hado! ¡Fortuna!' Y afirma emocionada a propósito de Augusta :
'Me he reconocido en aquella señora más amada por infiel y por
trapacera'. Luego, en esa bella carta apasionada, la escritora pasando
de lo literario a lo real, recuerda lo pasado en la primavera con afán
de explicarlo mejor y serenar a Galdós. Y, por fin insiste: 'Si quieres
enviarme algo que me guste envía pliegos de *Realidad*'.[7]

Al escribir su novela dialogada, Galdós soñaba ya con estrenarse
como dramaturgo, así lo afirma Dª Emilia en el largo estudio que
dedicó en 1892 a la obra teatral. Siendo conocido el grado de
intimidad de los dos escritores, no presta a duda la información. Al
exponer con gran lujo de detalles la génesis y nacimiento del drama

precisa que Galdós, decidido por fin a probar fortuna en las tablas resolvió adaptar *Realidad* en octubre de 1891.[8] Al extenderse sobre los motivos de esa elección y sobre las vacilaciones del autor, demuestra a las claras Dª Emilia que desde el principio estuvo al tanto de todo y debió discutir largo y tendido del asunto con Galdós.

Las tres cartas que tratan de *Realidad* cuyo texto se da a continuación datan de finales de 1891. En la primera, su autora da interesantes precisiones sobre *La piedra angular* que se prepara a publicar. Además, y es el principal objeto de su misiva, informa a Galdós de sus fructíferas gestiones acerca de los directores del Teatro de la Comedia: Vico y Mario. Manifiesta su entusiasmo la escritora a la idea de que iba por buen camino un proyecto en el que según escribe: 'tiene tanta parte'. No cabe duda pues que influyó no poco en la decisión de su correspondiente. No faltaban argumentos a favor de la elección de *Realidad* para una primera tentativa teatral: se prestaba a ella la forma dialogada de la novela. Insistiría además Dª Emilia en la vitalidad dramática del argumento y la novedad de su desenlace anticalderoniano, propio para crear sensación en la escena española. Pero obraría además poderosamente el factor sentimental, la secreta complicidad que la unía a Galdós en el caso particular y que resulta explícita en la firma de la carta: *Augusta*. No hay otro ejemplo conocido de esta firma, mientras es frecuente en el epistolario de 1889–1890, el uso de *Porcia*, seudónimo que reaparece en las dos últimas cartas (IV y V) reproducidas a continuación.

Debieron ser muchas las vacilaciones del novelista a propósito de la adaptación de *Realidad* en el teatro. Convida a pensarlo la actitud de Dª Emilia, enérgica y decidida como ella sola. Anima a Galdós, calma sus inquietudes, predice un éxito rotundo y le mete prisa para que se persone en Madrid. No disimula su impaciencia de ver al amigo y lo hace con una familiaridad y viveza expresiva que da mucho sabor a su prosa epistolar. Por fin, es manifiesto que la escritora no quiere quedar apartada de un asunto que ha tomado tan a pechos. Aunque, discretamente, lo deje al arbitrio de su correspondiente, solicita el favor de anticipar la noticia de la representación y también la de poner al novelista en contacto con los cómicos en su propia casa. Así es como, a la luz de esa correspondencia íntima, se aprecia mejor el estudio dedicado a *Realidad* en el *Nuevo Teatro Crítico*. Obligada a una indispensable reserva, Dª Emilia sin embargo cede a la tentación de ostentar en la parte I su personal conocimiento de la génesis y nacimiento del drama de Galdós. En cambio, conserva luego mayor distancia en su análisis de la obra que defiende, como fiel admiradora de su autor, sin desistir por ello de su sereno juicio crítico.

He aquí pues, la reproducción de esas páginas olvidadas en que se refleja tan a lo vivo la entrañable y fecunda amistad que unió dos de las figuras mayores de la literatura finisecular española.

Cartas a Galdós

I   Sr D. Benito Pérez Galdós

Ilustre amigo y maestro: si no le he escrito a V. antes, no es porque todos los días no lo recuerde y hable de V. con nuestros comunes amigos Pavlowsky y Savine. Con el primero he realizado varias excursiones del género de aquella famosa a la Paloma; y si le tuviésemos a V. aquí, nuestra satisfacción sería completa.

De la vida literaria por acá poco puedo decir aún, pues es el segundo año que vengo, y como no tengo gran empeño en trabar relaciones con la mayor parte de estas celebridades de palco, solo tengo conocimiento con las que buenamente se me vienen a las manos. En cambio tengo horas libres para trabajar mucho y la tarde y la noche entera para distraerme. Considero esta vida más sana para el cerebro que la de Madrid, donde se tropieza siempre a la misma gente y se renueva poco la atmósfera intelectual.

Desde que he llegado, sentí que recobraba el perdido aliento, y me puse a corregir, limar, rehacer mi casi abandonada novela. Ya está muy cerca de salir para Barcelona, donde la editará la casa Cortezo. No tengo resolución para lanzarme a editar yo misma.

¿Y la de V. la grande, en qué estado se encuentra? Supongo que bastante adelantada.

Díceme Alfonso en una carta que recibí pocos días hace, que V. le ha elogiado *El Guante*, con ciertas restricciones acerca del protagonista y de lo que Alfonso llama *lindeza y finura* de la obra y supongo que V. calificará de *relamidura* y *empalagosidad*, en su fuero interno. —A mí me pide parecer sea impreso o escrito, el caso es que no me ha alcanzado el valor para leer la novela entera, y que después de hojearla a los 10 minutos la he remitido a España con un cajón de libros ¿Qué le contesto yo a ese hombre? Echaré mano de una moratoria cualquiera, y haré equilibrios como V. pues desengañarle sería inútil, a juzgar por el tono de la carta, que revela verdadera satisfacción y orgullo ¡Dichosos los que así pueden ilusionarse acerca del valor de su obra! Y sé decir que las mías están cada día más lejos de mi aspiración y de mi propósito.

Me parece que me volveré a Galicia directamente sin pasar por ésa, pues Jaime se examina en Junio y yo necesito siquiera dos meses para prepararlo, y si me voy ahí a principios de Abril, me entretengo y no salgo ya para parte alguna, pues esa vida es muy absorbente. Me volveré pues a mi casa en derechura, con la esperanza de que V., que es una de las grandes tentaciones de la Corte para mí, no me jugará este año la mala pasada de no ir a acompañarnos un mes. Ya sabe V. que cuento con esta visita y no la perdono.

Le quiere muy de veras su amiga

Emilia P. Bazán

Hôtel d'Orient—rue Daunou

II   Amigo mío: aquí estoy, Plazuela de Santa Ana, 17. ¿Cuándo viene V.? Dígamelo para estar en casa, porque no quisiera tardar en verle.

Su amiga

Emilia Pardo Bazán

III   Hoy Sabado

Mi ratón del alma. Estos últimos días han sido para mí ocupadísimos, como que me cogió de medio a medio el limar y pulir los seis últimos capítulos de *La piedra angular*, que estaban informes y además no me gustaba el desenlace, por lo cual lo varié del todo. No sé lo que será esta novela sin amores y casi sin acontecimientos, o en que al menos los acontecimientos quedan en segundo término para dejar sitio a las ideas. Allá veremos, y Dios quiera no resulte algún ciempiés. Muy pronto estará el libro completamente impreso; pero no creo que lo pondré a la venta hasta el 1° del año de 92, porque no quiero faltar a mi compromiso con los editores y deseo dejarles ese respiro. —De todas suertes, en cuanto esté irá a las augustas manos de V. M. ratonil.

No por estos cuidados propios olvidé un instante otro que juzgo propio también, el de *Realidad*. Estoy entusiasmada con la idea, en

141

que tengo tanta parte, y será para mí un inmenso descordojo el verla salir a flote.

Bueno, pues para conseguirlo cité a mis dos directores de la Comedia, Vico y Mario. Como estaban de ensayos de una comedia miguelechegarayesca (parecía cosa de Miguel Ángel, pero hay viles falsificadores) tardaron en venir, y sólo el Lunes tuve el gusto de verles; que gusto es, pues son muy simpáticos. Excuso decirte que levantaron al cielo las manos, de placer, y que salieron de mi casa decididos a *estudiar* el libro a ver si aquello es escénico u no es escénico. Y hoy han vuelto, entusiasmados (sobre todo Mario) y sin más deseo que el de que te des la mayor prisa posible, y en las vacaciones que te tomes al venir acá, que ojalá sean prontito, traigas ya el drama hecho.

Hemos convenido en los puntos siguientes:

1°—El drama tendrá cinco jornadas, como la novela.

2°—Vico será *Orozco.* —Mario, Malibrán o el *padre de Federico.*— *Federico*, Thuilier. *Augusta*, La Cobeña. —*La Peri*, la Martínez. Y así sigue el reparto. —¡Vico será un *Orozco* soberbio!

3°—Le pintarán las decoraciones como V. M. disponga, y se arreglará la escena a su gusto y descordojo.

4°—Saldrá la sombra de Federico, al final, única sombra que creemos posible, pero ésta hará un efecto maravilloso. El mismo Thuilier proyectado, *impalpable*, a una luz misteriosa y rara. Ahora ¡porra! Sólo falta ponerse al telar, sólo falta poquita cosa: el arreglo del *manu auctoris.*

Será este drama el acontecimiento de la temporada, si se sublevan ¡mejor! y si aceptan una verdad tan grande, tan bonita, entonces mejor, nenico.

Se necesita que V. M. me escriba una cartita *oficial* que poder enseñar a los actores, y que sea contestación a la presente, para que puedan tener idea aproximada de *cuando* empezarán los ensayos y preparativos.

Y ahora, feo, mono, a mi vez digo yo ¿cuando tendré el descordojo de ver tu geta? Te vas a convertir en gasterópodo o en cefalópodo si permaneces mucho tiempo *cabe* el instituto de las profundidades *sup* marinas. Vente, carambita, que estas ausencias ya pican en historia.

Tuya

Augusta

IV Hoy 8

Cariño: ya estoy rabiando porque vengas, y los actores lo mismo. Les parece mentira que los hagas tan pronto el drama, y sobre todo que se los hagas. Quería decírtelo de palabra, y no me atrevía a escribirte, temerosa de que no te cogiese la carta ahí; pero ayer me dijo Meri Galiano que ella pensaba escribirte hoy y que sabía que te cogería ahí la carta... por consiguiente me aprovecho de la noticia.

Creo que son quiméricos tus temores de que nadie enfríe a los actores pintándoles un porvenir del tartareo querub con tu drama. Los actores ven al contrario un horizonte de célicos serafines: porque este año no tienen cosa que lo valga, y el acontecimiento será tu drama, no lo dudes. —Están locos de entusiasmo y en prueba de ello te incluyo la adjunta de Vico... Digo, no, no te la incluyo, porque sería poco maquiavélico, vale más que te la enseñe aquí.

Pero... vente pronto y tráete ese engendro divino. Ya verás, mono, ya verás el exitazo, *de ruido* sobre todo, además de la aprobación, que no será de esas aprobaciones convencionales y cursis, sino que llevará en sí la vitalidad de la discusión y de la batalla.

Por ahora se ha de guardar y se guarda maquiavélica reserva con la gente menuda de la prensa. Pero yo pido, por mi corretaje, el derecho de adelantar la noticia. ¿Es mucho pedir? Dime si en el n° de Enero del *Teatro* puedo hablar de eso ya y lanzar la cosa como se debe, en toda regla, con su 'Boca abajo todo el mundo' correspondiente.

Y ven pronto ¡porra!

Y contéstame avisando el día de tu regreso a *Mantua*.

Adios, feiño

tu Porcia

V Chiquito mío: por tu carta veo que quizás se encontrará en Santander esperándote la que yo te escribí última. —Te la escribí porque me dijo Meri Galiano que ella iba a escribirte el mismo día y que sabía que tenías que responderle desde tu refugio cantábrico antes de venir: de lo cual deduje que mi carta te cogería allí y que vendrías ya enterado del mucho entusiasmo y contento con que los actores supieron que estaba más próxima de lo que ellos creían

143

la hora de representar *Realidad*. — Pide a Santander tu correspondencia, que entre ella vendrá mi última carta. Quisiera incluirte la que Vico me escribió sobre el contenido de la tuya pero no sé donde la he metido: era breve y en sustancia decía lo que sigue: 'Estoy contentísimo y sólo deseo que todo sea cuanto antes. Creo que ni en el reparto ni en otra cosa alguna te pondrán la menor dificuldad. Les he comunicando mi entusiasmo sin esfuerzo, porque ellos estaban en igual tessitura.

Respecto a la fórmula de la entrevista con ellos, tu dirás. ¿Quieres que Mario vaya a tu casa? Pues se lo indicaré. Pero si me preguntas mi opinión, creo que, habiendo yo mediado en este asunto, la entrevista debiera verificarse aquí, en mi casa. Yo lo arreglaría de modo que ningún importuno viniese por ningún pretexto a molestarnos. Los actores vendrían a la hora y día que se les señalan, y tu también, por el corto espacio de tiempo que quisieras. Hecha la primera aproximación, lo demás ya sería cuenta tuya y cosa bien fácil de arreglar. —Para mi resultaba también más airoso el asunto, llevado de esta manera. Espero tu decisión, y entre tanto y con ganas de abrazarte soy tu

Porcia

9

Religion in Galdós's *Miau*

Eric Southworth

Still relatively few of Galdós's novels have been studied in the light of their earlier versions, although the novelist was careful about keeping sketches, drafts and printers' proofs of them. Pioneering work in this area was, however, published in 1964 by R.J. Weber, who examined the genesis of *Miau* through its two extant drafts to the final version dated April 1888.[1] Galdós, it is plain, worked quickly but not without care: he paid meticulous attention to his text as it evolved. We may conclude that the finished form of it is the result of sustained and concentrated effort.

Weber's textual study is extremely useful, therefore, but his literary judgements have been more open to question. His interpretative opinions on *Miau* set off a whole string of articles in the later 1960s and beyond, devoted to attributing blame for what happens in the novel either to the personal shortcomings of its protagonist, Villaamil, or to the social and political system within which the old man operates. Some critics presented Villaamil as victim of his environment; some depicted him as lazy and squarely responsible for his own and his family's problems: some sympathized while others condemned.[2]

By the later 1970s, the critical debate had become more balanced, however, and it is far easier to agree with the line taken by Eamonn Rodgers.[3] Rodgers's point is that in *Miau* Galdós wishes to undercut precisely the kind of partial opinionated responses that too many critics of the 1960s had gone in for. In *Miau*, we are presented with a case that it is, precisely, hard to form a judgement about. Different possible interpretations of events and characters have to be kept in tension in the reader's mind and not be resolved in a procrustean fashion. Galdós is concerned to ask how we may account for what happens to Villaamil and those around him, and the novel presents a wealth of information about the causes of the old man's ills.[4] A single satisfactory interpretation of it all is nonetheless hard to arrive at. People tend to have ready-made attitudes to questions such as those the novel deals in: views about the relative responsibilities of the state and of individuals; and views about such painful phenomena as suicide.[5] *Miau* treats a range of troubling, interrelated issues about which folk are prone to have stock responses, perhaps in an effort to protect themselves against the full pain of perplexity. Galdós wants to tease us out of such rigidities as these.

We are in fact warned that interpretations may be hard to formulate by an incident in the text itself, occurring near the end of Chapter 37. The penurious *cesante*, increasingly desperate and unhinged, haunts his former places of work, where he encounters younger civil servants of an all-too-familiar Galdosian sort. One of them nervously tries to humour the old fellow by pretending to go along with the wavering significances that the latter has come to attach to the letters MIAU, his personal version of the letters INRI set up by Pilate above the Cross of Christ. (Villaamil has madly come to think of himself as another Jesus.) The whole passage is a marvellous instance of Cervantine humour. First, Villaamil interprets the four letters MIAU as meaning 'Mis Ideas Abarcan Universo'; then he changes his mind: no, the letters stand for 'Ministro I Administrador Universal'... It is hard to humour someone who keeps on changing his views but his interlocutor still tactfully pretends to go along with him, only once more to be false-footed:

> —Pues mire usted, esa interpretación me parece una cosa muy sabia y con muchísimo intríngulis.

> —Lo que yo te digo: hay que examinar imparcialmente todas las versiones, pues éste dice una cosa, aquél sostiene otra, y no es fácil decidir...[6]

We as readers stand warned as well.

In addition to his concern with causes, with how things come about, Galdós is also centrally interested in how we interpret the results in moral terms, and it is here that we come to the question of religion, which is a crucial ingredient in the novel's examination of this question—the question of meanings, the grounding of value.

Eamonn Rodgers has pointed out that in *Miau*, religion is shown to be subject to wholesale trivialization, and is another area of the characters' lives in which clichéd responses supplant a sense of the truly and painfully problematic aspects of human experience. Rodgers is interested in how the novelist shows the superstitious nature of adults' religious practices and beliefs to be in fact childish (in the bad sense of that word) and immature.[7] In the present essay I want to pursue these matters a little further, in homage to Maurice Hemingway, whose own interest in theological reflection in the nineteenth-century novel is well known and has been seminal.[8]

Religion is a topic of central concern in *Miau*, as in so many of Galdós's novels, not least from *Fortunata y Jacinta* on. It is not that earlier than that, Galdós had not, as in his *novelas de la primera época*, explored the socially and politically destructive effects of religious prejudice, or that he had been unconcerned with that abiding emphasis of his, the nature of true charity. It is rather that in *Fortunata y Jacinta* and after, religion, as well as remaining a subject of socio-political concern, increasingly becomes a focus for imaginative thought about the nature of the Good and about theodicy (the problem of defending the goodness and omnipotence of God against objections arising from the existence of evil in the world), whilst deepening the reader's involvement with the paradoxes of Pauline Christology.

In the penultimate section of Part V of *Halma*, the sequel to *Nazarín*, José Antonio de Urrea is made to quote St Paul, as he responds to Father Nazarín's announcement that the Countess Halma is prepared to live in Christian matrimony with him:

> Dio un abrazo a Nazarín y no pudo expresar su alegría sino con frases entrecortadas:

> —Yo también, yo también... vi claro... no podía decirlo... a mí propio no podía decírmelo. Temía disparate... ¡Y no lo era, Cristo, no lo era! La suma ciencia parece locura; la verdad de Dios... sinrazón de los hombres.[9]

The relevant passage from Chapter 1 of the First Letter to the Corinthians runs as follows:

> Lo que parece loco en Dios, es mas sabio que los hombres; y lo que parece flaco en Dios, es mas fuerte que los hombres.[10]

By 1895, Galdós had certainly assimilated the Pauline writings on the 'hiddenness' of the Saviour—the logic-confounding redefinition of Messiahship revealed in the life and death of Jesus.[11] Similarly, though, in the novel published immediately before *Miau*, *Fortunata y Jacinta* of 1886–7, we already find a passage that is strongly reminiscent of another of St Paul's writings. I refer to the words of Fortunata, one of Galdós's most unlikely saints, that close Part IV, Chapter 1. (It is central to St Paul's teaching about Jesus and by extension, about those whose lives are hidden in His, that they are all 'unlikely' people in worldly terms.) Fortunata, Juanito Santa Cruz's working-class mistress, has just been stunned to be told that Jacinta, her lover's wife and in her eyes a moral paragon, has been having a affair with another character, Moreno Isla. The passage is worth quoting *in extenso*, given its importance:

> Fortunata no chistó. Aquella revelación la había dejado tan atontada, cual si le descargaran un fuerte golpe en la cabeza.
>
> Jacinta... ¡Jesús!... el modelito, el ángel, la mona de Dios... ¿Qué diría Guillermina, la obispa, empeñada en convertir a la gente y en ver la que peca y la que no peca?... ¿Qué diría?... Ja, ja, ja... ¡Ya no había virtud! ¡Ya no había más ley que el amor!... ¡Ya podía ella alzar su frente! Ya no le sacarían ningún ejemplo que la confundiera y abrumara. Ya Dios había hecho a todas iguales... para perdonarlas a todas.[12]

Now of course Fortunata does not 'intend' to cite or endorse a Pauline sense here. She means to refer to her own moral code of naturalness which is hypocritically condemned by the values of bourgeois society. However, the alert reader may catch here echoes that Fortunata was not herself aware of, so to speak, but which I think the author was.

The Pauline drift of what Fortunata says—she who ultimately in the novel dies claiming in her demented state that she is an angel like Jacinta[13]—may be caught in verses from the Letter to the Romans:

> Por las obras de la Ley no será justificado ningún hombre delante de él: porque la Ley es el conocimiento del pecado.
> Mas ahora sin la Ley se ha manifestado la justicia de Dios; [...]

Y la justicia de Dios es por la fé de Jesu-Christo para todos, y sobre
todo los que creen en él: Porque no hay distinción:
Pues todos pecáron, y tienen necesidad de la gloria de Dios.
Justificados gratuitamente por la gracia del mismo, por la redención,
que es en Jesu-Christo,
A quien Dios ha propuesto en propiciación por la fé en su sangre, á fin
de manifestar su justicia por la remisión de los pecados pasados.
En la paciencia de Dios, para demostrar su justicia en este tiempo: á
fin de que él sea hallado justo, y justificador de aquel, que tiene la fé
de Jesu-Christo.
¿Dónde está pues el motivo de su gloria? Excluida queda. ¿Por qué
ley? ¿De las obras? No: sino por la Ley de la fé.
Y así concluimos que es justificado el hombre por la fé, sin las obras
de la Ley.

Si Dios es por nosotros, ¿quién será contra nosotros?
[...]
¿Quién pondrá acusación contra los escogidos de Dios? Dios es el que
justifica.
¿Quién es el que condenará? [...]
¿Quién nos separará del amor de Christo?
[...]
Vencemos por aquel, que nos amó.
[...]
[Nada] nos podrá apartar del amor de Dios, que es en Jesu-Christo
Señor nuestro.
El que ama á su próximo, cumplió la Ley
[...] y así la caridad es el cumplimiento de la Ley.[14]

However misplaced or tendentious the reasoning that leads to it and
however little she may be aware of the fact as such, Fortunata's
conviction is St Paul's own, that if sin is everybody's problem, we are
all made equal by that fact. No one may properly stand in judgement
on others, making an exclusion zone for themselves and perhaps for
their friends. The only proper ethical response is love, received as a
free gift, as something beyond questions of calculation or deserving,
a love shared and communicated to others. The chief obstacle to
charity, to love in action, is pride, a lack of humility. It is something
that the rich, that capitalists, find hard to understand since it is a

value that transcends all talk of price. If *Fortunata y Jacinta* has a 'message', it is arguably this.[15]

Pauline sentiments are, then, to be found in *Fortunata y Jacinta*, with special emphasis on Paul's Letter to the Romans; in *Halma*, Galdós seems to have been especially taken also by the sentiments with which Paul's First Letter to the Corinthians opens, developing Deutero-Isaiah's preaching of a Messiah who reverses people's expectations by not being attractive or in worldly terms successful.[16] The preaching of the Cross is a vindication of salvation, by means that to the world and to the eyes of reason look like ignominious defeat. It is a radical anti-triumphalism, or rather, radical redefinition of a triumph.

What then of *Miau*? In this text, once all allowances have been made on the narrator's part for irony and on a character's part, for self-deception, *mauvaise foi*, special pleading and, not least, downright clinical insanity, one still finds lingering the idea that in some sense Villaamil might indeed be thought of as a *santo varón*, rather as Fortunata stirs us by dying claiming to be a angel. Villaamil's paranoia certainly has a religious edge to it: he sees himself as Christ and, to boot, identifies his grandson as a saint, 'San Luisito Cadalso'. It is all quite lunatic, but then, as St Paul told the Corinthians, that was also true of what the contemporary world thought about Jesus, blinded by its misplaced expectations.

In the context of the contemporary Catholic hierarchy's sympathy with theocracy, its promotion of the cult of Christ the King, and its bitter opposition to the modern liberal, secular state,[17] Galdós may be seen, whatever else, to remind people what theocracy really entailed—not ecclesiastical dominance over the secular power, but rather, something closer to what Paul's Letter to the Philippians had famously expressed as follows:

El mismo sentimiento haya en vosotros, que hubo tambien en Jesu-Christo:

Que siendo en forma de Dios, no tuvo por usurpación el ser él igual a Dios:

Sino que se anonadó á sí mismo tomando forma de siervo, hecho á la semejanza de hombres, y hallado en la condición como hombre.

Se humilló á sí mismo, hecho obediente hasta la muerte, y muerte de Cruz.[18]

The reader of *Miau* cannot fail to notice the wealth of religious references in the novel, and particularly the delicious visions of 'God' supposedly enjoyed by the epileptic Luisito in Chapters 3, 9, 19 and 40. Galdós shows his usual care in observing the symptoms which accompany the small boy's visions, which are an aspect of his epileptic attacks and, more widely, part of the author's case study of an 'unbalanced' family environment. With his insight into the world of children, Galdós makes plain to us that the deity Luisito encounters in the course of his attacks is a projection of the lad's own mind, borrowing from and recombining elements from his everyday existence, in a way similar to what happens in dreams. This God is a father-figure, with those ambiguous characteristics that fathers are wont to be perceived as having: the voice of authority, siding with Luisito's schoolteacher and with the Minister who cannot find a job for his grandfather, but also a friend and a supporter, in both aspects supplying a presence the family context cannot quite provide.[19] One readily takes Rodgers's point:

> We should be slow to jump to the conclusion that the figure who appears in Luisito's dreams is the God of Christian theology, or that his utterances have a special revelatory value, which is somehow different in kind from the rest of the novel.[20]

The local humour and the psychological acumen of the visions are real enough but, without disagreeing with Rodgers's observation, there is more, and talk of God can be a metaphorical way of commenting on 'how things are', on the nature of a world in which relatively decent people suffer and in which the wicked seem to thrive, a world in which God either cannot intervene or will not. This is, in short, a matter of theodicy—of the place of evil in the world and of the problematic expression of God's omnipotence, mercy and justice. Specifically, we are encouraged to ask how Villaamil's suicide and the human disasters that precede it are to be evaluated as a response to a Providence that in the 'real' world seems to operate on a par with the projections of Luisito's visions, rather than on a par with the fantasies involving Providence so frequently entertained by the novel's official adults. In his naivety, Luisito arguably sees straighter how the world actually wags than adults with more highly developed, more devious, more self-deceiving systems of 'moral' support.

The God whom Luisito meets is ineffectual: not the Almighty at all! He laments his little influence and control over earthly affairs. Here he is in Chapter 3:

> La excelsa persona que con Luis hablaba dejó un momento de mirar a éste y fijando los ojos en el suelo parecía meditar. Después volvió a encararse con el pequeño y suspirando —¡también él suspiraba!— pronunció estas graves palabras. (W 87)

In Chapter 9, God would have it that the world's troubles are more the fault of humans than of Himself; in Chapter 19, He laments how little notice anyone takes of him in Parliament; and in Chapter 40 he says much the same again. In the same chapter, he confesses on a different tack how little he grasps the aunt Abelarda's homicidal attack on her small nephew:

> Ya sé que te pasan cosas raras. Tú tía... ¡Parece mentira que queriéndote tanto...! ¿Tú entiendes esto? Pues yo tampoco. Te aseguro que cuando lo vi me quedé como quien ve visiones. (W 376)

Obviously transmitted here, with all the delicious humour of it, are not the author's but Luisito's insights, or lack of same. But clearly also, set in the novel's wider context, the words acquire a potentially wider significance. Divine Providence, in which so many of the text's adult characters claim to place their trust and which with varying degrees of 'success' they seek to manipulate to their own ends, seems in fact to be ineffectual or non-existent when it comes to rewarding average decent behaviour (not to speak of heroic virtue), effective perhaps only when it comes to doing such people down. God seems neither to prevent harm nor the success of evil men. In the context of such a world, to speak of God as omnipotent, loving and so forth could indeed seem like a figment of the imagination. An important focus of this comes in the final paragraph of Chapter 29, for all that what we read is skewed by emanating from an obviously 'tainted' source:

> Desde aquel día Villaamil frecuentaba la iglesia de un modo vergonzante. Al salir de casa, si las Comendadoras estaban abiertas, se colaba un rato allí, y oía misa si era hora de ello, y si no, se estaba un ratito de

rodillas, tratando, sin duda, de armonizar su fatalismo con la idea
cristiana. ¿Lo conseguiría? ¡Quién sabe! El cristianismo nos dice: *pedid
y se os dará*; nos manda que nos fiemos en Dios y esperemos de su
mano el remedio de nuestros males; pero la experiencia de una larga
vida de ansiedad sugería a Villaamil estas ideas: *no esperes y tendrás;
desconfía del éxito para que el éxito llegue*. Allá se las compondría en su
conciencia. Quizás abdicaba de su diabólica teoría, volviendo al dogma
consolador; tal vez se entregaba con toda la efusión de su espíritu al
Dios misericordioso, poniéndose en sus manos para que le diera lo que
más le convenía [...] y se proponía aguardar con ánimo estoico el
divino fallo, renunciando a la previsión de los acontecimientos, resabio
pecador del orgullo del hombre. (W 299)

This is a richly ironic passage. No properly cautious reader will
overlook such features as the comings and goings of its *style indirect
libre*, its parade of authorial ignorance and hypothesis, or Villaamil's
subsequent departure from the textbook Christian route of resig-
nation and acceptance. But still... Villaamil is not the first human
being to be perplexed by the apparent contrariness of heavenly
operations.

Rodgers has shown how Luisito's visionary conversations with God
need to be set in the broader context of other adults' religious
attitudes.[21] For the boy's childless aunt Quintina, for example,
religion is simply a source of income. She trades in *objets de piété*
imported from France, and otherwise, uses Christianity as a means to
manipulate Luisito in order to satisfy her frustrated maternal
instincts. For Luisito's grandmother Doña Pura, God is like a tap to
be turned on. Providence for her is what gets you out of a financial
tight spot and thus is credited with her windfalls, such as the return
of Víctor with his dishonest handouts or the death of Ponce's uncle
and the consequent legacy. Providence for her is a synonym of chance
and has no moral connotations whatsoever, beyond her conviction of
her own deserving.

In the case of Villaamil himself, his references to God are far more
numerous and have a consistently ironic direction to them, of which
he is himself semi-aware. Villaamil speaks of trusting in God but
when he does, no good ever comes of it. Thus, for example, when he
is about to approach him for some money, he praises Cucúrbitas as a
Christian gentleman, but then Cucúrbitas doesn't shell out.[22]

Likewise, when Villaamil says he is confident that God will touch the Minister's heart and cause him to be reinstated, this does not happen.

As the book progresses, and despite such divine rebuffs, Villaamil under his grandson's influence becomes more and more inclined to invoke the help of God (having no other cards to play). Thus, Luisito tells the old man to try prayer: 'Verás cómo Dios te da el destino' (W 250). We do see this: God doesn't give it to him. There seems to obtain a law of perverse effect, that adds up to a view of Providence which in so far as it helps anyone at all, helps only the least deserving.[23]

Luisito earlier, in Chapter 17, had voiced a pertinent insight: he had always been told that God helps good people, so if people are not helped, it must be because they are bad. If God does not find his grandfather a job and no longer appears when he feels unwell, it must be because God is angry with him for being in some way naughty. But then the text continues with a piece of narratorial comment:

> La lógica infantil es a veces de una precisión aterradora y lo prueba este razonamiento de Cadalsito: «Pues si no le quiere colocar, no sé por qué Dios se enfada conmigo y no me enseña la cara. Más bien debiera yo estar enfadado con El». (W 194)

In a similar vein, in Chapter 4 Villaamil had complained to God about not being reinstated:

> Villaamil decía: «Esto ya es demasiado, Señor Todopoderoso. ¿Qué he hecho yo para que me trates así? ¿Por qué no me colocan?» (W 97)

Again, in Chapter 30 the old man asks why God does not give him his daily bread: why not, when he is a no more spectacular sinner than those who do get fed (W 301). God, he says, seems only to protect *pillos* (W 306).

Such comments are equivocal of course, given who is making them and under what circumstances, and Villaamil in any case regards God as an instrument to serve his personal ends. The narrator actually comments directly at one point that the old man's prayers are a 'mezcla absurda de piedad y burocracia' (W 301), and readers can see for themselves that the remark is not unjust.

However, a consistent picture is emerging, put, if anything, euphemistically by Abelarda when she says, 'Dios a veces hace unos disparates' (W 304). She means by this that God does not arrange her love life according to her desires, but there seems to arise from the novel as a whole a more general sense in which one might agree with her. The confidence she had expressed in Chapter 27 that God would punish Víctor for his impiety and for his unprincipled way of treating her is utterly misplaced. Cadalso continues to enjoy worldly success, whereas she marries Ponce, whom she despises, on (of all days) the 'día de la Cruz'.

All in all, and extremely disconcertingly, the person who best might be said to sum up the evidence of the novel as a whole is Víctor Cadalso, the arch-villain: 'A Dios se le ve soñando' (W 146). Or as he puts it cynically to Abelarda in Chapter 37:

> La religión, entiendo yo, es el ropaje magnífico con que visten la nada para que no nos horrorice... ¿No crees tú lo mismo? (W 279)

Even so, the point is driven home from one source after another in this novel that evil is not punished on this earth; if anything, the contrary is true.

Villaamil in the light of this devises his crazy system by which since God never does what you want, you should pretend to want the opposite of what you really want, and then the perverse effect might actually come up with the goods. This system does not work of course, except for once, and that once is when the old man manages successfully to shoot himself.

No tangible evidence emerges from *Miau* that there is any benign Providence at work in the world at all. Inference from what happens to the Villaamil family suggests that there is no God at all, that the world is run by a malign agency, or at best, that God does really in fact resemble the depressed and powerless character with whom Luisito has his visionary interviews. God as a practical reality seems dead, and those who keep the word alive do so with varying degrees of self-serving dishonesty.

Traditional Christianity has always replied to such a critique that happiness is not to be looked for in this world at all, and that where accounts are properly settled is beyond the grave. Luisito himself reminds his grandfather of this, having been told it by his God in a vision (W 389–90). It is the child's sensitive insight that death is now his grandfather's only exit, but it may be noticed that when Luisito passes God's message on to Villaamil, it is this that actually confirms the old man in his decision to commit suicide. It is, one might say, God who finally pushes Villaamil over the edge into terminal despair.

The case of Fortunata had earlier led us to ask whether there is some metaphorical sense in which she might be said to be an angel, albeit of a highly unconventional sort. One might ask the same about that self-appointed *alter Christus*, Villaamil. At the end of the novel he is confident he will make it to heaven (W 410). Indeed, he forms, with the God the Father of his grandson's visions, and with the lad himself, whom he thinks of as San Luisito Cadalso, the third member of an unlikely alternative Trinity. Is there some sense in which, through his suicide, Villaamil might be considered, in terms of the reader's estimate of him, as entering into Glory or, at least, participating in the saving Passion of Christ? Is there some element in him which allows him to become a Christ-figure in the reader's eyes, in terms that are neither straightforwardly didactic nor, alternatively, simply those of grotesque parody? Is there a sense in which this crazy old man's self-inflicted death could be reinterpreted as a moral victory over a world in which the Gospel is normally disregarded point by point? My own sense is that one cannot simply agree with the view J.M. Ruano de la Haza has taken on this matter:

> The purpose of the parallel which Galdós draws in the novel between Villaamil and Christ is designed, not to allow us to detect the similarities that exist between the two, but to attract our attention towards the enormous differences between them.[24]

It is interesting to note how in the novel's final stages and as Villaamil gets more obviously madder and madder, he is invested with a certain moral dignity; the reader's sympathies are drawn towards him to a greater degree than before, guided in this perhaps by the narrator's deployment of epithets for him. He is spoken of as 'el infeliz cesante' (W 331, 334), 'el buen Villaamil' (W 359, 360), 'el anciano', and, at least three times, as 'el santo varón' (W 326, 328, 335). It is true that these phrases all contain their relativizing element of *style indirect libre*, reflecting how Villaamil feels sorry for himself. However, the old man is not simply laughed at by the narrator any more, or simply mocked, as earlier in the text. (His progress here somewhat recalls a comparable development within *Don Quijote*.) Villaamil becomes invested with a kind of dignity in the face of the inhuman treatment meted out to him by erstwhile colleagues; he is himself partly aware that he is mad and is distressed by it; he is in that and other ways as well quite like Don Quixote, a madman with lucid intervals, or so at least he seems to some. In Chapter 36, we read the following:

> Sevillano confirmaba con una sonrisa las acres observaciones del trastornado Villaamil, que no lo parecía al decir cosas tan a pelo. (W 346)

There is a good deal of Don Quixote in Villaamil: his monomania about the reform of Spain's tax system; his belief that the world should conform to his ideals whilst being himself ineffectual in putting them into practice; and so forth. Indeed, Galdós cunningly introduces an allusion to the Cervantine masterpiece when Argüelles relates that on the main floor of the house he lives in, there is a marquess:

> No me acuerdo del título; es valenciano y algo así como Benengeli, algo que suena a morisco. (W 347)

It might in fact be mentioned that the 'Romantic Approach' to Don Quixote readily lends itself to an interpretation of the Knight as 'a Christ-like figure, a man isolated by his noble ideals and misunderstood by his fellow-men'.[25]

Villaamil comes to see himself more and more determinedly as a Christ-figure (however much his language is embedded in popular usage): in Chapter 35, he reinterprets the insulting word '*Miau*' used against him as an INRI above his cross (W 344); in Chapter 37 he speaks of being crucified (W 356); in Chapter 41 he says 'apuremos el cáliz' (W 384); in Chapter 43 he says his marriage has been a Passion (as in Christ's Passion) of some thirty years' duration (W 400).

As he becomes increasingly unhinged from a clinical point of view, people find they cannot even so simply dismiss him as insane. Galdós does seem to want to leave the question of the evaluation of Villaamil open. Take the mixed reaction produced in Sevillano and Argüelles at the start of Chapter 36, on hearing Villaamil's self-identification with Christ:

157

> Sevillano y Argüelles, que al principio le habían oído con algo de respeto, en cuanto oyeron aquella salida titubearon entre la compasión y la risa, prevaleciendo al fin la primera. (W 345)

This is not straightforward narratorial endorsement of Villaamil's self-aggrandizing, self-pitying self-projection, one tinged perhaps with reminiscences of the kind of piety that encourages people to 'carry their cross' and identify in their sufferings with the suffering of Christ. Sevillano and his friend mainly exhibit in their reaction here a Christian compassion towards a former colleague who is off his head, in a way that echoes the reactions towards Don Quixote of some of that novel's more humanly sensitive other characters. But there is as well, alongside the nervous temptation just to laugh at him, an awareness of a sense in which Villaamil does resemble Christ, in being a man of sorrows, one rejected by a world in which it is the egregiously ungodly who seem to win out, a world in which Divine Providence, if operative, does not observe normal standards of decent behaviour, a world in which 'Christ' commonly seems left dangling on the Cross by his Father.

One should emphasize once more that the presentation of Villaamil is far from idealizing, including in the final period of his life, once he has resolved to kill himself. He has by then a quixotic anarchism and ridiculous randiness. He is, arguably, irresponsible in abandoning Luisito to his other aunt, Cadalso's sister Quintina. He is perhaps not reliable in his dismissive summing-up of his wife, it being notably comic when he of all people accuses her of knowing nothing of how to 'acomodarse a la realidad' (W 397, 399)!

That said, it is interesting to note the references we find to the Sermon on the Mount (*el sermón de la montaña*) in the novel's final chapters: parts of Villaamil's speeches are, after all, delivered near the Cuartel de la Montaña in Madrid. One has only to recall such Biblical injunctions as these, transmitted in St Matthew's Gospel:

> Por tanto os digo, no andeis afanados para vuestra alma, qué comereis, ni para vuestro cuerpo, qué vestireis. ¿No es mas el alma, que la comida: y el cuerpo mas que el vestido?
>
> Mirad las aves del cielo, que no siembran, ni siegan, ni allegan en troxes; y vuestro Padre Celestial las alimenta. ¿Pues no sois vosotros mucho mas que ellas?

¿Y por qué andais acongojados por el vestido? Considerad como crecen los lirios del campo: no trabajan, ni hilan.

Ya digo, que ni Salomón en toda su gloria fué cubierto como uno de estos.

Pues si al heno del campo, que hoy es, y mañana es echado en el horno, Dios viste así: ¿quánto mas á vosotros, hombres de poca fé?

No os acongojeis pues [...] vuestro Padre sabe, que teneis necesidad de todas [estas cosas].

Buscad primeramente el reyno de Dios, y su justicia: y todas estas cosas os serán añadidas.

Y así no andeis cuidadosos por el dia de mañana. Porque el dia de mañana se traherá su cuidado. Le basta al dia su propio afan.[26]

This allusion in the Sermon on the Mount to the birds of the air is taken up by Villaamil in Chapter 42, after he has lunched, what is more, at a tavern called La Viña del Señor:

A ver, esos pajarillos tan graciosos que andan por ahí picoteando, ¿se ocupan de lo que comerán mañana? No; por eso son felices; y ahora me encuentro yo como ellos, tan contento que me pondría a piar si supiera ... ¿Por qué razón Dios, vamos a ver, no le haría a uno pájaro en vez de hacerle persona?... Al menos que nos diesen a elegir. Seguramente nadie escogería ser hombre... .(W 396)[27]

Here is a man deranged, endorsing sentiments found in a Sermon which most sane people down the centuries have had the greatest difficulty in acting upon. Christian preaching so often has not seemed sensible or practical to 'realists', and such thoughts seem to lie behind the view of the narrator back in Chapter 7, when he comments sardonically about Doña Pura and the rest as follows:

Las tres *Miaus* estuvieron aquella tarde muy animadas. Tenían el don felicísimo de vivir siempre en la hora presente y de no pensar en el día de mañana. Es una hechura espiritual como otra cualquiera, y una filosofía práctica que por más que digan no ha caído en descrédito, aunque se ha despotricado mucho contra ella. (W 119)[28]

It is hard to miss the ironies being directed in all this against conventional Christian pieties. Folk repeat them, but no one in his right mind ever tries to act upon them. When an old fellow suffering from self-destructive paranoia endorses them, it hardly increases their credit-worthiness.

Galdós had evidently assimilated the criticisms levelled against one version of God by the *philosophes* of the eighteenth century, and he was equally wary of facile, infantile images of a deity like some cosmic fixer.

However, against these forms of idolatry, against a dream-world God, Galdós does, I think, set the God revealed in Christ that St Paul had preached in his First Letter to the Corinthians. God, according to Paul, is all about seeming mad. The very things that unbelievers level against the Gospel—its unreasonableness, its impracticality, and all the rest—are not distortions: the accusations are true, and are authentic marks of the divine as revealed in the life of God's only son. A man like Villaamil may not rank highly in terms of a conventionally, comfortably adjusted set of 'bourgeois Christian' values, but how does he seem when set alongside such shocking paradoxes as the following (one sentence of which, as we have seen, was later to be cited in *Halma*)?

> Nosotros predicamos á Christo crucificado, que es escándalo para los Judíos, y locura para los Gentiles;
> [...]
> Pues lo que parece loco en Dios, es mas sabio que los hombres; y lo que parece flaco en Dios, es mas fuerte que los hombres.
> Y así, hermanos, ved vuestra vocación, que no sois muchos sabios según la carne, no muchos poderosos, no muchos nobles.
> Mas las cosas locas del mundo escogió Dios, para confundir á los sabios; y las cosas flacas del mundo escogió Dios, para confundir á las fuertes:
> Y las cosas viles, y despreciables del mundo escogió Dios, y aquellas que no son: para destruir las que son:
> Para que ningun hombre se jacte delante de él.[29]

Such a view of the Christian message is not fundamentally at odds with the God revealed in Luisito's dreams, although the child's own view of matters is different. Luisito is afraid of the image of the Crucified starkly displayed in the church of Our Lady of Montserrat, as we read in Chapter 23:

En Montserrat, iglesia perteneciente al antiguo convento que es hoy
Cárcel de Mujeres, no se encontraba Luis tan a gusto como en las
Comendadoras, que es uno de los templos más despejados y más
bonitos de Madrid. A Montserrat encontrábalo frío y desnudo; los
santos estaban mal trajeados; el culto le parecía pobre, y además de
esto había en la capilla de la derecha conforme entramos un Cristo
grande, moreno, lleno de manchas de sangre, con enaguas y una
melena natural tan larga como el pelo de una mujer, la cual efigie le
causaba tanto miedo que nunca se atrevía a mirarla sino a distancia.
(W 245)

This *Cristo melenudo* seems to obsess Luisito particularly after
witnessing the illness, death and funeral of his school tormentor
Posturitas, described in Chapters 24, 27 and 28. He talks about the
image in Chapter 30 and it gives him almost fatal nightmares in
Chapter 32, in ignorance of his aunt's growing mental derangement.
It is, indeed, at this point that he makes a distinction between the
unthreatening figure of his epileptic attacks and the image from the
church of Our Lady of Montserrat that now haunts him.

—Tiíta, ahora le veo el faldellín todo lleno de sangre, mucha sangre...
Ven, enciende luz, o me muero de susto; quítamele, dile que se vaya.
El otro Dios es el que a mí me gusta, el abuelo guapo, el que no tiene
sangre, sino un manto muy fino y unas barbas blanquísimas... . (W
321–2)

It is, however, Christs of such a type that Unamuno would later
consider the authentically Spanish representation, one truer to the
New Testament than official 'political' or theologizing Catholicism
purveys, a figure to set alongside that of Villaamil when he projects
himself as Christ.[30] A comparable feeling is expressed by Azorín,
whereas later still, Lorca pointed out how these realistic Spanish
Christs stress everything about the crucified figure that made him
appear human, not divine.[31]

In this connection, one may usefully recall the scene in Chapter 32
where Abelarda has just been formally jilted by Cadalso in the course
of a rendezvous in the church of the Comendadoras. She takes refuge
in its Capilla de los Dolores, where there is a representation of the
Crucifixion, with Our Lady and St John at the feet of Christ. The

church of the Comendadoras too, in other words, for all its prettiness, is not devoid of references to the iconography of Christ's suffering and death, although this chapel shows signs of neglect and poverty. (The very sordidness of the chapel's decorations, when seen in a Pauline perspective, becomes indeed a mark of authenticity.)

> Mejor estaba allí, quieta y muda, rivalizando en inmovilidad con el San Juan del gallardete y con la Dolorosa. Esta se hallaba al pie de la Cruz, rígida en su enjuto vestido negro y en sus tocas de viuda, acribillado el pecho de espaditas de plata, las manos cruzadas con tanta fuerza que los dedos se confundían formando un haz apretadísimo. El Cristo, mucho mayor que la imagen de su madre, extendíase por el muro arriba, tocando al techo del templete con su corona de abrojos, y estirando sus brazos a increíble distancia. Abajo, velas, los atributos de la Pasión, ex-votos de cera, un cepillo con los bordes de la hendidura mugrientos, y el hierro del candado muy roñoso; el paño del altar goteado de cera, la repisa pintada imitando jaspes. Todo lo miraba la señorita de Villaamil, no mirando el conjunto, sino los detalles más ínfimos, clavando sus ojos aquí y allá como aguja que picotea sin penetrar, mientras su alma se apretaba contra la esponja henchida de amargor, absorbiéndolo todo. (W 318)

One notes how Abelarda there is likened to St John and Our Lady of Sorrows, especially the latter: women are not thus wholly left out of the novel's pattern of religious parallels. (The women, indeed, are certainly seen to suffer in this novel too, although it is the selfish male, Villaamil, that complains most loudly.)

Galdós was deeply suspicious of superstitious, childish religious beliefs in adults, functioning as one more way of failing to square up to painful facts about our lives as individuals and as members of the human race, and he was suspicious too of the triumphalist Catholicism of his day, about the ethos and attitudes of which much may be learnt from Frances Lannon's book,[32] or for that matter from Clarín's *La regenta*. Minter, in addition, has argued that later, in *Halma*, Galdós drew on St Augustine to challenge concepts of a militant Papacy that still sought to wield temporal power, and he links with this an interest in the ideals and structures of the early Church, pursuing a concept of sanctity inspired by *The City of God*.[33] Where our author was specifically and highly unusual, though, was in re-presenting a 'kenotic' Christology that was hardly dominant or standard currency amongst Spanish theologians at this period. By Kenotic Christology, one strictly means the views of those Lutherans who in the 1840s and 1850s had battened onto the text from Philippians 2 quoted earlier, and insisted that Christ emptied himself of his divine attributes of omnipotence, omniscience and cosmic sovereignty in order to become man.

I am not aware that these heretical views were canvassed in the Spain of the 1880s nor that Galdós could have known the writings of German theologians such as Thomasius or Gess.[34] One might, though, wonder to what extent Tolstoy's work was a contributing stimulus, with its emphasis on the teaching of the Sermon on the Mount. Vera Colin has written on Galdós's engagement with Tolstoyan Christianity in connection with the later novels *Ángel Guerra and Nazarín*.[35] Hans Hinterhäuser has also developed the link between Tolstoy's thought and *Nazarín*, in the context of a broader discussion of *fin-de-siècle* treatments of the figure of Christ.[36] Should one perhaps think of *Miau* in this connection too?

M.P. Alexeyev has interestingly shown that some interest in Russian literature had been briefly stimulated by the activity in the Madrid Ateneo of Russian priest, Father Kustodiev, in late 1869 and 1870. Kustodiev certainly stimulated Emilio Castelar to read Pushkin and Herzen. By 1889, a Russian visitor to Spain wrote that Galdós was a student of Turgenev.[37] Galdós's library contained a copy of Tolstoy's *Ma religion* dated 1885 and a copy of *La Guerre et la paix* dated 1884 (but one does not know when he purchased them).[38] What is more, in Autumn 1887, when we may imagine Galdós to be working on *Miau*, Pardo Bazán delivered in the Ateneo her important lectures *La revolución y la novela en Rusia*, which she published soon afterwards. She based these on Eugène de Vogüé's study, *Le Roman russe*, Vogüé having been someone with whom she had enjoyed detailed conversations on Russian literature during her recent stay in Paris. In her lectures, she discussed not only *War and Peace* and *Anna Karenina*, but also gave an account of Tolstoy's religious thought in *What I Believe (Ma religion)* and elsewhere, with its characteristic insistence on non-violence, its opposition to secular authority and its criticism of high culture and ameliorative education. I am not sure, however, that Tolstoy's writings alone account for the theological ideas that *Miau* presents; nor is there in this novel the explicit taking up of those specifically Tolstoyan issues like non-violence that the later novels confront. Tolstoy, however, did deny the divinity of Christ and preached that man's highest good was found in the practice of Charity: Galdós could readily sympathize with this. One's hunch, though, is that he got there on his own, by reading not only St Augustine but his own Bible.

Pardo Bazán's lectures also discussed Dostoyevski, stressing the Biblical inspiration of his *Memoirs from the House of the Dead and Crime and Punishment.* Critics have since drawn attention to the character of Prince Myshkin as reminiscent of Christ, in *The Idiot.* Dostoyevsky is perhaps another strand of potential Russian influence that it would be worth examining further.[39]

Miau has in common with earlier *novelas contemporáneas* its canvassing of other 'solutions' to problems characteristic of Restoration Spain as Galdós saw it, problems also characteristic of human life more widely. These are preoccupations that we see explored in, say, *La desheredada* and *Fortunata y Jacinta,* and here one thinks of both political intervention, especially insurrection, and also the role of education or of art as possible correctives. Galdós seems sceptical about the practical results of revolutionary activity, and pessimistically doubtful about any administrative or bureaucratic reforms in a world where the weakest always seem to go to the wall and in which the Cadalsos come out unfailingly on top. (Revolution if anything makes matters worse.) So, what of the Christian religion as another source of amelioration of the human lot?

Galdós's attitude to neo-Catholicism and Carlism as systems was a negative one and his suspicion of superstition ran deep.[40] He also had a liberal's special suspicion of the triumphalist, influence-hungry Jesuits, and that no doubt motivates his little joke in matching Villaamil as *alter Christus* with his grandson, as an ironic counterpart to the Jesuit St Luisito Gonzaga, patron of the then current Catholic youth organization, the *Congregación de los Luises,* with its anti-sexual obsessiveness.[41] His ploy in *Miau* is to suggest, I think, that God's official, self-appointed earthly representatives travesty the preaching that they should enact, the preaching of the Cross. Pauline 'kenotic' Christology, though, whilst in Galdós's view more authentic, is not something that his novels thereby endorse. A text like *Miau* confronts us with Christianity's irreducibly 'scandalous' nature, neither recommending nor rejecting it, but presenting its, in practical terms, eternally unfashionable response to the age-old problems of suffering and evil. One might, indeed, in this connection apply to Galdós a comment made about Tolstoy by Pardo Bazán:

> Sucédele a Tolstoi con el Evangelio lo que al profano que entra en un gabinete de física y, sin previas noticias, quiere [...] entender el manejo de tanto aparato y maquinaria.[42]

Galdós displays a characteristic scepticism, a distrust of nostrums of any sort, political, artistic or religious, but he does not fall into cynicism, any more than he deceives himself as to the efficacy of didacticism. He certainly wishes to canvass the problems of evil and suffering, aware of Enlightenment religious critique in the realm of theodicy but equally aware of the Pauline Christian response to that critique, one that seeks to place ethics beyond the reach of reason. He seeks to challenge readers to confront the issues of value and purpose in life, not least in the light of what one strong and central Christian understanding in this area has been. His reflections coalesce mainly around the figure of Villaamil, at first sight a preposterous *alter Christus* — until we recall, that is, that St Paul's preaching of the Cross was rooted in its very preposterousness when judged by worldly (rational, utilitarian) standards. For St Paul, the preaching of the Cross is a stumbling-block, and smacks of madness. Through a modern figure like Villaamil, a reader may perhaps recapture something of the original scandal of that preaching, a scandal that a more inert and conventional religiosity evades and dulls. Re-presenting the scandal of the Christian reply to basic problems in theodicy is not, though, necessarily to recommend it: it is to confront us with questions that in Galdós's eyes demand a response. My own sense is that Galdós's penchant remained for avoiding dogmatic answers to problems of human suffering and apparent purposelessness: he preferred practical responses, with their analogues or roots in the Gospels. These are non-judgementalism, the promotion of clear-sighted charity and the exaltation of humility, the capacity to live through uncertainty. In *Miau*, that is to say, we are well on the road towards such later novels as *Nazarín*, *Halma* and *Misericordia*.[43]

10

Los personajes secundarios de *Nazarín*[1]

Peter Bly

En el primer párrafo del *episodio nacional, O'Donnell,* número 2 de la cuarta serie, publicado en 1904, Galdós escribió:

> El nombre de *O'Donnell* al frente de este libro significa el coto de tiempo que corresponde a los hechos y personas aquí representados. Solemos designar las cosas históricas, o con el mote de su propia síntesis psicológica o con la divisa de su abolengo; esto es, el nombre de quien trajo el estado social y político que a tales personas y cosas dio fisonomía y color. Fue O'Donnell una época, como lo fueron antes y después Espartero y Prim, y como éstos, sus ideas crearon diversos hechos públicos y sus actos engendraron infinidad de manifestaciones particulares que, amasadas y conglomeradas, adquieren en la sucesión de los días carácter de unidad histórica. (4: 117)

Es algo arriesgado declarar, desde el principio, así, sin más, que en esta cita, sacada de una novela histórica, se encierra, hasta cierto punto, la clave al tema de nuestro estudio, pero lo indudable es que *Nazarín,* novela social, se diferencia de las otras de la Serie Contemporánea que asimismo llevan como título el nombre, o forma alternativa, de su protagonista.[2] Pues, en la mayoría de estas novelas 'onomásticas', se construye un andamiaje o red de relaciones en torno al protagonista central, en la que, en la buena tradición de la novela realista-naturalista del siglo XIX, la presencia de los personajes secundarios se explica y se justifica por su trato social o familiar con los protagonistas. A raíz de esta interacción se pone de relieve el desarrollo psicológico de éstos, o se desenlaza la trama de su historia personal, sin que por eso dejen algunos personajes secundarios de

166

cobrar, a veces, una identidad muy marcada y singular—pongamos por caso a Estupiñá, de *Fortunata y Jacinta*. Sin embargo, por muy inolvidables que sean estos tipos secundarios, no terminan por ensombrecer a los protagonistas, a quienes, justamente, recae la primacía de interés, por parte de los lectores. Al fin y al cabo, *Fortunata y Jacinta* no es la historia de Estupiñá ni siquiera de doña Guillermina, sino de las dos casadas epónimas. Ni tampoco es *La de Bringas* la novela de Milagros o de Manuel Pez.

Mas, ¿qué se puede decir de *Nazarín*? ¿Es, por casualidad, una rara excepción en que todo el interés crítico gira en torno al protagonista? Así nos lo daba a entender en parte Leonardo Romero Tobar, al observar: 'Desde el momento de su publicación la novela *Nazarín* (1895) ha sido leída con una atención singular referida a ... la función narrativa que desempeña la figura de su personaje central'(471). Efectivamente, en términos del espacio textual que él ocupa, se pudiera decir que, a partir del momento en que aparece en la novela, Nazarín casi nunca abandona el escenario, como si quisiera acaparar toda nuestra atención, y que el narrador no se interesara por ningún otro personaje. Aun en los pocos momentos en que el cura vagabundo no se encuentra ante la vista, como cuando hablan a solas Beatriz y Ándara, todavía está presente, porque las acólitas se refieren a él sin cesar. Esta obsesión narrativa con Nazarín, con que se quedaría sobradamente justificado el título de la novela, la parece prefigurar la manera como el cura entra por primera vez en el escenario: al abrirse la ventana estrecha de su cuartucho que da al corredor de la casa de huéspedes de la *señá Chanfa*, 'en el marco de ella apareció una figura' (31), como si en el marco de la historia siguiente no fuera a caber otra persona. Además vive apartado de los demás inquilinos, teniendo como vía de acceso a su habitación una escalera independiente por el portal. Más adelante, ya harto de los disgustos que acarrea la convivencia urbana, sale gozoso de la metrópoli para refugiarse en el campo circundante, donde 'la imaginación del fugitivo centuplicaba los encantos de cielo y tierra, y en ellos veía, como en un espejo, la imagen de su dicha, *por la libertad que al fin gozaba, sin más dueño que su Dios*' (105; el énfasis es mío). Todo parece indicar, entonces, que tenemos en las manos una novela muy diferente de las que le preceden en la biblioteca galdosiana: que se trata de la historia de un santo, un anacoreta, un hombre sin familia ni acompañantes, que prefiere la vida solitaria. Al abandonar la capital, Nazarín cree estar volviendo las espaldas a la vida constituida por una red de relaciones humanas. A otro nivel, se pudiera decir que Galdós está abandonando los moldes del realismo-naturalismo decimonónico. Mas, irónicamente, al lanzarse por los caminos ilimitados del campo castellano, Nazarín no va a encontrar la soledad anhelada, sino un mundo de personas aun más complicado que el de Madrid, mientras que Galdós, en tanto que novelista, va a resucitar la vieja narrativa de los libros de caballería renacentistas, en los que los héroes se cruzan con un sinnúmero de personas en sus andanzas. Como observa muy bien Romero Tobar, '*Nazarín* es novela de conciencia y novela de personajes' (474).

En efecto, pululan los personajes en las cinco partes de la novela, sin que se note apenas una variación en las cifras correspondientes a las etapas urbana y rural de la crónica de Nazarín: concretamente, en lo que a nuevos personaje se refiere, se introducen treinta y dos en la Primera Parte, veinticuatro en la Segunda, veintidós en la Tercera, treinta en la penúltima y diecisiete en la última, de los cuales muy pocos siguen y pasan a otras partes. Las dos notables excepciones, desde luego, son, primero, Ándara, que, al igual que su amo, va a estar presente en todo el libro, mientras que la segunda, Beatriz, entra en el escenario a partir de la Tercera Parte. La cuestión inmediata que se plantea es la siguiente: si Nazarín es el personaje central, que parece acaparar toda nuestra atención, ¿qué clase de personajes son los demás? ¿Secundarios o comparsas o aun principales, por muy estrambótico que parezca decirlo? Y, en segundo lugar, ¿cómo se puede justificar tal montón de personajes, aunque se trate de un libro caballeresco de plan abierto? En verdad, la razón del ser novelístico de estos personajes, hay que buscarla en el respectivo grado de su pertinencia al desarrollo temático de la vida de *Nazarín*, independientemente de qué espacio textual ocupen. Hasta se puede afirmar que la novela cuestiona la clasificación tradicional de roles que desempeñan los personajes ficticios y aun la misma definición de lo que constituye un personaje de novela. No carece de significación al respecto el que, en su reseña de *Nazarín* el mismo mes en que salió a la luz, Norberto González Aurioles declarara: 'Todos los caracteres están llenos de vida y de verdad, hasta el punto de que aún los personajes de segundo y tercer orden en la acción novelesca son tipos acabados cuyos modelos no es difícil encontrarlos en las más humildes capas sociales'. Opinión de la que, décadas más adelante, va a hacer eco Julián Palley al declarar: 'Los personajes secundarios— Ándara, Beatriz, el *Sacrílego*— están diestramente trazados'. En fin, ¿qué personajes tienen más interés o más protagonismo, para los lectores de esta novela?: ¿el titular, Nazarín, o los secundarios como Ándara, o Ujo, o aun algunos comparsas, como los Peludos, por ejemplo? Discutir, profundizar, si no descifrar, tales enigmas y rarezas literarias es la tarea que se propone emprender en este estudio.

El primer personaje al parecer secundario que se nos presenta al abrir las páginas de *Nazarín* es el reportero, que acompaña al narrador a la pensión de la *señá Chanfa*. A este tipo no se le bautiza con nombre alguno, ni es recipiente de una pintura física. Sin embargo, este señor es responsable de poner en marcha toda la trama de la novela, es propietario del texto, por así decirlo, pues a él le debe el narrador 'el descubrimiento de la casa de huéspedes de la *tía Chanfaina*' (21), cuando 'Un martes de Carnaval, bien lo recuerdo, tuvo el buen *reporter* la humorada de dar conmigo en aquellos sitios' (25). Asimismo, al reportero le corresponde fijar los parámetros del debate que se llevará a cabo en el resto de la novela sobre el verdadero carácter de Nazarín —si es un loco o un santo— precisamente con motivo de la entrevista que se celebra con él. Es éste un medio comunicativo ideal para la exposición de las ideas raras del cura, pues el reportero sólo sirve de máquina parlante que, con sus preguntitas, incita al entrevistado a abrirse al auditorio, o así lo parece. Mas antes de adjudicarle al reportero el mérito entero de esta puesta en marcha de la novela, se ha de recordar que tiene como compañero al mismo narrador, que, además de presentarse —por primera y única vez— como ente de ficción, forma con él una pareja, un dúo, el primero de muchos que se incluyen en el libro. Aquí los dos personajes secundarios anónimos comparten juntos el mismo espacio textual, repartiéndose las preguntitas que se han de hacer al entrevistado, al igual que destacando las diferencias de opinión que generan sus respuestas. Si, de una parte, el reportero queda convencido de que 'Este hombre es un sinvergüenza ... un cínico de mucho talento' (50), del que pronto se olvida, de otra, con él se obsesiona cada vez más el narrador, preocupado por si concluyera 'por construir un Nazarín de nueva planta con materiales extraídos de mis propias ideas, o llegué a posesionarme intelectualmente del verdadero y real personaje?' (56). Total que, lo único que se saca en limpio del interrogatorio es que el enigmático personaje central de la novela sólo consigue provocar una oposición de pareceres entre aquellos personajes secundarios que intentan profundizar en su carácter, y eso a base de una interrogación muy larga y muy franca.

A esta primera pareja de interviuadores corresponde otra que aparece más adelante en el relato, pero la simetría estructural resulta engañosa, ya que no se trata de una sola entrevista, sino de dos, colocadas en momentos culminantes de la historia. Por lo demás, se incorporan detalles que las diferencian de la primera, lo mismo que la una de la otra. Por ejemplo, es Nazarín el que, picada su curiosidad por lo que ha oído contar del carácter extraño de Belmonte, va en su búsqueda, en una clara inversión, subrayada por la estructura laberíntica de la casa del señor de Coreja, de lo que pasó en la primera entrevista de la calle de las Amazonas. Si esta segunda entrevista sigue teniendo como objetivo la exposición de las teorías e ideas de Nazarín, se le añade la variante de un mayor protagonismo por parte del interrogador. A diferencia del reportero y el narrador, Belmonte tiene una figura muy imponente, a cuya descripción se dedica más espacio que a la del mismo protagonista epónimo.

Propias de tal hombre son la testarudez con que mantiene su tesis de que Nazarín es un obispo armenio disfrazado, y la arrogancia con que trata a sus criados. Por más señas, a veces, a Nazarín, no le deja meter baza en la conversación. Como contrapartida de estos defectos, se pueden alegar su generosidad y trato afable, al obsequiarle al cura vagabundo con un festín, en el que muestra un verdadero interés en la necesidad de una regeneración espiritual del mundo. El hecho es que en la única ocasión en que aparece en la novela, Belmonte consigue ensombrecer al protagonista, sin que éste se dé cuenta de que el que tiene enfrente es un espejo humano en que verse a sí mismo, tipo como él por la convicción inquebrantable con que mantiene sus ideas e interpreta los aspectos más enigmáticos de la vida. Al revés de lo que pasa en la primera entrevista, Nazarín se ve obligado a hacer caso del personaje que tiene ante él, precisamente por el impacto muy directo que tiene en su vida. Y al comentar más tarde a sus dos acólitas la singularidad de Belmonte, se ve que el cura peregrino le ha calado bien al señor de Coreja: 'iAy qué señor, qué hombre tan raro es ese D. Pedro! ... No he visto otro caso. Cosas tiene de persona muy mala, esclava de los vicios; cosas de persona bonísima, cortés y caballeresca' (173). Evaluación ésta que dista mucho de ser tan simplista como la de la Polonia, para quien el viejo tirano 'está más loco que una cabra' (173). Pero, en última instancia, Nazarín se muestra incapaz de aprender la lección más pertinente para sí mismo: que él es igualmente enigmático para los demás personajes con que se encuentra en el camino.

La tercera entrevista, que forma la última sección sustancial de la novela, llevando a su mismo desenlace, como la primera la había puesto en marcha, es celebrada por otro personaje secundario destinado a no reaparecer en el relato: el alcalde de un pueblo que pudiera ser Méntrida o Aldea del Fresno, aunque nunca se resuelve esta confusión. Como al reportero y al narrador de la Primera Parte, no se le proporciona ni nombre, ni cuerpo, no obstante lo cual se destaca su personalidad, tan singular como la de Belmonte, por su locuacidad y su tendencia a bromear. Además, esta entrevista final tiene todos los indicios de ser un verdadero enjuiciamiento legal, pues tiene lugar en la cárcel del pueblo, una vez detenidos los tres delincuentes según órden de un juez de la capital. Mas el prendimiento parece bullanga de Carnaval, la cárcel es una cuadra con rejas, y la interrogación tiene trazas de ser una charla de tertulianos, aunque Nazarín se niega a hablar en su propia defensa. Lo que da pie para que el alcalde recuerde los hechos y dichos del sacerdote errante y que, simultáneamente, haga una apología de los adelantos y del progreso científico del siglo XIX. Se opone, claro, al espiritualismo de Nazarín, que, al optar por el mutismo, manifiesta hasta qué punto renuncia a dialogar con su contrincante ideológico: 'Señor mío, usted habla un lenguaje que no entiendo. El que hablo yo, tampoco es para usted comprensible, al menos ahora. Callémonos' (237). A pesar de sus simplezas, su estilo de hablar pomposo e incorrecto, y sus bromas, este alcalde articula unas verdades irrebatibles. A diferencia de Belmonte, que servía de espejo de carácter, el alcalde es una caja de resonancia ideológica, a la que Nazarín tampoco quiere prestar atención, ni siquiera para considerar lo que haya de justo, por muy poco que sea, en el discurso. Por otra parte, a este alcalde de Méntrida/Aldea del Fresno, hay que cotejarle con otro colega administrativo: el alcalde anónimo de Villamantilla, que, flaco y abrumado por los problemas prácticos que ocasiona la epidemia de la viruela, si está dispuesto inicialmente a despedir a los tres vagabundos a cajas destempladas, no se hace rogar cuando se ofrecen a ayudar a enterrar a los muertos.

Si, para sentar los fundamentos importantes de la ideología nazarinista, Galdós había echado mano de dos parejas de personajes secundarios, también recurre a una modalidad dualista para poner de relieve los efectos prácticos de su misión evangélica. La pareja más significante de este terreno narrativo es la de Ándara y Beatriz, cuyo acompañamiento del cura no se programa desde el principio, sino que se produce de una manera algo accidental. Una de las cuatro tarascas con que dan el reportero y el narrador al entrar en la casa de *Chanfaina*, Ándara reaparece al principio de la Segunda Parte al buscar refugio en el cuarto de Nazarín, suceso que conduce, a la larga, al autoexilio del cura de Madrid. Pero la definitiva participación en éste de la pintoresca fulana, a partir de la Tercera Parte, se produce pese a los deseos del clérigo. En cada una de las tres apariciones de Ándara, que comparte con el que va a ser su amo y maestro la distinción de llevar un nombre de muchas connotaciones (Bly, Clarke), su figura física resulta un enigma visual: en la primera, tiene la cara maquillada, en la segunda, es un bulto que tapa los cristales del cuarto de Nazarín, y en la tercera, le cuesta muchísimo trabajo a su antiguo protector reconocerla en un camino de las afueras de la capital, de venir tan transfigurada. De nuevo Galdós entra en detalles, más numerosos que los que dedica al cuadro físico de su protagonista, para fijar la inolvidable imagen esperpéntica, goyesca, de esta ex-prostituta, comparable —dígase entre paréntesis— a la que de su rival, la Tiñosa, ella misma había esbozado anteriormente. Andara tiene ya 'la piel erisipelatosa, arrugada en unas partes, en otras tumefacta ... No tenía el cuerpo ninguna redondez, ni trazas de cosa magra; *todo ángulos, atadijo de osamenta*' (110; el énfasis es nuestro). No es gratuita la pormenorización anatómica, puesto que sirve para poner de relieve la transformación más significante que ha sufrido Ándara, la interna, ya iniciada en la convivencia obligada de la Segunda Parte: 'Pero lo que más asombro causó a Nazarín fue que la mujercilla, al llegarse a él, parecía vergonzosa, con cierta cortedad infantil, que era lo más extraordinario y nuevo de su transformación' (110–11).

En un texto literario de tanta complejidad como la de *Nazarín*, sería muy arriesgado afirmar que Ándara representa un tipo totalmente opuesto al de Beatriz. Verdad es que, de las dos compañeras, ella es la más práctica y la más espontáneamente agresiva. Pero lo que importa en el desarrollo de su carácter, bajo la presión positiva del carismático Nazarín, es el progreso espiritual que se logra; en concreto, se puede hablar de un autoconocimiento y un autodominio impresionantes, si no completos, como se revela asombrosamente en la conversación que entabla con Beatriz en la cárcel de Navalcarnero: 'La verdad, [dice Ándara] ahora me pesa de todas las maldades y truhanerías que hice; pero como hemos de padecer tanto, porque así nos lo dice él, como no tenemos más remedio que aguantar y sufrir las crujías que vengan, yo no lloro, que tiempo habrá de llorar' (263–4). Tal clarividencia y sentido común, desde luego, se eclipsa poco después, cuando afirma en tono contundente que está dispuesta a convencer con violencia a todo el mundo de la santidad de Nazarín.

Ándara, además de ser el personaje secundario más destacado de toda la novela, es la prueba viva y fehaciente, aunque no intencionada ni perfecta, de la influencia sorprendentemente positiva que en el mundo contemporáneo podrán tener las ideas y el ejemplo práctico de Nazarín. También lo es Beatriz, cuya incorporación a la cuadrilla nazarinista se realiza en un momento bastante avanzado de la novela y de una manera también algo impremeditada. Precisamente se debe a una sugerencia por parte de la que va a ser su compañera de enseñanza y rival del cariño de Nazarín: la misma Ándara le insta al cura a entrar en Móstoles para curar a la hija enferma de Fabiana, hermana de Beatriz, lo que motivará su mutuo conocimiento. También Beatriz se contrasta con Ándara en lo que se refiere a la presencia física, pues, aunque es mujer del pueblo, tiene cierta finura de señora de ciudad. En efecto, ella pretende ser —aquí, primero, en términos de rango social— lo que no es. Por lo cual se justifica su inserción en la galería de cuadros enigmáticos de secundarios que pueblan la novela, tanto más cuanto que, por todo su exterior sereno y señorial, sufre de una enfermedad psíquica, la histeria. Tanto se ha comentado la oposición de valores que encarnan Ándara y Beatriz, que a menudo se hace caso omiso de aquellos en los que coinciden, aunque en proporciones inversas. He aquí otro ejemplo del dualismo del que, aparentemente, se inunda todo el libro, pero en cuya modificación se va insistiendo en este estudio. Si a la energía práctica de Ándara no le falta una dimensión de desarrollo espiritual, la meditación religiosa de Beatriz va acompañada de cierta actividad práctica, no exenta, por cierto, de una autosatisfacción. Es al final de la novela que Beatriz parece alcanzar el grado celestial que augura su nombre, que era un feliz cambio efectuado muy avanzada la composición del manuscrito al sustituirse por Martina, 'lógica elección', según Yolanda Arencibia, 'de la que viene a ser "compañera del mártir"' (149). En la visión final de Nazarín, se dan cita las dos vertientes del cristianismo: la contemplativa o mística, representada por Beatriz y la militante, encarnada en la figura de Ándara. Pero, como colmo del proceso mistificante del texto, hay que tener muy en cuenta que el lenguaje que se usa en la descripción de esta visión está teñido de una ironía, que se explica por el estado de gran fiebre en que se encuentra el cura al volver a Madrid. Mas no por eso deja de ser un indicio acertado e interesante de lo mucho que han venido a representar para el cura estas dos mujeres, que han compartido su recorrido por el campo castellano.

Lo que sí que pudiera haber anticipado, hasta cierto punto, eran las complicaciones y problemas que acarrearía la aparición repentina de Pinto en la plaza de Méntrida/Aldea del Fresno. Las relaciones que ha mantenido Beatriz con él no sólo explican su histeria, sino también que contribuyen —indirectamente— al desarrollo de la trama, a lo menos en sentido hipotético, pues de haber alcanzado su meta de llevarse a Beatriz a Madrid, la historia se hubiera desarrollado de otra manera. Lo mismo que *La Chanfa*, el ex-amante de Beatriz tiene un nombre cuya forma es discutible, pues no se sabe si es Pinto o Pintón. Muy acertadamente comenta Jo Labanyi, que quizás haga eco este nombre del modismo, 'estar entre Pinto y Valdemoro' (que son dos aldeas situadas al este de Móstoles), lo que significa: 'ser incapaz de decidir entre dos alternativas', que resume muy bien la actitud de Beatriz frente a él, pues aunque se siente muy atraída hacia él, no quiere abandonar a Nazarín. Pinto no es, en rigor, personaje secundario, sino un comparsa, pero, lo mismo que tantos otros, recibe una caracterización cuya extensión es desproporcionada, si sólo se piensa en términos del poco espacio narrativo que ocupa, pero, de otra parte, enteramente aceptable, y sobre todo, adecuada y verosímil, por ser proyectada a través de la mente de la amante a la que tanto hostiga. Sin embargo, y a pesar de todo —sus modales bárbaros y los solecismos que le ridiculizan como portavoz del código de honor calderoniano—, la cuestión que le toca plantearle a Beatriz es fundamental para cualquier persona que quiera seguir al misionero: 'Por la cuenta que te tiene, Beatriz, no seas terca, y arrepara en tu honor, que está tirado como una alpargata vieja por los caminos. Vas y hablamos' (196).

Este triángulo 'amoroso' se intersecta con el que forman Nazarín, Ándara y Ujo, constituyendo estos dos otro dúo de un personaje secundario y un comparsa, si se quiere, pero el retrato físico del enano es uno de los más inolvidables de toda la galería galdosiana. Lo que sí que no puede por menos de ser muy sorprendente, dado no sólo el poco espacio textual que ocupa, sino, lo que es, después de todo, lo chiquito de su cuerpo:

> La primera impresión que producía el verle era la de una cabeza que andaba por sí, moviendo dos piececillos debajo de la barba. Por los costados de un capisayo verde que gastaba, semejante a las fundas que cubren las jaulas de machos de perdiz, salían dos bracitos de una pequeñez increíble. En cambio, la cabeza era más voluminosa de lo regular, feísima, con una trompa por nariz, dos alpargatas por orejas, y unos pelos lacios en bigote y barbas, y ojuelos de ratón que miraban el uno para el otro, porque bizcaban horriblemente. (207)

Al igual que su contrafigura del otro triángulo 'amoroso', Ujo sale de improviso para luego desaparecer del escenario, pero en contraposición a la de Pinto, su aparición en la novela es totalmente inesperada, pues no se ha dicho palabra alguna de él hasta el momento. A mayor abundamiento, la intensidad de la luz, en parte irónica, en parte seria, que proyecta Ujo, junto a Ándara, sobre las actividades y actitudes de *Nazarín* es superior, a lo que parece, a la de la pareja Pinto-Beatriz. Lo de siempre, no se producen paralelos o inversiones simétricamente iguales en la estructura temática de *Nazarín*. En el caso de la pareja Ándara-Ujo, se añaden dimensiones que no se ven en el de la pareja 'hermosa'. Primero, a diferencia de Nazarín, que principia su viaje al campo jugando a la mendicidad, el enano lo hace de verdad, entrando y saliendo de las casas de Méntrida/Aldea del Fresno a la busca de mendrugos de pan y otras cosas de comer y de vestir, que luego comparte con las dos discípulas de Nazarín, y como consecuencia, aguantando toda clase de injurias: 'era objeto de chacota y befa ... los chicos del pueblo tenían con él un Carnaval continuo' (206–07). Pero, este monstruo con voz de niño, emplea el lenguaje más rico y complicado de cualquier personaje de la novela, y en este respecto indica Labanyi con perspicacia (xxiv) que Ándara se apropia del taco o muletilla que emplea el enano, 'caraifa', de este modo manteniéndose la presencia anímica de Ujo en la novela, aunque ya hace tiempo que ha desaparecido por completo del escenario.

Al invitar Ujo a Ándara a abandonar a Nazarín y quedarse con él en el pueblo, se repite, ahora desde una perspectiva cómica y más irreal, (pues Ándara ya es prisionera de la Guardia Civil), la prueba de fidelidad a Nazarín a la que había sometido Pinto a Beatriz. No obstante todo lo irreal del episodio, la declaración de Ujo es una expresión de verdadero cariño, y se hace dentro de una iglesia en la única ocasión en que en esta novela, supuestamente tan religiosa, el narrador, si no el protagonista, nos conduce al interior de un templo. No sería un despropósito declarar que Ujo encarna mejor que el cura Nazarín o que ningún otro personaje de la novela el verdadero espíritu del evangelio de Jesucristo, como nos lo da a entender el narrador en su característico estilo irónico y desorientador: 'Parecía que no; pero era un buen hombre, mejor dicho, un buen enano o un buen monstruo, el pobre Ujo' (208).

Al mismo tiempo, Ujo se nos presenta como un objeto artístico y aun escultural, pues, inicialmente Beatriz le tiene por 'algún demonio escapado del retablo de las Ánimas benditas' (207) y el narrador sentencia: 'era como parte integrante del pueblo mismo, como la veleta de la torre, o el escudo del Ayuntamiento, o el mascarón del caño de la fuente. No hay función sin tarasca, ni aldea sin Ujo' (208). Para Labanyi (xix), Ujo es una figura simbólica que encarna lo monstruoso y lo carnavalesco, con que insistentemente se asocia el mismo Nazarín, sobre todo en la Primera Parte de la novela. En efecto, Ujo tiene la forma física de un cabezudo, tan común en las fiestas españolas. Por lo tanto Ujo parece reflejar el intento de Nazarín, con sus prácticas cristianas tan revolucionarias, de meter patas arriba el mundo establecido (Labanyi 200, nota 138). El único reparo que tengo que poner a tal idea, por otros conceptos muy aceptable, es que Ujo, lo mismo que Nazarín, es también persona de carne y hueso, capaz de desarrollo emocional y espiritual en su contacto con otros seres humanos.

Como si no bastaran Ujo y Pinto como puntos de referencia desde los que asesorar las respectivas transformaciones de Ándara y Beatriz, Galdós incluye otra pareja de comparsas para destacar cómo puede efectuarse inmediata y eficazmente la influencia de Nazarín sobre cualquier desconocido con quien se cruce en el camino. Los dos presidiarios, el *Parricida* y el *Sacrílego*, forman otra pareja que se instala en la galería de retratos secundarios. Pero el contacto de los dos criminales con Nazarín es mucho más breve y se produce de una manera fortuita, si bien ineludible, y en ínfimas condiciones: cuando los tres presos descansan la noche en las inhóspitas cárceles de los pueblos situados cerca de Madrid. A pesar de, mejor dicho, a causa de estos factores, la conversión espiritual del *Sacrílego* parece tener aun mayor trascendencia que la de Ándara y Beatriz. Parece una conversión totalmente sincera que han ocasionado las palabras pronunciadas por Nazarín en la cárcel: '—Señor —afirmó el *Sacrílego* con aflicción sincera—, yo soy muy malo, y no merezco ni tan siquiera que usted hable conmigo' (259). Mas, con este tono humilde se contrasta el lenguaje violento y enérgico con que ha amenazado a los otros de la cadena. Y en la visión apocalíptica de Nazarín al final de la novela, también se transforma el físico del reo: del de un hombre 'enjuto de carnes, fisonomía melancólica, ceja corrida y barbas ralas, la mirada en el suelo, el paso decidido' (268) en el de un 'mancebo militar y divino' (281). En fin, como todos los personajes de segunda categoría discutidos hasta ahora, es una figura enigmática y algo confusa: ¿hasta qué punto se puede confiar en la regeneración futura y permanente del *Sacrílego*? Es una cuestión imposible de contestar definitivamente, dentro de los límites de una novela en que se ha subrayado lo muy poco que se ha de fiar de la palabra escrita y hablada. Por otra parte, una variante de esta pareja, la ofrece el *Parricida* que no experimenta conversión espiritual de ninguna clase, ni siquiera se arrepiente de sus malos tratos verbales y físicos del cura.

Curiosamente, en su primera aparición en la novela, los dos criminales habían fingido ser lo opuesto de lo que eran: agentes del orden social, una pareja de la Guardia Civil disfrazada, encargada por el Gobierno de detener 'a cuantos ladrones encontrasen, quitándoles los objetos robados' (217). Irónicamente, el *Sacrílego* y el *Parricida* serán capturados por una legítima pareja de Guardias Civiles, quienes, como el primero de estos reos, se ven al final obligados a rectificar sus impresiones originales del cura. Si lo habían tenido por un redomado hipócrita, pronto 'la humildad de sus respuestas, la paciencia callada con que sufría toda molestia, su bondad, su dulzura, les encantaban, y acabaron por pensar que si D. Nazario no era santo lo parecía' (248). En un cambio total de ciento ochenta grados, los guardias al final le tienen mucha compasión, prediciéndole que por loco, aunque no por santo, ser absuelto, como los 'dos tercios de los procesados que pasan por nuestras manos, por locos escapan del castigo, si es que castigo merecen' (283). Y esto que el guardia que es amigo de Beatriz, Cirilo Mondéjar, había defendido con gran energía su deber a la Benemérita cuando en la cárcel de Méntrida/Aldea del Fresno su paisana le había sugerido que les dejara escaparse a los tres peregrinos. Su negativa no pudiera haberse expresado más rotundamente: 'El Cuerpo no sabe lo que es compasión, y cuando el alma, que es la Ley, le manda prender, prende; y si le manda fusilar, fusila' (238). Mayor contraste entre estas dos frases no se podría concebir. Y no se habla de cosas triviales, puesto que se trata de nada menos que el mismo destino de Nazarín, que se narrará en la novela siguiente, *Halma*. Lo que aquí nos importa es subrayar que las únicas opciones que Nazarín tendrá abiertas —dos en este momento: ser libertado por idiota o agarrotado por reo—, se las presentan dos funcionarios insignificantes de la Administración del país, dos comparsas de esta novela.

Hasta ahora, hemos examinado a los personajes secundarios y algunos comparsas con que van emparejados, de acuerdo con una configuración dualista que ha permitido el planteamiento de una serie de contrastes en torno al cura protagonista. Mas, en cierta medida, esta estrategia interpretativa ha resultado ser otro engaño, pues, aunque mediante ella se han podido comprobar las diferencias, por ejemplo, entre los componentes de las parejas (Beatriz–Ándara; reportero–narrador; Belmonte–alcalde de Méntrida; Ujo–Pinto; el *Parricida*–el *Sacrílego*), con mayor frecuencia se han registrado semejanzas de actitud o de comportamiento entre los dos elementos supuestamente opuestos. Por otro lado, se hallan interconectados estos dualismos de una manera mucho más complicada de lo que se pudiera imaginar a primera vista: pongamos por caso a Ujo y Pinto. No es cuestión de un dualismo básico y de nada más: de si Nazarín es un loco o un santo, punto; de si Ándara es símbolo de la cristiandad práctica y Beatriz, el de la contemplativa, etcétera. De consistir la novela *Nazarín* en una serie de contrastes y oposiciones de esta clase, sin complicaciones ni irregularidades, quedaría descalificado su tejido esencialmente enigmático. En vez de una perspectiva dualista, hay que pensar más bien en términos pluralistas, al abordar este texto polifacético, así como nos invitan a hacerlo la estructura física de la casa de huéspedes, el cuerpo de *Chanfaina*, el mismo título de la novela y, en fin, la alargada discusión al final de la Primera Parte sobre la autoría de la misma (Bly, Gullón, Smith, Urey).

Son los comparsas, los de la figuración, en términos cinematográficos, quienes sirven para amplificar y aclarar, mediante contrastes y paralelos, lo que significa la relación del protagonista y sus personajes secundarios. Y elevadísima es la cifra de los comparsas que aparecen una sola vez en la novela. Como lo ha señalado muy bien Labanyi (xxiii), son, en general, tipos del pueblo marginado. Pero no sólo se destaca su lenguaje singularísimo, sino su caracterización, realizada en breve, para contribuir, a su manera, al mosaico de apariencias y sucesos enigmáticos y paradójicos que forman la fibra esencial de esta novela. A modo de prólogo emblemático, miniaturista, se podría citar a los dos mieleros con quienes tropiezan el narrador y el reportero en el patio de la casa de la calle de las Amazonas, los cuales son 'enjutos, con las piernas embutidas en paño pardo y medias negras, abarcas con correas, chaleco ajustado, pañuelo a la cabeza, tipos de raza castellana, como cecina forrada en yesca' (25). Sobran las palabras acumuladas para trazar a dos tipos que van a desaparecer al instante de nuestra visión. Pero ni por eso dejan de ser inolvidablemente graciosos, al ofrecerse un contraste evidente entre su físico amojamado y el dulzor del líquido que salen a vender por las calles de Madrid.

En una novela de clara filiación religiosa y cuyo protagonista central es un cura, no podría faltar la presencia de otros clérigos, sobre todo al principio cuando se trata la grave cuestión de la complicidad de un cura en el crimen de la calle de las Amazonas. El basurero amigo de Ándara, *Bálsamo*, de joven había querido ser sacerdote antes de perder la vista. A otro cura, que se llama a secas 'cleriguito', y vive con su mamá, le toca un mayor protagonismo. Aparentando ser buen amigo de Nazarín, a quien le da cobijo, le gusta entrometerse en el asunto, sólo, como se entera uno más tarde, para codearse con las autoridades. Y cuando las cosas se le ponen negras a Nazarín, el dicho 'cleriguito' recoge velas, y echa a su buen amigo de la casa en un discurso que es un verdadero 'tour de force' lingüístico, por la yuxtaposición cómica de latinismos y vulgarismos, formando un inolvidable conjunto macarrónico. Así se capta a la perfección la hipocresía y ambivalencia de este supuesto amigo, que, frente a la cuestión fundamental de la novela, que había planteado inicialmente el reportero —la de la locura de Nazarín— se ve precisado a expresar su duda en términos también ambiguos: 'Pues el juez, que es todo un caballero, lo primero que me preguntó fue si usted está loco. Respondíle que no sabía... No me atreví a negarlo, pues siendo usted cuerdo, resulta más inexplicable su conducta' (93).

También algo inexplicable resulta la conducta de los Peludos, otra pareja de comparsas que reciben a Nazarín cuando tiene que abandonar la casa del cleriguito. Otra vez se nota una diferencia de actitudes frente a Nazarín, pues, si el marido no quiere que el cura se marche a correr aventuras, la mujer no se entristece tanto ante tal posibilidad. Y a pesar de que demuestran una caridad genuina al llenar su mochila de comestibles y ropa vieja, transparentan cierta autocongratulación las palabras con que le despiden: 'dijéronle que no se afanase por el pago de la corta deuda, pues ellos, como gente muy cristiana y con su poquito de santidad en el cuerpo, le hacían donación del comestible devengado' (101).

A partir del momento en que el cura abandona la choza de los Peludos, las ambivalencias y los enigmas a los que tiene que hacer frente, por parte de personajes de la comparsa, son más bien de índole física. El tipo pintoresco, al que otros llaman Paco Pardo o 'el hijo de la Canóniga', sin que nunca se sepa su verdadero nombre, recibe una descripción física muy breve pero muy expresiva: 'un hombre muy mal carado, flaco de cuerpo, cetrino de rostro, conde-corado con más de una cicatriz, vestido pobremente' (99). Su importancia estriba en el contraste que con ella forman sus modales de cortesía, manifestados de modo verbal en su muletilla 'con respeto'. Pero, a pesar de este encuentro significativo, y para colmo de con-fusión, al día siguiente, cuando se cruzan los dos hombres en el camino, no se reconocen ni el uno al otro, con más justificación Paco Pardo, porque Nazarín ya anda disfrazado de mendigo.

Otro tipo campesino, con que Nazarín se tropieza, nada más iniciar su trayecto, el cabrero que le pide pan, tiene un lenguaje marcado por solecismos puestos en letra cursiva en el texto. Pero a este personaje, que transita fugazmente por el texto, le corresponde el honor de anticipar el desenlace, al informarle a Nazarín de que los Guardias Civiles tienen órdenes de capturar a todos los vagabundos y llevarlos a Madrid, donde se quedarán puestos en libertad, por estar atestadas ya de gente las cárceles.

Con un reparto de comparsas tan extenso, el problema funda-mental que se le plantea a Galdós es cómo variar su función temática para evitar el aburrimiento. Ahora bien, en los primeros encuentros de su odisea, Nazarín cree que se le ha caído la buena suerte, pues, le regalan legumbres dos mujeres y un chico; recibe una moneda de tres hombres, a quienes ayuda a liberar una carreta que se ha atascado en una cuneta al lado del camino. En concepto de experiencias negativas se han de registrar el rechazo inmediato que recibe de un propietario bien vestido que le tiene por mendigo, o la despedida cruel de unas personas que cavan viñas a orillas de un río, después de haberle regalado un conejo. La realidad de la vida es tan compleja y variada, que las experiencias humanas que experimenta Nazarín nunca son iguales, por muy similares que parezcan. Dentro de las coordenadas del bien y del mal se encuadran una multitud de matices y correspondencias.

El cuidado con que Galdós presenta tanto a los personajes secundarios como a los comparsas, que a veces ni siquiera entran en las tablas, solamente puesto su nombre en boca de otros, que es el caso de la Tiñosa verbalmente pintada por Ándara, es una clara señal de su intención de revolucionar el concepto tradicional de los personajes novelescos. Punto de referencia imprescindible en torno del cual gira todo el texto aun cuando salga momentáneamente del escenario, Nazarín no monopoliza, ni con mucho, la atención de los lectores, precisamente porque hay tantos otros personajes cuya importancia es difícil de determinar de forma definitiva. ¿Se puede asegurar rotundamente, por ejemplo, que Belmonte es personaje más trascendente que el *Sacrílego*, en lo que atañe al impacto del mensaje cristiano de Nazarín, porque ése se destaca más por sus idiosincrasias? Habida cuenta de la conversión aparentemente verdadera del criminal, sería difícil aceptar que las observaciones de Belmonte tengan más peso en la novela. Lo que sí que logra hacer Galdós en esta novela es desafiar a sus lectores regulares, instándoles a cuestionar las normas narrativas. La caracterización, por ende, es uno de los muchos laberintos de significación que configuran el terreno interpretativo de la novela. De ahí que sea erróneo aceptar cien por cien lo que asevera el narrador en la primera página de la novela acerca de la 'eterna *guasa* de Madrid' cuando en este cuadro de Carnaval se inscriben escenas tan trágicas como las del entierro de los muertos de Villamanta y Villamantilla o del niño de dos años cuyo cadáver es sacado en ataúd de la casa de huéspedes de *Chanfaina* en el instante en que entran en el patio el reportero y el narrador. Y este difunto es un comparsa cuyo cuerpo físico y lenguaje singular no se reproducen en la imaginación o la memoria de otros. El comentario del narrador al respecto, intercalado en la descripción de las otras actividades de los inquilinos en día tan festivo, es uno de los más amargos que jamás escribiera Galdós: 'Salió sin aparato de lágrimas ni despedida maternal, como si nadie existiera en el mundo que con pena le viera salir' (27).

Tampoco se debe tomar al pie de la letra lo que ante el reportero y el narrador en la Primera Parte opina Nazarín de los libros:

> Nada quiero con libros ni con periódicos. Todo lo que sé bien sabido lo tengo, *y en mis convicciones hay una firmeza inquebrantable; ... Sólo añado que los libros son para mí lo mismo que los adoquines de las calles o el polvo de los caminos.* Y cuando paso por las librerías y veo tanto papel impreso doblado y cosido, y por las calles tal lluvia de periódicos un día y otro, me da pena de los pobrecitos que se queman las cejas escribiendo cosas tan inútiles, y más pena todavía de la engañada humanidad que diariamente se impone la obligación de leerlas. (44; el énfasis es nuestro)

La ocurrencia del sacerdote, que da tanto que reír a los dos interviuadores, ya que termina abogando por la conversión en estiércol de todo el contenido de las bibliotecas, encierra una gran ironía, que sólo se puede apreciar de una manera retrospectiva, puesto que los episodios que constituyen el meollo de esta novela tienen como marco físico los adoquines de las calles de Madrid y el polvo de los caminos de Castilla la Nueva. Es más, debido a este relato impreso, se eterniza la figura del cura y se valora a más no poder el mérito de su aventura evangélica, no del todo previsible al principio, ni definitivamente calificable al final, pero apreciable, bajo cualquier concepto.

Agnes Moncy Gullón ha dicho de *Nazarín* que es 'una novela polifónica, distinta de la característica novela homofónica de Galdós, y por ser polifónica, está hecha de contradicciones' (221). Sí que lo está, digo yo, pero de contradicciones que no son contraproducentes sino que, al contrario, obligan a los lectores a reconciliarlas, aceptándolas a la vez, sin discriminación, como que se complementan la una a la otra, fundiéndose —para adaptar la frase unamuniana— en 'una feliz incertidumbre'. Por esto, a la 'firmeza inquebrantable de convicciones' de que hace tanta gala Nazarín en su filípica contra la

Imprenta, se le ha de contrapesar la perplejidad total que experimenta en la página final de la novela cuando, sumido en un gran
delirio, cree oír la voz de Jesús. Para Jo Labanyi, en *Nazarín* Galdós
prolonga los límites del realismo, al intentar representar lo que es,
por definición, irrepresentable (xvii). Mas, es precisamente a fuerza
de la palabra impresa de la novela, tan despreciada por Nazarín, que
Galdós realiza lo imposible: recrear en toda su complejidad el mundo
que recorre Nazarín y a la vez hacerlo comprensible, en medidas
respectivamente diversas, para los lectores. De ser Nazarín el único
personaje, la novela no sería tan complicada. Pero, a fuerza de
presentar a tantos personajes secundarios y comparsas en una red,
no de relaciones, como en la novela naturalista galdosiana, sino
de 'encuentros', directos o indirectos, lejanos o cercanos, con el
protagonista, Galdós consigue dotarles de una significación que
rebasa con creces su mera presencia textual. Constituyen ellos los
ángulos (comparables a los del techo de la casa de *Chanfaina*) desde
los que es necesario enfocar a Nazarín. Cada uno aporta su rayito de
luz enigmática al gran conjunto de perplejidades que es la novela
socio-religiosa *Nazarín*.

Volviendo al párrafo del *episodio nacional, O'Donnell*, que sirve de
prólogo a este estudio, tal vez no sería un despropósito sugerir en
último término que el nombre *Nazarín* al frente de nuestro libro
significa, además del ambiente espiritualista del final del siglo XIX
español, un mundo entero de personajes de segundo y tercer orden
que son influidos por, a la vez que influyen al protagonista epónimo,
pero todo de una manera difícil de evaluar definitivamente.

Bibliografía
ALAS, Leopoldo, *Galdós* (Madrid: Renacimiento, 1912).
ARENCIBIA, Yolanda, 'Tanteos de estilo. *Nazarín* de Pérez Galdós' *Anales
    Galdosianos* 27–28 (1992–3) págs 145–56.
BLY, Peter, *Pérez Galdós: Nazarín* (London: Grant and Cutler/Tamesis Books, 1991).
CLARKE, Anthony H., 'Ándara, Ujo and a Handful of "amazonas", "peludos" and
    Outcasts: A Footnote to *Nazarín*' *Anales Galdosianos* 26 (1991) p gs 83–8.
GONZÁLEZ AURIOLES, Norberto, '*Nazarín*, novela por D. Benito Pérez Galdós' *El
    Correo* 5,571 (25 de julio de 1895).
GULLÓN, Agnes, 'Escenario, personaje y espacio en *Nazarín*' en *Actas del Segundo
    Congreso Internacional de Estudios Galdosianos* (Las Palmas: Excmo Cabildo
    Insular de Gran Canaria, 1980).
LABANYI, Jo, ed. *Benito Pérez Galdós: Nazarín* (Oxford: Oxford University Press,
    1993).

PÉREZ GALDÓS, Benito, *Nazarín* (Madrid: Alianza, 1984).

—, *O'Donnell*, en *Obras completas*, ed. F.C. Sáinz de Robles, tomo 4 (Madrid: Aguilar, 1968).

ROMERO TOBAR, Leonardo, 'Del "Nazarenito" a *Nazarín*' en *Actas del Quinto Congreso Internacional de Estudios Galdosianos* (1992) [sic] (Las Palmas: Ediciones del Cabildo Insular de Gran Canaria, 1995).

SMITH, Alan E., 'Una posible fuente panfletaria de *Nazarín*: "Evangelio de don Juan; el moderno precursor en la segunda y anunciada venida del mesías"' *Anales Galdosianos* 26 (1991) págs 51–6.

UREY, Diane F., *Galdós and the Irony of Language* (Cambridge: Cambridge University Press, 1982).

11

The 'History' of José María Fajardo in the Fourth Series of Galdós's *Episodios Nacionales*

Eamonn Rodgers

The problem of how to cast a history of Spain in an appropriate narrative form was an issue with which Galdós had to grapple continually as he attempted to construct his own semi-fictionalized account in the *Episodios nacionales*. As Geoffrey Ribbans has pointed out, Galdós experienced recurrent dissatisfaction with the balance between historical content and narrative form, a dissatisfaction which had become acute by the fourth series, written between 1902 and 1907.[1]

The solution adopted in the early volumes of the fourth series is adumbrated in *Bodas reales* (the last volume of the third series). Towards the end of Chapter 3, the anonymous third-person narrator describes certain kinds of historical account of the recent past of Spain as a 'tejido de vanidades ordinarias'.[2] Not only is the narrative of history couched in conventionally rhetorical terms, but the actual behaviour and thinking of individuals is externalized according to patterns derived from literary stereotypes. Thus, the life of the politician Joaquín María López is described as a *novela*, and, from the terms in which Galdós describes it, a bad romantic one at that:

> Mil veces más que la historia de don Joaquín María López vale su novela, no la que escribió ... sino la suya propia, la que formaron los desórdenes, las debilidades y sufrimientos de su vida, y que remató una muerte por demás dolorosa. Vivió su alma soñadora en continuos aleteos tras un ideal a que jamás llegaba ... (II, 1323)

The debate on the Olózaga affair is described in terms of 'la semejanza de tal función con las de un drama o comedia' (II, 1330), the ill-fated love-affair between Eufrasia Carrasco and Terry develops against a background of theatre-going (II, 1349), and the young revolutionary officer Solís is described as a poet, 'no porque hiciera versos, sino porque veía la política y las revoluciones en artística y sentimental forma' (II, 1376).[3]

This tendency of characters to see reality in terms of literary stereotypes is developed in more depth in three of the first four volumes of the fourth series, *Las tormentas del 48* (1902), *Narváez* (1902), and *La revolución de julio* (1904), which mark a clear progression in Galdós's search for an appropriate blend of fiction and history. By making the act of narration itself constitute a piece of historically-representative behaviour, Galdós achieved a closer fusion of both these elements than he had attempted before. Though each of these novels is, like all the *Episodios*, a self-contained unit, their effects can only fully be appreciated if they are considered as a series of interlinked narratives. The fact that so many of the *Episodios* end with various issues left unresolved suggests that Galdós intended them to be read in this way. Besides, his bid for commercial success in the third and subsequent series presupposed the continuing loyalty of a reading public interested in seeing particular storylines continued. It is therefore meaningful to see a specially close link among three novels which share the same fictional narrator.

Las tormentas del 48 opens with José García Fajardo recording the fact that he has decided to begin writing his *Memorias*. Immediately, the narrative tone is established, and we learn a great deal about Fajardo's character. The tone is flippant, mock-portentous, and disingenuously self-deprecating:

> Antes de que mi voluntad desmaye, que harto sé cuán fácilmente baja de la clara firmeza a la vaguedad perezosa, agarro el primer pedazo de papel que a mano encuentro, tiro de pluma y escribo: 'Hoy, 13 de octubre de 1847, tomo tierra en esta playa de Vinaroz, orilla del Mediterráneo, después de una angustiosa y larga travesía en la urca *Pepeta*, ¡mala peste para Neptuno y Eolo!, desde el puerto de Ostia, en los Estados del Papa ...'
>
> Y al son burlesco de los gavilanes que rasguean sobre el papel, me río de mi pueril vanidad. ¿Vivirán estos apuntes más que la mano que

los escribe? Por sí o por no ... he de poner cuidado ... en alumbrarme
y guiarme con la luz de la verdad y en dar amenidad gustosa y picante
a lo que refiera; que sin un buen condimento son estos manjares tan
indigestos como desabridos. (II, 1413)

Here and in similar passages where Fajardo comments explicitly on
the act of composition, the picture which emerges is of a character
who is easy-going, somewhat cynical, and self-indulgent. His claim to
sincerity is based on his assertion that his memoirs, which he also
refers to as *Confesiones*, will not be read by anyone else in his
lifetime, but his frequent references to *la Posteridad* betray the
vainglorious assumption that his deeds will be of interest to future
generations: he declares himself 'resuelto a perpetuar la verdad de mi
vida para enseñanza y escarmiento de los venideros' (II, 1415).
Besides, his memoirs are not the only product of his writing activity,
for while in Rome, he and an equally wayward fellow-student compose
essays on the topical subject of the unification of Italy:

Y escribíamos sobre el mismo tema político sendas parrafadas
ampulosas, que nos leíamos *ore alterno* buscando el aplauso, y éste
fácilmente coronaba nuestras lucubraciones. (II, 1424)

Fajardo's ready pen is matched by considerable oral facility, of which
he makes ample use in the *tertulias* of his home town, Sigüenza, after
his return from Italy. Though he encounters a sceptical response
from the ex-Carlist parish priest, the other members of the gathering
listen with rapt attention to his 'fácil palabra' (II, 1431) as he
describes the opulence of the Papal court, the monuments of ancient
Rome, and outlines his view of the potential of the Papacy for
exercising leadership of a new democratic and liberal Italy (a theory
which he has culled at second hand from his reading of Gioberti's
Primato degli italiani). It would be a mistake to see this merely as
Galdós using Fajardo as the vehicle for the inclusion of authentic
historical events,[4] for, although he undoubtedly does this, such
episodes have the wider effect of raising a question-mark over
Fajardo's character, and his reliability as a witness. Only in the
previous chapter, he had recorded how he personally experienced the
full weight of the tyranny of the Church at the hands of Cardinal
Antonelli, who forcibly separated him from his peasant lover,

Barberina, and had him expelled from Italy under police escort (II, 1428). Whether wilfully or otherwise, he appears blind to the contrast between this treatment and the hope that the Papacy will espouse the liberal cause (an irony of which Galdós's readers would have been well aware in the light of subsequent events), and simply basks in his momentary status as an oracle.

This episode is a typical example of how Fajardo tends to drift with the tide, accommodating himself to the role and persona that others suggest for him. He makes no attempt to correct his mother's idealized picture of him as a paragon both of moral virtue and learning (II, 1432–3), and he allows himself to be absorbed into the network of patronage inhabited by his brothers Gregorio and Agustín and his sister Sor Catalina, whose manipulative power among the monied classes parallels the political influence exercised historically by Sor Patrocinio. Fajardo's tendency to allow circumstances to dictate his actions is, significantly, illustrated by his attitude towards his writing activity. When he discovers after his move to Madrid that the manuscript of the first part of his memoirs (containing all that he wrote up to that point) is missing, he is dismayed at the thought that 'aquellas hojas en que vertí la verdad de mis sentimientos y los secretos más graves' (II, 1434) might be read by someone else. This setback dampens his enthusiasm for writing, though ironically it coincides with his appointment to a job in the official *Gaceta* (thanks to Agustín) which, in theory, should enable him to exercise his pen in the service of the country. In reality, however, no one in the office does any work: his colleagues spend their time writing plays or poetry, and he himself is exempted from duty because he is wrongly supposed to be researching a major scholarly work (*ibid.*). There is an even more profound irony in the fact that, as he later discovers, the manuscript of his memoirs has, in fact, been read by his sister Sor Catalina, and by others of her traditionalist circle, such as Eufrasia, with consequences which, as we shall see, draw Fajardo even more deeply into the world of corruption and patronage, a process which he makes little or no effort to resist.

The doubts that Galdós strives to raise in the reader's mind about Fajardo's character do not, however, mean that he is systematically unreliable about everything. He is a shrewd and accurate observer of the general climate of Madrid society in the late 1840s, particularly with regard to the efforts of the middle classes to keep up appearances, which cause them to live beyond their means. Nor is he devoid of a moral sense: he is appalled to discover that his brother Gregorio, with whom he lives after his move to Madrid, is a moneylender, and though he correctly ascribes the existence of usury to 'la holganza y la vanidad' of the aristocracy and the upper bourgeoisie, he is also aware of 'la negra y pavorosa mina' and 'la región de dolor y tinieblas' which support Gregorio's comfortable lifestyle (II, 1438).

Fajardo's reliability, however, is predominantly the reliability of someone who has a keen sense of the corruption of society at large, but fails either to realize clearly how much he is implicated in it, or to find the courage to distance himself from it.[5] Once again, his role as a writer plays an important part in the development of this theme, which is illustrated in one of the most revealing episodes in the entire novel. A mere seven weeks after obtaining the job in the *Gaceta*, he is assigned low-grade, repetitive work which he considers incompatible with 'mi grande erudición' (II, 1449). In a fit of exasperation he insults his immediate superior, Cuadrado, as a result of which he expects to be dismissed. But it is Cuadrado who loses his job, through the intrigue of Sor Catalina, and because of the illusory prestige attaching to Fajardo through the phantom *Historia del Papado* he is believed to be composing (II, 1452). Though Fajardo promises to help Cuadrado and his family, the episode has a long-term consequence which he is unable to prevent. In desperation at his dire financial straits, Cuadrado takes a marginal part in a political conspiracy, for which he is arrested and transported to the Philippines, a fact reported by his distraught wife, who appears at Fajardo's house one morning surrounded by 'un enjambre de chiquillos de diferente edad, rotos y sucios, mocosos y famélicos' (II, 1514–15). Fajardo's reaction to this is equivocal. On the one hand, he is moved by their suffering, and offers to help, appealing unsuccessfully to the Interior Ministry to revoke the transportation order. On the other, his feelings of guilt are quickly suppressed as he abruptly terminates the narration of this episode by turning his attention to the letter from his mother with which the novel ends, in which she expresses her joy at the news that he is to marry María Ignacia Emparán.

Mention of Fajardo's marriage returns us to a different sector of the circle of corruption, in which, once again, his sister Sor Catalina is deeply involved, and which embraces a dense cluster of financial and political interests. Here, too, a link is provided by Fajardo's literary activities, for the idea of marriage is first suggested to him by Catalina after she secretly reads the missing manuscript narrative of his youthful dalliance in Italy, which has come into her possession, and which she has shown to several members of her traditionalist circle, including Eufrasia. What Fajardo had tried to present to the reader as a private record of his secret thoughts and actions, to be read only by *La Posteridad*, has not only come into the public domain, but has itself become part of a larger story in which he is, for the most part, an unwitting protagonist. For Catalina's motives go far beyond the desire to steer him into the path of moral virtue. His future father-in-law, Feliciano de Emparán, is a right-wing clericalist with a chronically uneasy conscience, for his wealth has been amassed as a result of buying up disentailed Church property. Catalina encourages Don Feliciano to quieten his scruples by paying a substantial sum into the coffers of her convent, La Latina, and accepting as son-in-law a person designated by her (II, 1509). The added advantage for him is that he marries off a daughter who is physically unattractive and has the reputation of being stupid.[6]

Fajardo only comes gradually to realize the existence of this dense network of intrigue, as he strives to make sense of various items of information. This is arguably the only time when he acts like a true historian, as he tries to arrive at an overall understanding by connecting random pieces of evidence. For most of the time, he presents himself to the reader as an omniscient and reliable chronicler, who is already in possession of the complete picture, even to the extent of claiming that he can give an authoritative account of the Queen Mother's words to her daughter after the fall of the *Ministerio relámpago*, a conversion at which he was not present (II, 1626). In other words, he writes more like a novelist than a historian. His initial reaction to Catalina's advice that he should take a wife is not only a characteristic piece of wishful thinking, but also displays his tendency to see reality in terms of romantic literary models. He immediately supposes that Catalina might be intending to marry the mysterious woman whom he met at a masked ball shortly after arriving in Madrid (who turns out to be Eufrasia Carrasco, now married to Saturnino Socobio, a member of the same traditionalist circle as Emparán), and with whom he is by now infatuated.

The speed with which Fajardo falls in love with the masked woman is only one instance of his susceptibility to female charms, shown by his affair in Italy with Barberina, his flirting with Serafín Socobio's two daughters, Virginia and Valeria, and his affair with a working-class married woman, Antoñita *la cordonera*. This part of Fajardo's personal history hardly augurs well for a life of marital fidelity, but it also has wider moral and political implications. Though his failure to overcome the social gulf between himself and Antoñita is inevitable, given the prevailing attitudes of society, it nevertheless casts an ironic light on the revolutionary disturbances which coincide fortuitously with her death and funeral. As Fajardo watches over her corpse, he falls asleep and dreams that she is lying in state in a kind of sumptuous pagan temple. His mind typically interprets the dream in aesthetic terms:

¿Será esto ... el tipo de un arte que, andando los siglos, vendrá potente a derrocar los tipos y módulos que hoy componen nuestra arquitectura y nuestras artes decorativas? (II, 1494)

As well as characterizing himself once more as a literary dilettante, Fajardo unconsciously points to the possible future vindications of victims like Antonia, which can only be brought about through the overturning of existing conventions and institutions, as will later be achieved by Virginia and Leoncio (*La revolución de julio*). For in the dream, Antonia's funeral takes on the character of a triumph, with acclamations and military salutes which merge into the sound of gunfire in the street outside as Fajardo slowly comes awake. The real, historical revolution of 1848, of course, produces no such radical change as far as Spain is concerned, but fizzles out in a 'fiesta de pólvora' (II, 1496). Far from bringing about the vindication of people like Antonia, this revolution involves her being exploited even in death, together with her uncouth husband Sotero, when the fugitive Nicolás Rivero, while uttering predictable rhetoric about the 'pueblo crucificado', seizes the opportunity to escape from the police by taking Sotero's place in the cortège (II, 1496).

Fajardo's reluctance to end his affair with Antonia illustrates a lack of will-power which parallels the way in which he allows himself to be swayed by his sister and Eufrasia. This, too, has political implications, for he is soon persuaded to abandon, or at least conceal, his views, which, though ill-formed and inconsistent, still include certain progressive elements, such as his belief in Pius IX's willingness (short-lived, as history would soon reveal) to reach an accommodation with liberalism. When he begins to be invited to Saturnino Socobio's house, his hostess, Eufrasia, prevails upon him to modify his opinions: 'Siempre que se trate de griegos o romanos, llámelos *gentiles* o *idólatras* ... y póngalos que no haya por donde cogerlos' (II, 1456). And she is particularly concerned to ensure that he does not raise issues that are even more likely to touch on raw nerves: 'Por las llagas de Cristo, no hable usted mal de los que antes abominaron de la desamortización y ahora compran los bienes raíces que fueron de frailes y monjas' (*ibid.*), a description which would apply not only to Feliciano Emparán, but also to the two Socobios, her husband and brother-in-law.

Nevertheless, Fajardo is not wholly without some capacity for independent decision, and for a substantial period of time he resists the attempts of Catalina, aided and abetted by Eufrasia, to marry him off to María Ignacia Emparán, whom he finds lacking in sexual attractions of any kind, a disadvantage which is not compensated for by her undoubted wealth:

> Se casa uno con una mujer, a la cual no estorban sus talegas si está de buenas y bellas cualidades adornada; pero no se casa nadie con un capital personificado en una criatura que carece hasta de los atractivos más elementales. Esto sería venderse, no casarse ... (II, 1480)

These honourable sentiments, however, crumble under the impact of two events which combine to effect a radical change in Fajardo's attitude. In the first place, he is faced with a financial crisis to which the most immediate and convenient solution is marriage to María Ignacia: '... lo primero que en la profundidad vi fue la pingüe fortuna de don Feliciano de Emparán, que por una combinación social de las más sencillas vendría pronto a mis manos pecadoras' (IL, 1508). Simultaneously, his relationship with Eufrasia moves onto a new plane of intimacy when she begins to address him as *tú* (*ibid.*). Though Galdós does not spell out at this stage the probable consequences of this increased closeness, it is clearly implied that at least Eufrasia, and possibly Fajardo as well, are not disposed to regard marriage to María Ignacia as an obstacle to the further deepening of their relationship, as, indeed, events will later prove:

> Retiréme sin comprender bien la intrincada psicología de aquella mujer, mas con la esperanza de entenderla y desentrañarla pronto,

algún día ... Desde la sala próxima, volviéndome para mirarla, vi que en mí clavaba sus negros ojos, y en ellos se me reveló su soberano talento, su apasionada corazón ... y su profunda inmoralidad.
Eran sus ojos el signo de los tiempos. (II, 1514)

The change in his financial prospects not only modifies Fajardo's adverse view of María Ignacia's attractions ('en estos días no me ha parecido mi novia tan desgraciada de figura como la describí en otra ocasión' [II, 1512]), but changes his political views as well. The passage is worth quoting at some length, to illustrate the subtle graduations whereby Fajardo arrives at a position which contrasts markedly with the one he held immediately before:

¿Qué organismo social es éste, fundado en la desigualdad y en la injusticia, que ciegamente reparte de tan absurdo modo los bienes de la tierra? Retumba en mi mente, al pensar en esto, el fragor de las tempestades que pavorosas estallan en toda Europa. Mis conocimientos de las teorías o utopías socialistas reviven en mí, y reconozco y declaro la usurpación que efectúo casándome con Mariquita Ignacia ...

Comprendo el terror que causan estas ideas en la sociedad en que vivo ... Me pone carne de gallina la idea de que una súbita y despiadada revolución venga a despojarme de todo esto que será mío ... A más de poseer bienes raíces y valores públicos, tendré coches, caballos de silla (no me contento con menos de tres), casas de campo, cotos para mis cacerías ...

... La tormenta que venga por Europa ... ha de ser, andando el tiempo, furioso torbellino que arrase el vano edificio de nuestra propiedad, sin que contra él nos valgan falanges ni falansterios ... ¿Tardará meses, años, lustros; tardará siglos? ... Que a mí no me coja es lo que deseo, y que cuando estalle, ya estén leídas y dadas al olvido mis deslavazadas *Confesiones* ... ¡Yo, que quizás habría sido revolucionario, y que sentí en mi alma vagos estímulos de rebeldía y protesta, ahora me coloco entre las víctimas de la revolución, y ya no seré pueblo justiciero, sino aristocracia justiciada, como enemigo del pobre y ladrón de propiedad! (II, 1510–11)

Undoubtedly, there is a degree of wry self-knowledge in this, but this simply confirms what we know already about Fajardo's tendency to swim with the tide, and let circumstances determine his conduct: the whole passage is an apologia for acceptance of the status quo. Nor does this remain purely at the level of rational reflection, for it issues in concrete action a few paragraphs later, when Fajardo begins to dispense largesse to his relatives in the shape of promised titles of nobility (II, 1513).

To say, therefore, that Galdós has dramatized in fictional form the events of the years 1847–8 in Spain, by causing them to be narrated by a fictitious participant, accounts only partly for the complex effects of these novels. Additionally, and more significantly, what he has done is to recreate the moral atmosphere of the period, and its political culture, by making the character of the narrator and his equivocal manner of writing history appear fully representative of his time. As has been well said by Diane Urey, 'The period of history to which these historical novels correspond ... is one of decadence, immorality, and spiritual anticlimax. So if the protagonists are to continue to characterize the spirit of the age ... they must represent "abulia", as Pepe Fajardo does ...'[7]

Las tormentas del 48, then, provides us with a perspective from which to judge Fajardo's version of events in *Narváez*. At first, he seems to have settled down happily to married life with María Ignacia, in whom he discovers unsuspected gifts of shrewd judgement: '... los chispazos de razón fueron bien pronto un luminoso rayo que todo lo encendía y alumbraba. Discurría sobre todo lo divino y lo humano con un sentido que era mi mayor gozo ...' (II, 1526). María Ignacia's capacity for discernment soon develops in a surprisingly radical direction, when she begins to chafe under the excessive religiosity of her family, and criticizes the superstitious character of much of what passes for spirituality in Spanish society as a whole. Her unorthodox views appeal to the strong element of scepticism in Fajardo's character, but his cautious reaction shows how far he has compromised with the reactionary culture in which his wealth and connections have immersed him:

> —...¿no te parece que sobre todas las estupideces humanas está la de adorar a esos santos de palo, más sacrílegos aún cuando los visten ridículamente? ...
>
> —Lo mismo pienso ... Pero nosotros ... hemos de disimularlo ... Seamos cautos, mujer mía, que nada cuesta decir a todo *Amén*, y vivir en santa paz con la familia. (II, 1557)

Despite his delight at what he sees as María Ignacia's rapid intellectual development, it is not long before Fajardo is committing to the pages of his memoirs the admission that 'el afecto que le doy débilmente corresponde ... al exaltado amor que ella tiene por mí' (II, 1553). The romantic susceptibility which he displayed in *Las tormentas del 48* soon causes his interest to wander. As with the story of his marriage, this new infatuation has implications for how the reader evaluates his historical account. In order to illustrate this, it is necessary to analyse the context in some detail.

During his honeymoon in Atienza, Fajardo makes the acquaintance of the semi-nomadic Ansúrez family, who enjoy a somewhat unenviable reputation for living on the fringes of the law. The patriarch of this clan, Jerónimo Ansúrez, presents himself in the character of an honest but proud man who is the victim of an unjust system, causing Fajardo to wonder whether 'teníamos que habérnoslas con un pillete de finísimo sentido y trastienda' (II, 1534). A contrasting view, however, is held by the eccentric antiquarian Buenaventura Miedes, for whom the Ansúrez family are pure representatives of the ancient Celtiberian race, 'esta soberana raza, la más bella, señor don José, la mejor construida en estéticas proporciones ... la que mejor personifica la dignidad humana, la indómita raza que no consiente yugo de tiranos ...' (II, 1532).

At first, Fajardo treats these absurd lucubrations with the amused scepticism they merit: he, after all, is a 'serious' historian, both in his own eyes and in the eyes of the deluded society which credits him with the non-existent *Historia del Papado*. In a matter of days, however, his view of Jerónimo has changed:

> ... hubo de parecerme aún más gallarda ... la figura del viejo Ansúrez, y su rostro más impregnado de exquisita nobleza ... Su afable sonrisa, su despejada frente, sus cabellos blancos, todo el conjunto de su vejez vigorosa me hacían el efecto de ver reproducidos en él los caballeros de remotas edades, que seguramente no irían mejor vestidos ni hablarían con más entonada y cortés gravedad. (II, 1540)

Fajardo's belief that Jerónimo cuts a handsome figure is shared by other characters, but his perception of him at this moment as the personification of the austere, independent, noble spirit of the ancient Castilian is later shown up in an ironic light when, in *Los duendes de la camarilla*, Jerónimo proves to be as affected as anyone by the prevailing *empleomanía*, accepting employment first as a doorkeeper in the Teatro Real, then as a spy for the hated police chief, Chico, and eventually depending for his subsistence on a loan from the priest Merino, the would-be assassin of the Queen. The more important implication of Fajardo's idealized view, however, is that it has less to do with Jerónimo as an individual than with his beautiful daughter, Lucila, with whom Fajardo has fallen hopelessly in love. The fact that this love remains unrequited means that he is free to idealize the figure of Lucila as the personification of the true spirit of the people, or History, or some similar abstraction, a process which is closely connected with his own professed role as the historian of his time. The first ten chapters of *Narváez*, which contain the narrative of his marriage and his stay in Atienza up to the time of writing, are composed after the death of Miedes, when the pretext of going through the antiquarian's papers gives Fajardo the leisure to write, which his family obligations have denied him. By that time, he has met Lucila, and his whole approach to his writing task is coloured by his infatuation, so that he persuades himself that he is composing 'la historia de mi vida en contacto con la vida y alma españolas' (II, 1550).[8]

It is in the light of this infatuation with Lucila that we must interpret some of Fajardo's more overtly political statements. At one level, his utterances can be taken as a reliable reflection of Galdós's view of Isabelline society, if only because they are echoed many times in both his fictional and his non-fictional writings:

> Todo lo que no sea pueblo no es más que una comparsería indecente, figuras de un carnaval, que a lo chocarrero llama elegante, y a las pesadas bromas da el nombre de cultura. Los días del vivir actual, esto que con tanto énfasis llamamos *nuestro siglo, nuestra época*, ¿qué es más que un lapso de tiempo alquilado para fiestas? El plazo de alquiler a su fin se aproxima, y en ese momento del quitar de caretas, volveremos todos a ser pueblo, o no seremos nada. (II, 1586)[9]

At a deeper level, however, the immediate context makes it clear that this is not the cool detachment of the impartial observer, but is inspired by an overwhelming sexual frustration. Shortly before he pens these lines, he has caught a tantalizing glimpse of Lucila in the street, but has failed to locate her after a frantic pursuit. His state of mind in the immediate aftermath is so turbulent that he begins to fear for his sanity: 'Pienso que he perdido la razón' (II, 1585). When he declares, 'me siento demagogo, me descubro anárquico' (*ibid.*), his sudden upsurge of radicalism is simply the effect of his agitation, and is an extension to the *pueblo* as a whole of his passion for Lucila. Though he says, 'Amo a Lucila porque amo al pueblo' (II, 1586), the chronological sequence of the narrative makes clear that his love for Lucila is the cause of his professed political enthusiasm rather than its effect. Apart from his earlier passing comments on the type of government represented by the major of Atienza, under whose rule the 'infeliz rebaño de hombres sencillos ... gimen en efectiva esclavitud' (II, 1539), there is very little evidence at this stage of sustained democratic sympathy in Fajardo, independently of his feeling for Lucila. On the contrary, his political views, as has been suggested above, evolve towards acceptance of a very conservative and authoritarian status quo as he acquires a comfortable position in the establishment: 'Vívame mil años mi *espadón de Loja*, y durmamos tranquilos los que juntamente somos usufructuarios y sostenedores del orden social' (II, 1556).

The picture Fajardo paints of Isabelline society as a *comparsería indecente*, then, describes the historical reality accurately enough as far as it goes, but it remains incomplete so long as the reader leaves out of the reckoning the fact that the narrator is himself a part, only half-consciously at best, of that reality. The effect of the fusion between fiction and history which Galdós has achieved here is that political developments, and the general intellectual and moral climate, are seen to be determined not only by the interplay of large social forces, but also in large measure by the emotional reactions and self-interest of individuals,[10] who, furthermore, are prone to rationalizing their own part in the prevailing carnival in the accounts they commit to the judgement of posterity. It is striking how often in these three *episodios* Fajardo depends for his 'evidence' on narratives woven by others, with varying levels of reliability. Thus, for example, Eufrasia takes issue with Fajardo's optimistic view of Narváez by providing her own account, 'con voz y autoridad de Historia para echar abajo esa mentira novelesca' (II, 1578), of an incident during the Carlist War, when Narváez supposedly executed an innocent civilian simply for being from the same village as Espartero, whom he allegedly envied for his military success and popularity. Eufrasia, however, admits that she was not an eye-witness of this incident, and relies on secondhand accounts and rumours. More significantly, before she begins her narrative, it is revealed that her own objectivity is suspect, as she is furious with Narváez for a remark he is reported to have made, but for which the only foundation is, once again, rumour and gossip (II, 1577–8).

What Narváez is alleged to have said is in turn part of the dense interplay of fiction and truth which is the main constituent of these novels. Eufrasia's husband, Saturnino Socobio, is interested in acquiring a title of nobility, and Narváez reportedly proposes that he be styled *marqués de Capricornio*, suggesting that he is being cuckolded (II, 1577). As the result of an earlier interview with Narváez, Fajardo is aware that, independently of whether this anecdote is true or not, the general believes him to be Eufrasia's lover, something which to his chagrin he knows is not the case (II, 1567)—at least not yet. While continuing to enjoy the proximity of temptation, Fajardo tries to convince both himself and his readers that his duty to María Ignacia will prevent him succumbing:

> Si contemplando a Eufrasia y oyendo su gracioso divagar de política pude repetir para mis adentros el verso de Leopardi *E il naufragar m'è dolce in questo mare*, caminito de mi casa, y acercándome a este refugio bien templado, me dije: 'En ese mar bonito y placentero podré pasearme sin que nadie me vea; pero nunca naufragaré'. (II, 1581)

Eufrasia, for her part, is not restrained by any such feelings of duty, but merely by the desire not to undo her strenuous efforts to regain her social standing, seriously damaged by her elopement with Terry six years before (*Bodas reales*). When it becomes clear that society at large shares Narváez's belief about her relationship with Fajardo, she decides to prove the hitherto false rumours true, receiving willing co-operation from a Fajardo still recovering from the shock of his sighting of Lucila:

> ... el Acaso me deparaba quizás un grande alivio de mis murrias; deparábame asimismo el gusto de dar la razón al penseque mundano, y de convertir el cronicón apócrifo en historia verídica, espejo de la vida real. Me molestaba la mentira, ¡y era tan fácil trocarla en verdad! (II, 1587)

There could hardly be a more ironic reflection on Fajardo's pretensions as a reliable historian than this conscious assimilation of his conduct to those false standards of society that he has earlier professed to condemn. A striking, as well as amusing example of the same process occurs in *La revolución de julio*, where he is mistakenly taken by an over-excited crowd in Torrejón for an agent of the revolutionary movement begun by O'Donnell, and, after a token attempt to correct the error, allows himself to be carried along on the wave of popular emotion (III, 67–8). Yet here there is an important difference. The tone of self-justification found in the two earlier novels is much less to the fore: instead, he shows a greater awareness of the farcical nature of the event, and ascribes his own part in it to the infectious nature of communal enthusiasm:

> Arrastrado por aquel vértigo y metido en él, llegué a creerme que soy, en efecto, la cabeza civil de la revolución ... Ni recuerdo bien lo que dije, ni hago por traer aquellos disparates desde las neblinas de mi memoria a la claridad de estas páginas. (III, 68)

Fajardo's character and opinions have, in fact, evolved significantly in the six years since the events recorded in *Narváez*. Two crucial experiences have contributed to this evolution. The first consists in his witnessing the ritual degradation of the priest Martín Merino after his attempt on the Queen's life. Prior to his execution by garrotting, Merino is ceremonially stripped of his priesthood in a harrowing scene in which he is made to vest as if for Mass, after which the vessels are snatched from his hands, and each of the vestments is removed to the accompaniment of a solemn anathema in Latin. The scene has a profound effect on Fajardo, and causes him to question seriously, for perhaps the first time since his social promotion in *Las tormentas del 48* and *Narváez*, the whole basis on which the Isabelline regime rests:

> Llegué a mi casa con dolor de cabeza, desconcertado de todo el cuerpo, amarga la boca y los espíritus muy caídos. El frío que cogí en la odiosa cárcel me molestaba menos que el recuerdo de lo que allí vi, la vileza y procederes bajunos del brazo secular, por una parte; por otra, el bárbaro formalismo del brazo eclesiástico. !Con tales brazos, valiente tronco social nos hemos echado! (III, 18)

The second experience appeals to Fajardo's romantic nature. Virginia Socobio (who is referred to in his novel predominantly by her nickname *Mita*), with whom he used to flirt innocently (or so he persuaded himself), marries a conventional and boring rich young man, but shortly afterwards elopes with her real love, Leoncio Ansúrez (whom she calls *Ley*). At first, Fajardo acquiesces in the censorious judgement of the rest of his social milieu, and even agrees to approach the police chief, Chico, with a view to tracing the fugitives. His perception is transformed, however, by the letters he receives from Virginia from their hiding-place in the countryside, which occupy a substantial part of the first half of the novel. The picture she paints of simple contentment, far from the corruption of the capital, is saved from sentimentality by the realism with which she describes their frugal and hard-working life, and her witty pun on the words *moral/morral*, which suggests the burdensome nature of conventional morality:

> Este vivir libre y sano no lo conoces tú, ni ninguno de los desgraciados que se pudren en ese presidio, condenados a pensar en el sastre, en la modista, en lo que traerá el cartero, en lo que dirá el periódico, en si cae el Gobierno ...
>
> Conque, mi buen Pepín, haz el favor de poner a un lado la moral, o *morral*, que gastáis vosotros para disimular tantos crímenes, y dejarnos aquí en paz ... (III, 37)

The same idea is given even more powerful expression in a later missive, which moves María Ignacia deeply, and finally convinces Fajardo that *Mita* and *Ley* have discovered a truth which is hidden from him and from most of society. After Leoncio has been near to death with a fever, Virginia, confident that he is on the way to recovery, leaves him briefly and goes out into the sunshine of a peaceful spring morning. Realizing it is Sunday, she walks on hoping to reach a church, but finds that the nearest village is still some distance away, and that she would have to leave Leoncio alone for too long. It suddenly occurs to her that there is a simple solution:

> ... tuve una inspiración, Pepe ... : tuve la idea de oír misa en el mismo cerro donde me hallaba. Me arrodillé, mirando al campanario, y, rodeado de sol y del viento, con tanto mundo de campiñas y montes delante de mis ojos, le dije al Señor y a la Virgen todo lo que se me

ocurría ... , que no fue poco ... , y cosas muy sentidas y de mucha religión se me vinieron al pensamiento, y del pensamiento a la boca, puedes creérmelo. (III, 43)

Even the sceptical Fajardo seems to recognize that there is a genuine spirituality here which contrasts markedly with the external and ritualistic view of religion held by conventional society, and makes nonsense of their stigmatization of Virginia and Leoncio as 'criminals'. Furthermore, he soon realizes that the letters constitute a narrative account of personal experience which, in its sincerity and lack of specious embellishment, is very different from his own, a realization which is no less genuine for being expressed in characteristically sententious language:

> —Algo de arte hay siempre en todo lo que se escribe [he tells María Ignacia], y los hechos, aun referidos en forma descarnada, se revisten de un extraño resplandor, más o menos vivo, según la sensibilidad de quien los refiere. En la carta de Virginia resplandece la narradora, que no carece de habilidad: adorna un poquito. Pero bien se ve que es cierto lo que nos cuenta, y en el sello de verdad está todo el interés y todo el encanto de lo que hemos leído. (III, 45)

In this changed frame of mind, Fajardo sets off in search of the fugitive couple, not now with the intention of returning Virginia to her 'duty' and delivering Leoncio up to justice, but with a view to helping them. On the way, he hears the news of O'Donnell's *pronunciamiento*, and once again displays his capacity to be swayed by circumstance when he turns aside from his mission to witness this 'página histórica': 'Mi alma necesita hoy, más que nunca, un poco de drama' (III, 65). Yet he is less under the influence of the passion which fired his facile revolutionary enthusiasms in *Narváez*, and retains sufficient detachment to be critical of O'Donnell's platitudinous rhetoric:

> Vulgar y breve fue su arenga, limitándose e las frases de ritual en la literatura de pronunciamientos ... 'Que él no daba aquel paso por vengar agravios personales, sino por sacar a la Patria de su envileci-miento ... , que para esto era menester el esfuerzo de todos sus hijos ...', y pitos y flautas ... (III, 66)

An even more ironic light is cast over the whole idea of revolution when, after the inconclusive battle of Vicálvaro, Fajardo meets up with the cynical libertine Bartolomé Gracián, who, unknown to him, is the former lover of Lucila Ansúrez, whom he abandoned for the inveterate intriguer Domiciana Paredes (*Los duendes de la camarilla*). Gracián's involvement in revolutionary conspiracies contrasts markedly with the genuine liberation achieved by the rebellion of Virginia and Leoncio. It is inspired by pure hedonism, and is devoid of any trace of political idealism: social upheaval offers a pretext for abandoning all moral restraint:

> Los amores ilegítimos desatan lazos, aflojan vínculos. La volubilidad y el capricho de la mujer extienden por toda la sociedad un cierto espíritu de rebeldía, que es el principal elemento de las alteraciones políticas. (III, 79)

This, together with the rather tawdry character of *Vicalvarada*, throws Fajardo into a mood of disillusionment both with politics and with his own efforts to record history as it happens: 'La página histórica tras la cual corrí, resúltame ahora como pliego de aleluyas o romance de ciego' (III, 82). The only way in which he can lift himself out of his depression is to think in aesthetic terms: his problem is accordingly identified as *ansia de belleza* (III, 83). When, however, the revolution reaches Madrid, the heady atmosphere of popular revolt only makes him aware of the unflattering contrast between the vigour and energy of the *pueblo* defending its freedom and his own effete and self-serving inertia. While he has been an observer and a self-styled chronicler of history, they have taken history into their own hands, and are in the process of shaping it:

> Ellos trabajan rudamente todo el año para vivir con estrechez, y yo vivo de riquezas que no he labrado y de rentas que no sé cómo han venido a mí. Y viviendo en la inactividad, amenizando mis ocios con el recreo de ver pasar hombres y cosas, ellos se lanzan a la hechura de los acontecimientos, a impulsar la vida general y a desenmohecer los ejes del carro de la Historia. (III, 108)

Inevitably, however, Fajardo, cut off by his education and social status from real participation in the concerns of the *pueblo*, can only articulate his inchoate enthusiasm in poetic images drawn from his dormant passion for Lucila, rekindled by the knowledge that she is now near at hand in Madrid: 'En los ojos de tu hermana', he tells Rodrigo Ansúrez, 'están todas las revoluciones' (III, 109). And he even goes so far as to express his emotional turmoil in the exaggerated language used by the antiquarian Miedes, which he had earlier decried:

> ... vosotros, los Ansúrez, sois celtíberos, la raza primaria. Tu padre es el perfecto tipo de la nobleza española, y tu hermana, el ideal símbolo de nuestra querida Patria ... (*ibid.*)

Fajardo's feeling of inferiority *vis-à-vis* the *pueblo* makes him strive after some heroic act to forward the struggle, and an opportunity presents itself when he foils an attempt by Gracián to abduct Lucila by shooting him dead. As so often in these novels, however, the reality is somewhat less exalted than the narrator's perception of it, for the 'heroic' quality of Fajardo's action is diminished by the fact that it is a bystander who incites him to kill Gracián, and hands him the pistol, which he fires in the tipsy, automaton-like state in which he had gone about all day, after a breakfast of *aguardiente* and *buñuelos*.

This incident provides an overall characterization of the revolutionary events recorded in this volume, and supplies the keynote which closes the novel, and ends both Fajardo's 'history' (his attempts to chronicle his epoch), and 'the history of Fajardo', (his autobiography). It is at this point that he probably reaches his peak of self-knowledge, and his greatest reliability as a narrator, for he has abandoned his pretensions both to achieve something notable as an individual, and to providing a definitive account for posterity. As Diane Urey rightly says, 'No one interpretation, inspiration, historical account, or verisimilar representation remains fixed in the text. Rather, there is a constant alternation among contradictory accounts.'[11]

It does not follow, however, that 'the terms history, truth, fiction, and lie' are interchangeable, or that 'neither seemingly historical nor the clearly imaginary version is more valid than the other'.[12] Fajardo's account ends, not on a note of relativistic scepticism, but with a ringing testimony to something of enduring worth, which has defied all his literary expectations as a historian, and his social assumptions as a member of the upper bourgeoisie, namely the love of Virginia and Leoncio. Though obscure and insignificant by the standards of those who write the official history of great events, their relationship stands for a freedom, honesty and loyalty which transcend the petty posturings and artificial restrictions of conventional society:

> Ved aquí el juicio y la fría opinión, una vez pasado el hervor revolucionario y entibiadas las pasiones que del corazón de los demás pasaban al mío: Todo es pequeño, en conjunto. Relativa grandeza o mediana talla veo en la obra del pueblo sacrificándose por renovar el ambiente político de los señoretes y cacicones que vivimos en alta esfera. Menguados son los políticos y no muy grandes los militares que han movido este zipizape. Pobre y casera es esta revolución, que no mudará más que los externos chirimbolos de la existencia, y sólo pondrá la mano en el figurón nacional, en el cartón de su rostro, en sus afeites y postizos, sin atreverse a tocar ni con un dedo la figura real que el maniquí representa y suple a los ojos de la ciega muchedumbre. De mezquina talla es asimismo mi hazaña, la rápida muerte que di a Gracián, en defensa de la paz obscura de una mujer ... , única paz que en lo humano existe ... Todo es pequeño, todo; sólo son grandes *Mita* y *Ley*. (III, 115)

12

La recepción de *Pequeñeces* del Padre Luis Coloma*

Jean-François Botrel

Una 'archicélebre' novela

El asombroso y sonado éxito en 1891 de la novela *Pequeñeces* del Padre Coloma S. J. requiere, por lo insólito de la 'algarada', 'algazara' o 'alharaca' que armó,[1] alguna explicación: novela 'ejemplar' en sus fines didácticos e ideológicos, también puede servir para una privilegiada observación *in vivo* de la recepción inmediata y de la génesis de un inesperado 'acontecimiento' así como del papel desempeñado por los intermediarios —los 'corrillos' y la prensa— en la creación de una corriente de opinión pública.

El estudio cronológico del éxito medido por el ritmo de venta/adquisición de los ejemplares y la duración y amplitud del ruido y de los ecos producidos suministra claves para la interpretación del fenómeno caracterizado en nuestra opinión por la irrupción en lo que se contemplaba oficialmente como debate interno a los sectores católicos y aristocráticos de actores y receptores (tal vez también de lectores) foráneos, con la consiguiente traición o subversión del propósito inicial: de ahí el 'escándalo'. En un contexto de agotamiento del modelo de la novela 'naturalista', incluso la de temática aristocrática (*La Montálvez, La espuma*) (Botrel, 1989).

Estudiemos, pues, a través de la recepción inmediata de la novela, la génesis del éxito, así como las interpretaciones a que dio lugar.

El éxito de *Pequeñeces*

Los estudiosos de la recepción no suelen disponer de tan abundantes datos o documentos como los a que dio lugar el proceso de comunicación organizado alrededor de *Pequeñeces:* anuncios, noticias, artículos originados por un verdadero 'ataque de hiperestesia crítica',[2] un 'Juicio público' abierto por *El Heraldo de Madrid* el 2 de abril de 1891, o sea: más de 1 'ecos' en total de marzo a mayo de 1891 a los cuales es preciso añadir los folletos, las cartas de y a Coloma, etc. El examen y explotación sistemática de todo este material suministra informaciones y formulaciones de gran provecho para este estudio.[3]

Vale recordar, desde el punto de vista meramente editorial, que la novela se publica primero de enero de 1890 a marzo de 1891, 'a retazos' como 'folletín 'de *El Mensajero del Corazón de Jesús,*[4] revista de los jesuitas, pues, y como tal de público muy *sui generis,* adscrito y reducido. De hecho, pocos ecos se encuentran hasta después de su publicación en dos tomos durante la primera quincena de febrero de 1891 coincidiendo con la última entrega de la revista.[5]

Los primeros ecos públicos y más o menos convencionales de su publicación en dos tomos se encuentran en la *Revista Contemporánea* (28–11), *El Movimiento Católico* (I–III), *La Ilustración Nacional* (6–III), *La Ilustración Española y Americana* (8–III) y *La Controversia* (9–III), hasta que en *Los Lunes de El Imparcial* (11–III) Mariano de Cavia ponga en solfeo la condición de 'padre'/'padrastro' del autor de ese 'sermón' y 'pasquín'. El 13–III, el también liberal *Correo* —sagastino—, con un titular de inusitados tipos, anuncia la publicación de *Pequeñeces,* reproduciendo a continuación el capítulo II.

A partir de entonces, durante cuatro semanas (hasta mediados de abril), la novela se vuelve noticia y tema de actualidad.[6]

El momento clave de la recepción se ha de situar en la primera quincena de marzo, cuando poco después de anunciarse, en dos semanas se agota la primera edición de 5,000 ejemplares.[7] El 30 de marzo alude el propio Coloma a la edición 'que a toda prisa se imprime en estos instantes', edición de 7,000 ejemplares. Se observa una especie de frenesí por parte de un público poco adicto habitualmente a tantas y tales lecturas que ahora 'devora', 'lee con avidez': una nueva edición de 8,000 ejemplares (la tercera) 'desapareció de las librerías —se habla de 'asalto'—, por arte de birbiloque como desaparecen butacas y palcos de un teatro en noche de interesante estreno'.[8] El número de ejemplares efectivamente vendidos de marzo a agosto habrá alcanzado los 20,000, o sea un ritmo mensual de venta de unos 3,300, lo cual es a todas luces excepcional en la España de la época: recuérdese que de *La puchera* había vendido

Pereda unos 4,000 ejemplares entre enero de 1888 y enero de 1889,[9] que de cada título de la primera serie de los *Episodios Nacionales* de Galdós se vendían entonces unos 1,200 ejemplares al año (Botrel, 1984–5), pero también que de *La Débâcle* de Zola se ponen 176,000 ejemplares en circulación entre mayo y diciembre de 1892... De ahí que Mariano de Cavia vea, con cierta ironía, en el Padre Coloma 'nuestro pantagruelesco Zola, nuestro Gargantua literario. Jamás han disfrutado de tan buen puesto ni de tan abundantes raciones en el festín editorial... Alarcones, Valeras, Peredas y Galdoses. El éxito ha sido considerable... y el reclamo también'.[10]

Desde la prensa, con la participación de más de 30 diarios o revistas, empiezan a 'llover' o 'granizar' artículos, sueltos, gacetillas, diatribas, agudezas, exclamaciones y dicharachos a propósito de *Pequeñeces* (son más de cien items entre el 13–III y el 18–IV), con silencio de las voces más autorizadas, exceptuando a E. Pardo Bazán quien publica su primer artículo el 4–V. Puede decirse con V. de la Cruz en *Más pequeñeces,* que 'la prensa ha secundado poderosamente el impulso dado al libro'.[11]

Después, al calor de 'la barahunda de la prensa' y del éxito, empieza a menudear la crítica libresca con la publicación de folletos, de iniciativa propia como el de Juan Valera,[12] o por encargo de los editores que presienten la oportunidad de un buen negocio como en el caso de Bobadilla o Martínez Barrionuevo.[13] Estos folletos alimentan, a su vez, el debate instaurado, dando lugar a sendas (y varias) reseñas en la prensa.[14] Hasta la Pardo Bazán 'madrina de *Pequeñeces*', según Martínez Barrionuevo,[15] se verá 'obligada a quebrantar (sus) propósitos de no publicar impresiones relativas al Padre Coloma hasta que se apaciguase el estrépito y algazara que movió su novela *Pequeñeces*...' dando a luz *Españoles ilustres. El P. Luis Coloma. Biografía y estudio crítico.*[16]

Toda esta expresión pública ha de interpretarse teniendo en cuenta lo más notable, que son las reacciones, comentarios y el animado debate en la esfera semi-pública o privada: si el 30–III el Padre Coloma se refiere al 'aluvión de cartas y periódicos que han invadido en estos días (su) soledad' será esto poco comparado con las conversaciones o sea el 'juego que ha dado' en Academias, Ateneos, Casinos, tertulias de los cafés, círculos literarios y sociales, círculos políticos y literarios, reuniones aristocráticas y mesocráticas, salones y boudoirs, despachos y estudios, en la plaza pública en los corrillos y hasta en las sacristías, por lo visto, todos lugares de la sociabilidad al uso, mencionados en la prensa.[17]

Se produce pues —fenómeno interesante— una interacción entre las dos esferas, la privada y la pública, la escrita y la oral: 'a medida del éxito van creciendo en exageración las opiniones contrarias acerca de su mérito literario', observa *El Imparcial* el 13–IV, quien destaca la 'zambra y bullicioso regodeo con que se comenta, tilda y aquilata el último libro del traído y llevado Padre Coloma 'con los inevitables rumores (sobre la inminente visita del Padre Coloma a Madrid, sobre sus nuevos proyectos de novelas: *Grandezas bizantinas, El diputadito),* y los desmentidos de tales 'grillas': según E. Pardo Bazán 'murmuraciones, dicterios, invectivas, reflexiones, protestas, risas, artículos en verso y en prosa, chanzonetas, cabildeos, caricaturas,[18] folletos y disquisiciones religiosas' se alimentan mutuamente, gracias al decisivo apoyo de *El Heraldo de Madrid* que toma la iniciativa de un debate 'nacional' que permita 'decir en voz alta lo que hoy se dice en voz baja': la novela se encomia o discute 'con pasión' ante una opinión 'hipnotizada',[19] con severas apreciaciones por parte de Castelar, Clarín o el P. Conrado Muiños de ese primer intento —interesado— de 'democratización' de la 'crítica'. En junio de 1891, según Emilia Pardo Bazán, no lleva traza de pasar la arroyada de artículos, diatribas y folletitos más o menos punzantes'.[20] Nada extraño, pues, que a fuerza de oir y leer juicios más o menos apasionados sobre *Pequeñeces* hayan llegado muchos a 'olvidarse de lo que en realidad dice el libro y a sustituirlo con lo que otros dicen que digo', se queja el Padre Coloma a E. Pardo Bazán en una carta de mayo.[21]

Por primera vez un libro, una novela ('de las que entran pocas en libra', según Fr. Candil), un autor, se han vuelto noticia 'nacional' en España, 'país en que se lee poquísimo, por desgracia nuestra' recuerda V. de la Cruz[22] y no se puede descartar que la voluntad de entrar de esta manera en el concierto de usos y costumbres foráneas extranjeras haya tenido alguna consecuencia sobre la participación de todos los medios a mantener el debate a cierto nivel de intensidad.

Si ahora se traduce en términos de audiencia, se ve, a todas luces, que el Padre Coloma 'ha conseguido variar de público y extender su esfera de propaganda':[23] el público habitual de Coloma (católico medianamente culto e 'inteligente' y 'timoratas siervas') y de la novela

realista (gente del oficio, 'círculo de personas más que medianamente educadas') tal vez se haya ampliado por primera vez a aquéllos
que según Castelar 'aprenden a leer para no coger nunca un libro',[24]
a los 'iliteratos' (Bobadilla), a los 'lectores superficiales'(Martínez
Barrionuevo), al 'vulgo' sobre el cual ha producido la novela un
'efecto mágico' (Clarín) y al tan famoso como misterioso 'gabinete'
de las señoras ya que se escribió la novela, 'para que la leyeran todas
y todas la leerán': lo afirma Martínez Barrionuevo.

Lo evidente es que que la audiencia de la novela ha rebasado con
mucho los que, sin ser 'popular' como equivocadamente lo afirma
algún contemporáneo, nada tiene que ver con los 20,000 lectores
'habituales' de Valera ni los 3 a 4,000 lectores-compradores de las
Novelas Españolas Contemporáneas de Galdós,[25] ya que pudieron ser
unos insólitos 70/100,000, lo cual es a la vez mucho y poco en
una España con 12.5 millones de analfabetos y 5 millones de
analfabetizados: *Pequeñeces* pudo pasar entonces por 'la novela más
leída' y después por 'una de las obras de mayor éxito de librería del
siglo XIX'.[26]

De todo esto da cuenta el debate abierto por *El Heraldo de Madrid*
que, después de publicar 46 cartas o juicios 'cortos' (algunos 'de
proporciones excesivas' no se podrán publicar) de lectores 'literatos y
aficionados', la mayor parte con seudónimos, afirma el 18–IV que
'podría llenar todavía muchas columnas con la inserción de los
trabajos que (ha) recibido' y hace el siguiente balance: 'el ensayo de
interesar a la opinión haciéndola tomar parte activa en todo lo que la
conmueve y la importa, ha dado un feliz resultado (...) Personas de
todas las clases sociales y de diversidad de opiniones y cultura nos
han escrito acerca del famoso libro, y en nuestra mesa se confundían
todos los días el papel satinado y elegante y la tosca cuartilla, la letra
clara y redonda del joven y la temblona del anciano, de estilo suelto
del acostumbrado a escribir para el público y el giro indeciso del que
no tiene costumbre de expresar por escrito su idea' además de
'señoras y sacerdotes'. De lo publicado, estima la redacción de *El
Heraldo de Madrid* que 'se puede deducir el juicio exacto que el país
se ha formado acerca del famoso libro'.

El impacto de tal éxito se puede observar en los títulos de novela,[27]
el teatro,[28] en las cajas de cerilla ('apogeo del aura popular'), en el
lenguaje corriente —'pequeñeces' es la palabra/expresión de moda y
sirve de título para numerosos artículos de prensa[29]—, y en el

extranjero, en la mismísima Francia poco adicta a traducir novelas españolas contemporáneas.[30]

Bueno es recordar para entender el asombro general ante el éxito de la novela que cuando el Padre Coloma publica *Pequeñeces* es un novelista casi desconocido : si algún periódico cree poder recordar que Manuel de la Revilla predijera el futuro éxito del Padre Coloma, los más habían de atenerse al diagnóstico de Luis Alfonso en *La Epoca:* 'por haberse no más impreso en periódicos de la Compañía o por haberse reunido en volúmenes que no se han puesto a la venta o se han puesto no más en determinadas librerías de ortodoxia irreprochable (sus producciones anteriores) han llegado a conocimiento de poquísimas personas'; hasta tienen los periódicos que recurrir a fuentes jerezanas para conseguir algunas noticias biográficas.[31] De ahí que aparezca aún más extraño el intenso y duradero revuelo a que da lugar: es un 'suceso bien extraño aquí donde solemos dar de lado con olímpico desdén, no vencidas las 48 horas, las producciones de nuestros primeros novelistas';[32] un 'fenómeno tan inexplicable y tan apartado de las vías y cauces aquí seguidos por lo general';[33] un 'caso prodigioso (ya que) acaso por primera vez, una novela española acaba de lograr, no sólo inusitada venta sino el privilegio de dar pasto a las conversaciones y contingente a la prensa diaria durante muchos días...';[34] '¿ Quién lo había de decir? La literatura ocupando, siquiera algunos días, puesto de honor entre los españoles'.[35] Si se buscan antecedentes ni la publicación de Fray Gerundio ni la de... *El escándalo* de Alarcón han dado lugar a algo comparable : Valera/Currita no recuerda... 'éxito tan extraordinario alcanzado por un libro español como el de Vd'.[36] La publicación de *Pequeñeces* se ha vuelto pues 'un acontecimiento que ha hecho salir de su habitual indiferencia a las gentes'.

Conviene ahora intentar explicar el fenómeno hasta ahora sólo descrito.

El éxito y el escándalo

Tradicionalmente, se atribuye el sonado éxito de *Pequeñeces* al escándalo a que dio lugar.[37] Pero el examen de las modalidades de inserción en el proceso de la comunicación social y sus consiguientes sucesivas recepciones por el/los público(s) desde distintos horizontes de espera —entre otros, ideológicos— o sea la génesis del éxito, permite matizar o completar tal interpretación.

El propósito del Padre Coloma al escribir su novela aparecía muy claramente —según él creía— en el prólogo al lector publicado el l° de enero de 1890: hacer, con conciencia del mal que 'en el mundo, en cierta clase del mundo sobre todo (...) suele desconocerse a si mismo', 'obra de defensa de la sociedad cuando la relajación es general', advirtiendo a una aristocracia pasiva o comprometida con la alta burguesía (la aristocracia del dinero) la necesidad de volver a si misma, a su esencia utilizando, con una instrumentalización bastante corriente en la Iglesía católica de entonces de la novela —su forma— como púlpito para poder alcanzar 'a los que sólo podrán tragar esa misma celestial doctrina envuelta en una salsa lícitamente profana'. Para Luis Alfonso, el Padre Coloma confirmará el 30–III este propósito comentándolo así como su puesta por obra con la idea de proponer una lectura conforme y en una carta a éste reafirma su 'recta, sana y exclusiva intención de defender a la sociedad': 'lo que allí se encierra, lejos de ser un ataque, es una verdadera defensa de la sociedad'[38] y años después Baroja podrá confirmar este propósito con su lectura al ver en la novela un 'libro de adulación'.[39]

El contexto político de la novela, con el intenso debate —no terminado— entre los carlistas integristas de Ramón Nocedal representados por *El Siglo Futuro* y los 'contemporizadores' —carlistas templados— y sobre todo los 'mestizos' o sea los católicos pidalinos favorables a la colaboración con Cánovas, puede confirmar, para la historia política, la verosimilitud de 'los puros y los contaminados' (Campomar, 1989).[40]

Ahora bién: la recepción —la interpretación— no corresponde a la intención: la novela se tiene por un libelo de un sacerdote/de la Compañía de Jesús contra la aristocracia.

Lo del sacerdote hay que situarlo en un contexto en el que el propio Padre Coloma tiene que prevenir las objecciones de los habituales lectores de *El Mensajero*... acostumbrados a advertencias acerca del género nefando y vitando,[41] al salir a un campo considerado por los habituales lectores de la novela como propio de los laicos y seglares (Botrel, 1982; Hibbs, 1997). De ahí, el que la calidad sacerdotal del novelista —jesuita, además— y lo novedoso de la situación —'la adaptación a nuestra literatura, a nuestro idioma y al criterio católico más ortodoxo del género realista' escribe *El Clamor* el 4–IV–1891[41]— hayan podido cobrar tanta importancia en la lectura de la novela.

De la recepción de la novela por los lectores de *El Mensajero*... no sabemos apenas nada: en la segunda quincena de febrero, más de un año depués del principio de la publicación, sólo conocen la obra 'las contadas personas a quienes el autor tuvo la bondad de adelantarla y los lectores de *El Mensajero* que se contentaban con susurrar bajito, algo alarmados, que era 'cosa muy notable' afirma E. Pardo Bazán en *La Ilustración Ibérica*, el 4–V–1891. Entre los 18,000 suscritores de esta revista que 'por acá nadie conoce' dice Clarín y 'que no leen los de la acera de enfrente' según fórmula de Pereda, figuran 'al lado de místicas abadesas señoras muy del mundo y junto a congregantes de San Luis, hombres despreocupados y hasta jóvenes alegres'.[42] Para estos que por lo visto ya habían ido reaccionando a la lectura de algunos detalles de la novela había tenido el novelista o la revista que puntualizar bajo forma de advertencias en febrero, junio y septiembre de 1890 (reproducidas en la edición en volumen) hasta enero de 1891 en que se precisa que 'yerran por completo los que han creído ver en algunos personajes de la presente novela retratos de individuos determinados...', lo cual sugiere una primera sospecha por el público 'natural' de la novela de posibles claves y, por consiguiente, de la asimilación de determinadas personas con personajes que son las 'figuras más salientes', pero 'muy escasas', la 'charca que abomin(a)' el moralista Coloma.

Pero el impacto de la intencionada novela sobre el debate interno no pasa de discreto; al menos no percibimos ecos mayores.

Tampoco se van a encontrar alusiones o referencias a la dimensión 'escandalosa' de la novela en las opiniones de la *Revista de España* (Vidart), el *Nuevo Teatro Crítico* (E. Pardo Bazán), la *Revista Contemporánea* que insisten más bien sobre la dimensión de novela aristocrática (mencionando a *La espuma* de Palacio Valdés), ni por supuesto en el elogioso artículo de Cesáreo del Castillo en *El Movimiento Católico* del 1–III.

El germen del alboroto está en la lectura por otro círculo de lectores de 'las figuras más salientes' y de los demás personajes que bullen en segundo término, que llegan a hacer olvidar a los 'numerosos hermosos modelos, y nobles caracteres oscurecidos por el propio peso de sus virtudes' dice Coloma: por tratarse de un público con otro horizonte de espera y de otra cultura literaria la referencia moral e ideológica no funciona correctamente pero sí la dimensión estética.

Como novela de costumbres aristocráticas donde un jesuita buen conocedor del medio fustiga con formidable látigo las malas costumbres de la vida elegante, 'excita la curiosidad de sus lectores y del público en general' como escribe *El Correo* —diario sagastino— el 13–III, al calificar a una novela cuyo 'criterio político es radicalmente contrario de las escuelas liberales de todos los órdenes'; y llega a vaticinar : 'La novela, o mucho nos equivocamos nosotros, o hará ruido en el gran mundo, y también entre la gente de letras'. Lo cierto es que ya desde el 14 se barajan públicamente posibles claves para los 'acertijos' a que pronto se reduce la novela (o casi). Pero si el 18 hace una semana que, en Madrid, no hay conversación posible fuera del libro del Padre Coloma —el 'libro de moda'—, los artículos en la prensa no han sido abundantes: los comentarios no pasan del microcosmos del gran mundo, de 'ecos de la sociedad' en los que se perciben 'las voces de los perpetuos adalides de la aristocracia al uso, acusando al Padre Coloma de seguir la rutina y de desconocer por completo la sociedad actual': de hecho en *La Época* 'defensor de las clases fustigadas por el Padre Coloma y que tiene tanto aristocrático lector' es donde el 21–III se encuentran oficialmente expresadas las reacciones de la 'aristocracia moderna' bajo la denominación de 'círculos literarios y sociales' con denuncia de la novela de un clérigo ex-calavera, de la tolerancia de la Compañía de Jesús, del crimen de lesa-sociedad y de la infamante picota, reproduciendo además, el 24, un suelto de *La Correspondencia de España* del 22 en que se da una interpretación política de la novela como intento 'carlista' de desestabilizar al régimen pactado, en una fase delicada de la Regencia, 'un ataque a la dinastía conjurando nada menos que el destino sobre la cabeza de un niño inocente' según palabras indignadas del propio Padre Coloma quien supone que los artículos de Luis Alfonso en *La Época* son artículos teleguiados por el Marqués de Valdeiglesias en nombre de Cánovas. Parece ser, pues, que, después de una fase informal de 'corrillos' observada por los sagastinos de *El Correo,* la reacción pública, a través de *La Época,* por parte de la fracción de la aristocracia aludida ante la formidable sátira 'de las que levantan ampollas' del sacerdote novelista y la confirmación por la voz pública de muchas claves para la interpretación de la novela desde la actualidad —Marqués de Molíns (cf. Hibbs, 1991), Felipe Ducazcal— dé lugar a un cambio de opinión y dé la señal de partida para un debate público de amplias dimensiones en las que las clases medias van a 'meter cuchara' (y periódico), con una especie de traición de las intenciones del novelista fijándose en algunos aspectos de la novela, con preocupaciones o segundas intenciones muy poco estéticas. Lo cierto es que después de poner, con mucha cautela, las cosas en su sitio en *La Epoca* del 30–III[43] el Padre Coloma, por decisión de la Compañía de Jesús, va a callarse, esperando en silencio que 'pase el chubasco'.[44] La aristocracia, *La Epoca* y demás, lejos de salir a su encuentro se contentaron 'con el papel de Cimodocea', según Martínez Barrionuevo, y bajo la amenaza del Primero de mayo obrero, se hacen más discretos, despolitizando el asunto. Ahora bien: cuando 'la escasa (prensa), digamos así, la alta que (le) había hecho la oposición comenzaba a calmarse y aun a volverse a favor (suyo)', empieza a desbordarse... la prensa liberal ('baja y francmasónica', según el Padre Coloma) que se apodera de la 'escandalosa' novela tomando el acontecimiento 'un giro canallesco'.[45]

El Liberal y La República, diarios poco favorables a la aristocracia en general, destacan en seguida tal hostilidad y sacan las consecuencias dando su propio parecer sobre esa arremetida desde la otra acera a lo que se denominará 'la alta sociedad', 'lo que llaman ahora *high life*', 'la alta goma', 'la buena sociedad', 'el gran mundo', 'las clases elevadas', 'las clases aristocráticas y pudientes', la aristocracia dorada color de billete de Banco —aristocracia 'de talega', según Pereda— reunión de cuantos han adquirido posición y riqueza en la industria, en el comercio, en la política o cultivando algún arte, oficio o ramo del saber, olvidándose por completo de la otra aristocracia, la 'azul', 'espejo fiel en que se han reflejado las virtudes de nuestro país y ejemplo constante a las clases inferiores de honradez y proceder correcto'.

La novela ha llamado la atención de toda especie de gentes, y aun del periodismo liberal, constata *El Siglo Futuro* el 30–III, y ha sido despertada la curiosidad, perceptible en las conversaciones de casinos y tertulias: de ahí el que se 'arrebaten' los 7,000 ejemplares de la nueva edición; como dice *El Resumen*: '¿Cómo (...) no han de devorar ansiosamente las clases inferiores este manjar tan fuerte, —grato lenitivo a las contagiosas tristezas del bien ajeno', impresión fortalecida por el temor por parte de las clases altas que esto fragilice las bases del régimen pero también de la sociedad. A esta dimensión, es preciso añadir las expresiones anticlericalistas y antijesuíticas a que dan lugar la ingratitud de la Compañía de Jesús cuyos vínculos con la aristocracia se recuerdan: 'el vulgo, dice Currita/Valera, sobre todo el liberalesco, arma acerca de los jesuitas un carmillo semejante al que arma usted acerca de los masones' y en los artículos de Martínez Barrionuevo, pero también en algún 'juicio' publicado por *El Heraldo de Madrid* se encuentran varias de esas 'virulentas impugnaciones'[46] provocadas por la calidad de Jesuita del Padre Coloma, la 'Casa Coloma y Cía'. Según Valera 'nadie se hubiera calentado la cabeza tratando de descubrir las tendencias y los fines si no hubiera pertenecido el autor a una asociación poderosa e influyente. Si *Pequeñeces* fuera la obra de un literato lego, todos acaso nos hubiéramos divertido leyéndola, pero nadie o casi nadie hubiera hablado ni escrito sobre lo *tendencioso e intencionado*, como se dice ahora, de la novela'. A través de lo publicado por la prensa liberal como *La República, La Librtad, El Liberal,* etc. se llega a un corpus de doctrina liberal y anticlerical que podría ser el siguiente: la aristocracia española no sirve para maldita de Dios la cosa y de ahí casi se llega a interrogaciones sobre el régimen de la Restauración; sin embargo no debiera un sacerdote atacarla de tan mala e ingrata manera, tratándose además de un Jesuita...

El hecho es que, en un tercer momento, el debate público, gracias al sensacionalista y más bien sagastino *Heraldo de Madrid* de Felipe Ducazcal, toma otro giro al permitir la intervención degente que no solía manifestar públicamente su opinión; lo hace en prosa y en verso, de manera a veces muy extensa: aun cuando el seudónimo puede encubrir plumas 'autorizadas' enrevesadas estrategias y no permite confirmar la calidad anunciada, no se puede dudar de la participación de lectores —incluso mujeres— de toda España y de distintas condiciones, no acostumbrados a escribir en los periódicos.[47]

No obstante, aun cuando se llega a comentar algún detalle de la novela y se convocan referencias a Zola, Galdós, Pereda y hasta Ubaldo Romero Quiñones, la lectura que resulta de los 'juicios' es más bien global, poco personal u original, con referencias a la opinión de los demás y sólo tiene en cuenta la dimensión ideológica y política del asunto sin apenas referencias al hecho de que de una novela se trata, votando en contra o en pro, con una mayoría de opiniones sobre la calidad sacerdotal del Padre Coloma ('novelista con manteos') y sus consecuencias y en contra de la Compañía de Jesús. Lo más notable, acaso sea que el juicio público permite un metadiscurso alimentado por los comentarios leídos en el *Mismo*

Heraldo (reacciones a los 'juicios' de F. Ducazcal o Nocedal, por ejemplo) o en otros periódicos (*'El Liberal* de ayer...'): la novela ha sido captada por un público al que no iba destinada, en un principio, y de ella sólo se tiene en cuenta la dimensión ideológica y política, con predominio de las censuras sobre los elogios, con el siguiente balance hecho por la redacción de *El Heraldo* el 18 de abril: 'un literato bueno, un sectario apasionado, un libro escandaloso y un acontecimiento que ha hecho salir de su habitual indiferencia a las gentes'.

Pero incluso para *El Heraldo de Madrid,* lo que llega a preocupar principalmente 'en estos momentos' es la cuestión obrera: 'el movimento socialista se acentúa; la figura del obrero se destaca y adquiere importancia'; de ahí que a los hijos de Loyola no les desagrade poder decirle: 'Olvida lo que dijo Eugenio Sue y acuérdate de lo que ha dicho el Padre Coloma'. Se llega a una especie de consenso entre conservadores y liberales temerosos de una posible expresión y emergencia de una tercera España. No tiene desperdicio, a este respecto, el comentario de M. Martínez Barrionuevo quien sospecha que al dar la espalda a un sol que ya consideran en su ocaso ' los maquiavélicos jesuitas se van aproximando a 'otro sol que no luce aún en Oriente, pero cuyos reflejos, sin dejarse ver, queman ya las retinas'. La coincidencia de la celebración por segunda vez de la 'huelga general' o fiesta socialista del Primero de Mayo, de la promulgación de *Rerum Novarum* o la creación de la Liga de contribuyentes del Ribagorza pudo inspirar otra interpretación de *Pequeñeces,* como máquina de guerra utilizada por la Iglesia 'para resistir en lo posible al naufragio tenebroso captándose el aprecio de los oprimidos de hoy, que podrían muy bien tarde o temprano imponer el yugo, aunque fuese de pasada, pero con tiempo suficiente, para tomar sabroso desquite'...[48]

Una obra cerrada...abierta

En el éxito de *Pequeñeces* habrán podido influir otros factores aquí apenas tenidos en cuenta como el modelo francés, la 'inverosímil baratura' del libro,[49] las cualidades literarias, el naturalismo, la tendencia antimadrileña (Madrid como Síbaris o Babilonia 'levantada a costa del resto de España' —visión compartida por el propio Padre Coloma—), la evocación de la misteriosa masonería, etc.

Lo interesante, pues, es 'lo que ha resultado a despecho del propósito':[50] la explicación está en 'la pluma de hierro' con que ha sido escrita la novela;[51] la cosa rechispea y ha de levantar ampollas en ciertas epidermis de allí arriba', pronosticaba Pereda.[52] Pero el peligro de la novela correccional es que 'con sus escollos aguza el público maleante' recuerda el clarividente Currita/Valera.

Los anteriores intentos de novelas satíricas contra la 'alta goma' habían podido despertar la consciente o inconsciente animosidad de la mayoría social, que es la clase media, contra la minoría de ciertos círculos llamados elegantes y de buen tono y *Pequeñeces*, a pesar de su propósito aparentemente unívoco, por sus calidades de novela y de escritura, pudo dar pie, a causa del o gracias al proceso descrito, a una expresión mágica de la frustración de unas clases marginadas de un poder confiscado que puede explicar otras adhesiones a formas de populismo antimadrileño y antiestablishment de origen católico e integrista.[53]

La cooperación interpretativa en esta obra aparentemente cerrada, según los criterios de U. Eco, por las preocupaciones latentes y por la conjunción 'astral' de factores que no volverán a ser reunidos, ha podido convertir momentáneamente y por primera vez en España, a una novela en noticia y pretexto para un casi debate 'nacional', más democrático en cualquier caso, en el que acaban por participar, oralmente o por escrito, aunque a menudo sucesivamente, casi todos los portavoces consagrados de la opinión e incluso algunos nuevos representantes de un lectorado en vías de emergencia.

En este sentido, para la historia literaria, no poco son *Pequeñeces*.

Bibliografía

BENÍTEZ, Rubén (ed.), L. *Coloma, Pequeñeces* (Madrid, Cátedra, 1982, 4a ed.).

BOTREL, Jean-Francois (1982), 'La Iglesia católica y los medios de comunicación impresos en España de 1847 a 1917: doctrina y prácticas' en M. Tuñón de Lara (ed.) *Metodología de la historia de la prensa española* (Madrid, Siglo XXI, 1982, pp. 119–176).

—, 'Le succès d'édition des oeuvres de Benito Pérez Galdós: essai de bibliométrie' *Anales de Literatura Española* 3–4 (1984–5), pp. 119–57 y 29–66.

—, 'Le roman en Espagne au temps de *La Regenta*: tendances et statistiques' *Cotextes* 18 (1989) pp. 5–22.

CAMPOMAR FORNIELLES, Marta M. (1989), '*Pequeñeces*: la novela integrista del siglo XIX en su contexto histórico y lingüístico' *Incipit* IX (1989) pp. 57–91.

ELIZALDE, Ignacio, '*Pequeñeces*, de Coloma, y su interpretación socio-política', *Boletín de la Biblioteca Menéndez Pelayo*, LXIII (1987).

—, 'Centenario de *Pequeñeces*, novela del P. Coloma: su intención y su sentido', *Razón y Fe* (1991) pp. 448–63.

—, *Concepción literaria y socio-política de la obra de Coloma (Kassel,* Reichenberger, 1992).

HIBBS, Solange, 'Le personnage de Butrón: le Marquis de Molíns/Cánovas dans *Pequeñeces* du Padre Coloma' en *La construction du personnage historique,* (Lille, Presses Universitaires de Lille, 1991, pp. 53–63).

—, 'Le roman édifiant catholique (1840–1900)' en J. Maurice (éd.) *Regards sur le roman espagnol au XXe siècle,* Paris, Université de Paris X, 1998.

HORNEDO, Rafael María de, 'El escándalo de *Pequeñeces* en el centenario del P. Luis Coloma' *Razón y Fe,* CXLIV (1951).

MOLHO, Blanca (1978), *Le roman bien-pensant dans l'Espagne de la Restauration: le Père Luis Coloma (Contribution à une étude de mentalités),* Thèse pour le Doctorat d'Etat (Université de Paris-Sorbonne, 1978).

13

Sentimental Battles
An Introduction to the Works of Alberto Insúa

Frank McQuade

During the first decades of the twentieth century in Spain are to be found a considerable number of prose fiction writers who, though now forgotten, nevertheless occupy a curious and largely unexplored place in the history of the Spanish novel for their popularity in their day and for their prodigious output: Felipe Trigo, Eduardo Zamacois, Ricardo León, Concha Espina, José López Pinillos, Antonio de Hoyos y Vinent, Rafael López de Haro, Pedro Mata, Joaquín Belda, and Alberto Insúa, to name but a few. Whereas the works of Spanish novelists of *segunda fila* such as Felipe Trigo and Eduardo Zamacois have received some critical attention and are still somewhat remembered[1], in literary and historiographical surveys, Alberto Insúa occupies a hazily defined space in twentieth-century Spanish letters. His case is interesting for the degree to which he exemplifies the status of these writers in literary historiography, in the vagueness of the generic labels applied to him, the extraordinary popularity of his work during his own time, his uneven but occasionally high-quality literary production, and his almost total consignment to oblivion today. In youth he starts out among the largely forgotten epigons of the Generation of 1898, and his writings exhibit traits of modernism, decadence, realism and naturalism in differing degrees. A glance at the relatively scant critical evaluations of Insúa reveals the varied, often positive appraisals, whose critical approval wanes with the passage of time. Cejador praises him in 1920 as a 'novelista psicólogo, sobresaliendo en la finura y tino con que observa los estados, mudanzas y variedad de las almas, y en la propiedad certera y sobria con que los pinta'.[2] Hurtado and Palencia in 1925 point to his place in the genre of the erotic novel, noting that as an 'escritor culto, ha evolucionado hacia más sanas tendencias.'[3] Cansinos Assens in 1927 discerns a nineteenth-century debt in 'los fondos galdosianos de su novela, la humanidad de sus argumentos y su honrado propósito literario.'[4] Francisco Carmona Nenclares, in a study full of hyperbolic and generalized praise, finds that 'los dolores que él [Insúa] descubre, que muestra realizados bellamente en una forma sabia y compleja, dejan entrever, por el recóndito prestigio de la hermosura intelectual, un contenido inagotable de ternura y sensibilidad.'[5]

The reader of Insúa today is most likely to view these appraisals with surprise, not to say incredulity in certain cases (Carmona Nenclares's 1928 study, one of the very few lengthy studies of Insúa, is an extraordinarily ardent, verbose and inaccurate eulogy). Later surveys ring more true in their restraint. Eugenio García de Nora's useful overview in his monumental *La novela española contemporánea*, discusses Insúa's writerly flaws, showing that even thirty-five years ago the latter's style was regarded as thoroughly dated:

> Insúa, con un arte equilibrado, insinuante y discreto (lo que no supone ausencia de defectos; sin duda hay también aquí situaciones inverosímiles, psicologías artificiales y estereotipadas, rasgos muy abundantes de lo que hoy nos parece imperdonablemente 'cursi': pero todo ello entra en las limitaciones genéricas de este tipo de novela).[6]

Insúa was born in Cuba and moved to Spain in the turmoil of the Spanish–American War, and throughout his life would retain an affinity for Cuba which surfaces in several of his novels. His novelistic development in the first decade and a half of the twentieth century was interrupted by a sojourn as a reporter in France during the First World War. During the period 1920 to 1936 he was regarded as one of the most popular —and prolific— authors in Spain, forming, with Wenceslao Fernández Flórez and Pedro Mata, what Entrambasaguas described as the 'triunvirato de los escritores mejor cotizados de nuestra patria.'[7] For Bernard Barrère, in his meticulous study of marketing forces and influences in the Spanish novel, Insúa is simply 'le romancier le plus lu de son époque.'[8] A major part of Insúa's huge literary production found an outlet in many of the serial and magazine publications of the time, such as *El Cuento Semanal* and *Los Contemporáneos*, both founded by Eduardo Zamacois (in 1907 and 1909 respectively). He also published eleven short novels[9] in the significant and prestigious *La Novela Corta*, a serial which began in January 1916 with the publication of Galdós's *Sor Simona*, and was to include works by most of the major literary figures of the day, including Trigo, Benavente, Pardo Bazán, Baroja, Blasco Ibañez, Palacio Valdés, Valle-Inclán and Azorín.

Alberto Insúa was born in Havana on 22 November 1883, son of a Cuban mother and Spanish father. 'Insúa' appears to be the pseudonym of Luis Galt y Escobar, but this name appears nowhere in his memoirs, apart from a mention of his grandfather as one Alfredo Escobar; but his father, a lawyer and also a writer of some reputation, wrote under the pseudonym Waldo Insúa (1858–1938). Insúa spent the first years of his childhood in Cuba, and was educated in a Jesuit school in Havana. In October 1898 the family moved to Spain, and Insúa gained his *bachillerato* at the Instituto de La Coruña. In 1899 he moved to Madrid to study law, but from a very early age appears to have been more drawn to a literary and journalistic career, attending *tertulias* and debates at the Ateneo. His first articles were published in *Nuevo Mundo, El País* and *El Liberal*. By 1906 he seems to have been contributing regularly to the latter paper and in *Los Lunes del Imparcial*. His first book, *Don Quijote en los Alpes*, appeared in 1907. This was followed by his notable trilogy *Historia de un escéptico* and, among other works, *La mujer fácil*, from which he gained both success and a dubious notoriety. This vigorous start to his literary career was suspended from 1915 to 1921, when he lived in Paris reporting as a war correspondent for *ABC*, *La Correspondencia de España* and *La Nación*. His extensive and strongly Francophile war correspondence seems to have had some impact, and at the end of the war he was awarded the Cross of the Legion of Honour.

On returning to Madrid in 1921, Insúa continued his journalistic career, and from 1922 contributed extensively to *La Voz*.

He appears to have spent most of the 1920s and early 1930s resident in Madrid (with the exception of a long return visit to Cuba in 1927) and this was the period of his greatest popularity, in which he published such bestsellers as *La batalla sentimental* (1921) and *El negro que tenía el alma blanca* (1922). Between 1907 and 1933 Insúa published some thirty-one novels, and the number of editions of many of these testifies to his popularity. *El negro que tenía el alma blanca*—by no means one of his better works—was phenomenally popular, going to three editions in one year. Writing his *Memorias* in 1956, Insúa could boast of three film versions of the novel, an adaptation for the theatre, and translations into nine languages.

In 1936, to escape the national conflict, Insúa left Spain to live for a time in Paris, and then for many years in Buenos Aires. He returned to Spain in 1950 to a very different literary and cultural setting in which he found his work largely forgotten. In the 1950s most of his energy seems to have gone into his *Memorias*, which ran to three volumes from 1952 to 1959, but which cover Insúa's life only up to and including his 1927 visit to Cuba. There were to be more volumes, but the series ended with Insúa's death in Madrid in November 1963.

The range and scope of Insúa's work, along with a prodigious output over some five decades, makes it problematical to find a niche, a label, or a generic group in which to place him, an exercise which would in itself be of dubious value if not for the fact that his work is so sparsely documented or studied. The Generation of 1898, for example, has proven to be an ineffectual cover term for the brilliant and diverse constellation of writers it proposes to demarcate, whilst Spanish prose literature in the years following this point, up to the Spanish Civil War, seems to lack focus for want of useful categorization, however tentative this might be. Insúa has been described as forming part of a group that Federico Carlos Sáinz de Robles has called 'Promoción de 1907 o de *El Cuento Semanal*.'[10] He has been described by José Luis Abellán as forming part of the Generation of 1914, and is mentioned by Eugenio de Nora as one of four 'novelistas "eróticos"'[11] worthy of consideration (the others mentioned are Pedro Mata, R. López de Haro, and Antonio de Hoyos y Vinent). Although this classification again seems limiting, Nora points out later in his study that Insúa does not by any means derive from this rather immature genre of erotic writing. Fascinatingly and puzzlingly, he evolves towards it after his first efforts, the idiosyncratic *Don Quijote en los Alpes* and his serious, if flawed and over-earnest, trilogy, *Historia de un escéptico*.

Don Quijote en los Alpes is a medley of *costumbrismo*, travel-writing, literary musings, and an account of a personal literary pilgrimage to Geneva in search of the relatives of the Swiss professor of philosophy and man of letters, Henri Frédérique Amiel (1821–1881), author of a single great work, the posthumous and monumental *Journal intime*, philosophical reflections in the form of a diary in heavily Romantic vein. The early sections of Insúa's book are in the form of a diary, describing the author's encounters with a cosmopolitan array of characters in his Genevan *pensión* looking out on Mont Blanc, and he spends much time musing on their background and destinies, taking particular interest in the virginal beauty of a twelve-year-old North American girl. There are numerous references to swans, *hojas secas*, and the melancholy effect on the author's spirit as he contemplates the natural world. There are, therefore, strong hints of *modernismo* and *romanticismo* not characteristic of most of the later work, and among the reviews supplied at the back of early editions there is a complimentary notice by Rubén Darío. One wonders what to make of Insúa's posturings as an anguished Romantic spirit, knowing the writer that he is to become; and he also seems to be a long way from the sensibilities of the hermetic and asexual Amiel whom he emulates and for whom he professes such admiration, principally in an account of a college for young ladies in which he expresses a barely disguised penchant for very young girls, and the description (or fantasy) of a lesbian encounter in the garden of the academy. In a new edition of 1921 Insúa somewhat grandiosely recognizes the contrast of sensibilities present in the work:

> En *Don Quijote en los Alpes* están los gérmenes de mi carácter: un anhelo inefable de perfección espiritual y un decaimiento del lado de la materia, especie de resignación desesperada. Este combate continúa en toda mi obra. El idealismo alado y la materia torpe no dejan nunca de librar batalla. Y ambos salen malheridos siempre.[12]

There is, here, a characteristic note of bombast and self-regard which is often a feature of Insúa's introductions to new editions of his own work, but also an element of truth which certainly applies to aspects of his next major work, the trilogy *Historia de un escéptico*, comprising *En tierra de santos* (1907), *La hora trágica* (1908), and *El triunfo* (1910). The two principal characters are don Alfredo Sangil and his devoted friend and assistant Bermúdez. Don Alfredo is a wealthy, free-living philanderer who nonetheless has an intellectual and philosophical nature. Bermúdez is down-to-earth, pragmatic and outspoken, even anarchical, especially in his opposition to the Church. This thinly disguised Quijote–Sancho device provides the opportunity for many debates on idealism and pragmatism, religion and atheism, action and inertia, responsibility and commitment, and the contemporary plight of Spain.

En tierra de santos begins when, to Bermúdez's consternation, don Alfredo has decided to relinquish all pleasures of the flesh—and Madrid—to seek solitude and spiritual purification in Avila. For a while Sangil succeeds in living a morose and withdrawn existence, though almost from the outset he is beset by thoughts of his Madrid consort Luisita. He is gradually coaxed into exploring the city, contemplating the wild surrounding landscape, the religious aura of the city, its cathedral and churches. Soon, however, he has his sights on Asunción, youngest daughter of his host, don Batalla. He writes her a love letter (though he has never spoken to her) which is intercepted by a priest who is preparing her for the Church. This romantic failure leads to Sangil's further disillusionment with life, and he becomes physically and emotionally debilitated to the point that Bermúdez has to call on the help, from Madrid, of Luisita. She succeeds in bringing Alfredo back to health, first by sisterly nursing, then by the resumption of their amorous relationship. Having succeeded in breaking free of his melancholia, Alfredo resolves to live life to the full: 'Por de pronto, estoy dispuesto a luchar por algo indefinido que ya la vida se encargará de concretar. No tengo plan. Ni falta, ¿verdad?'[13]

En tierra de santos, written when Insúa was twenty-two, shows a writer of considerable promise, and some of the ideas and sentiments expressed have more in common with *Don Quijote en los Alpes* than with the facile pulp he was to produce in such measure in the course of his career. When not indulging in repetitious and almost obsessive descriptions of female beauty, with 'manos blancas' and 'rojos labios', he shows a gift for description of landscape and for the religious architecture and artefacts of Avila. The novel is a rite of passage in which the protagonist undergoes suffering in order to find fulfilment and self-knowledge. To the modern reader Don Alfredo's sufferings seem ridiculous, posturings of Romantic torment from an earlier age (contemplations of suicide because of unrequited love, reading aloud his thoughts on love by a moonlit fountain, being driven almost to his death-bed by melancholy), and it would be hard to disagree with an exasperated Bermúdez when he calls his master 'un onanista espiritual' (p. 210) The struggle in Sangil's soul between the spiritual and the sensual reveals again the author's increasingly blatant fascination for virginal beauty and purity, and the desire to despoil the latter with all haste, along with a disillusionment which befits the fatigue and weariness characterized as *abulia* at the turn of the century in a Spain bereft of national pride and many of the moral and spiritual certainties of an earlier age.

A synopsis of the second novel of the trilogy, *La hora trágica*, suggests something of its melodramatic and psychologically unconvincing nature. It opens with Sangil's return to Madrid after his Avila adventure. Here he explores the life of bars and theatres and recovers something of his *joie de vivre*. He becomes romantically involved with a theatre starlet, Amparito Ruiz, while still claiming to love Luisita, and in fact proposes a *ménage à trois* to the latter, who finds this unacceptable and leaves him. Sangil is also faced with the unwanted return of Amparo's ex-lover, Gerardo, but is sanguine about the prospect of a duel. The climax, Sangil's *hora trágica*, is a confrontation in which the jealous Gerardo shoots Amparito dead. Sangil is also carrying a gun and in turn shoots Gerardo dead. An epilogue has Sangil's political associate, Ruiz-Prieto, visiting him to announce that he has been entirely exonerated by the authorities, and that his action has been accepted as self-defence, and evidence to his friends of Sangil's will to live. He again needs to get away from Madrid and recover from this traumatic experience. In the comforting arms of Luisita, he decides to go to his family home in Orillamar.

The novel continues the theme of reconciling the need for carnal and sensual satisfaction with the attainment of a higher philosophical purpose. There are several passages of a floridly erotic character, such as Amparito's seduction of Sangil, though the sexual encounter actually takes place behind closed doors. The suggestion of a threesome may have been risqué at the time, but to the modern reader seems almost comic as Sangil earnestly proposes this as a solution to his indecision, only to be flatly rejected. On the other hand, Bermúdez's long-held belief in Sangil's vocation as a politician becomes increasingly absurd. The long debates about political commitment and philosophical passivity continue, but Sangil persists in his asceticism, and is indecisive, apolitical, even if his capacity for 'la voluptuosidad' has temporarily been revived. At the latter's refusal to engage in politics, Bermúdez himself is tempted to enter the political arena, even though he is convinced that his master is the man to carry through the mighty task of Spain's renovation.

The final volume of this trilogy, *El triunfo*, sees the return of Sangil to his childhood surroundings for the first time in ten years. Although still weighed down by the memories of Gerardo and Amparito in Madrid, he is moved by memories of childhood and the landscape that formed his life until he went to study in a Jesuit college in Madrid. He also feels some spiritual relief at the sight of the sea (a small prefiguration of the end of the novel). In a passage rich in sensuous description, Luisita and Sangil walk in their orchard, and later make love on a bed of ebony. Bermúdez is happy at this indication of a return to normality, for he knows that apart from Sangil's bout of neurasthenic debilitation in Avila, he has always needed carnal love ('Había necesitado siempre sacrificarse en los brazos de Venus').[14] There is soon talk of a baby, but by now Sangil is on a seemingly inexorable slide into enervation and *abulia*. By Chapter XXI, however, he and Ruiz-Prieto have managed to persuade Sangil to stand for political office, and Bermúdez's joy is typically hyperbolic:

> '¡Oh gracias! Al fin, al fin se porta usted como un hombre. La hora de nuestro triunfo ha sonado; mis sueños comienzan a realizarse... Dentro de poco nos hallaremos en nuestra casa en Madrid, y el talento de usted estará siempre al lado de la razón y la justicia. Este pueblo oprimido encontrará en usted un defensor...' (p. 198)

Even the unworldly Sangil can point out to his friend that he is hardly in a position to effect revolutionary legislation as a member of the Conservative Party; moreover, he feels he can do more humanitarian and patriotic work for the small community of his own *pazo* than for Congress. Triumph and depression alternate in Sangil (*triunfo* is used repeatedly in the novel in ironic prefiguration of Sangil's end), and following the announcement of his political victory ('El momento más glorioso en la vida de Bermúdez') and the meal in his honour, 'las ideas melancólicas volvían a apoderarse de él' (pp. 228–9). In Chapter XXV there is a fiesta in Sangil's honour, involving a boat excursion. He has reached his limit, and in contemplating his past and present situation decides that life is a dream. He confesses to Luisita that he is ill, and that the memory of Amparito keeps returning.

> —Alfredo, por Dios, no te preocupes ahora, ahora que has triunfado, ahora que...

El la interrumpió dulcemente:

—¡Ah! ¿Pero tú también crees que he triunfado? (p. 236)

The triumph of the title is clearly the irony of Sangil's suicide by drowning. The final chapter has the melodramatic image of the inconsolable Bermúdez wandering into the sea with Sangil's child in his arms, calling out for don Alfredo, whose body is never found.

Historia de un escéptico is an intriguing depiction of the turn-of-the-century sensibility in which the national political malaise is related to the artist's choice of engagement or hermeticism. It is highly uneven, and the neurasthenic Sangil, ranting Bermúdez and vapid Luisita lack psychological plausibility. However, it is clear that the consignment of Insúa to the subgenre of the erotic pulp novel hardly does him justice. This trilogy clearly shows a continuation of the preoccupations of writers of the Generation of 1898, and we are reminded in particular of two novels of 1902: Baroja's *Camino de perfección* and *La voluntad* by Azorín. Both are 'character' novels featuring a main protagonist suffering from an abulic condition, and share the common theme of the individual in search of himself. In both cases the search for a meaningful existence leads to death. Also of major importance is the treatment of the Castilian landscape. Just as the terrain of Yecla exerts a powerful influence on Antonio Azorín, and Toledo and its surrounds influences Baroja's Fernando Ossorio in their pursuit of the contemplative life, so does Avila on the enervated sensibility of Alfredo Sangil.[15]

It is with the publication of *La mujer fácil* in 1911 that we begin to see a style and subject-matter that will more closely typify much of the rest of Insúa's literary production — or rather how his work has been perceived. This novel was apparently the source of some controversy when it first appeared. In an edition of 1931 Insúa provides a postscript (actually written in October 1920) in which he regards the novel as a 'un mal paso'[16] in his career. 'Es que *La mujer fácil* no es un libro malo sino un libro "mal hecho"' which he wrote in only two months. Insúa is not usually given to regret or self-criticism, but here clearly finds it difficult to find a positive re-evaluation of the work:

Esta falta de unción literaria podría perdonársele a *La mujer fácil* si fuese una obra fuerte, una obra dolorosa. Pero *La mujer fácil* es un

227

libro débil y un libro frívolo. A veces se asoman una inquietud ideológica y una angustia moral, pero se desvanecen pronto. Yo tenía veintitrés años al escribir lo que muy pronto observé que no merecía sino honores de una conversación de café. *La mujer fácil* es eso: una conversación de tenorios madrileños, en un rincón de Fornos, del antiguo Fornos. Y nada más, desgraciadamente. (op. cit., pp. 314–5)

Insúa found it unfortunate that the book should have earned him the reputation of a pornographic author, even though he does not necessarily despise that genre. He claims to have known and liked Felipe Trigo, but not to have been influenced by his work. Perhaps most interestingly Insúa records here the disdain felt for the book by his literary mentor, Alfredo Vicenti, who had made Insúa a reporter for *El Liberal* in 1903 when the latter was only twenty. In the first volume of his *Memorias* Insúa refers to the book: 'En octubre de 1909 publiqué un libro de cuyo nombre no quiero acordarme.'[17] Forty-two years after its appearance Insúa claims to receive letters and read articles criticizing 'ese pecado de la juventud' (p. 590). Again he laments Vicenti's reaction to the book, but also that of his father Waldo, and the fact that on this one occasion doña Emilia Pardo Bazán chose not to acknowledge his latest work.

The novel concerns the amorous adventures of Arturo Morales, a respectably married minor politician with five children. He is, however, a womanizer, whose main consort is Magda, a married woman herself and the best friend of Morales's wife Ernestina. He also has encounters with a succession of 'easy women'. He is pursued by Charito, a young virgin, with whom Morales at first hesitates because he does not want to dishonour her father, a disabled ex-army officer. He eventually gives way and conceives a passion for Charito. She agrees to flee with him if they can go to Paris. This they do, until one day he surprises her with an old admirer from Madrid. After attempting to strangle her, Morales faints; when he comes round Ruiz explains that she has been unfaithful from the start. Morales takes the first train to San Sebastián, to be reunited with his wife.

Morales's amorous liaisons and sub-liaisons are mesmerizing. Charito is freely bisexual and takes the active role with Magda, and there are several fairly explicit erotic lesbian scenes, not to mention heterosexual descriptions. In a scene with Aurora, a go-between figure who lets out a room to Morales for his trysts, fellatio is suggested with coy euphemism ('ciertas caricias exquisitas', p. 111; 'une autre chose...plus belle...plus délicate', p. 115; 'Ella extendió por el vientre y los muslos de Arturo la gravedad de sus pechos. Y sutil y voluptuosa, comenzó la caricia', p. 116, and so forth).

Arturo Morales is almost a Bertie Wooster figure without the filter of authorial wit or irony. He is popular enough at his club, enjoys amorous liaisons when they do not lead to retribution or responsibility. He possesses neither brains nor moral sense, and yet has certain standards, for example in understanding his wife's attitude in cutting Charito's family in public because they have no money:

> A Morales, un poco conocedor de las mujeres, en particular de la suya, no le extrañaba aquella condenación tan absoluta por motivo tan frívolo: había aprendido que la frivolidad es una de las leyes fundamentales de la vida moderna, sobre todo de la *hig-life* [sic], y la respetaba.' (p. 87)

He holds conventional ideas about men and women's sexual behaviour but when Magda points out the illogicality of his views (double standards for men) he has no answer. Similarly when he surprises Charito and Magda having sex, he finds Charito's arguments unanswerable.

The narrative is told from Morales's point of view, and little indication is given of where the narrator stands on the protagonist's moral trajectory. Is this a moral tale, a modern *exemplum vitandum?* If it is a tale of moral decline it hardly succeeds, because Morales was never a figure of any substantial character in the first place. Indeed, by the end of the novel he seems only to feel a complacent relief that he has avoided complete disaster (in terms of financial ruin, or succeeding in killing Amparito, or having to fight a duel). Despite his philosophical turn of mind at the end, Morales appears to have learned nothing. The broader context of Insúa's work suggests that here he is simply straining to be bold, 'modern', erotic, or has simply not worked out fully his views on bourgeois respectability and the meaning of a fulfilled life.

In spite of Insúa's disappointment at the reception of *La mujer fácil* by those associates whose opinion he so respected, it is this novel that is more characteristic of the bulk of his work to come. In *Don Quijote en los Alpes* and *Historia de un escéptico* we see with hindsight glimpses of a serious, if somewhat facile, writer of considerable promise. From the publication of *La mujer fácil* the mould of Insúa's art seems to have set, and a spate of erotic, sentimental melodramas follows, including *Las neuróticas* (1910), *La mujer desconocida* (1911), *El demonio de la voluptuosidad* (1911), *Las flechas del amor* (1912), and the 'two-part' novel, *Los hombres: Mary los descubre* (1913) and *Los hombres: Mary los perdona* (1914).

Los hombres is essentially a kind of *éducation sentimentale* of its heroine, Mary Pacheco, a rich girl educated in Geneva in the protective environment of a select ladies' college, is now married to Isaac, a successful lawyer in Madrid. The voice of wisdom throughout is that of Mary's brother Félix ('bilioso y pesimista')[18] who is concerned that she has not had any preparation for life's harshness, and gives several disquisitions on 'los hombres', that there is good and bad, something of the gallant and the rogue, in all of them. Mary's perspectives on life are much more mature when she has her first child, a boy, but she is revulsed by the discovery that she is still attractive to men, and is shocked to learn of her close friend, the Condesita's, extramarital affair. She develops a distaste for men, and yet is rearing one herself. Her anxiety for the development of her son is expressed in terms typical of the simplistic, naturalistic thesis underpinning the novel: 'Mary se preguntaba melancólicamente si "los hombres eran malos antes de nacerse". Y sospechando que el egoísmo fuera acaso el verdadero pecado original, quería redimir a su hijo, en lo posible, de los malos instintos heredados' (p. 288).

From 1914 there is something of a hiatus in Insúa's prodigious fictional output, when he went to Paris as a war correspondent and remained there until well after the war. In 1930, in the prologue to a new edition of his 1916 novel *De un mundo a otro*, Insúa writes:

> En 1921, al restituirme a España, después de haber vivido en Francia los cuatro años de la guerra y los tres primeros de la posguerra, tuve que luchar para reconstruir mi crédito de novelista, casi agotado. Todo un lustro sin publicar libros de imaginación. Siete años de periodismo activo —y aliadófilo— en *ABC* y *La Correspondencia de España*. Frialdad, impopularidad, en torno mío. Se me acusaba de francofilia exagerada. Y tal vez venal…Vendido a los franceses. Pero yo volvía a España con dos cosas limpias: la bolsa y la conciencia.[19]

As Claire-Nicolle Robin points out, Insúa's journalistic activity during the First World War makes for perhaps a unique case, in that he was a novelist almost at the height of his career when he relinquished it, only to go to another country for a considerable time to devote himself to a journalistic effort that was not of a directly national nature. Insúa appears to have gone to Paris in part for personal reasons, and to keep solidarity with friends he already had there. He also appears to have been one of the first Spanish journalists to have urged that the future of Spain be seen in the context of a unified Europe.

Between 1918 and 1921 Insúa published *Maravilla, Las fronteras de la pasión, Un corazón burlado*,[20] and *La batalla sentimental*. These novels are described by him as 'estudios psicológicos en torno al sentimiento amoroso y cuadros de costumbres españoles'.[21] A summary and examination of the latter novel may provide us again with a confirmation of the limitations of these novels in terms of psychological depth or otherwise.

In *La batalla sentimental* the young Spanish aristocrat Enrique Vélez is living in Paris and is in love with the young and beautiful Cristiana de Gamboa.[22] His affection is reciprocated, but he is constrained from pursuing her further by his sense of honour. Cristiana's father is a rich and powerful banker in Paris whose morality and honour are both suspect (he has made his money by dubious means, and both he and his wife conduct extramarital liaisons). Enrique knows that his own father, 'don Rafael Vélez de Castro, de una hidalguía tan irreductible, de un pundonor tan recio'[23] could never tolerate Gamboa ('será siempre para mi padre un bandido', p. 93). The marriage takes place, but from the start he is uneasy. The Gamboas are pleased to be associated with Enrique's noble extraction, whilst he himself has been disowned by his father. Meanwhile, he is concerned about his wife's continued extravagance, a fact which eventually necessitates his taking a post in her father's bank. At a birthday party for Cristiana, a friend admires Cristiana's pearl necklace which Enrique had always taken to be false. He secretly has the necklace valued and finds that it is worth a fortune. He is contemplating suicide, but when he expresses his sorrow and fury that she has deceived him, she gets the chance to explain. She *stole* the necklace, and her great vice is not adultery but kleptomania. Reconciled, they see the cure for her 'sickness' in escaping the tawdry world of Paris for a new life. The novel ends with a cry of joy from Enrique's father as he sees his son returning to *la patria* with his bride, and all is forgiven. Before he dies, don Rafael will have the chance to hold his grandchildren, while 'Enrique sentía latir en sus hijos las dos sangres con que se habían formado, tan enteros, en el molde mágico del amor' (p. 231).

Psychological analysis of a sort, and *costumbrista* observations are present in the novel, but the general effect is highly unconvincing to this reader, who so often comes away from reading these novels wondering what the lover sees in the beloved. On several occasions it is made clear that Cristiana is nothing like as angelic as her appearance, and Enrique himself is tormented by the thought that his wife carries the corrupt blood of the Gamboas in her veins. She is unashamedly materialistic and unscrupulous, and admits to the horrified Enrique that they are together because she desired him, and would have captured him anyway, if not as a husband then as a lover. Enrique's own weakness, his giving in to a carnal passion, his disregard for his revered father's wishes, his servility towards Gamboa, would all suggest a destiny of unhappiness. In spite of the inherent inadequacies in the characters, the only problem is deemed to be kleptomania. The naturalistic thesis being presented—however unconvincingly—is eventually ignored by an unexplained family reconciliation, or at least the notion that love can overcome the curse of a tainted lineage. The strong temptation is to wish for the subject-matter and the exploration of the psychological themes to be in the hands of a Galdós. Another temptation, that a surface reading of the novel may be ignoring an ironic treatment, need not be entertained for long. A pattern emerges that Insúa tends to choose one of two dramatic outcomes: either death as the result of emotional or philosophical unfulfilment (*Historia de un escéptico, El negro que tenía el alma blanca*), or else a forced happy ending in which love is seen as the cure to all differences, in terms of politics, age, family and social status. By and large, then, these novels are not especially or overtly erotic, nor psychological studies. Rather they are highly competent 'potboilers'.

El negro que tenía el alma blanca was Insúa's greatest popular success, and contains many of the ingredients of his typical *novela sentimental*, a story of fame without fulfilment, virtue unrecognized, success without happiness. Peter Wald, the hero to whom the title refers, is reminiscent of Alfredo Sangil in having money, looks, intelligence and, in this case, a genius for the foxtrot and the 'shimmy', for which he has achieved fame and fortune. Sangil succeeds in committing suicide, whilst Peter Wald withers away, a victim of love unrequited. The novel is a fairly entertaining—if typically turgid—melodramatic yarn, with a strong element of *costumbrismo* in the portrayal of life in the *farándulas* of the lowly Madrid theatres of the early decades of the century, and the ugly and avaricious figure of don Mucio, father of the innocent Emma Cortadell. It contains some mild examples of Insúa's erotic writing, but is generally more pious than prurient. What does make the novel hard work for today's reader is the treatment of the racial issue at the core of the novel. As a boy, Pedro's repeated humiliations at the hands of the young aristocrat Néstor lead to his abandonment of the family he grew up with, and under whom his parents were slaves. The brutal treatment of slaves in late nineteenth-century Cuba is less hard—or plausible—to accept than the values Peter himself holds: the tragedy of being black, and his lifelong desire to be white-skinned. His disillusionment culminates with the realization that he can never possess his beautiful dancing-partner except in the dance, other than through the influence of her father don Mucio, over whom he has gained total control through money. The wealthy and honourable Peter Wald, now only a slave to love, can only achieve spurious fulfilment through material means: 'El, nieto de esclavos, *había comprado una blanca.*'[24]

Reading the novel today one has to make a certain effort of imagination to see why it was such a success. The novel contains many features likely to have inspired a popular appeal in the early 1920s. It is in part a tale of theatre life, from the backstage intrigues of a Madrid *farándula* to the fame and glamour Peter achieves on the stages of Paris, London and New York. Part of the novelty interest of the book must have come from the fact of a black protagonist. Peter Wald is not of the tradition of the black and white minstrels of vaudeville, but more the outsider, a genius with a tragic flaw. The fact that the flaw happens to be the colour of his skin, and that the sympathetic treatment of his tragedy nonetheless implicitly accepts the legitimacy of this characteristic *as* a flaw, is likely to make the novel particularly unpalatable to a modern reader. It is hard not to agree with Eugenio de Nora, writing more than three decades ago, that the treatment of an impossible love leading to a tragic death, and the forced happy ending to the novel's sequel (*La sombra de*

Peter Wald, 1937) is a formula in which 'la amalgama de idealismo cursi, sensualidad dulzona y superficialidad mundana no pueden ser más flagrantes' (p. 412).

A relatively extensive reading of Insúa's remarkable output begins to persuade the reader that his novels are irredeemably lacking in sufficient merit to warrant reappraisal, except for their character of quaintly typifying a long-disappeared popular sensibility, and *El negro que tenía el alma blanca* exemplifies this judgement. It is a pleasant surprise then to find later novels which though far more obscure than his bestsellers are yet of superior literary quality. One of these, *El amante invisible* (1930), is a reworking of the Faust legend. Pandoro is a gossip, intriguer and voyeur whom a traditionally world-weary Satan tempts with the gift of invisibility in return for his soul. The plot provides licence for a number of erotic situations, along with the tale of yet another character who fails to find fulfilment through love, as well as containing some fairly clear references to the dictatorship of Primo de Rivera. This departure into fantasy is also represented in another late novel, *El barco embrujado*, subtitled *Novela de magia* (1929). Another surprise is *Ha llegado el día* (1932), a vivid evocation of the days leading up to the formation of the Second Republic, set partly in Madrid and partly in Málaga during Holy Week. When Jorge de Cisneros, artist, playwright and liberal intellectual, spends a period away from Madrid to visit Málaga (after the poor reception of one of his oft-misunderstood plays) he finds out how different the situation is in the provinces. The essential conflict in Spanish society of the period is represented by the contrasting beliefs and values of Jorge and his lover Cristina: he a progressive liberal in favour of the new Republic, and agnostic; she part of a wealthy landowning family, pro-Alfonso XIII and a devout Catholic. The arguments between the two as they struggle to reconcile their differences for the sake of their growing love are typical of Insúa in their didactic artificiality, and the characters are largely mere representations of opposing points of view. The novel offers an intriguing view of this turbulent period of modern Spanish history (and was written startlingly soon after the action it depicts—late 1931 and early 1932), but still bears out an old theme of Insúa, that true love conquers and redeems all. It is also strikingly reminiscent of the early trilogy *Historia de un escéptico*. The main protagonist is an intellectual who seeks escape from Madrid to the provinces in order to rethink his life, but who in fact falls in love. He has a devoted friend who idolizes him and yet is opposed to his political inactivity. Like Alfredo Sangil, he is torn between being an observer of the drama of life and being an engineer of events, a political man of action. Sangil never resolves this dilemma except in death, whilst Cisneros does find fulfilment and love after a cathartic experience of violence and danger. Yet the similarities between the two works also provide a hint to their different places in Insúa's artistic trajectory and the time span between them. The backdrop of the trilogy was a Spain disorientated and dispirited, and the hero debilitated by an abulic temperament; in *Ha llegado el día* Spain is in a state of vertiginous change, but the mood is positive, and hope for the future is expressed in part by the lovers' conciliation in spite of political differences.

Assessments of Insúa's works (including that of Insúa himself) often mention their treatment of psychological motives and a penchant for sketches of a *costumbrista* nature. As Nora points out, Insúa is prone to the facile psychological perceptions inherent in the sentimental and saccharine plot resolutions usually required by the *novela galante*, and often contrives happy endings and lovers' reconciliations without too much regard for thematic coherence or psychological plausibility. He is more convincing and engaging, however, in the observation of the natural landscape, regional descriptions, religious and secular rituals, and commentaries on the Spanish character, although the term *costumbrismo* should be taken in its broadest acceptance. We have seen how this interest in the streets and churches of Avila and its contrast with Madrid make up the more interesting aspects of the early novel *En tierra de santos*. An exploration of Madrid low-life reminiscent of Galdós is present in *Las flechas del amor* (1912); the processions and rituals of *Semana Santa* in Málaga are described and analysed at considerable length in *Ha llegado el día*, along with the amusing transcriptions of the strong accents of the Malagan fishermen as they expound their crude understanding of Marxist concepts in the social upheavals on the eve of the Second Republic. These experiences are crucial to the main character Jorge de Cisneros's meditations on his own political beliefs and religious agnosticism. In a discussion of eighteenth-century Spanish sculpture, Jorge's friend Branting makes these observations on the Spanish religious and artistic tradition:

Esta sensibilidad no es filosófica, ni teológica. Sino dramática. El español no quiere pensar, sino sentir. Y no sentir suavemente, sino con angustia. Necesita lágrimas y llagas. Vírgenes de los siete dolores con sus siete cuchillos. Cristos de la columna o del madero con la faz contraída y cianótica, la espalda amoratada por los verdugos [...]. Pide la sensibilidad española este arte tremebundo, pues el español sólo siente cuando tiembla. Por eso, sus principales espectáculos son...la religión y los toros.[25]

Memorias is possibly the most unjustly forgotten of all Insúa's works. It is a formidable three-volume work, begun in 1948 when Insúa was still in Buenos Aires, and appeared between 1952 and 1959, under the titles *Mi tiempo y yo; Horas felices, tiempos crueles*; and *Amor, viajes, literatura*. Jorge Febles describes it as 'una pseudoauto-biografía incompleta'[26] covering the period 1888—his earliest childhood memories—to 1927 when, as a successful writer, Insúa enjoyed a triumphal return to Havana. In large part it is made up of brief journalistic sketches, its tone discursive and anecdotal rather than historical, and Insúa gives free rein to his many enthusiasms and prejudices. The first tome runs to 614 pages, and the other two contain 516 and 580 pages respectively: all this taking Insúa's memories up to approximately the half-way point of his lifespan. They typify not only Insúa's admirable zest for life and sheer literary energy, but also his want of moderation and a penchant for redundancy and bombast.

Much of the first half of *Mi tiempo y yo* is devoted to Insúa's early formative years in Havana, and is striking in its melancholy, almost lachrymose yearning for a lost age and a lost colonial Cuba. Insúa was not only an energetic observer of the age in which he lived, but also actively engaged in it. His presence in Paris in the war years is testament alone to this. *Memorias* provides a fascinating window onto Insúa's life and times, of interest to the social historian, but in particular the literary historiographer investigating reading and publishing trends, life in the publishing houses, editorial offices, and presses of Madrid. Insúa also seems to have known almost all of the leading Spanish literary figures of the day, including Galdós, Unamuno, Blasco Ibáñez, Ricardo León and in particular doña Emilia Pardo Bazán, whose friendship he prized and whose literary approval he craved (and did not always receive). A visitor at Valle-Inclán's famous *tertulias*, he refers to the latter as 'amigo Valle' even though he was once on the point of demanding satisfaction following insults over an advance on the publication of a new book by Valle.

In a climate of literary investigation which is today less concerned with a hierarchical canon of literary excellence than with the attempt to inscribe literary production within the cultural milieu in which it is generated, reading the forgotten bestsellers such as Insúa can provide a perspective on the tastes of a popular Spanish readership of the early twentieth century to which literary surveys rarely do credit. It is hoped that in bringing to light this forgotten body of work, at least knowledge of its existence and its contemporary popular impact might fill a gap in a neglected period in the development of modern Spanish prose fiction. This is not to urge that Insúa merits extensive literary reconsideration, but that his work certainly does deserve to be rescued from what Maurice Hemingway described as 'este olvido casi sepulcral',[27] and take its place in the endeavours of scholars and specialists to chart and clarify the intertextual relationships between the popular writers of the period and their major contemporaries.

14

Boundaries and Black Holes
The Physics of Personality and
Representation in Unamuno

Alison Sinclair

W.R.D. Fairbairn, writing on the structure of the self, pointed out
that Freud's theory of the self was one produced in an atmosphere
'dominated by the Helmholtzian conception that the physical universe
consisted in a conglomeration of inert, immutable and indivisible
particles to which motion was imparted by a fixed quantity of energy
separate from the particles themselves'. In postulating his alternative
view of the structure of the self, Fairbairn considered that it was
proper to reflect advances in other branches of science.[1] In the spirit
of Fairbairn, I would like, in my discussion of the issues and
difficulties in the representation of the personality in Unamuno, to
draw on a concept of our times, the black hole, as understood in
physics, and as utilized for the understanding of primitive states of
mind in psychoanalysis.[2]

Fairbairn had a further observation on Freud which is central to
Unamuno, namely that Freud's earliest work was on hysterics, and
later moved on to an interest in melancholia.[3] The emphasis within
Freud (as with Lacan later) was hence with the Oedipal, and the post-
Oedipal self. Fairbairn, by contrast, along with other theorists of the
Object Relations School, identified the earlier stages of the self, the
pre-Oedipal, and frequently the pre-verbal, as stages at which crucial
changes and responses were made and which would affect later
development and behaviour.

In undertaking the following reading, I start from the premise that
in many of the fictional works of Unamuno the self is conceptualized
and represented as being in an extremely primitive state. Oedipal

concerns are therefore of little import. I have argued in relation to *Niebla* that Augusto Pérez engages in a hysterical (presumed post-Oedipal) narrative of courtship as a defence against the threat of non-identity.[4] That is, in response to the two questions formulated by Lacan, the obsessional's question of 'Am I alive or dead?', is replaced by the diversionary hysteric's question of 'Which sex am I?'[5] Likewise, Augusto's attempts to define himself through language, to enter, as it were, into the Symbolic, is a project doomed to failure, since in so doing he enters into a world of misrecognition, of posturing and imitation. Language in *Niebla*, as so powerfully articulated by Orfeo in the *Epílogo*, is used for purposes of concealment and self-deception, for covering over, or diverting from crucial issues of the self.

In the majority of Unamuno's fictional works, we could regard post-Oedipal 'hysterical' narratives and situations as ones which are entered into defensively, in order to deal with irresoluble dilemmas and problems at the level of dyadic relationships (as in *Abel Sánchez*), or simply at the level of the definition of the self (*Niebla, El otro*). Thus, for example, the strange manoeuvring of Joaquín Monegro into a triangular relation between himself, Abel and Helena (as light, almost normal, relief from the pathology of the envious Cain/Abel dyad in which he finds himself with Abel), and thus also the ill-fated attempts of the twin brothers in *El otro* to establish difference between one another through their marriages.

In *La novela de don Sandalio, jugador de ajedrez* (1930) hysterical, Oedipal diversion is not only at a minimum, but its presence is consciously rejected. The text is in the form of a series of letters, directed from an unknown male writer to Felipe. Purportedly these letters come into Unamuno's hands. Later, in the *Epílogo*, Unamuno is, as ever, at pains to undermine and destabilize any sense of security that the reader might have had in construing the narrative situation, and suggests, among other things, that the letters might actually have been written by Don Sandalio himself. The nature of Unamuno's suggestion here is, I would suggest, not the diversion of a hysterical narrative that would lead us off on a false trail, but a reiteration of the splits and dislocations of the original narrative, a further sketching out of refractions rather than reflections. As in *Cómo se hace una novela*, and indeed in *Niebla*, Unamuno appears to regard the text not as a discrete and confined object to be offered to the reader, but one which will be used as a playful object of transaction in that writer/reader relationship. A less benign interpretation of Unamuno's attitude is that the concept of play in this context is one in which the reader becomes the object that is played with by the author, and in which the text is the accessory used in this sadistic teasing operation.[6]

In Chapter 22 of *Don Sandalio* it appears that Felipe has suggested that somewhere in the unsolved mystery of Don Sandalio there is a woman. The writer reproaches him: 'Te veo venir, Felipe, te veo venir. Tú has echado de menos en toda esta mi correspondencia una figura de mujer y ahora te figuras que la novela que estás buscando, la novela que quieres que yo te sirva, empezará a cuajar en cuanto surja ella.'[7] The introduction of a woman, or the request for such an introduction into the narrative, indicates that, for the writer, Felipe is misfiring in two directions. First, he appears by his enquiry to show an interest in that *other* existence of Don Sandalio, that which is unknown to the writer, and to show an interest in the way it might reflect what the writer scathingly calls '¡La ella del viejo cuento!' (1180). Second, in having this interest in how the seemingly puzzling events of Don Sandalio's reported life might be explained, he is, as it were, missing the whole point of the letters which have been addressed to him. He is missing the fact that the principal, indeed the whole concern of the writer, is with the relationship of himself to Don Sandalio, and whatever each represents for the other.

The black hole and the event horizon as psychoanalytic concepts

In order to discuss the relationship of the writer of the letters to Don Sandalio, I would like to draw on a number of different but over-lapping concepts. Partly, as indicated in my title, I would like to use the imagery of the black hole as an explanation for the experience of a style of relationship with others or with the external world. This is a relationship which is as bizarre as it is terrifying. The analogy is that just as the concept of the black hole stands outside the 'normal' laws of physics, so the style of relationship articulated over and over again in *Don Sandalio* is one of the 'pre-self', standing outside the supposedly more settled state of a post-Oedipal relationship. It delineates the self engaged in struggle with a single, unknown and terrifying Other, without the reassuring structures of Oedipal triangulation to de-marcate its boundaries.

The term 'black hole' was coined by John Wheeler of Princeton University in 1967, and denotes a star of such immense gravitational field that even the light escaping from it would be sucked back into it. It is thus not a simple emptiness, but rather a site of gravitational collapse. Moreover, the black hole is a place from which it is impossible to escape. In the use made of the black hole as concept by both Tustin and Grotstein in their psychoanalytic writings, the concern is with the idea of an implosion of the self into itself, a falling inwards or collapse which ensues as a reaction to intense terror. Tustin's elaboration is within the framework of her study of autism, which she characterizes as a formation produced in reaction to and defence against what she terms as '"the black hole" of nonrelationship'.[8] Grotstein's discussion of this concept again uses it to characterize a falling into the self. Specifically, he relates the gravitational pull of the black hole of physics to Bion's idea of 'beta elements', which are de-cathected chards of abandoned meaning.[9] That is, the black hole phenomenon occurs, in psychical terms, when there is experience which cannot be tolerated, and in relation to which the self is unable to organize itself. The experience cannot be obliterated; nor can it, in Grotstein's terminology, be 'regulated'. It thus fills the self, and pulls into it that which comes too close.

In the discussions of both Tustin and Grotstein, the emphasis in the first instance is, then, on the black hole as a process of the self, a process in which the self implodes. But Grotstein also explores at some length, in his second article on the topic, the varied ways in which parallels can be drawn between the properties of the black hole of physics and the processes that can be observed in the self. Of particular interest here is his discussion of the concept of the event horizon, which he characterizes as the border between sanity and psychosis.[10] Hawking's graphic image of this boundary in space reveals the potential drama of the psychological analogy I would like to suggest:

> The event horizon, the boundary of the region of space-time from which it is not possible to escape, acts rather like a one-way membrane around the black hole: objects, such as unwary astronauts, can fall through the event horizon into the black hole, but nothing can ever get out of the black hole through the event horizon. [...] One could well say of the event horizon what the poet Dante said of the

entrance to Hell: 'All hope abandon, ye who enter here.' Anything or anyone who falls through the event horizon will soon reach the region of infinite density and the end of time.[11]

This aspect of the theory is central to my analysis of *Don Sandalio*, in so far as this novel situates the black hole, and that which risks being sucked into it, into different characters. The event horizon is thus the uncertain boundary between them. Which two characters are at issue, is, as suggested by my initial remarks on the novel, not easy to decide, and the most plausible manner of construing the intention of the complex structure is to view it (as suggested by the multiple mirrors in the Casino) as a series of echoing dyads which all represent to the reader the complex effects of the confrontation between self and other, and the drama within the self of how to manage or relate to impingement upon it of 'foreign' or 'beta' elements. In the case of each dyad, including the dyad composed of the reader and the text, there is the issue of an event horizon, with the force which draws one member of the dyad into the black hole of the other. At a surface level, and one most easily comprehensible, the dyad is that between the narrator and Don Sandalio, and, as I shall argue, the terrifying attraction is one which will draw the narrator over the event horizon into Don Sandalio. My contention is, however, consistent with Unamuno's final suggestions about the story, namely, that all parts and personae of the story are in fact parts of the self, so that the tense structuring of the relationships between various proposed dyads in the story is one which arguably reflects the dynamic between parts and processes of the self.

The image of the black hole for this mode of relationship conjures up for us what is a terror of early experience, a terror to be re-enacted at moments of crisis in later life.

The style of relating I would suggest it illustrates is one which derives from and reaches back to a point characteristically anterior to the formation of a boundaried self that will be able to relate to others.[12] It is, significantly, a form of relating imbued with terror, an early schizoid state resorted to with massive defensive splits in order to protect the nascent self.[13] In order to discuss these primitive, as yet not fully formulated, states of the self, which I believe are characteristically exemplified in Unamuno's fiction, I shall have in mind the context of theory which conceptualizes such primitive schizoid states. Most specifically, I shall draw on Balint's concept of the basic fault, a stage or state of the personality which is again primitive, anterior to social relationships, and in which difficult experience will characteristically lead to a schizoid reaction to the environment and its occupants.

Balint theorizes two key ideas related to the experience of the nascent self, the ocnophil and the philobat. These, for Balint, are the options open when the emerging self has a difficult or painful relation to the not-self—whether it be the environment or the objects (people) within the environment. If what occurs is a painful passage through to relationship, then the emerging self may, if engaging in what Balint terms as an ocnophilic relation to the world, have a primary cathexis to the emerging objects. The spaces between them will, however, be experienced as 'threatening and horrid'. If, on the other hand, a philobatic relation to the world (related to the original undifferentiated environment experienced by the nascent self) is retained, then the objects will be experienced as 'treacherous hazards', but the environment between them will be felt to be safe and friendly.[14]

It may be asked whether it is appropriate to apply this area of psychoanalytic theory to a fictional text of the early twentieth century, which was almost undoubtedly written in ignorance (or innocence) of such theory. I think there are two main reasons for an affirmative response. First there is the context and history of this particular area of theory. Object Relations theory from the 1920s onwards grows out of, extends and builds upon the theoretical framework of Freud and Abraham. Further, it is not contextually independent, in that it theorizes concerns beyond the parameters of psychoanalytic thought which had become central at the period at which Unamuno was writing. Thus, just as within the European novel we observe a move from a bourgeois realist *bildungsroman* narrative of external social event to the modernist concern with what might or might not be the demarcations of the self, so within the theory of psychoanalysis there is also the move from the narrative of the bourgeois family structure, with its stresses and gendered roles, to a concern with the self before it is integrated into that social nexus.[15] Lacan, in his return to Freud, and writing after Unamuno, could be said in many ways to integrate these two diverging strands, in that the concept of the Symbolic foregrounds the inevitability of our integration with the social nexus in which we live (and which we need, in order to defend the self from the lure of the psychotic in the form of the Imaginary), and yet acknowledges the difficulty of coming to terms with the psychotic. Oddly, although object relations and Lacanian theory are frequently considered to be either opposed or irreconcilable, it is arguable that the intricacies of the formation of the self as explored in certain areas of object relations theory are as questioning of the ease of defining the boundaries of the self as is the theory of Lacan.

The second justification for this approach lies in the strong testimony of Unamuno himself, expressed through the fiction. He makes it clear that his interest is not in the narratives of social life and exchange in which we habitually engage, but rather, as he puts it in *Don Sandalio*, it is to do with the very question of being: 'El problema más hondo de nuestra novela, de la tuya, Felipe, de la mía, de la de Don Sandalio, es un problema de personalidad, *de ser o no ser*, y no de comer o no comer, de amar o ser amado' (1180, emphasis mine). I would argue that what Unamuno says here needs in a very basic sense to be taken literally. That is, when he refers to the 'problema de personalidad', it is the personality or the self that he has in mind, rather than any concept of 'alma' which would be inflected with religious meaning.

There is a further, and extremely pertinent, point. All readers of Unamuno are familiar with his concern with the self, with the personality. There has been a tendency to construe that concern primarily within the framework of either a philosophical context, based upon Unamuno's known interests, or on a religious context. What is less familiar to most readers is the degree to which Unamuno was interested in mind, personality and psychology. This is evidenced not only by his interest in the works of William James, which has received some attention, notably by Pelayo H. Fernández, Farré and Jurkevich, but more strikingly by numerous items in his personal library which reveal a wide-ranging scientific interest, including areas such as insanity and criminality.[16] Of particular interest and relevance are the items on these areas published in the first two decades of the twentieth century. If we put aside a theoretically justifiable *caveat*, namely to state that the presence of works in Unamuno's library does not imply that he read them at any particular time, and instead make the more reasonable assumption that they are likely in some manner to indicate his personal intellectual context at the time of writing his major fictions, their relevance to his conceptualizing of the self must be taken seriously.

Don Sandalio

La novela de don Sandalio, jugador de ajedrez is one of Unamuno's later fictions, appearing some three years after *Cómo se hace una novela*, and forming part of the *San Manuel Bueno* collection. It represents, and reiterates for us, a problem that will not go away. That is, after the middle-period novels, *La tía Tula* and *Abel Sánchez*, in which Unamuno has explored problematic areas such as envy and triangulation,[17] *Don Sandalio* returns us to a schematic, virtually silent world, in which the spirals and evasions of closure that were given formal articulation in *Cómo se hace una novela*, are now clothed in the form of a chess-player and his partner. The *novela* signals from the outset, in its title, that its concern is the self and the self's problematic relationship with existence. It does so by highlighting two of the opposing poles which will engage the attention of the letter-writer in the text. One is the concept of a self, that the letter-writer may come to know, and that he may come to be in relation with. The other is the occupation Sandalio engages in, which is, to quote Víctor Goti of *Niebla*, 'para pasar el rato': the playing of chess. What Sandalio eschews, however, is that engagement in dialogue valued in novels by the wife of Víctor Goti, for whom a 'novela para matar el tiempo' had to be of 'mucho diálogo y muy cortado'.[18] Language is here not engaged in, and is indeed to be rejected as trivial and diversionary. The actions of chess are substituted.

What is equally diversionary is the direction of the reader's interest onto the self of Sandalio and his occupation, in a situation where what will actually be at stake in the narrative is the nature of the narrator's strategies in relation to 'pasar el rato', and the problem of how to live through the state of *tedium vitae*.

A prime question of this text is 'What is the issue from which we are diverted?' It is evident that a central invitation to the reader is to become interested, as is the letter-writer, and as the letter-writer persuades Felipe to be, in the figure of Don Sandalio. Yet as we saw from the discussion of whether it was appropriate to *chercher la femme* in the story, the letter-writer clearly feels that Felipe is on the wrong track in becoming interested in that social existence of Don

Sandalio that lies outside the chess-playing dyad. In this sense, Don Sandalio's external, merely reported, history is a type of black hole, full of matter, urgently pulling the reader into it. As readers, we stand on the edge of that black hole, finding ourselves in a tension which replicates that of the narrator when faced and attracted by Sandalio and what he signifies.

We can pursue the parallel relationship of reader/text with letter-writer/Sandalio through a series of manoeuvres, in which there is a defensive drawing back from the dangers of being drawn into a black hole (of narrative focus, or of the personality of the other, respectively). In this way the different levels of narrative, and the complexity of relationship between them, can be understood and experienced as a mirroring of the letter-writer's anxious manoeuvres of withdrawal and defence in the face of the dangers and threats posed by a relationship with an Other which, it is feared, will be totally engulfing.

Thus, if, as readers, we draw back from the edge of the allegedly diversionary black hole of whether the heart of the story is the Oedipal issue of '¡La ella del viejo cuento!', we see that a possible focus of attention is then formulated in the sense of relationship between the letter-writer and Don Sandalio, as expressed through the chess ritual. This, in its turn, again becomes weighted with significance, so that we, as readers, are drawn into it. At a further stage of withdrawal from the black holes of the narrative, we have the activities of the letter-writer which form an alternation between, on the one hand, an intense ocnophilic experience of Sandalio as object, with the encircling *mirones* as a hostile outer environment, and on the other, a seeking out, in philobatic manner, of the open spaces of nature, the non-urban. At yet a further remove of withdrawal is the relationship between the letter-writer and his own self. This is expressed through the relationship with Don Sandalio and Felipe who is called on to witness that relationship with all its mysteries and fluctuations. Felipe is almost totally absent from the text, save as the implied sympathetic reader of the letters. Yet it is Felipe who is identifiably the reader *not* tuned in to the letter-writer and the other relationships I have just outlined. He demonstrates this by being the source of the unwelcome questions about whether there might not be a woman in the story of Sandalio's external world. Felipe is the source, arguably, of *the* significant relationship in the text, since he is so entirely absent, and on to him can be projected the extremities of the letter-writer's split and vacillating tendencies in relationship.

Having postulated the existence of these spirals of defensive withdrawal, so that the ultimate relationship of withdrawal is formulated as being between the absent Felipe and the letter-writer (with its parallel relationship between the reader and that absently formulated area of the content of the narrative), a further speculation is made available to us. That is, we should, in the spirit of Lacan's purloined letter (an object of central power and significance, which is hidden in the most obvious place, and thus cannot be found),[19] look to that obvious clue we are given to the centre of the narrative. What we are *told* is that the point of the narrative is not a woman, and we are seduced into believing that this is an explanation that we should indeed reject, in the belief, in the fantasy that what is implied is an amorous relationship with a woman. What other 'la' could there be, but woman implied in an amorous narrative? But the self that contemplates a 'la' of a post-Oedipal narrative is a self that might be presumed to be established, boundaried. The alternative is the further absent figure from the letter-writer's world, namely the first Other, the mother, the original '¡La ella del viejo cuento!', an Other that cannot be either named or alluded to. In the light of this central absence which I have postulated, the whole of the narrative can then be construed not simply as defensive, but as a screen-narrative, a memory and account of the pains and defences of relationship in terms that can be contemplated, which stands in the place of the terrors and pains of an original relationship.

What we learn about most directly from the text are two central relationships: that of the letter-writer who swings between an ocnophilic attachment to Sandalio, and a philobatic compulsion to seek object-free or at least person-free spaces, and that of the letter-writer with himself. The relationship with Felipe is one that essentially is to be inferred from the way that the other relationships are narrated. To reach the relationship with Felipe would be, as it were, to reach the end of the story. We might bear in mind here Lacan's account of what happens in analysis: first there is story, and finally there is contact, and the end has been reached: 'the subject begins by talking about himself, he doesn't talk to you—then, he talks to you but he doesn't talk about himself—when he talks about himself, who will have noticeably changed in the interval, to you, we will have got to the end of the analysis'.[20]

The link between the two relationships—letter-writer and Don Sandalio, and letter-writer with himself—can in part be deduced from a simple observation: the frequency of the letters. They span autumn, from late August to the end of December. In the two outer months the frequency of the letters is generally four or five days. In October, however, the frequency is more often of two days, with a gap in the centre when the letter writer is ill, or—as we might construe—goes into a temporary retreat, a flight into convenient illness from the relationship with Sandalio which has by this stage become complicated. As the relationship with Sandalio peaks, and is further complicated by the increasing impingement of puzzling external information, so the letters to Felipe keep pace with the ensuing anxiety. The month of October is, as it were, the black hole of the narrative, the place into which everything might be pulled by irresistible gravitational force.

It is not until Chapter 16 that the letter-writer defines himself, and refers to the loss of his *hogar* as the cause of his ills: 'Tú sabes, mi Felipe, que yo sí que no tengo, hace ya años, hogar; que mi hogar se deshizo, y que hasta el hollín de su chimenea se ha desvanecido en el aire, tú sabes que a esa pérdida de mi hogar se debe la agrura con que me hiere la tontería humana' (1173). This explanation seems to be Unamuno lapsing into the superfluous, the trite. It is evident from the whole of the preceding narrative that the letter-writer is engaged with a loss of his *hogar*, a container whose absence leaves him vulnerable and afraid.

The letters open with the writer in a state of retreat coloured by fear. It is 'un nuevo ataque de misantropía, o mejor de antropofobia, pues a los hombres, más que los odio, los temo' (1159). The vacillation between hate and fear is a significant one. For Freud, hate was one of the most primitive of mechanisms. Older than love, says Freud in 'The Instincts and Their Vicissitudes', an essay in which his conceptualization of the self tracks the besieged state of the infant in its earliest stages, hate 'derives from the narcissistic ego's primordial repudiation of the external world with its outpouring of stimuli. As an expression of the reaction of unpleasure evoked by objects, it always remains in an intimate relation with the self-preservative instincts'.[21] For Winnicott, hate was an emotion denoting a more advanced stage of the ego in its development for (as intimated above by Freud) it implies a reaction of the whole ego to the outside, or to an object. Arrival at the capacity to hate is simultaneously arrival at a full apprehension of death.[22] Guntrip, meanwhile, sees the presence of hate as a desperate defensive measure, which is to 'fend off a breakdown into a schizoid state; for in that condition the individual feels always on the brink of hopeless despair'.[23]

Our letter-writer opens as a philobat, unable even to gather himself into the position of hate, seeking the peace and continuity of nature. Occasional human contact comes his way. This he relates to in the way that Robinson Crusoe reacted to finding the print of a human foot. The terror he feels could be due to the fact that the evidence of the existence of others acts as confirmation to him of his condition as isolate. This confirmation is double-edged. It guarantees his independence (and thus he is free of the *tonterías* of men), but it also guarantees the presence of the others, a terrifying alternative existence.[24]

The allusion to the *huella* is central to the understanding of the story. The continuing tension in the narrative is between relating and not-relating, between the kindling and awakening of interest, and the fleeing from or deadening of contact that might arouse such interest. The *huella* is the trace where humanity has been, the imprint in the sand being a faint hollow, in human form, that sketches out the possibility of a container for the human foot. It is the first in a series of containers, or potential containers, signalled by the text. In the terms of Object Relations theory, the container is provided for the newly-born infant by a parental (usually maternal) presence, and as the infant projects out terrifying or uncomfortable initial experiences, the parental presence is able to act as a membrane which catches and detoxifies the projections.[25] The *huella* of Chapter 1 is followed by the image of the hollow oak, with its empty heart, an image instantly appealing to the narrator (as there are no human connexions apart from the human ones the narrator ascribes to it). The oak seems unthreatening. If it is literally and visibly a black hole, and the *corteza* through which sap still runs is a type of event horizon, it is an image which appears to console the letter-writer, and not one that invites him to a type of annihilation by its attraction. The oak consoles because, significantly, it is empty, the *vacío* being all that the black hole is not. In this, a space to be filled, a receptacle that might contain, the oak is distinct from subsequent black hole images, particularly that of the seemingly bottomless pit of Don Sandalio and his world. Indeed, as a *vacío*, it cannot be a black hole.

In the dynamic between the letter-writer and Don Sandalio, a critical point is reached in mid-October, and the letter-writer falls ill. What has been taking place between him and Don Sandalio is a type of alternation of interest and defensiveness, of merging and of separation, and in response to this the letter-writer retreats (hysterically?) into illness. The alternation of moods or states within the state of illness is more benign, being between the accommodating container of the bed ('ime entretenía tanto la cama, se me pegaban tan amorosamente las sábanas!' [1169]) and the comforting philobat's delight, the view of the mountain with its *cascada* seen through the safely containing frame of the window, and filtered further by the containing and limiting *prismáticos* with which he views it. And the doctor's name? Casanueva. One feels this is hardly accidental—the new container, the new *casa*, the new *hogar* (the other enticing image for the letter-writer being the old *caserío*, another empty space which (deceptively, one imagines) reminds him of Don Sandalio [1163, 1172]). The obviousness of Casanueva's name alerts the reader retrospectively to another possibility, namely that Sandalio has been viewed (erroneously perhaps) as another potential safe container. Sandalio's name can be playfully re-construed as the masculinized form of *sandalia*, the sandal that 'contains' the human foot, which otherwise would leave its clear, and all-too-human print on the sand. Sandalio is therefore safe, or apparently so. That he is the container, all things to all men, is further signalled in his full name, Don Sandalio Cuadrado y Redondo, finally cited in Chapter 16, when the letter-writer is called on to witness to Sandalio in court. The full name blatantly requires the reader of the letters to abandon any fiction that Sandalio might be real, but this is at the very point at which the narrative constructing the fiction of Sandalio's external life is intensified in that now there is a definite move to *draw the letter-writer in*.

Here I need to retrace steps in the narrative, to the relationship between the letter-writer and Don Sandalio. What I want to concentrate on is first the vacillation between the ocnophilic and philobatic modes of relation, and second on what we might consider to be the dangerous functioning of Don Sandalio, experienced by the letter-writer as a black hole into which he may be drawn, and from which he may not emerge.

Don Sandalio is a welcome point of quiet amid the trivial occupants of the Casino, with their inane chatter, and their habit of being *mirones*. The way in which the letter-writer describes him is careful, cautious: '*le llaman o se llama* Don Sandalio, y su oficio *parece ser* el de jugador de ajedrez' (1162, emphasis mine). He appears to wish to take no responsibility for the description of Don Sandalio that he produces in his text, and in the caution of his description he conveys what is presumably his own caution and detachment in the act of drawing near to Sandalio. At a more general level, he conveys his hesitation in relation to life. In coming to the place from which the letters are written, the letter-writer is in retreat, injured by what he experiences as the 'astillas de conversaciones' (not unlike Bion's chards of experience which are characteristically produced for the person in schizoid state) and which reach the wound (what Balint would term the 'basic fault') that he bears, and which he has come to recover from.

We might pause for a moment over the detail the letter-writer gives us of 'las astillas de conversaciones que me llegan me hieren en lo más vivo' (1161). This is, of course, in one sense a simple image which evokes the way in which the talk of others is experienced not as something separate, which can be *listened* to, but as something which enters and wounds the self. But we could also relate it to the observations of Bion about the experience of fragmented states of the self. In his discussion of the development of schizophrenic thought, Bion indicates projective identification as a crucial process. By this, there is a 'splitting off by the patient of a part of his personality and a projection of it into the object where it becomes installed, sometimes as a persecutor, leaving the psyche from which it has been split off correspondingly impoverished'.[26] For Bion, what was split off had a nature so definite as to be concrete, and projections for him are variously referred to as 'particles', 'expelled fragments' and 'bizarre objects'. The resulting circumstance was that the patient would feel a sense of imprisonment which would be 'intensified by the menacing presence of the expelled fragments within whose planetary movements he is contained'.[27] While the text offered to the reader by the letter-writer does not convey the acute conditions described by Bion in relation to his schizophrenics, the strong sense of hostility

251

emanating from the *mirones* and their language refers us back to the embattled state of the letter-writer's mind. Furthermore, if we follow the theory that the letter-writer has projected out these fragments, and that the main recipient of them in the text is Sandalio, the functioning of Sandalio as a black hole with increased gravitational force is reinforced. What is of interest is that Sandalio is not experienced as aggressive or hostile, whereas the *mirones* are. This supports further the concept of Sandalio as a black hole, as a container which does not give back, or as a recipient from which objects not only never return, but cannot be perceived once they have moved over the event horizon.

The attraction of Don Sandalio appears to be his condition as isolate, and the way that others desist from impinging on him. He gives out the impression that there is no world beyond what he does to pass the time, his chess-playing (1162). His is the appeal to the ocnophil in the letter-writer, 'el que más me ha interesado' (1162). What the writer notes most is the way in which, through his stupidity, Don Sandalio appears to offer him a type of self-definition: '*le llaman o se llama* Don Sandalio, y su oficio *parece ser* el de jugador de ajedrez' (1162, emphasis mine). That is, he offers excitement, even desire in the letter-writer, but most of all that awakening of irritation that could become *odio*, and thus confirm the boundaries of his self, within Winnicott's understanding of the function of hate. When Sandalio's chess-partner fails to arrive, the letter-writer contemplates his face 'mirando al vacío', and responds: 'no pude contenerme' (1164). But if he is drawn to Sandalio, it is not clear whether it will be to be related to him, or whether he will be subsumed in Sandalio: 'Era como si yo no existiese en realidad, y como persona distinta de él, para él mismo' (1164). Meanwhile, Sandalio himself appears to be ocnophilic, concentrating his attention upon the chess-pieces, in response to which the letter-writer reflects: 'acaso tenga razón' (1164). It is apparently not Sandalio's self that attracts the letter-writer, but his manner of playing. It is as though this activity, seemingly safe, is like the attraction of the trunk of the hollowed-out tree, the place where life remains. In focusing his attention on the pieces, it is as if Sandalio allows the letter-writer to be alone, in the Winnicottian concept of that capacity.[28] We might also note one of the many manifestations of mirror-functioning here, for if it is the case that the presence of Sandalio allows the letter-writer to be

252

alone, Sandalio himself (1164) is observed waiting for his chess-partner as though he also needed the presence of another in order to have that experience of being alone, or even—one might speculate—to tolerate the experience of being alone.

Both the letter-writer and Sandalio use the activity of playing chess as a type of substitute container, an object into which it appears to be safe to project unwanted or intolerable parts of the self. Chess in *Niebla* is the activity which is used to focalize the need of Augusto to take action, and to be committed to it. As Victor Goti reminds him with insistent severity, '¡Pieza tocada, pieza jugada!'[29] There is an implied distinction in *Don Sandalio* between chess and cards, the latter being the activitity of the mindless (perhaps linked to what Grotstein characterizes as 'meaninglessness'),[30] the former valorized as the dyadic activity in which the two exceptions in the Casino, the letter-writer and Don Sandalio, engage. Chess, moreover, is special when engaged in by these two, since this game, 'ese vicio solitario de dos en compañía' (1162), is silent, and not subject either, in the case of the writer and Sandalio, to the gaze of the *mirones* which surrounds other games, nor indeed to their mischievous interventions, as when the *mirones* move the chess-pieces of the magistrate and the engineer. The brief vignette of these two, the magistrate so anxious that the other will move the chess-pieces when he goes to relieve his bladder that he insists that his chess-partner accompany him, is in part a simple comic piece. As part of the multiple mirroring of the text, however, this anecdote indicates two more serious possibilities. It highlights the possibility that the dyadic relationship, seemingly of such comfort between the letter-writer and Don Sandalio, is also one fraught with suspicion and fear of betrayal. It also highlights the vulnerability of such a self-absorbed dyad: the magistrate and the engineer are both victims of the mischief of the *mirones*, suggesting that there is no level of paranoia so high as to be unjustified, and suggesting that the move into the comforts and consolations of a dyad is a move that simultaneously exposes the participants to attack from the outside. They are so engaged in the dyad that they become unable to perceive dangers from elsewhere. The only safe option for either of them is to relate only to the game of chess, or to the relationship through the other as mediated through the objects of chess, rather than to engage in any direct relationship with one another. Hence the rebuttal, in Chapter 11, by Sandalio of the letter-

253

writer's offer to engage his interest, by proposing to him 'la solución de un problema de ajedrez' (1168). Here Sandalio represents the denial of interest or need. While he represents an ideal state of detachment for the letter-writer, a withdrawal from need for extraneous stimuli, his detachment is clearly a source of frustration, since the letter-writer, while envisioning a state of detachment as embodied for him by Sandalio, cannot tolerate the possibility that for Sandalio there is no need for stimuli—an economic and devastating dismissal of the importance of the letter-writer for Sandalio.

When he returns to the scene of his philobatic longings, the beach, the letter-writer is now object-oriented. Don Sandalio is with him, in spirit, and he reflects that if Sandalio is the trace, the *huella* of humanity for him, it is one that no longer terrifies him (1165). A sense, a terrified sense, of full merging or absorption, has, however, reached the letter-writer by Chapter 8, and his fear is that he has thought so much about Sandalio, has so absorbed him, that he has been overtaken, so that he now suffers from 'doble personalidad' (1167).

From this point onwards the narrator moves back and forth, between an object-driven interest in Sandalio, and a philobatic return to the horizons of nature. Sandalio appears to give out nothing of himself that would render him interesting as object, except perhaps the appearance of an apparently efficient carapace that defends him against the *mirones*, an event horizon beyond which nothing can be known. In Chapter 12, the letter-writer tries hard to awaken Sandalio's interest, pushed on by the thoughts recorded in Chapter 10: '¿Qué pensará de mí? ¿Cómo seré yo para él? ¿Quién seré yo para él?' (1168). In this intensifying need to awaken Sandalio's interest, the letter-writer tries to engage him, is rebuffed by a look of fear, and makes the retreat into illness mentioned earlier. At this point in his vacillations, not unlike Guntrip's characterization of the schizoid mechanism of half-in/half-out,[31] fragments of the external world of Sandalio begin to impinge: a son who has died, the news that Sandalio is in prison, the request from Sandalio's son-in-law that the letter-writer testify, and finally the death of Sandalio.

The apparent difficulty that the letter-writer has with this external information is that it is in conflict with his construction of Sandalio as a being who has kept himself clear of the stupidities and trivialities of the world. I would suggest, however, that there is another, more vital issue. The relationship between them has expressed the letter-writer's interest, and has apparently been unreciprocated. But the news of the turbulent home life of Sandalio raises the possibility that Sandalio has not simply cut himself off from his surroundings, but has, arguably in the manner described by Fairbairn, internalized a series of difficult objects in order to retain control over them.[32] What other fate, then, can await the letter-writer, but that he too will be pulled in by the massive gravitational force of these accumulated other objects, into the black hole of Sandalio's imploding self? What is at stake is the letter-writer's survival.

If we read Sandalio as the mirroring of the letter-writer, then the model which is suggested is not simply that of the terror of being sucked into the black hole of another, which at least presupposes a self which exists with its own separate boundaries in the first place, but rather that of being sucked into one's own black hole. In so far as Sandalio represents a projection outwards of the letter-writer's state of mind, then the threat (and the attraction) presented by him is precisely that of a collapse inwards. The model suggested is thus of an inward-turning of self-regulation from which there is no escape—the Kleinian bottle. This 'has a spout which involutes into itself so that the contents being poured out from the bottle through the spout re-enter the bottle—theoretically—but actually enter into an invisible dimension which is contained within the visible bottle but which is not identical with it'.[33] The *Epílogo* posits this type of schema, an inward-whirling vortex where no foothold on reality can be retained once one has opted into moving over the event horizon of deciding that all is in motion, and that no boundaries are to be held.

Bibliography

BALINT, Michael (1968), *The Basic Fault: Therapeutic Aspects of Regression*. Repr. 1979, pref. by Enid Balint, London: Tavistock/Routledge 1992.

BION, Wilfred (1962), *Learning from Experience*, London: Heinemann.

— (1967), *Second Thoughts: Selected Papers on Psycho-Analysis*. Repr. 1984. London: Karnac.

FAIRBAIRN, W. R. D. (1952), *Endopsychic Structure Considered in Terms of Object-Relationships* (1944), In *Psychoanalytic Studies of the Personality*. Tavistock Publications, pp. 82–136.

FARRÉ, Luis (1967), *Unamuno, William James y Kierkegaard*. Buenos Aires: La Aurora.

FERNÁNDEZ, Pelayo Hipólito (1961), *Miguel de Unamuno y William James: un paralelo pragmático*. Salamanca: n.p.

FREUD, Sigmund (1915), 'The Instincts and Their Vicissitudes', in *On Meta-psychology: The theory of Psychoanalysis*. Trans. under James Strachey, ed. Angela Richards. Pelican Freud Library, vol. 11, (1984). Harmondsworth: Penguin Books, 113–38.

GROTSTEIN, James S. (1990a), 'Nothingness, Meaninglessness, Chaos, and the "Black Hole" I: the Importance of Nothingness, Meaninglessness, and Chaos in Psychoanalysis'. *Contemporary Psychoanalysis* 26 (2), 257–290.

— (1990b), 'Nothingness, Meaninglessness, Chaos, and the "Black Hole" II: the Black Hole'. *Contemporary Psychanalysis* 26 (3), 377–407.

— (1991), 'Nothingness, Meaninglessness, Chaos, and the "Black Hole" II: Self- and Interactional Regulation and the Background Presence of Primacy Identification'. *Contemporary Psychoanalysis* 27 (4), 1–33.

GUNTRIP, Harry (1968), *Schizoid Phenomena, Object-Relations and the Self*. Repr. London: Karnac and the Institute of Psycho-Analysis (1992).

HAWKING, Stephen W. (1988), *A Brief History of Time: From the Big Bang to Black Holes*. London: Bantam Press.

HUTCHINSON, Peter (1983), *Games Authors Play*. London and New York: Methuen.

JAMES, Colin (1984), 'Bion's "Containing" and Winnicott's "Holding" in the context of the Group Matrix'. *International Journal of Group Psychotherapy* 34 (2) (April 1984), 201–213.

JURKEVICH, Gayana (1991), *The Elusive Self: Archetypal Approaches to the Novels of Miguel de Unamuno*. Columbia and London: Univ. of Missouri Press.

LACAN, Jacques (1956), '*Le Séminaire sur "La lettre Volée"*'. Repr. 1966 in *Ecrits*, 11–61 (Paris: Editons du Seuil).

— (1981), *The Psychoses: the Seminar of Jacques Lacan*, ed. by Jacques-Alain Miller. Book III, 1955–1956 (1993). Contains 'The Hysteric's Question'. Translated with notes by Russell Grigg. Cambridge: Cambridge University Press.

SASS, Louis (1992), *Madness and Modernism: Insanity in the Light of Modern Art, Literature, and Thought*. New York: Basic Books.

SINCLAIR, Alison (1991), 'The Envy of Motherhood: Destructive Urges in Unamuno' in *Feminist Readings on Spanish and Latin-American Literature*, ed. Lisa Condé and Steve Hart. Dyfed: Edwin Mellen Press, 47–61.

— (1995), 'Unamuno and the unknown: responses to primitive terror', forthcoming in *Belief and Unbelief in Hispanic Literature*, proceedings of a conference held December 1995 at the University of Hull, ed. Helen Wing and John Jones. Warminster: Aris and Phillips, 134–145.

TUSTIN, Frances (1998), 'The "black hole"—a significant element in autism'. *Free Association* 11, 35–50.

UNAMUNO, Miguel de (1966), *Obras completas*. Ed. M García Blanco. 9 vols. Madrid: Escelicer. Refs are to *Niebla* (1914) and *La novela de Don Sandalio, jugador de ajedrez* (1930) in vol. II.

— (1914), *Niebla*. Repr. 1963. Madrid: Austral.

— (1930), *La novela de Don Sandalio, jugador de ajedrez*, in '*San Manuel Bueno, mártir' y tres historias más*. Madrid: Austral (1969).

VALDÉS, Mario J. and Valdés, María Elena (1973), *An Unamuno Source Book: a Catalogue of Readings and Acquisitions with an Introductory Essay on Unamuno's Dialectical Enquiry*. Toronto: University of Toronto Press.

WINNICOTT, D. W. (1965), *The Maturational Processes and the Facilitating Environment: Studies in the Theory of Emotional Development*. International Psycho-Analytical Library, vol. 64, ed. John D. Sutherland. London: The Hogarth Press and the Institute of Psycho-Analysis.

— (1969), 'The Use of the Object and Relating through Identification', *International Journal of Psycho-Analysis* 50, 711–716.

Notes

Chapter One

1. Not least by the present author himself in the opening lines of the Critical Guide to *Pío Baroja: El mundo es ansí*, (London: Grant & Cutler, 1977), p. 9 —'1902 is a year of special significance in the history of the Spanish novel'. Another example of the magical attraction of 1902 is found in Robert C. Spires, *Transparent Simulacra. Spanish Fiction 1902–1926*. (Columbia: University of Missouri Press, 1988), p. xi—'The year 1902 is fundamental to the efforts of renovating Spanish fiction'. Roberta Johnson uses the less loaded date of 1900 for the title of her *Crossfire. Philosophy and the Novel in Spain, 1900–1934*, (Lexington: University Press of Kentucky, 1993), but the 1902 novels remain the effective starting point ('1902 saw a dawning of artistic maturity', p. 34).

2. Malcolm Bradbury, *Possibilities. Essays on the State of the Novel*, (Oxford: OUP, 1973), p. 85. In their well-known critical anthology on Modernism, (*Modernism, 1890–1930*, Harmondsworth: Penguin Books, 1976), Bradbury and McFarlane also see Modernism as getting under way in the 1890s.

3. David Daiches, *The Novel and the Modern World*, (Chicago and London: University of Chicago Press, 1960). Very recently, and on the basis of Conrad's Modernism, Alan Sandison has argued that similar Modernist features are found in the novels of Robert Louis Stevenson (*Robert Louis Stevenson and the Appearance of Modernism*, London: Macmillan, 1996).

4. Quoted in Miriam Allott, *Novelists on the Novel*, (London: Routledge, 1965), p. 74.

5. Joseph Conrad, 'Henry James: An Appreciation' (1905). Reproduced in *Joseph Conrad on Fiction*, edited by Walter F. Wright, (Lincoln, Nebr: University of Nebraska Press, 1964), pp. 82–8, at pp. 86–7.

6. Virginia Woolf, 'Modern Fiction', reprinted in *The Common Reader*, (London and New York: Harcourt Brace, 1925); reproduced in Ellman and Feidelson, *The Modern Tradition. Backgrounds of Modern Literature*, (New York: OUP, 1965), pp. 121–6, at p. 122.

7. Ellman and Feidelson, p. 123.

8. 'Nada más ambiguo que eso que se llama realismo en el arte literario. Porque ¿qué realidad es la de ese realismo?' (*Tres novelas ejemplares y un prólogo,* in *Obras Completas*, 9 vols, Madrid: Escelicer, 1966–71, at II, 972). Cf. Baroja: 'No sé si puedo llamarme realista; no sé lo que es la realidad' (*Obras Completas*, 8 vols, Madrid: Biblioteca Nueva, 1946–51, vol. V, p. 414).

9. *Tres novelas ejemplares y un prólogo*, in *Obras Completas*, vol. II, p. 974. All further references to the *Obras Completas* of Unamuno will be given in the text as OC.

10. It should be unnecessary to add that Modernism, despite the impossibility of defining it in simple terms, had little to do with the earlier doctrine of art for art's sake that became fashionable in certain European circles (Wilde, Huysmans). There has been a regrettable tendency among some Continental Hispanists to equate the two, almost certainly due to the connotations of aestheticism acquired by the Spanish word *modernismo*. It is worth insisting that the Modernists' (and I include most of the so-called *noventaiochistas* under this label) persistent defence of the primacy of the individual conscious-ness of the artist is not the same thing as art for art's sake, especially that propounded by the more extreme aesthetes of the late nineteenth century. Modernism was by no means as inward-looking as some of its Marxist and Social-Realist critics have tried to make out. It was concerned with art, certainly, but in terms of its relationship with something else, whether the author, the reader, language, or indeed history and social circumstance.

11. Ángel Ganivet, *España filosófica contemporánea*, in *Obras Completas*, (2 vols, Madrid: Aguilar, 1951), vol. II, p. 625-6. All further references to the *Obras Completas* of Ganivet will be given in the text as OC.

12. Juan Ignacio Ferreras sees Naturalist Determinism at work in the novels of Zamacois, whether erotic or not. See his *La novela en el siglo XX (hasta 1939)*, (Madrid: Taurus, 1988), pp. 58–9. Another name associated with Naturalism is that of Felipe Trigo, but I am not sufficiently familiar with his novels to place him in any literary current. Ferreras classifies him quite unambiguously as a Naturalist but José Carlos Mainer sees him as a rather more complex figure who combines 'el cientifismo implacable de la novela positivista-naturalista con un modernismo, por el que entiendo una preceptiva moral basada en la exaltación del instinto y la redención literaria de lo extrasocial' (*Literatura y pequeña burguesía en España*, Madrid: Cuadernos para el Diálogo, 1972, p. 64). In Spain, Naturalism spawned a vast production of inferior, erotic, and sensationalist novels. See Jean-François Botrel, 'España, 1880–1890: el naturalismo en situación', in *Realismo y naturalismo en España*, ed. Yvan Lissourgues, (Barcelona: Anthropos, 1988), pp. 183–97. For a mention of some other Naturalists, and quasi-Naturalists see Juan Ignacio Ferreras, *La novela en el siglo XIX (desde 1868)*, (Madrid: Taurus, 1988).

13. Manuel Fernández Cifuentes, *Teoría y mercado de la novela en España: Del 98 a la República* (Madrid: Gredos, 1982), pp. 38–74.

14. Cited by Fernández Cifuentes, p. 41.

15. Cited by Fernández Cifuentes, p. 43.

16. Referring to Ramón María Tenreiro's (the leading critic of *La Lectura*) 1913 description of the new novel as having abandoned plot in favour of 'esbozos de sensaciones del artista', Manuel Fernández Cifuentes writes: 'La actitud de Tenreiro es representativa del conjunto de la crítica en por lo menos tres de sus aspectos: alude constantemente a la ruptura de antiguos patrones; muestra esa ruptura en obras de Valle-Inclán, de Pérez de Ayala y de Pío Baroja; y se declara partidario de un vago "realismo" que se tenía por nuevo' (*Teoría y mercado de la novela en España*, p. 40).

17. Quoted by Walter T. Pattison, *El naturalismo español*, (Madrid: Gredos, 1965), p. 159.

18. Jean-François Botrel, 'España, 1880-1890; el naturalismo en situación', p. 193.

19. 'Once upon a time and a very good time it was there was a moocow coming down along the road and this moocow that was coming down along the road met a nicens little boy named baby tuckoo' (James Joyce, *A Portrait of the Artist as a Young Man*, first published 1916 but first redaction 1904).

20. Pío Baroja, 'Hacia lo inconsciente', *Obras Completas*, vol. VIII, p. 851. Baroja appears to use 'inconsciente' and 'subconsciente' as synonyms. Further references to Baroja will be given in the text as OC unless otherwise indicated. It should be noted that the pagination of Baroja's *Obras Completas* published by Biblioteca Nueva was changed between printings without any warning or indication whatsoever and therefore page references can appear to be wrong.

21. Pío Baroja, 'Literatura y bellas artes' (1899), reproduced in *El modernismo visto por los modernistas*, introducción y selección de Ricardo Gullón, (Barcelona: Labor-Guadarrama [Colección Punto Omega], 1980), pp. 75–81, at p. 77. Preceding quotations also from this source.

22. In a 1926 lecture entitled 'Tres generaciones' Baroja was to insist that the writers who were born a few years either side of 1870 were formed in an age when the old ideas were breaking down and the new ones were a confused admixture: 'Las teorías positivistas estaban ya en plena decadencia y apuntaban otras ideas antidogmáticas. [...] Esta época nuestra fue una época confusa de sincretismo. Había en ella todas las tendencias, menos la de la generación anterior, a quien no se estimaba' (OC, V, 575). This repeats an idea which he first enunciated in an article published in 1899 (see 'Figurines literarios' in Pío Baroja, *Hojas sueltas*, ed. Luis Urrutia Salaverri, 2 vols, Madrid: Caro Raggio, 1973, vol. II, pp. 79–83).

23. Pío Baroja, 'Figurines literarios' in *Hojas sueltas*, vol. II, pp. 79. Further references to this edition will be given in the text as HS.

24. It has to be said that Dostoyevski was becoming known in Spain in the 1890s through translations of his work. The earliest of these (*El crimen y el castigo*, and *Los hermanos Karamazov*), are undated but probably appeared in the late 1880s. *La casa de los muertos*, a rather more curious choice, appeared in 1892 with an introduction by Pardo Bazán. Translations into French had been appearing regularly throughout the 1880s and it was these French versions that Baroja had been reading. The French academician Eugène Marie de Vogüé first published his enormously successful *Le Roman russe* in 1886, a work which Baroja obviously knew since he borrowed substantially from it. But in the Spain of the time few readers could have intuited the key position that Dostoyevski was to be accorded not simply in Russian but more importantly in European literature. The use of subconscious motivation was pioneered by Dostoyevski and recognized by Baroja. Nietzsche was still little more than a name, as his work did not begin to be translated until 1900.

25. What Baroja is doing here is continuing a hoax perpetrated by Amorós himself, who 'killed' his pseudonymous personage in one of his works and

from then on presented himself as compiler, editor and publisher of Silverio Lanza's posthumous works.

26. In his still indispensable study *Azorín as a Literary Critic* (New York: Hispanic Institute, 1962), Edward Inman Fox wrote: 'Azorín explains the apparent novelty of Baroja and Benavente to be nothing more than a result of the evolutionary process in literature. Their work at the beginning of the twentieth century is exactly the same as that of Lope and Cervantes in the seventeenth century: the final disintegration of the old and the integration of the new' (p. 69).

27. Azorín, *Ante Baroja*, in *Obras Completas*, (9 vols, Madrid: Aguilar, 1963), vol. VIII, p. 150. Further references to Azorín will be given in the text as OC.

28. I have argued elsewhere that Baroja went through a quasi-Symbolist phase which is virtually explicit in *Camino de perfección* ('*Camino de perfección* and the Modernist Aesthetic', in *Hispanic Studies in Honour of Geoffrey Ribbans*, ed. Ann L. Mackenzie and Dorothy S. Severin, *Bulletin of Hispanic Studies*, Special Homage Volume, Liverpool: Liverpool University Press, 1992, pp. 191–203). As we shall see, one can find Symbolist traits too in some of his early short stories written in the period 1893-8. But Symbolist or not, what is incontestable is Baroja's conscious attempt to describe through the mind rather than simply through the eyes, and it is this that struck Azorín and several other critics—those of a progressive tendency, such as Tenreiro, who defended his style, and those of a traditional outlook, such as Francos Rodríguez and José Nakens, who called Baroja's stories 'pedantescos, petulantes y ridículos' (see *Pío Baroja. Escritos de juventud*, ed. Manuel Longares, Madrid: Cuadernos para el Diálogo, 1972, p. 19).

29. Ramón Pérez de Ayala, 'La aldea lejana', in *Obras Completas*, (4 vols, Madrid: Aguilar, 1963), vol. I, p. 1094. Further references to Ramón Pérez de Ayala will be given in the text as OC.

30. Unfortunately the term 'novela psicológica' is useless for our purposes since it can be made to apply equally to an offshoot of Naturalism (for example the novels of Paul Bourget or the later works of Pardo Bazán) and an early phase of Modernism (Baroja, Azorín). Whether there is a psychological interest or not is not and cannot be by itself the key to the question of a changing aesthetic, since psychology was very much 'in the air' in the later decades of the nineteenth century and affected many different kinds of writers. We have to look at the manner of presentation of the psychological interest.

31. Having been taken to task on a previous occasion for referring to Galdós's narrator in *La de Bringas* as an 'inorganic I-narrator' I should perhaps explain that the adjective inorganic is not intended to carry any value judgement whatsoever. It is shorthand for the kind of narrator who occasionally uses first-person narration and therefore has a self-recognized existence, but who nevertheless has not been assigned a circumscribed role *within* the story as character witness, recipient of information, etc., and who, moreover, uses omniscient narration. It is, of course, a common form of narration (omniscient but not impersonal) in the nineteenth-century novel, but one whose intrusiveness came to be resented by some purists, such as Henry James.

32. *Style indirect libre* is significant because it foreshadows one of the Modernists' innovations, stream of consciousness. There are numerous examples of *style indirect libre* in the novel, but Galdós seems hesitant to continue it for any length. In the following passage, for example, what starts off as *style indirect libre* becomes thought-quotation through the standard use of guillemets (chevrons) or other quotation marks: 'Día más *perro* que aquél no se había visto en todo el año, que desde Reyes venía siendo un año fulastre, pues el día del santo patrono (20 de enero) sólo *se habían hecho* doce *chicas*, la mitad aproximadamente que el año anterior, y la Candelaria y la novena del bendito San Blas, que otros años fueron tan de provecho, vinieron en aquél con diarios de siete *chicas*: ¡valiente puñado! «Y me *paice* a mí —decía para sus andrajos el buen Pulido, bebiéndose las lágrimas y escupiendo los pelos de su barba— que el amigo San José también nos vendrá con mala pata [...]»' (B. Pérez Galdós, *Obras Completas*, 6 vols, [5th edition] Madrid: Aguilar, 1967, vol. V, p. 1878). Further references to *Misericordia* will be given in the text as OC.

33. Thirty-three years later Unamuno was to echo Galdós in *La novela de Don Sandalio*, where the narrating character invents his own version of Don Sandalio which he furiously defends against competing versions. He, too, talks of 'Mi Don Sandalio, el mío', just as Benina talks of 'el mío, mi D. Romualdo'. Another echo of Benina's 'Los sueños, los sueños, digan lo que quieran [...] son también de Dios; ¿y quién va a saber lo que es verdad y lo que es mentira?' is to be found in Ángela Carballino's 'Y yo no sé lo que es verdad y lo que es mentira, ni lo que vi y lo que soñé' (*San Manuel Bueno, mártir*).

34. For an excellent study that places rather greater emphasis on the meta-fictional aspects of the novel see Nil Santiáñez-Tió, *Ángel Ganivet, escritor modernista,* (Madrid: Gredos, 1994). See, also, Francisco García Sarriá, '*Los trabajos del infatigable creador Pío Cid* como antinovela y prenivola', in *Estudios de novela española moderna: texto y subtexto de Galdós a Guelbenzu,* (Madrid: Playor, 1987), pp. 45–52; and Germán Gullón, 'La modernidad de Ganivet: nueva lectura de *Los trabajos del infatigable creador Pío Cid*', *La Torre*, III, 10 (1989), pp. 243–57.

35. Of this, Baroja wrote in 1900: 'En France et en Angleterre, le bourgeois aisé destine une somme plus ou moins considérable de son budget a l'achat des livres; en Espagne, il trouve toute la littérature concentrée dans le journal' ('Chronique des lettres espagnoles', *L'Humanité Nouvelle,* April 1900, reproduced in HS, vol. II, at pp. 27–37).

36. Jeremy Sanders has shown that parts of *Camino de perfección* were written when Baroja was just twenty. See 'A Missing Link to the Work of Pío Baroja', *Bulletin of Hispanic Studies*, LXI, 4 (1984), 14–30.

37. 'El dolor: estudio de psico-física' was the title of Baroja's MD thesis submitted to the University of Madrid in 1894. It was published in 1896.

38. All the stories referred to may be found in *Hojas sueltas*.

39. There is a famous passage in *Point Counter Point* in which Huxley, starting from the Gidian *mise en abîme*, satirizes the idea of an experimental novel in which the narration takes on a wholly scientific appearance: 'At about the tenth remove you might have a novelist telling your story in algebraic symbols

or in terms of variations in blood-pressure, pulse, secretion of ductless glands and reaction times' (Chapter 22). Twenty-five years earlier Baroja had already satirized the concept of a scientifically-based novel.

40. Darwin's theory of natural selection is of course the best-known example of this movement from external manifestation to internal mechanism, but exactly the same approach holds for Comte's Positivism (establishing causal connections between phenomena, thereby inferring the laws that governed them), or Marx's historical materialism, or Spencer's scientific sociology. The realization that these thinkers were actually intuiting the theory first and finding the supporting facts second came only much later. The well-known incompatibility between Marxism and Modernism is itself revealing. Marxism is based on the belief that social or historical existence determines individual consciousness. The Modernists rejected this, which is one reason why Modernism was anathema to Marxist critics like Lukacs.

41. This is a question that appears to have preoccupied Baroja, for he repeated it in the story of Fernando Ossorio, first introduced in *Silvestre Paradox* and greatly expanded in *Camino de perfección*.

42. A rather more complex interpretation of this work, according to which Baroja was exploring the role of mental illness and the unconscious in artistic creativity, has been put forward by J.L. Sanders in his unpublished PhD dissertation 'From Medicine to Psychology: The Early Work of Pío Baroja, 1890–1903', University of Leeds, 1979.

43. For a reading of *Niebla* from a Modernist perspective, see John Macklin, 'Competing Voices. Unamuno's *Niebla* and the Discourse of Modernism', in *After Cervantes: A Celebration of 75 Years of Iberian Studies at Leeds*, (Leeds: Trinity and All Saints College, 1993), pp. 167–93.

44. Maurice Hemingway, *Emilia Pardo Bazán. The Making of a Novelist*, (Cambridge: CUP, 1983).

Chapter Two

1. 'Asfixia', reprinted with the title 'La pérdida de las colonias: El carlismo' in Emilia Pardo Bazán, *La vida contemporánca (1896 1916)*, compiled and with an introduction by Carmen Bravo-Villasante, Serie Literatura Española: Periodismo, Siglos XIX–XX (Madrid: EMESA, 1972), pp. 61–7 (p. 61).

2. Emilia Pardo Bazán, *La España de ayer y la de hoy: (Conferencia de París)* (Madrid: Administración, [1899]), p. 61.

3. Emilia Pardo Bazán, *Al pie de la torre Eiffel: (Crónicas de la Exposición)* (Madrid: La España Editorial, [1889]), p. 185.

4. Raymond Carr, *Spain: 1808–1939* (Oxford: Clarendon Press, 1966; repr. 1970), p. 387, n. 2.

5. For an assessment of the work of these two dramatists and of the dramatic output of other practitioners of the *alta comedia*, see David Thatcher Gies, *The Theatre in Nineteenth-Century Spain* (Cambridge: Cambridge University Press, 1994), pp. 231–91.

6. For example, in her 1891 essay entitled 'Un jesuita novelista: El padre Luis Coloma', Pardo Bazán notes: 'No cabe duda: el período de estabilidad política

que desde la Restauración atraviesa España se deja sentir en las letras', in Emilia Pardo Bazán, *Obras completas*, Tomo III, *Cuentos/Crítica literaria (Selección)*, ed. by Harry L. Kirby, Jr (Madrid: Aguilar, 1973), pp. 969–80 (p. 971).

7. *Mi romería*, 4th edn (Madrid: Administración, 1909), p. 197.
8. *Al pie de la torre Eiffel*, pp. 274–5.
9. See, for example, *Mi romería*, p. 196.
10. Emilia Pardo Bazán, *Obras completas*, Tomo I, *Novelas/Cuentos*, ed. by Federico Carlos Sáinz de Robles, 4th edn (Madrid: Aguilar, 1973), p. 313. Further textual references to this novel and also to *Insolación* will be to this edition and volume.
11. Emilia Pardo Bazán, *Por Francia y por Alemania: (Crónicas de la Exposición)* (Madrid: La España Editorial, [1890]), p. 248.
12. 'Veraneo de los autores: Emilia Pardo Bazán', *El Heraldo de Madrid*, 3 September 1899, pp. 1–2 (p. 1).
13. Emilia Pardo Bazán, *Obras completas*, Tomo II, *Novelas/Cuentos/Teatro*, ed. by Federico Carlos Sáinz de Robles, 3rd edn (Madrid: Aguilar, 1973), p. 588. Further textual references to *El Niño de Guzmán* will be to this edition and volume.
14. Miguel de Unamuno, *En torno al casticismo*, Colección Austral, 403 (Buenos Aires: Espasa-Calpe, 1952), p. 28.
15. Emilia Pardo Bazán, *Cuarenta días en la Exposición* (Madrid: Administración, [1900]), p. 119.
16. See my article, 'Continuity, Change, and the Decadent Phenomenon in Pardo Bazán's Late Fiction', *Neophilologus*, 78 (1994), 395–406.
17. A version of this article was given as a paper at the one-day conference, 'The 19th-Century Novel in Spain and Latin America', held at the University of Liverpool on 4 November 1994.

There are no notes to Chapter Three

Chapter Four

1. '[...] a la mañana siguiente no me acerqué al hotel donde se alojaba la Sra. Pardo hasta última hora de la tarde; pero ella no estaba. Regresé al mediodía siguiente y tampoco. Por la noche, me dijo que había hecho una excursión con Lázaro a Arenys de Mar, de donde volvía encantada. (Algunos quisieron suponer después que *Insolación* es un reflejo de ello)'. Agradezco la traducción de este texto a mi colega la Profesora María Mercè López Casas.
2. En la primera edición de su biografía (Bravo-Villasante, 1962: 158) la alusión era muy indirecta: '*Insolación* va dedicada a Lázaro Galdiano, admirador vehementísimo de la escritora, a la que ha poco acaba de conocer en la Exposición de Barcelona, siendo presentado por el escritor catalán Narcís Oller'; en la segunda edición (1973: 150) es más explícita: 'Lo de Arenys [fue] transformado todo más tarde en el episodio de la Pradera de San Isidro en *Insolación*'. Entre ambas ediciones, en una comunicación presentada en el Cuarto Congreso Internacional de Hispanistas (Salamanca, 1971), la misma investigadora precisaba aquella noticia: 'al enterarse de lo de Arenys y Lázaro

(transformado todo más tarde en el episodio de la Pradera de San Isidro y de la señora de *Insolación*) Galdós reprocha en su carta esas cosas a Emilia [...]; el episodio [de Arenys] se refleja en la novelita *Insolación*, y la Pardo atribuye la caída de su protagonista en brazos del apuesto andaluz a las circunstancias de un calor excesivo, es decir a la insolación en la pradera, con lo que se disculpa a sí misma de su abandono en Arenys, atribuyéndolo a factores externos.' (Bravo-Villasante, 1982: 200–1; y también en Bravo-Villasante, 1975: 5–7).

3. Clémessy, 1973: 214–15: 'L'oeuvre [*Insolación*] fut dédiée par son auteur à José Lázaro Galdiano. Sans aucun doute la clef de l'histoire est-elle à rechercher dans cette dédicace. D'aucuns se sont défendus de voir dans les personnages de l'appétissante veuve et de son sémillant séducteur, Emilia elle-même et don José. Cela se chuchota fort à l'époque et avec quelque raison. La correspondance inédite [en 1973, fecha de publicación de este libro] entre la romancière et Galdós confirme ces présomptions. A la lumière de cette correspondance on peut affirmer aujourd'hui sans risque de faire fausse route que *Insolación* est l'adaptation, fort libre cela s'entend, d'une expérience partagée avec Lázaro à qui doña Emilia offrit ensuite, en guise de souvenirs affectueux, cette évocation littéraire pleine d'esprit'; sigue contando cómo se conocieron en Barcelona y refiere la 'aventura de Arenys', aduciendo (nota 58, en p. 215) el testimonio de Oller que ya conocemos; y añade: 'Tout porte à croire que dans la brûlante journée madrilène, à la fête de Saint-Isodore, évoquée dans *Insolación*, l'écrivain a reflété les heures chaleureuses passées sur les rivages catalans'. Más adelante comenta que 'la correspondance de la romancière avec Lázaro, si jalousement gardée encore actuellement, pourrait sans nul doute éclairer la question', precisando (en nota 59) que la existencia de tales cartas le fue confirmada por Rodríguez Moñino, en la época en que fue director del Museo Lázaro Galdiano en Madrid, pero que su consulta no le ha sido permitida. Como enseguida diré, hoy conocemos una carta de aquella correspondencia, muy pertinente a nuestro objeto.

4. Mayoral, 1987: 11–12: 'Fácilmente puede deducirse que la amistad de doña Emilia con Lázaro Galdiano era del dominio público en el mundillo literario [...] *Insolación* reproduce en su esquema argumental las circunstancias [de la aventura de Emilia Pardo y José Lázaro]'. Aunque más adelante advierte: 'La relación entre doña Emilia y don José Lázaro y la aventura de Arenys de Mar como foco generador de *Insolación* ha de considerarse sólo como una hipótesis de trabajo' (13).

5. Whitaker, 1988: 364: 'The novel, according to many critics, is a veiled autobiographical version of one of Doña Emilia's own adventures: her infatuation with Lázaro Galdiano for a few days in Barcelona in 1889'.

6. Ortiz Armengol, 1996: 454: 'La aventura que parece relatar *Insolación* semeja, más bien, la aventura verdadera de la dama que se encuentra con alguien diverso, distinto —un hombre joven, empleado en alguna empresa mercantil, si bien con deseos de fundar una revista de letras y arte— que la conquista en pocos días —¿u horas?— después de una alegre excursión a un pueblecito bañado por el sol un día de mayo. La malicia humana pronto

relacionó la novelita *Insolación* con la resonante y súbita amistad del señor Lázaro Galdiano con la escritora'.

7. DeCoster, 1984: 121; Santiáñez-Tió, 1989: 118; Ávila Arellano, 1993: 308–10. Pero también —como la antes citada de Mayoral— hay opiniones más prudentes: 'There is little wonder that some persons thought that Asís and her adventures were taken from Doña Emilia's own experience. Attempts were made to identify Pacheco with some of her acquaintances. Yet, although Pardo Bazán was undoubtedly subject to erotic impulses, no complete identification of her with Asís es possible' (Pattison, 1971: 61). 'Autobiografismos aparte —que reclamarían el testimonio complementario de Lázaro...' (Penas, 1993–4: 332).

8. Cronología confirmada por sus comentarios a *Fortunata y Jacinta*: confiesa haber devorado en el viaje los tres primeros tomos y pregunta cuándo podrá leer el cuarto; como ha recordado Ortiz Armengol, 1987: 15, 'A comienzos de 1887 [Galdós] está trabajando en la cuarta parte [de *Fortunata y Jacinta*], que concluye en el mes de junio'; y añade que en una de sus cartas en *La Prensa* de Buenos Aires se excusa de un 'no pequeño plazo de interrupción epistolar', debido al 'cuarto tomo de una novela que debía publicarse en junio y por fin, forzando un poco la máquina, ha salido en los últimos días de julio', según escribe el 29 de julio de 1887; (el texto de Galdós, en Shoemaker, 1973: 250).

9. He de advertir que, según las estrictas normas del archivo de la Casa-Museo Pérez Galdós, las cartas inéditas que allí se custodian no pueden transcribirse ni siquiera parcialmente, aunque sí parafrasearse.

10. En varios trabajos posteriores la misma investigadora ha vuelto a mencionar esa carta: en dos artículos de 1994 ('Diario de un viaje', 173; 'La Condesa, la Revolución', 186), comentando las opiniones allí formuladas sobre *Fortunata y Jacinta*; en otro de 1997 ('La poética de Galicia', 154), repitiendo la noticia de que en aquel viaje en tren de Madrid a Galicia, en junio de 1887, 'Doña Emilia concibió la idea de *Insolación*'. Es de notar que, mientras en su libro de 1992 fechaba la carta el 16 de junio, en los artículos de 1994 y 1997 indica que el documento conservado en la Casa-Museo Pérez Galdós está datado el 'Corpus Cristi [sic] 1887', o el 'Día del Corpus 1887'. Mas, como he advertido antes, la única fecha que consta en el manuscrito es '16 de junio' (añadido '87'); y en aquel año dicha festividad —que es móvil y depende de la Pascua— cayó en el jueves anterior (9 de junio), según informe que agradecemos al franciscano Padre José Isorna.

11. González-Arias, 1992; conviene advertir que tal libro es versión corregida de su tesis doctoral presentada en 1985 (González-Arias, 1986), en la cual no hay referencia a esta cuestión; lo que parece indicar que su conocimiento de esta carta es posterior.

12. Quien ha llamado también mi atención sobre un texto del capítulo XIX de *La Madre Naturaleza* (1887) que podría ser una versión previa de esa especie de embriaguez propiciada por un sol ardiente (y que, a su vez, facilitará la entrega amorosa): 'entre el sol que le requemaba la sangre y el vaho que se elevaba de la ebullición de la tierra [...] Manuela sentía como un comienzo de

embriaguez, el estado inicial de la borrachera alcohólica...' (Pardo Bazán, 1887: II, 20–1). Conste aquí mi agradecimiento por esa y otras valiosas sugerencias suyas a la primera redacción de este artículo: una muy eficaz y generosa manera de sumarse a este homenaje a su admirado Maurice Hemingway.

13. Aunque es de notar (como sutilmente lo hace González Arias, 1992: 121) la coincidencia entre la circunstancia en que brotó la idea —un viaje en tren de Madrid a Galicia— y un momento especialmente significativo de la novela: la pesadilla de la protagonista en el capítulo XXI ('Lo que veía Asís, adormecida o mal despierta, puede explicarse en la forma siguiente, aunque en realidad fuese harto más vago y borroso: Encontrábase ya en el vagón...', Pardo Bazán, 1889: 298–9; y sigue una descripción de las impresiones que percibe la viajera —en el tren de Madrid a Galicia—, muy similares a las que explicaba en aquella carta a Galdós).

14. A este propósito es curioso advertir que en la nota 7 de su 'Introducción' a la novela, Marina Mayoral alude a esta misma carta —entonces inédita—, recogiendo el dato de que en ella 'le anuncia la salida de *Insolación*'.

15. '[...] mero galanteo o *flirtación* (como dicen los ingleses)', leemos en el capítulo VI de *Insolación*. (Pardo Bazán, 1889: 102).

16. En González Herrán, 1997, doy noticia de esa colección, de la que se está ocupando el equipo de investigadores que dirijo en la Universidad de Santiago de Compostela.

17. Aunque —según Eva del Valle, que prepara bajo mi dirección un estudio sobre esas galeradas— hay una realmente notable, nada menos que en el título, en la página inicial: si bien la tachadura es tan enérgica que imposibilita leer lo impreso, en un examen cuidadoso y al trasluz mi discípula cree advertir la palabra *Irradiación*; aunque así fuese, no me parece que de ello pueda deducirse una vacilación de la autora (en cuyas cartas nunca indica otro título que *Insolación*), sino tal vez una errónea lectura de su manuscrito en la imprenta, explicable por la similitud gráfica entre ambas palabras.

18. Quien, según Ortiz Armengol, 1990: xxi, 'estaba con frecuencia al pie de obra, junto al regente de la imprenta, o más bien junto a los cajistas, pasándoles papelitos rectificadores, o haciéndoles correcciones de viva voz y, por supuesto, introduciendo muchas modificaciones en las galeradas de pruebas'.

19. Llamo la atención sobre esta palabra, que podría ser error de lectura por 'viniendo'; en cuyo caso la autora aludiría a los pliegos de pruebas que se le envían para corregir. Algo similar sucede con la otra novela suya editada también en 1889 por la misma editorial; en la carta XVII, del 3 de junio, comenta que las ilustraciones de *Morriña* van gustándole más que las de *Insolación* y añade: 'Felicitémonos, pues. Espero más pliegos'. Y en la carta XVIII, del 29 de agosto, pregunta: '¿Qué le sucede a *Morriña*? Dejé de recibir pliegos hará dos meses y no sé en qué anda la cuestión' (Torres, 1997: 406 y 407, respectivamente).

20. En estas cartas doña Emilia se refiere a los editores como Henrich y como Ramírez, indistintamente; ello se debe a un cambio de denominación de la

empresa editorial —y de su imprenta—, siempre con el mismo domicilio en Barcelona: primero como 'Sucesores de N. Ramírez y Cª-Editores' (así consta en la portadilla de la primera edición de Insolación) y luego como 'Henrich y Cª en Comandita-Editores. Sucesores de N. Ramírez y Cª' (así, en la segunda edición de *Insolación*, 1895); el cambio se produjo precisamente en el otoño de 1889: la primera edición de *Morriña*, aparecida en octubre, es de Ramírez y la segunda (que en realidad es una reimpresión), en ese mismo año, es de Henrich. Hay otros testimonios coetáneos sobre este asunto: en carta a su editor M. Fernández Lasanta, escribe Clarín en septiembre de 1889: '*Tambor y Gaita* [...] está vendido [...] a los Sucesores de Ramírez en Barcelona, para hacer un tomo como el de *Insolación*' (en Botrel-Blanquat, 1981: 47); Pereda, en carta a Yxart del 3 de julio de 1890, alude a 'los Sres. de Henrich y Cía', que han editado *Morriña* y que en la misma colección van a publicar su *Al primer vuelo* (en Torres, 1980: 302); una nota en *La Correspondencia de España* del 11 de julio de ese año anuncia que Pereda 'ha entregado a la casa de Barcelona sucesores de Ramírez la novela que le encomendó y que se titula *Al primer vuelo*' (en González Herrán, 1983: 387). En la misma colección que *Insolación* y *Morriña* aparecieron en los años siguientes, entre otros títulos, *La espuma*, de Armando Palacio Valdés (1890), *Las personas decentes*, de Enrique Gaspar (1890), *Al primer vuelo*, de José María de Pereda (1891), todas ellas con el pie editorial Henrich y Compañía.

21. 'He preguntado si estaba el libro a la venta y me han dicho que aún no'. Y comenta las estrategias para que la crítica madrileña se ocupe del libro: 'los Madriles publicarán el trozo con un suelto-anuncio de la novela [...] Dígales usted a los Sres. Henrich [de nuevo, la comentada vacilación en el nombre de la empresa] si tienen bien asegurado aquí el servicio de prensa y si además de mis ejemplares enviarán cierto número para que yo trabaje aquí hasta donde me sea posible.' (Torres, 1977: 403–4).

22. Tomo los datos de Clémessy, 1973: 216, y en su bibliografía: 716–27; menciona también críticas de Clarín, en *Madrid Cómico* (11 de mayo), J. Sardá, en *La España Moderna* (mayo) y 'Fray Candil', en *Madrid Cómico* (agosto).

23. Este trabajo se enmarca en el Proyecto de Investigación *Inventario y catálogo bio-bibliográfico de la obra completa de Emilia Pardo Bazán. Ediciones y estudios*, que dirijo en la Universidad de Santiago de Compostela, con financiación del Programa Sectorial de Promoción General del Conocimiento de la DGCYT (Proyecto PS94–0159).

Chapter Five

1. Carmen Bravo-Villasante, *Vida y obra de Emilia Pardo Bazán con varias ilustraciones*. (Madrid: Revista de Occidente, 1962), pp. 99–102.

2. Nelly Clémessy, *Emilia Pardo Bazán, Romancière (la Critique, la Théorie, la Pratique)* (Paris: Université de Paris, Centre de Recherches Hispaniques, 1973), p. 511.

3. David Henn, *The Early Pardo Bazán: Theme and Narrative Technique in the Novels of 1879–89* (Liverpool: Francis Cairns, 1988), pp. 36–7.

4. Lou Charnon-Deutsch, *The Nineteenth-Century Short Story: Textual Strategies of a Genre in Transition* (London: Tamesis, 1985), p. 87.

5. All references to Pardo Bazán's work are to the 1957 Aguilar *Obras Completas* edited by Federico Sáinz de Robles and are given in parentheses in the text of the article. The roman numeral indicates volume number, the Arabic numeral page number and the letter a or b the column.

6. There is no textual indication of the narrator's gender, but I have used the female pronoun throughout for the sake of concision. I am not necessarily equating the narrator with Emilia Pardo Bazán.

7. For a representative sample of the fifteen short stories Pardo published in the 1880s, see *La Mayorazga de Bouzas* (1886. I, 1316–21); *Nieto del Cid* (1883. I, 1323–28); *El indulto* (1883. I, 1109–14); *El rizo del Nazareno* (1880. I, 1114–19) and *Morrión y Boina* (1889. I, 1076–89).

8. There is one, fairly neutral reference to his physical appearance (I, 909a), and some necessary statements summarizing his actions, or reactions to his interlocutor (I, 908b).

9. Charnon-Deutsch, *The Nineteenth-Century Short Story*, p. 20.

Chapter Six

1. The references are taken from Richard Ford, *A Hand-book for Travellers in Spain and Readers at Home*, edited and with an introduction by Ian Robertson, 3 volumes. Carbondale, Illinois: Southern University of Illinois Press, 1966).

2. W. B. C. Lister, LLB, FRGS, *A Bibliography of Murray's Handbooks for Travellers and Biographies of Authors, Editors, Revisers and Principal Contributors,* (Dereham: Dereham Books, 1993), p. 40.

3. Lister, op. cit., p.155.

4. Ulick Ralph Burke, *A History of Spain from the Earliest times to the Death of Ferdinand the Catholic*, 2 volumes. London: Longmans, Green, & Co., 1895. The work was four years in preparation, during which time he consulted Juan Riaño in Madrid 'that much abused but to me ever sympathetic city' (vol. I, xvi). Burke also edited George Borrow's *The Bible in Spain* which was published posthumously by John Murray in two volumes in 1896. In a footnote he states that he 'was on the point of starting for Compostella, where I might have investigated the incident detailed [concerning Benedict Mol], and I had actually paid for my ticket to Irún (May 2, 1895), when I was summoned to a more distant shrine on the slopes of the Southern Pacific' (vol. I, 190).

5. *The Hand-book for Travellers in Spain*, by the late Richard Ford, revised and corrected, eighth edition, London: John Murray, 1892, I, 192.

6. *A Hand-book*, ed. Ian Robertson, vol. II, 965; fourth ed., 1869, vol. I, 184; eighth ed., 1892, vol. I, 192.

7. Karl Baedeker, *Spain and Portugal. Handbook for Travellers*, (Leipsic: Karl Baedeker, 1898), p. 462.

8. Baedeker, op. cit., pp. 481–4 and 491–500.

9. Henry George O'Shea, *Guide to Spain and Portugal*, ninth edition, ed. John Lomas, (London: A. & C. Black, 1892), p. 146.

10. O'Shea, op, cit., pp.145–6 and p. 365.

11. Dr Charnock, [Richard Stephen], FCA, FRGS, &c. , *Bradshaw's Illustrated Hand-book to Spain and Portugal: Complete Guide for Travellers in the Peninsula,* (London: W.J. Adams and Sons, New edition, 1895) Preface.

12. Op. cit., pp.42–3.

13. Op. cit., pp. 101–4.

14. Op. cit., p. 9.

15. Albert F. Calvert, *The Traveller's Handbook for Spain,* (London: Thos. Cook & Son, 1912), preface.

16. Wendy Birman, 'Albert Frederick Calvert' in *Australian Dictionary of Biography,* ed. Bede Nairn, Geoffrey Serle, and John Ritchie, (Melbourne: Melbourne U. P., 1966–1996), vol. II, pp. 528–9.

17. Albert F. Calvert, FRGS, *Impressions of Spain,* (London: George Philip & Son; Liverpool: Philip, Son & Nephew, 1903), preface, p. vii.

18. Calvert, *Impressions,* p. 195–196.

19. Op. cit., pp. 200–1 and 204–7.

20. *Impressions,* p. 200; Cook's *Traveller's Handbook,* p. 349.

21. Op. cit., p. 349, although Street actually stated that it is ' in plan and design a very curiously exact repetition...'; George Edmund Street, ARA, *Some Account of the Gothic Architecture in Spain,* (London: John Murray, 1865), p. 145. He also points that the architect of the Cathedral at Lugo 'copied, not from any foreign work, but from that at Santiago', thus establishing the existence of 'several subordinate variatons' (p. 417).

22. Street, op. cit., p. vi.

23. Op. cit., p. 140.

24. Op. cit., p. 141.

25. Andrew Noble Prentice, *Renaissance Architecture and Ornament in Spain,* (London: B. T. Batsford, 1893; new edition, with introduction and additional illustrations by Harod W. Booton, London: Alec Tiranti, 1970).

26. Op. cit., pp. 24–5.

27. *A Guide Book to Books,* edited by E. B. Sargant and Bernhard Whishaw, (London: Henry Frowde, 1891), pp. 3 and 286–90.

28. Hugh James Rose, *Untrodden Spain and her Black Country; being Sketches of the Life and Character of the Spaniard of the Interior,* second edition, 2 vols, London: Samuel Tinsley, 1875; this second edition was published in the same year as the first). Amongst the citations of this work may be mentioned Revd Wentworth Webster, *Spain,* (London: Sampson Low, Marston, Searle, & Rivington, 1882), who refers to this book as 'going out of the common round' (p. 243).

29. Op. cit., vol. I, pp. 355–66.

30. Abel Chapman and Walter J. Buck, *Wild Spain (España Agreste), Records of Sport with Rifle, Rod, and Gun, Natural History and Exploration,* (London: Gurney and Jackson, 1893). The later collaborative volume on the Iberian Peninsula was *Unexplored Spain,* (London: Arnold, 1910).

31. *Wild Spain,* pp. 4–5, and 328–9.

32. Jane Leck, *Iberian Sketches, Travels in Portugal and in the North-West of Spain,* with Illustrations by Robert Gray, FRSE, (Glasgow: Wilson & McCormick, 1884).

33. Op. cit., Preface, p. V, and pp. 39–61, especially p. 59.

34. John Lomas, *Sketches in Spain from Nature, Art and Life,* (Edinburgh: Adam and Charles Black; London: Longmans, Green, 1884). The second edition, identical to the first, and from which the present quotations are taken, was published in 1888.

35. Op. cit., pp. 407–13; the quotations above are taken from pp. 407, 409, and 411.

36. Hans Gadow, MA, PhD, FRS, Cambridge, *In Northern Spain,* with map and eighty-nine illustrations, (London: Adam and Charles Black, 1897). Gadow was also in Portugal in 1885 (p. 373).

37. *Through Southern Mexico, being an account of the Travels of a Naturalist,* (London: Witherby & Co., 1908).

38. Miguel de Unamuno, 'Del elemento alienígena en el idioma vasco', *Zeitschrift für Romanische Philologie,* 1893; Gadow comments on Unamuno's article on pp. 310–11.

39. Op. cit., pp. 223–33.

40. Op. cit., p. 215.

41. The vast majority of the 150 species described by Dr Gadow and taken home with him were collected in the Asturian and Cantabrian mountains (pp. 383–97).

42. Katharine Lee Bates, *Spanish Highways and Byways,* illustrated with many engravings from photographs, (New York and London, Macmillan, 1900).

43. Op. cit., pp. 409–22.

44. Edgar T. A. Wigram, *Northern Spain,* (London: Adam & Charles Black, 1906).

45. Op. cit., pp. 86–7.

46. W. W. Collins, RI, *Cathedral Cities of Spain,* (London: William Heinemann, 1909).

47. Op. cit., pp. 171–2.

48. Annette M. B. Meakin, *Galicia, the Switzerland of Spain,* 105 illustrations and a map (London: Methuen, 1909).

49. Op. cit., p. 209.

50. Op. cit., p. 357.

51. Op. cit., pp. 357–8.

52. E. Boyle O'Reilly, *Heroic Spain,* (London: Burns & Oates, 1911; also published in New York by Duffield and Company in 1911, copyright, 1910, with the same pagination).

53. Op. cit., pp. 130–1.

54. Op. cit., pp. 343–5.

55. Walter Wood, *A Corner of Spain,* with an Introduction by Martin Hume, Illustrated in Colour and Line by Frank H. Mason, RBA, and with numerous reproductions from photographs, (London: Eveleigh Nash, 1910).

56. Op. cit., Chapter X, pp. 39, 175, 144–5 and 181–94.

57. C. Gasquoine Hartley [Mrs Walter M. Gallichan], *Spain Revisited. A Summer Holiday in Galicia,* with coloured frontispiece and 57 illustrations in half-tone, (New York: James Pott & Company, 1911); and *The Story of Santiago de Compostela,* illustrated by Frank H. Mason, RBA, The Mediaeval Towns Series (London: J. M. Dent, 1912).

Chapter Seven

1. Espasa Calpe, Colección Austral, to appear shortly.

2. 'Viaje y llegada de Julián a los Pazos y otros viajes y llegadas afines', in *Estudios sobre Emilia Pardo Bazán In Memoriam Maurice Hemingway*, (Edición de José Manuel González Herrán, Universidade de Santiago/ Consorcio de Santiago de Compostela), 1997, pp. 67–83.

3. 'Madre, madrastra Naturaleza: una imagen compartida entre Pardo Bazán y Pereda', in *Estudios sobre Emilia Pardo Bazán...*, cited above, pp. 41–65; 'Hacia *Peñas arriba*: Pereda y la tierra', in *'Peñas arriba', cien años después. José María de Pereda; crítica e interpretación*, edited by Anthony H. Clarke, (Sociedad Menéndez Pelayo, Santander 1997), pp. 87–137.

4. *Los pazos de Ulloa*, end of chapter II. The precise form of words does not occur again in the text, althought their gist is omnipresent. Henceforward, page references to the Alianza Editorial, 'El Libro de Bolsillo', 2nd edn., 1969, will be given in the text.

5. It should be made clear that Hawthorne's *The House with Seven Gables* and Dickens' *Bleak House* do not follow the journey/arrival pattern; nevertheless, the dominating presence of house and setting places them in a kindred category which may have had a knock-on effect. *Great Expectations* offers a symbolical rather than a real journey.

6. See especially pp. 73–5 of 'Viaje y llegada de Julián...', above, note 2.

7. See his article '*Los pazos*, novela en la encrucijada', in *Estudios sobre los Pazos de Ulloa*', edited by Marina Mayoral, (Ediciones Cátedra, Ministerio de Cultura, 1989), and also *El polen de ideas*, (Colección Literatura y Pensamiento, *PPU*, 1991).

8. Perhaps deliberately so. Written between the summer of 1892 and December 1894 (see details in J.M. González Herrán, *La obra de Pereda ante la crítica literaria de su tiempo*, Santander: (Colección Pronillo, Ayuntamiento de Santander y Ediciones de Librería Estvdio, 1983), pp. 406–11) the novel not only looks back to a period twenty-five years before but seems to recreate all the literary assumptions that go with it. As has been noted before, it is scarcely credible that *Peñas arriba* and Galdós' *Angel Guerra* were written at about the same time.

9. Maurice Hemingway, amongst others, has commented on the psychological implications underlying Julián's new gloves and his consciousness of them in 'Emilia Pardo Bazán, *Los Pazos de Ulloa*: punto de vista y psicología', in *Estudios sobre Emilia Pardo Bazán...*, cit., pp. 389–403, and especially p. 400. This short, previously unpublished essay by Maurice dates from 1977 and, as González Herrán explains (pp. 389–90), was probably the text of a talk and relates closely to the second chapter of his book, *Emilia Pardo Bazán. The Making of a Novelist*. It is suggestive that, in *Peñas arriba*, Marcelo's preoccupation with and evident consciousness of the newness and expense of his hunting gear has a similar role to Julián's gloves.

10. 'Un país de lobos', in *Estudios sobre 'Los Pazos de Ulloa'*, op. cit., p. 14.

11. In 'Viaje y llegada de Julián a los Pazos...' I have sought to link these same castle-like features with similar ones attributed to the House of Usher in Poe's story.

12. In establishing the links between *Pedro Sánchez/Penas arriba* and certain archetypal folk tales, González Herrán uses the term 'la llamada' to refer to the summoning of Marcelo to the Montaña, see ' "Erase un muchacho (de la corte) que emprendió un viaje (a la aldea)…": Pereda, *Peñas arriba'*, in *'Peñas arriba' cien años después*, pp. 63–86.

13. In recent studies on *Peñas arriba* (the Cátedra edn., 1988, with Introduction and Notes by A. Rey Hazas; the above-mentioned article by J.M. González Herrán at note 12; my edition of *Peñas arriba*; J.M. López de Abiada's article *'Agrum manibus suis colebat*: imágenes del protagonista y conceptos de regeneracionismo en *Peñas arriba'*, in *'Peñas arriba' cien años después*, pp. 231–42), Marcelo's 'pruebas' are seen as the necessary steps of his conversion, occasionally with incursions into the language of mysticism on Pereda's part.

14. All of these quotations are from Chapter II, between pp. 37 and 42 in the Suárez edn. (Madrid, 1924). They highlight the hostile, austere, 'hard' role of Nature. The opposition and intertwining relationship between stone/hardness and water/softness has been exhaustively studied by Laureano Bonet in his article 'Hacia *Peñas arriba*: Pereda y la tierra', op. cit.

15. A further parallel, with the opening chapters of Galdós' *Doña Perfecta*, suggests itself here. See 'Viaje y llegada de Julián a los Pazos…', in *Estudios sobre Emilia Pardo Bazán…*, cit. pp. 80–1.

16. The relevant passages are reproduced in the Introduction to my edition of *Peñas arriba*.

17. Though it seems likely that she had read *Los hombres de pro* much earlier, she does not make reference to it in her writings until March 1891, in 'Pereda y su último libro', first published in *Nuevo Teatro Crítico*, and reproduced in *Polémicas y estudios literarios*, *Obras Completas* Madrid, n.d., vol. VI, pp. 67–97, The phrase 'mezquina historieta de campanario', used of *Los hombres de pro* by Pardo Bazán in 'Pereda y su último libro', was one that stuck.

18. See José Manuel González Herrán, 'Emilia Pardo Bazán y José María de Pereda: algunas cartas inéditas', *Boletín de la Biblioteca de Menéndez Pelayo*, LIX, 1983, 259–87, and especially pp. 262–5; and 'Emilia Pardo Bazán en el epistolario de Marcelino Menéndez Pelayo'; *Cuadernos de Estudios Gallegos*, XXXVI, no. 101, 1986, pp. 325–42.

19. See J.M. González Herrán's edition of *Pedro Sánchez*, (Colección Austral, Espasa Calpe, 1990), pp. 11–12.

20. *La cuestión palpitante*, edited with Introduction and Notes by J.M. González Herrán, (Editorial Anthropos, 'Autores, textos y temas', co-published by Anthropos/Universidade de Santiago de Compostela, 1989), pp. 311–13.

21. Op. cit., p. 313.

22. 'ċPor qué *Pedro Sánchez*? (La salida de Pereda hacia dentro)' in *Nueve lecciones sobre Pereda*, edited by J.M. González Herrán and Benito Madariaga, (Santander: Institución Cultural de Cantabria, 1985), pp. 91–118.

23. 'Cartas de Pereda a José María y Sinforoso Quintanilla', *Boletín de la Biblioteca de Menéndez Pelayo*, XLIV, 1968, note 254, p. 262.

NOTES TO PAGES 129–139

24. *Desde la Montaña*, edited with Introduction, Notes and Appendix by J.M. González Herrán and J.R. Saiz Viadero, (Santander: Biblioteca San Quintín, Ediciones Tantín, 1997).
25. *Desde la Montaña*, op. cit., Introduction, p. 18.
26. *Desde la Montaña*, op. cit., Introduction, p. 12.
27. Letter to Juan León Mera, April 1893, reproduced in J.M. de Cossío, *José María de Pereda. Selección y estudio*. Santander: (Antología de escritores y artistas montañeses, XLVIII, 1957), pp. 163–4.
28. See especially J.M. González Herrán's edition of *Pedro Sánchez*, cit., (Introduction, p. 29) and A. H. Clarke, 'El regreso a la tierra natal: *Peñas arriba* dentro de una tradición europea', *Boletín de la Biblioteca de Menéndez Pelayo*, LX, 1984, pp. 213–69.
29. 'Pereda y los nacionalismos (regionalismos) peninsulares', in *'Peñas arriba' cien años después*, cit., pp. 97–229.
30. In addition to the article by Enrique Miralles referred to above, see the same author's *Cartas a Víctor Balaguer*, (Barcelona: Puvill Libros S.A., 1995) and Laureano Bonet, *Literatura, regionalismo y lucha de clases (Galdós, Pereda, Narcís Oller y Ramón D. Perés)*, (Publicaciones i Edicions de la Universitat de Barcelona, 1983).
31. See note 3 of this article.
32. *La madre naturaleza*, Alianza Editorial, 'El Libro de Bolsillo', 1972, p. 320.
33. This aspect, together with the eventual 'aprobación' or 'visto bueno' of Marcelo by the river Nansa and the valley of Tudanca, is covered in my article 'Marcelo entre dos ríos; el *visto bueno* del Nansa', in *'Peñas arriba' cien años después*, cit., pp. 23–42.
34. In 'Cartas de Pereda a Laverde', ed. A.H. Clarke, *Boletín de la Biblioteca de Menéndez Pelayo*, LXVIII, 1991, p. 261.
35. J.M. González Herrán, 'Emilia Pardo Bazán y José María de Pereda: algunas cartas inéditas', cit., pp. 283–4.
36. See J.M. González Herrán's edition of *Pedro Sánchez*, cit., p. 25, note 38, and his article in *'Peñas arriba' cien años después*, cit.
37. See F. Pérez Gutiérrez, *El problema religioso en la generación de 1968*, (Taurus Ediciones, 1975), pp. 177–8.

Chapter Eight

1. Op. cit., NYC, Madrid 1973, pp. 142–57.
2. Biblioteca Nacional de Madrid, S/XIX, MSS, 22, 325, 49–53.
3. *Cartas a Galdós*, prólogo y edición, Carmen Bravo-Villasante, ed., (Madrid: Turner, 1978).
4. Op. cit., p. 56.
5. Id., p. 53 y 78.
6. Id., p. 49.
7. Id., pp. 79–82.
8. *Nuevo Teatro Crítico*, N° 16, abril de 1892, in Emilia Pardo Bazán, *Obras Completas* (Madrid: Aguilar, 1973), Tomo III, pp. 1105–1119.

Chapter Nine

1. Robert J. Weber, *The Miau Manuscript of Benito Pérez Galdós: A Critical Study*, University of California Publications in Modern Philology, 72 (Berkeley: University of California Press, 1964).

2. See A.A. Parker, 'Villaamil: Tragic Victim or Comic Failure?', *Anales Galdosianos*, IV (1969), 13–23; Theodore A. Sackett, 'The Meaning of *Miau*', *Anales Galdosianos*, IV (1969), 25–38; R.O. Jones and Geraldine M. Scanlon, '*Miau*: Prelude to a Reassessment', *Anales Galdosianos*, VI (1971), 53–62; H. Ramsden, 'The Question of Responsibility in Galdós's *Miau*', *Anales Galdosianos*, VI (1971), 63–78.

3. Eamonn Rodgers, *Pérez Galdós: 'Miau'*, Critical Guides to Spanish Texts, 23 (London: Grant & Cutler, 1978).

4. A useful study is Stephen Miller, 'Villaamil's Suicide: Action, Character and Motivation', *Anales Galdosianos*, XIV (1979), 83–96.

5. In Chapter 9 of Galdós's earlier novel *Marianela* (1878), there is an interesting discussion of suicide, in which the character Teodoro Golfín insists that compassion is the best response to it and that one should attempt to understand its causes, including whether 'la sociedad' has contributed towards the disaster in a given instance. See Benito Pérez Galdós, *Obras completas*, ed. by Federico Carlos Sáinz de Robles, 6th edn. (6 vols, Madrid: Aguilar, 1966), vol. IV, pp. 714–15.

6. W (= *Miau*, ed. by R.J. Weber, Textos Hispánicos Modernos, 25 [Barcelona: Editorial Labor, 1973]) 356.

7. Rodgers, pp. 50–68 (p. 58, p. 67).

8. One thinks of his monograph *Emilia Pardo Bazán: The Making of a Novelist*, (Cambridge: Cambridge University Press, 1983), and the articles 'The Religious Content of Pardo Bazán's *La sirena negra*', *Bulletin of Hispanic Studies*, XLIX (1972), 369–82; 'Grace, Nature, Naturalism, and Pardo Bazán', *Forum for Modern Language Studies*, XVI (1980), 341–49; 'Pardo Bazán and the Rival Claims of Religion and Art', *Bulletin of Hispanic Studies*, LXVI (1989), 241–50.

9. *Obras completas*, vol. V (7th edn, 1970), pp. 1864.

10. I Corinthians 1:25. All Biblical quotations are from *La Biblia Vulgata Latina traducida en Español*, trans. by Felipe Scio de San Miguel, 2nd edn, (19 vols, Madrid: Benito Cano, 1794–97), XVI and XVIII (1797). (References follow the verse-numbering of this translation. I have retained its spelling, punctuation and accentuation.) Galdós owned an edition of it in 5 vols (Madrid: Gaspar y Roig, 1852–54), that is still in his library. See Sebastián de la Nuez, *Biblioteca y archivo de la Casa Museo Pérez Galdós* (Exmo Cabildo Insular de Gran Canaria, 1990), p. 57.

11. Curiously enough, this Pauline reference was not spotted by G.G. Minter in his careful study of our author's 'extensive debts' to a great Patristic figure: '*Halma* and the Writings of St Augustine', *Anales Galdosianos*, XIV (1979), 73–97.

12. *Fortunata y Jacinta*, ed. by Francisco Caudet, Letras Hispánicas, 185 & 186 (2 vols, Madrid: Cátedra, 1983), vol. II, p. 330.

13. Fortunata's being an angel has been the subject of much critical study, an interesting recent instance of which is Catherine Jagoe, 'The Subversive Angel in *Fortunata y Jacinta*', *Anales Galdosianos*, XXIV (1989), 79–91. This article, though, is interested in how Galdós subverts stereotypical views of a desirable female submissiveness, such as Pilar Sinués's *El ángel del hogar* of 1859. Beyond this, due acknowledgement should be made of James Whiston, 'The Materialism of Life: Religion in *Fortunata y Jacinta*', *Anales Galdosianos*, XIV (1979), 65–91.

14. Romans 3: 20–28, 8: 31–39, 13: 8, 10.

15. There are many studies of the virtue of Charity in Galdós, including Arnold Penuel, *Charity in the Novels of Galdós* (Athens: University of Georgia Press, 1972). Minter for his part stresses how St Augustine is also behind Galdós's concern with humility and un-self-consciousness, selfless devotion to others (p. 84).

16. See Isaiah 52: 13–15; 53.

17. See Frances Lannon, *Privilege, Persecution and Prophecy: The Catholic Church in Spain 1875–1975* (Oxford: Clarendon Press, 1987).

18. Philippians 2: 5–8.

19. This general drift was underscored by Sackett, (p. 32). Also important is J.M. Ruano de la Haza, 'The Role of Luisito in *Miau*', *Anales Galdosianos*, XIX (1984), 27–43.

20. Rodgers, p. 51.

21. See note 6.

22. See Chapter 2. *Cucurbita* is the Latin botanical name for the gourd family— *calabazas* in Spanish. *Dar calabazas* means to snub someone, as Cucúrbitas does by refusing charity to his former colleague. One notes as well that he lives in the Calle del Amor de Dios, a 'real' streetname in Madrid, but obviously chosen for its ironic connotations.

23. One is reminded of Psalm 73 [Vulgate, 72], especially its first sixteen verses.

24. Ruano, p. 30.

25. Nicholas Cronk, 'The French Don Quixote, or How to Know Cervantes' Novel Without Reading It', in *Don Quixote, Massenet/Cain* (opera programme, English National Opera, 1994). See also A.J. Close, *The Romantic Approach to 'Don Quixote'* (Cambridge: Cambridge University Press, 1977).

26. Matthew 6: 25–34.

27. Galdós had earlier made ironic reference to the Biblical passage at the end of *La desheredada*, Part II, Chapter 8: 'Isidora, Riquín y el viejo [...] eran efectivamente pájaros, porque no tenían más que lo presente y lo que la Providencia divina quisiera darles para pasar del hoy al mañana. El mundo se diferencia de los bosques en que es necesario pagar el nido' (*Obras completas*, vol. IV, pp. 1102–3).

28. Compare, contrastingly, the passage where Villaamil comments sarcastically to Luisito 'Sí, hijo mío, bienaventurados los brutos, porque de ellos es el reino... de la Administración' (W 98).

29. I Corinthians 1: 23–29.

30. See, for example, 'El Cristo yacente de Santa Clara' in Miguel de Unamuno,

Obras completas, ed. by Manuel García Blanco, (9 vols, Madrid: Escelicer, 1966), vol. VI (1969), pp. 517–20.

31. See José Martínez Ruiz, 'Azorín', *La voluntad*, ed. by E. Inman Fox, Clásicos Castalia, 3 (Madrid: Castalia, 1968), pp. 136–7 (Part I, Chapter 15), and 'Los Cristos', in Federico García Lorca, *Impresiones y paisajes*, ed. by Rafael Lozano Miralles, Letras Hispánicas, 379 (Madrid: Cátedra, 1994), pp. 137–40.

32. See note 16.

33. Minter, pp. 86–97.

34. See *The Oxford Dictionary of the Christian Church*, ed. by F.L. Cross and E.A. Livingstone, 2nd edn (London: Oxford University Press, 1974), p. 777.

35. 'A Note on Tolstoy and Galdós', *Anales Galdosianos*, II (1967), 155–68; 'Tolstoy and *Angel Guerra*', in *Galdós Studies*, ed. by J.E. Varey (London: Tamesis Books, 1970), pp. 114–35. Mention should also be made of G. Portnoff, 'The Influence of Tolstoy's *Anna Karenina* on Galdós's *La* [sic] *Realidad*', *Hispania*, California, XV (1932), 203–4.

36. *Fin de siglo: figuras y mitos* (Madrid: Taurus, 1980), pp. 15–39. In addition to Galdós, Hinterhäuser studies the work of Hauptmann, Fogazzaro and Bloy.

37. M.P. Alexeyev, 'Russian Language and Literature at the Madrid Ateneo in the 1860s', *Anales Galdosianos*, XX (1985), 122–30.

38. De la Nuez, p. 230.

39. I am grateful to Dr Ronald Truman for this suggestion. Hinterhäuser also draws attention to the influence of Dostoyevsky, pp. 20–21.

40. On Galdós and Carlism one may for example consult Geoffrey Ribbans, *History and Fiction in Galdós's Narratives* (Oxford: Clarendon Press, 1993).

41. For a robustly negative view of the cult of San Luisito by Unamuno, see his essay of 1906, '¿Qué es verdad?', in *Obras completas*, vol. III (1968), pp. 854–64 (pp. 861–62).

42. *La revolución y la novela en Rusia*, in *Obras completas* III, ed. by Harry L. Kirby, Jr (Madrid: Aguilar, 1973), pp. 760–880 (p. 869).

43. I am grateful to fellow members of the Oxford Sub-Faculty of Spanish for their encouragement when an earlier version of this article was read to its Graduate Seminar in January 1995. I particularly wish to mention the kindness of Louise Johnson, Ronald Truman and Daniel Waissbein in commenting on my text.

Chapter Ten

1. Este estudio es una refundición de una ponencia que se presentó en el seminario, 'Crisis histórica y evolución de las ideologías: *Nazarín* de Pérez Galdós', organizada por la Cátedra Pérez Galdós de la Universidad de Las Palmas de Gran Canaria del 12 al 14 de junio de 1996.

2. Son muy contadas las excepciones: *La Fontana de Oro, Lo prohibido, La incógnita, Realidad* y *La loca de la casa*.

Chapter Eleven

1. Geoffrey Ribbans, *History and Fiction in Galdós's Narratives* (Oxford: Clarendon Press, 1993), p. 228.

2. Benito Pérez Galdós, *Obras completas: Episodios Nacionales* (Madrid: Aguilar, 1968) Vol. II, p. 1315. All references are to vols. II and III (1970) of this edition and will be given in the text in parentheses in the form II, 1315.

3. For further examples of the same feature, see Diane Faye Urey, *The Novel Histories of Galdós* (Princeton University Press, 1989), pp. 113–14.

4. Ribbans considers the space given to Fajardo's Italian experience as insufficiently justified (op. cit., p. 87).

5. While I agree with Ribbans that Fajardo is an 'involved commentator on the course of Spanish politics' (op. cit., p. 88), I am less certain that one can describe him as 'a dissident from within the Establishment, who comments freely from an independent point of view on the events he describes' (op. cit., p. 89). This description would apply more accurately, in my view, to the position towards which Fajardo evolves by the end of *La revolución de julio*, rather than one which he consistently maintains. Similarly, Antonio Regalado García shrewdly remarks that Fajardo is a 'catador entusiasta de costumbres castizas y turista de la historia integral', but also describes him, more controversially, as 'juez imparcial de los demás y de sí propio' (*Benito Pérez Galdós y la novela histórica española: 1868–1912* [Madrid: Insula, 1966], p. 370).

6. Catalina's plot seems to raise a question-mark over Brian Dendle's assertion that 'the novelistic intrigues are less complex and well knit' than those of earlier series (*Galdós: The Mature Thought* [The University Press of Kentucky, 1980], p. 79). Diane Urey makes a similar point: 'The fourth series . . . seems to lack the cohesive artistic unity of plot development that characterizes . . . the first three series' (op. cit., p. 101).

7. Urey, loc. cit.

8. Urey, in my view, pays insufficient attention to context and the implications of presentation, accepting largely at face value the 'identification between Lucila, [Queen] Isabel, and the "pueblo español", which intensifies as the narrative progresses' (op. cit., p. 104). This interpretation begs the question of the reliability of Miedes's view of Spanish history, and of Fajardo's contemporary account, all the more surprisingly because in another part of her study she clearly emphasizes Miedes's insanity (p. 121).

9. Compare, to take but one example from the *Episodios*, the way in which the unprepossessing façade of the Buen Suceso church is transformed for the Queen's wedding festivities in *Bodas reales*, by means of 'tela pintada, a modo de teatro' (II, 1401).

10. A minor, but significant example is that of the Andalusian *Moderado* deputy who becomes a Progressive after he receives brusque treatment from Narváez (II, 1564). As Dendle rightly remarks, 'On a national plane, ideologies and heroes provide convenient focal points for the yearnings of individuals' (op. cit., p. 95). I am less convinced by Dendle's assertion that 'Galdós rarely seeks to explain the past by the interplay of historical forces or individual decisions' (op. cit., p. 184). The kind of financial corruption that arose from *desamortización*, Narváez's efforts to govern in the face of clerical intrigue, the power of the *camarilla*, are all realized in concrete detail on both an individual and a national level.

11. Op. cit., p. 113.

12. Urey, op. cit., pp. 116–17, 121.

Chapter Twelve

* Después de haber buscado y encontrado en la prensa española de 1891 —a finales de los años 60—, parte de la información necesaria para estudiar a *Pequeñeces* desde la perpectiva de la sociología del libro y de la lectura vigente en la época, he venido aplazando la realización del ambicioso estudio entonces proyectado. El transcurso de los años y la muerte de Maurice Hemingway me aconsejan ahora renunciar a demasiadas ilusiones y dedicar a la memoria del investigador desaparecido en plena madurez esta escueta y humilde contribución.

1. Son los términos más empleados. De 'singular, nunca visto, fenomenal y estrepitoso éxito' lo califica la Pardo Bazán en *Nuevo Teatro Crítico* de mayo de 1891 al referirse a la 'archicélebre' novela.

2. Como dice *La Ilustración Artística*.

3. Los recortes de prensa conservados en el archivo de Padre Coloma y utilizados por R. M. Hornedo y B. Molho quien los reproduce en el tomo tercero de su tesis (1979) pueden completarse, pues, con unos 60 ecos. Llama la atención la participación 'masiva' de la prensa en el debate pero también el total silencio de algunos periódicos, algunos reacios a la información literaria y otros por motivos que se podrían interpretar como indiferencia voluntaria (cf., por ejemplo, *El Popular, La Fe, La Iberia, El Estandarte, El Diario Español, Las Ocurrencias, El Globo, El Siglo, La Izquierda Dinástica*).

4. Véanse al respecto las quejas de Pereda en su carta del 18–II–1891 al Padre Coloma en Coloma, L., *Obras completas, XIX. Relieves y críticas* (Madrid/ Bilbao: Razón y Fe/ El Mensajero del C. de J., 1950), p. 61.

5. Pereda la recibe entre el 13 y el 18 (cf. Coloma, L. *Obras completas, XIX*, op. cit., pp. 60–1).

6. Los demás temas de actualidad son, en abril, el crimen de la calle de la Justa, la discusión del Mensaje en el Senado, el aplazamiento de la constitución del Congreso, la cercana manifestación del proletariado universal (según *El Siglo Futuro)*. Luego el calor, la dispersión veraniega habrán de calmar o apagar del todo 'la hoguera de rencillas y disputas encendida por un hijo ... de Loyola' (E. Pardo Bazán, *La Ilustración Artística*, 4–IV).

7. 'Ya se han agotado los ejemplares en las librerías y hay que esperar la nueva remesa' según *El Resumen* de 18–III–1891, hecho confirmado por *El Imparcial* el 23.

8. Por lo visto la Compañía de Jesús dudó en publicar la 3a edición (cf. carta de J. Valera a Morel Fatio de 10–V–1891, *Bulletin Hispanique* LXXIV (1972), p. 457) y según la Pardo Bazán, en julio de 1891 'ya está despachada también, antes de salir, la edición cuarta (que) constará de 10,000 ejemplares', no puesta en venta aún a fines de agosto (*El Mensajero*... alude en su número de junio 'al considerable aumento de trabajo en nuestra imprenta').

9. Como suele suceder cuando de ediciones se trata, las cifras van y vienen: el Padre Hornedo adelanta 50,000 ejemplares en 1891, *La Libertad* habla, el

27–III, de 20,000 ejemplares 'arrebatados' en pocas horas. Las declaraciones del Padre Coloma a José Castro y Serrano reproducidas en *El Correo* de 25–XI–1891 (cf. Molho, 1978, 747–5l) me parecen más de fiar: 'una edición de 5,000, después otra de 7,000, luego una tercera de 8,000 y, en la actualidad, una de diez que está comprometida; es decir lo que los franceses llaman *treinta ediciones*' o sea: 30,000 ejemplares. 'También hay algunas fraudulentas' añade el P. Coloma ...

10. *El Cascabel*, 16–IV–91.

11. Apenas se tiene en cuenta la prensa de provincias que también se interesó por el tema (cf., por ejemplo, en *El Avisador de Badajoz* del 14–V–1891, 'Pequeñeces y sus críticos', o *El Defensor de Granada*, antes del 26–IV).

12. El 12–IV anuncia *El Clamor* la publicación dentro de tres días de un folleto 'combatiendo valerosa y razonadamente el libro *Pequeñeces*'; será *Pequeñeces... Currita Albornoz al Padre Coloma* (Madrid: Imp. de A. Pérez Dubrull, 1891), anónimo debido a la pluma de Juan Valera.

13. El folleto de Fray Candil (Emilio Bobadilla) *(Críticas instantáneas. I. El Padre Coloma y la aristocracia*, Madrid, Est. tip. Sucesores de Rivadeneyra, 1891, 80 p.), escrito en pocas horas, al correr de la pluma para aprovechar las 'proposiciones ventajosas de un editor amigo', se publica en los primeros días de mayo. En cuanto a la Librería López de Barcelona, propone a M. Martínez Barrionuevo la reunión de sus artículos publicados en *La Ilustración Ibérica* que da lugar, a fines de mayo, a un folleto de 60 páginas *(Un libro funesto ('Pequeñeces'... del P. Coloma))* que alcanza la 7a edición en 1891.

14. Cf., por ejemplo, *La Libertad* de Salamanca del 21–V–1891 'A Currita Albornoz en Madrid'.

15. Para una interpretación del interés de Emilia Pardo Bazán por *Pequeñeces* y su defensa e ilustración, léase la hipótesis de B. Molho (1979).

16. Madrid, Imp. de A. Pérez Dubrull, s. a., 122 p., 2 pesetas. El 1–IX–1891 se anuncia *Caricias de un lego al P. Fray Luis Coloma, a su novela Pequeñeces y a la Compañía de Jesús, por un veterano de la primera guerra civil*, 62 p. El Marqués de Figueroa, publicará *La novela aristocrática. Las Pequeñeces del Padre Coloma* (Barcelona: Romero imp.).

17. Es la novela 'objeto preferente de las...', 'asunto de todas las...', 'tema del día', 'no hay otra cosa que hablar', 'mucho ha dado y da que decir...', es 'tema obligado de conversación', 'tema único de discusión', '¿ Han leído Vds. la novela del Padre Coloma? Esta es pregunta que está al orden del día' *(passim)*.

18. Un cura inspeccionando un cepillo, clara alusión al 'negocio' que se supone será la venta de tantos ejemplares de la novela.

19. *El Cascabel*, 16–IV.

20. *Nuevo Teatro Crítico*, p. 83.

21. *Nuevo Teatro Crítico*, p. 91.

22. Dice E. Pardo Bazán: 'si con justicia podemos lamentar el corto espacio que los periódicos dedican a la crítica literaria (probablemente porque a los lectores no les gusta el género) menos sitio aún consagran a las noticias literarias propiamente dichas'(*Nuevo Teatro Crítico*, marzo de 1891, p. 89).

23. Melchor de Palau, *Revista Contemporánea*, 15–V–189l.

24. *La Ilustración Artística*, 27–IV–1891.
25. Cf. Botrel, J.-F., 'Juan Valera et l'argent' *Bulletin Hispanique* LXXI (1970) p. 307 y Botrel, J.-F., 'Galdós et ses publics' in *Mélanges offerts à Albert Dérozier* (Besançon: Annales littéraires de l'Université de Besançon, 1994), pp. 215–32).
26. Según Pío Baroja, 'El aristocratismo en España' in *Obras completas, V* (Madrid: Biblioteca Nueva, 1948), p. 959a.
27. *Más pequeñeces... El cuarto estado, Más pequeñeces... El jesuíta,* novelas de Vicente de la Cruz publicadas en 1891.
28. Se alude a un proyecto de arreglo de la novela para el Teatro Eslava. Lo cierto es que en 1897 se representa en el teatro Eslava *Currita Albornoz* de Ceferino Palencia.
29. Cf. *El Heraldo,* 23–V, 21–VIII, 12–X–1891, *La Justicia,* 10–IV–1891, *La Libertad,* 28–IV–1891, *El País,* 13–VI–1891, *El Popular,* 23–III–1891 (lo toma de *La Epoca* del 22–III), *El Resumen,* 12–XII–1891, *La Unión Católica,* 9–VII–1891, etc. M. Campomar Fornielles (1989) observa que 'Pequeñeces' era el rótulo con que encabezaba el periódico mestizo de Pidal y Mon, *La Unión,* sus columnas de dimes y diretes ...
30. *Bagatelles* (Pequeñeces), adapté de l'espagnol par Camille Vergniol, avec une préface de Marcel Prévost, Paris, Alphonse Lemerre Ed. (juin 1893), además de las traducciones alemana e inglesa a que alude la Pardo Bazán. Antes del 6–IV–1891 había recibido el Padre Coloma propuestas de traducción por parte de editores de París y Berlín. La primera reseña publicada por la *Revue Hispanique* en su primer número (1894) será la de *Pequeñeces,* a cargo de H. Peseux-Richard, hecha a partir de la 5a edición de 1891.
31. Cf. *El Liberal* del 24–III.
32. *El Resumen,* 3–IV.
33. *El Correo,* 3–IV.
34. *La Ilustración Artística,* 4–V.
35. Martínez Barrionuevo, op. cit., p. 9.
36. *Obras completas, II,* (Madrid: Aguilar, 1958), p. 841.
37. Cf. el estudio del Padre R. Hornedo (1951).
38. 6–IV–1891 in L. Coloma, *Obras completas, XIX,* op. cit., p. 183.
39. 'En el Padre Coloma, con su supuesta hostilidad por la aristocracia, trasciende el adulador (...) Claro que en *Pequeñeces* se ataca a la aristocracia; pero es a la improvisada, no a la antigua y a la buena católica. Esa es la posición del aristocratista, del que maneja el incensario' ('El aristocratismo en España', *loc. cit.,* p. 958).
40. Para más interpretaciones del 'sentido' de *Pequeñeces,* véanse las opiniones de Molho (1979), Benítez (1982) y Elizalde (1987, 1991, 1992).
41. 'aunque novelista parezco, sólo soy misionero', afirma el Padre Coloma, consciente de que, según sus lectores, puede 'rebaj(ar) el carácter sacerdotal al escribir cosas tan baladís'.
42. Se le atribuye entre 1,500 y 36,000 suscriptores, cifra 'increíble para lo que suelen ser estas cosas en España' según J. Bonet y C. Martí (*apud* Hibbs, 1995, 402); según el propio Padre Coloma (declaraciones a José de Castro y

Serrano, loc. cit.) 'vino *El Mensajero* a nuestras manos con una tirada de 300 ejemplares y hoy la tiene de 18,000'.

43. Por su correspondencia se sabe que el Padre Coloma consulta, el 26–III, al Conde de Guaquí, quien a su vez hablará al Marqués de Casa Trujillo y a A. Pidal y Mon y Esperanza.

44. Carta al Conde de Guaquí de 6–IV–1891 en *Epistolario del P. Luis Coloma S.J. 1890–1914* (Santander: *Anejos del Boletín de la Biblioteca de Menéndez Pelayo 2, 1967).*

45. En los 79 'ecos' encontrados entre el 2–IV y el 18–IV predominan los de la prensa 'liberal', recordando que para *El Siglo Futuro* es 'liberal' *La Epoca...*

46. *Nuevo Teatro Crítico*, Octubre de 1891.

47. Se conoce, por ejemplo, por el que escriben en las dos caras de la cuartilla. Al lado de las contribuciones/juicios de Felipe Ducazcal, E. Pardo Bazán, A. Miralles, Narciso Campillo, Luis Vidart, Ramón G. Rodrigo Nocedal, Navarro Ledesma, Kasabal, abundan las de 'anónimos lectores' (Un hombre práctico, Un aprendiz de psicología, Uno que guarda el retrato de Da María Victoria, Fray Silvestre, Una señora de la clase media, Un amigo de la verdad, Un imparcial, Una duquesa, Un aguilucho, Un aristócrata, Cualquiera, Un lector, Un lector de El Heraldo, Lord Dear, Diógenes, Un liberal imparcial, Expósito, un juez jubilado, Un chico de la mayoría, un Cronista indecentillo, Vivasca, el presbístero M.R., M.R. y Ll., Julio de Lanzas, M. García Rey, M.R. Moriano, Fernando Dori, E.G. San Martín, Ricardo de Cienfuegos, Pedro Arbués, Vicente Casanova, Millán Miguel, Antonio de Zayas, J. Mas.

48. Op. cit., p. 40.

49. 3 pesetas los dos tomos. '¿Quién es el que no tiene tres pesetas?', dice Narciso Campillo. Podemos contestar que no las tiene el que tenga que eligir entre 8 o 10 kilos de pan y los dos tomos de *Pequeñeces.*

50. J. Valera, *Obras completas, II,* op. cit., p. 845b.

51. '[...] Hay que sacar sangre de esas carnes podridas, [escribe J.M. de Pereda el 10–XI–1891], o dejarlas para pasto de gusanos. Los paños calientes tratando de ellas, son inocentadas de que se ríen los mismos aludidos... ¡Dichosos los flageladores que, como usted, tienen el conocimiento de las flaquezas a la medida de los bríos y de la autoridad !' (L. Coloma, *Obras completas, XIX,* op. cit., p. 60).

52. Pereda, 18–II–1891 en L. Coloma, *Obras completas, XIX,* op. cit., p. 60.

53. Cf., por ejemplo, mi estudio sobre 'Antonio de Valbuena et la langue espagnole: critique et démagogie' *Bulletin Hispanique,* 96 (1994), p. 485–96.

Chapter Thirteen

1. See for example, Luis S. Granjel, *Eduardo Zamacois y la novela corta* (Salamanca, 1980); Angel Martínez San Martín, *La narrativa de Felipe Trigo* (Madrid: CSIC, 1983); José Ma. Fernández Gutiérrez, *La novela corta galante: Felipe Trigo* (1865–1916) (Barcelona: PPU, 1989).

2. Cejador, Julio, *Historia de la lengua y literatura castellanas,* XII, 1920, p. 209.

3. Hurtado, J.H., Palencia, A.G., *Historia de la literatura española,* 1925, p. 1069.

4. Cansinos Assens, R., *La nueva literatura,* IV, 1927, p. 168.

5. Francisco Carmona Nenclares, *El amor y la muerte en las novelas de Alberto Insúa* (Madrid, 1928), pp. 59–60.

6. García de Nora, E., *La novela española contemporánea (1898–1927)*, p. 410.

7. Entrambasaguas, J. de, *Las mejores novelas contemporáneas*, VI, 1967, p. 312.

8. Barrère, Bernard, 'La crise du roman en Espagne, 1915–1936. Le cas d'un romancier: Alberto Insúa', *Bulletin Hispanique*, LXXXV (1983), 3–4, p. 274.

9. These were *Los hombres (Mary los descubre)* (48), *Los hombres (Mary los perdona)* (49); *La agonía de don Juan* (167), *Los filántropos* (261), *Memorias de un asesino genial* (270), *Las cigarras* (279), *Hebes del arroyo* (297), *Una aventura termal* (318), *El hijo golfo* (332), *El manuscrito del padre Clarencio* (355), *Mi tia Manolita*. For further details of the contents of the pages of *La Novela Corta*, see José Ma. Fernández Gutiérrez, op. cit, pp. 99–106.

10. Sáinz de Robles, Federico, *La novela corta española* (Madrid, 1952), p. 23.

11. Op. cit., p. 387.

12. Insúa, Alberto, *Don Quijote en los Alpes* (Renacimiento, 1921), p. 9.

13. *En tierra de santos* (Villavicencio, 1907), pp. 278–9. Further page references to this edition are included in the text.

14. *El triunfo* (Renacimiento, 1914), p. 39. Further page references to this edition are included in the text.

15. For a further analysis of Insúa's trilogy in relation to his more illustrious contemporaries, see Isabel Román Gutiérrez, 'Aproximación a la *Historia de un escéptico*, de Alberto Insúa', *Mosaico de varia lección literaria en homenaje a José M. Capote Benot* (Sevilla: Publicaciones de la Universidad, 1992), pp. 331–54.

16. *La mujer fácil* (Renacimiento, 1931), p. 313. Further page references are to this edition.

17. *Memorias*, I (Tesoro, 1952), p. 590.

18. *Los hombres: Mary los descubre* (Renacimiento, 1913), p. 26. Further page references are to this edition.

19. *De un mundo a otro. Novela de la guerra*, (Renacimiento, 1930), 7th edition, pp. 7–8.

20. This novel, published in 1921, also appears under the title *La virgen y la fiera* (El Libro de Todos, Cosmópolis, 1927), and exemplifies Maurice Hemingway's observation that 'Insúa no era reacio a reciclar su obra', in 'Alberto Insúa (1883–1963): Ensayo Bibliográfico', *Revista de Literatura*, Vol. LVI, No. 112, 1994, pp. 495–512 (p. 498). Without this painstaking bibliographical investigation the tracing of works by Insúa would have been difficult in the extreme, both here and for other researchers in the future.

21. *Memorias,* III (Tesoro, 1959), p. 212.

22. In its entry on Albert Insúa, *The Oxford Companion to Spanish Literature* (1978) mentions this novel with the single comment that it 'advocated divorce'. This is incorrect; the work that does deal with the theme of divorce is *Las fronteras de la pasión* (1920).

23. *La batalla sentimental* (Renacimiento, 1921), p. 93. Further page references are to this edition.

24. *El negro que tenía el alma blanca* (La Novela Mundial, 1926), p. 301. Further page references are to this edition.

25. *Ha llegado el día*, (Sociedad Española General de la Librería, 1932), p. 148.

26. Febles, Jorge, 'Encuentro, desencuentro, reencuentro: España frente a Cuba en las Memorias de Alberto Insúa', *Letras Peninsulares*, Spring 1992, 5(1), pp. 57–74.

27. Op. cit., n. 17 (p. 497).

Chapter Fourteen

1. W. Ronald D. Fairbairn, 'Endopsychic Structure Considered in Terms of Object-Relationships' (1944), in *Psychoanalytic Studies of the Personality*. (London: Tavistock Publications, 1952), pp. 82–136, at pp. 126–7.

2. James S. Grotstein, 'Nothingness, Meaninglessness, Chaos, and the "Black Hole"', Parts I, II and III in *Contemporary Psychoanalysis* 26.2 (1990), 257–90; 26.3 (1990), 377–407; 27.4 (1991), 1–33. Frances Tustin, 'The 'Black Hole'—A Significant Element in Autism', *Free Association*, 11 (1988), 35–50.

3. Fairbairn, 'Endopsychic Structure', p. 92.

4. Alison Sinclair, 'Unamuno and the Unknown: Responses to Primitive Terror', in *Belief and Unbelief in Hispanic Literature*, ed. Helen Wing and John Jones (Warminster: Aris and Phillips, 1995), pp. 134–45.

5. Jacques Lacan, 'The Hysteric's Question', in *The Psychoses: The Seminar of Jacques Lacan*, ed. Jacques-Alain Miller, trans. Russell Grigg. Book III, 1955–6 (Cambridge: CUP, 1993), p. 171.

6. For discussion of the varied dimensions of play of this type, see Peter Hutchinson, *Games Authors Play* (London and New York: Methuen, 1983).

7. Miguel de Unamuno, *La novela de don Sandalio, jugador de ajedrez*, in *Obras Completas*, ed. M. García Blanco, (9 vols, Madrid: Escelicer, 1966), vol. II, pp. 1155–84, at p. 1180. All subsequent references to *La novela de don Sandalio*, given parenthetically in the text, will be to this edition.

8. Tustin, 'The "Black Hole"', p. 39.

9. Grotstein, 'Nothingness, Meaninglessness', vol. I, p. 267. Wilfred Bion, *Learning from Experience* (London: Heinemann, 1962), pp. 7, 11, 25. The de-cathexis of such 'chards' of meaning is an act of desperate defence: they are not abandoned, but rejected. Since they have failed to be assimilated, they remain, disconnected, cluttering the self, and absorbing and attracting energy. As such, they constitute a type of inner-world counterpart to the disconnected perception of the objects of the external world so graphically signalled by Sass as characteristic of the schizophrenic.

10. Grotstein, 'Nothingness, Meaninglessness, vol. II, pp. 385–94 and 388.

11. Stephen W. Hawking, *A Brief History of Time: From the Big Bang to Black Holes* (London: Bantam Press, 1988), p. 89.

12. Although the comparison between the concepts of the self in Object Relations theory and Lacanian theory characterizes the latter as understanding the self as constructed through social relations, whereas the former is viewed as in some sense 'given' from the outset, such a distinction oversimplifies the

Object Relations view. Theorists ranging from Klein to Winnicott, Fairbairn and Bion understand the self as composed over time through a series of confrontations with the external world, the impingement on the self of that experience, and its consequent responses, defences and adjustments. My reading of Unamuno here views the self as understood by these Object Relations theorists working on the early stages of the self, and the re-formulations of the early stages in primitive and violence reactions in later life to experience.

13. This concept of an early schizoid state is originally that of Klein. It is given one of its fullest elaborations in Fairbairn, who specifically views the activity of the self in relation to objects that are a source of terror as a necessary introjection of them in order to control them, or as Fairbairn puts it, as a measure of coercion. See Fairbairn, 'Endopsychic Structure', p. 111.

14. Michael Balint, *The Basic Fault: Therapeutic Aspects of Regression*, preface by Enid Balint (London: Tavistock/Routledge, 1992 [First published 1968]), p. 68.

15. This is articulated particularly in Louis Sass, *Madness and Modernism: Insanity in the Light of Modern Art, Literature and Thought* (New York: Basic Books, 1992), where he argues that the characteristics of modernism are not, as has frequently been argued, a return to the wealth and excitement of the unconscious, but rather a defence against the terror of a world that has been perceived in a hyper-intellectualized manner. Sass associates this type of 'over-activity' of the consciousness with the disorders of psychosis, or schizo-phrenia, which have tended to be viewed more as 'loss of mind', rather than 'over-possession of mind'.

16. Pelayo Hipólito Fernández, *Miguel de Unamuno y William James: un paralelo pragmático* (Salamanca: n.p., 1961); Luis Farré, *Unamuno, William James y Kierkegaard* (Buenos Aires: La Aurora, 1967); Gayana Jurkevich, *The Elusive Self: Archetypal Approaches to the Novels of Miguel de Unamuno* (Columbia and London: Univ. of Missouri Press, 1991); Mario J. Valdés and María Elena Valdés, *An Unamuno Source Book: A Catalogue of Readings and Acquisitions with an Introductory Essay on Unamuno's Dialectical inquiry* (Toronto: Univ. of Toronto Press, 1973). In her chapter I, Jurkevich covers certain aspects of Unamuno's *formación* in relation to psychology, but privileges James and Bain. The bulk of references later in her study privilege analytic thinkers such as Rank, whose link with Jung's ideas is well accepted.

17. Alison Sinclair, 'The Envy of Motherhood: Destructive Urges in Unamuno', in *Feminist Readings in Spanish and Latin American Literature*, ed. Lisa Condé and Steve Hart (Dyfed: Edwin Mellen Press, 1991), pp. 47–61.

18. Miguel de Unamuno, *Niebla, Obras Completas* (Madrid: Escelicer, 1966), vol. II, p. 615.

19. Jacques Lacan, 'Le Séminaire sur "la lettre volée"', in *Écrits* (Paris: Editions du Seuil, 1966), 11–61.

20. Jacques Lacan, *The Psychoses*, p. 161.

21. Sigmund Freud, 'The Instincts and their Vicissitudes', in *On Metapsychology: The Theory of Psychoanalysis*, trans. James Strachey, ed. Angela Richards.

Pelican Freud Library, vol. 11 (Harmondsworth: Penguin Books, 1951), pp. 113–38, at p. 137.

22. D. W. Winnicott, *The Maturational Processes and the Facilitating Environment: Studies in the Theory of Emotional Development*, ed. John D. Sutherland. International Psycho-Analytical Library, vol. 64 (London: The Hogarth Press/ Institute of Psycho-Analysis, 1965), p. 47.

23. Harry Guntrip, *Schizoid Phenomena, Object-Relations and the Self* (London: Karnac/Institute of Psycho-Analysis, 1992 [First published, 1968]), p. 106.

24. D.W. Winnicott, 'The Use of the Object and Relating through Identification', *International Journal of Psycho-Analysis*, 50 (1969) 711–16.

25. 'Container' is Bion's term; the equivalent in Winnicott is the concept of 'holding'. See Colin James, 'Bion's "Containing" and Winnicott's "Holding" in the context of the Group Matrix', *International Journal of Group Psychotherapy* 34.2 (April 1984), 201–13.

26. Wilfred Bion, *Second Thoughts: Selected Papers on Psycho-Analysis* (London: Karnac, 1984 [First published in 1967]), pp. 36–7.

27. Bion, *Second Thoughts*, p. 39.

28. Winnicott, *The Maturational Processes*, pp. 29–36.

29. Unamuno, *Niebla*, p. 564.

30. Grotstein, 'Nothingness, Meaninglessness', vol. I.

31. Guntrip, *Schizoid Phenomena*, pp. 36–7.

32. Fairbairn, *Endopsychic Structure*, pp. 110–11.

33. Grotstein, 'Nothingness, Meaninglessness', vol. I, p. 278.

Index of Names